Ian McPhedran is the Sydney
Limited. He has been a journ
conflicts in Burma, Somalia, C
East Timor, Afghanistan and Iraq. In 1993 he won a United Nations
Association Peace Media Award and in 1999 the Walkley Award for best
news report for his exposé of the navy's Collins class submarine fiasco.
His first book, *The Amazing SAS: the inside story of Australia's special forces*,
is a national best seller. McPhedran lives in Balmain with his wife
Verona Burgess and daughter Lucy.

AIR
FORCE

IAN McPHEDRAN
INSIDE THE NEW ERA OF AUSTRALIAN AIR POWER

HarperCollins*Publishers*

For my dad Colin, who experienced the cruelty of war and the mercy of life-saving aid delivered by courageous airmen.

HarperCollinsPublishers

First published in Australia in 2011
by HarperCollinsPublishers Australia Pty Limited
ABN 36 009 913 517
harpercollins.com.au

Copyright © Ian McPhedran and Verona Burgess 2011

The right of Ian McPhedran and Verona Burgess to be identified as the authors of this work has been asserted by them in accordance with the *Copyright Amendment (Moral Rights) Act 2000.*

This work is copyright. Apart from any use as permitted under the *Copyright Act 1968*, no part may be reproduced, copied, scanned, stored in a retrieval system, recorded, or transmitted, in any form or by any means, without the prior written permisson of the publisher.

HarperCollinsPublishers
Level 13, 201 Elizabeth Street, Sydney NSW 2000, Australia
31 View Road, Glenfield, Auckland 0627, New Zealand
A 53, Sector 57, Noida, UP, India
77–85 Fulham Palace Road, London W6 8JB, United Kingdom
2 Bloor Street East, 20th floor, Toronto, Ontario M4W 1A8, Canada
10 East 53rd Street, New York NY 10022, USA

National Library of Australia Cataloguing-in-Publication data:

McPhedran, Ian, 1957-
    Air force : inside the new era of Australian air power / Ian McPhedran.
    ISBN: 978 0 7322 9025 2 (pbk.)
    Includes index.
    Australia. Royal Australian Air Force--History--21st century.
358.40994

Cover design by Heath McCurdy
Front cover photograph: RAAF fighter combat instructor Flight Lieutenant Marq Saunders at the controls of an F/A-18 Hornet fighter jet above the NSW countryside with two other Hornets flying in close formation. PHOTO RAAF
Back cover photograph: A RAAF F/A-18F Super Hornet fighter jet creates its own vapour cloud. PHOTO ADF
Typeset in Bembo 11.5/16.5pt by Letter Spaced
Printed and bound in Australia by Griffin Press
70gsm Classic used by HarperCollinsPublishers is a natural, recyclable product made from wood grown in sustainable forests. The manufacturing processes conform to the environmental regulations in the country of origin, Finland.

5 4 3 2 1   11 12 13 14

ACKNOWLEDGMENTS

This book is a collaborative effort and would not have been written without the constant support, hard work and dedication of my wife, Verona Burgess.

The year 2010 was tough, not least because of the death of my father Colin, but Verona remained focused on the job of producing this book, which is a tribute to her editing skills.

She and our daughter Lucy endured my absences with their usual patience and tolerance. As ever, my stepchildren Daniel and Jenna Cave were constant supporters.

Many thanks are due to the air force liaison person for this project, Andy Anderson, whose good humour and unflappable optimism were a joy to behold and whose ability to achieve outcomes quietly was a constant source of wonder. Thanks also to Leigh Harris who guided it through its final stages.

Former Chief of Air Force, Air Marshal Mark Binskin, now Vice Chief of the Defence Force, was an enthusiastic backer of the book from day one. I am grateful to him and to former Chief of the Defence Force, Air Chief Marshal Angus Houston, for opening the door so this story could be told in the Royal Australian Air Force's ninetieth anniversary year.

Former RAAF chief Geoff 'Shep' Shepherd was a mine of information and great stories.

Wing Commander Bill Talbot did a great job in the Middle East where a packed schedule yielded a mountain of material.

To all the air force personnel who took time out of their busy lives to tell me their stories, thank you. Although by now many have been promoted or have moved on, I have retained the ranks and roles that were current at time of interview.

I hope this book goes some way to demonstrate that not everyone seen on television doing good work in a camouflage uniform is from the army.

To Ken Morton from Boeing, the US Navy, the RAAF Central Flying School and Matt Hall, thank you for giving me the joy flights of a lifetime.

Thanks also to the many people who facilitated interviews and organised my visits to RAAF bases and aerospace facilities around the world.

I am most grateful to Andy Sloan, who was very generous with his time and encouragement, and also Tom Burbage and staff at Lockheed Martin.

Thanks to United States Air Force Colonel Gavin Ketchen from the US Embassy in Canberra for his help.

Janette Doolan once again went above and beyond as she transformed hours and hours of more than 150 audio interviews into written transcriptions.

I am indebted to my employer, News Limited, for its tolerance and flexibility.

Finally, many thanks to Shona Martyn and her terrific team at HarperCollins Publishers, especially Julian Gray and Jennifer Blau, who showed their usual professionalism, support and patience during the long process of producing this book, our third together.

Ian McPhedran
Sydney, July 2011

CONTENTS

Acknowledgments vii
Glossary xii
Prologue 1

AIR LIFT

1 Workhorses of the Air 7
2 East Timor — The Air Bridge 14
3 John Oddie 29
4 Bali Bombings 36
5 Loadies 53
6 Bye Bye 'Bou' 62

EYES ON THE TARGET

7 Aussie Roulette 77
8 Pigs and Caterpillars 91
9 Pigs Did Fly 99
10 Survival 109

IRAQ

11 Baghdad or Bust 123
12 Top Gun 135
13 Bombs and Babies 152
14 Fighter Pilots — The Aftermath 162

EYES IN THE SKY

15 Operation Resolute — Ocean Hunter 175
16 Afghanistan — the Convoy 185
17 The Buzz 197

ON THE JOB

18 Black Handers, Heat Stroke and Curry   209
19 Soldiers of the Air   221
20 Very Heavy Air Lift   228

EYES ON THE MIDDLE EAST

21 The Nerve Centre   241
22 Calling in Air   251
23 In a Box at Kandahar   259
24 Air Traffic Controllers   264

PEOPLE

25 Very Important Passengers   279
26 Saving Lives   290
27 In the Face of Trauma   301

THE FUTURE

28 Lightning Strikes   313
29 Test Pilots   327
30 The Super Hornet   335
31 The Flyers   348
32 Next Generation   358

GLOSSARY

AAA	anti-aircraft artillery
ACO	air combat officer
ADFA	Australian Defence Force Academy
ADG	Air Defence Guard
AMRAAM	Advanced Medium-Range Air-to-Air Missile
AEA	airborne electronic analyst
AESA	active electronically scanned array
AEWAC	Airborne Early Warning and Control
AME	aeromedical evacuation
ASLAV	Australian Light Armoured Vehicle
ATC	air traffic control
BBJ	Boeing 737 Business Jet
CAOC	Combined Air Operations Centre
CAF	Chief of Air Force
CDF	Chief of the Defence Force
CFS	Central Flying School
CHOGM	Commonwealth Heads of Government Meeting
CISCON	communications information system controller
CIVPOL	Civilian police
CPP	close personal protection
CRC	Control and Reporting Centre
CRM	crew resource management
CTOL	conventional takeoff and landing
CSTS	Combat Survival Training School
CSU	Combat Support Unit
DCA	defensive counter-air
DCP	Defence Capability Plan
DMO	Defence Materiel Organisation
ECM	electronic countermeasures
EO	electro-optical
EW	electronic warfare
FAC	forward air controller
FCI	Flight Combat Instructor
FLIR	forward looking infrared
FTS	Flying Training School (1FTS) (2FTS)
HUD	head up display
Huey	UH-1 Iroquois helicopter
HMD	helmet mounted display
ICU	intensive care unit
ISR	intelligence, surveillance and reconnaissance

IR	infrared
IED	improvised explosive device
INTERFET	International Assistance Force in East Timor
ISAF	International Security Assistance Force
ISR	intelligence, surveillance and reconnaissance
JSF	Joint Strike Fighter
JTAC	joint terminal air controller
MEAO	Middle East Area of Operations
NAVCOM	navigator/communicator
NACC	New Air Combat Capability
NVG	night vision goggles
OAS	offensive air support
OCU	Operational Conversion Unit (2OCU)
RAAF	Royal Australian Air Force
RAF	Royal Air Force
RPG	rocket-propelled grenade
RPV	remotely piloted vehicle
SAM	surface-to-air missile
SAR	search and rescue
SAS	Special Air Service
SCAR	strike coordination and reconnaissance
SECDET	security detail
SEM	sensor employment manager
SENGO	Senior Engineering Officer
STOVL	short takeoff and vertical landing
SIEV	suspected irregular entry vessel
Super MEZ	Super Missile Exclusion Zone
TACCO	tactical coordinator
TIC	troops in contact
TK	Tarin Kowt
TNI	Indonesian military
UAS	unmanned aerial system
UAV	unmanned aerial vehicle
UNAMET	UN Mission to East Timor
USAF	United States Air Force
VVIPs	very, very important passengers
'wisso'	weapons specialist

Prologue

MARCH 2003

Australian fighter pilot Matt Hall felt suddenly confused. Dark clouds had just appeared around the bubble canopy of the United States Air Force F-15 jet he was flying over Iraq.

His first thought was that they were storm clouds. Then the Australian 'top gun' realised that the dark puffs appearing at 15,000 feet were exploding anti-aircraft artillery (AAA) shells. His jet was under attack from Iraqi ground forces.

Operation Shock and Awe had begun and the Royal Australian Air Force pilot was flying an early bombing mission over the most dangerous piece of real estate on earth — Baghdad's infamous Super Missile Exclusion Zone, the 'Super MEZ'.

'That's a funny looking cloud,' Hall thought. 'Why is there a storm cloud above the target area, this really weird-looking black cloud in the middle of nowhere?'

Then, 'That's not fair! They are shooting back! It shouldn't be happening that way!' It was the first time he had been shot at with live ammunition.

The RAAF squadron leader was flying on exchange with the USAF's 336 Expeditionary Fighter Squadron known as The Rockets. Hall's mission was deep inside the Super MEZ, which was supposed to be Saddam's impenetrable shield above Baghdad. Intelligence warnings had predicted that a virtual wall of missiles and anti-aircraft fire would render it impossible to penetrate.

Earlier stealth-bomber missions and cruise-missile attacks had taken out the bulk of Saddam's air defences, but Hall and his weapons specialist, or 'wisso', who sits in the back seat of the tandem fighter, were still expecting attacks from missiles or AAA. However, now that they had been in the target area for about 45 minutes and were on their seventh attack, Hall's personal defences had dropped; he had started to think, 'This is a walk in the park!'

'I felt a false sense of security. It had become surreal. I was dropping bombs in Baghdad but — nothing. I was expecting to get shot at in the first pass [and] the second pass. I'd had to shoot missiles on that particular flight; I was expecting a big fight,' Hall says. But nothing had happened.

The aircraft's electronic countermeasures can only detect radar-guided AAA, but the one that nearly got them was guided visually by Iraqi operators on the ground.

The Iraqis were desperate to 'bag' an American fighter and its crew. Had that crew included an allied Australian pilot, the propaganda value would have been enormous. Along with every other pilot attacking Iraq, Hall was acutely aware of the consequences of being captured and paraded on TV screens around the globe.

He had swept in at a steep angle from 20,000 feet, aiming to release his bombs as close to the 12,000 foot tactical floor — a level known as the 'hard deck' — below which he was forbidden to fly. That was when he saw the ominous black cloud above the target area and realised a split second later that it was Iraqi AAA.

'It was kind of weird, the realisation it was triple A,' he says. 'All of a sudden there was more of it. Time to get the hell out of here. We jink our way up, get away from it, do a quick battle damage assessment. Are we okay, is the wingman okay? Yep, we've got two more bombs left to drop — we were dropping two bombs at a time at this stage — [so] go through for one more pass. We were jinking and diving and we got a hit on that one. It was a successful tactic except I had put us in more of a risk environment than I had planned.'

Despite the enemy fire, Hall's desperate evasive flying and a busy radio, his wisso had done a fantastic job recording the successful two-bomb attack. Following a swift battle damage assessment, Hall decided it was time for a change of tactics to put their remaining weapons into the fight in a slightly less risky fashion.

'So then I re-briefed my wingman for the next pass, that we'd probably go with a combination of the two, a little less steep, a little less low and be very wary of the fact they are now fighting back … We weren't at that level yet where we were fighting for everything, so don't take any unnecessary risks to get the bomb off, abort the pass if you are getting shot at.

'The next pass, we did get shot at but it wasn't as effective because we were higher and less predictable. We got our bombs off on that one and we went home.'

AIR LIFT

Chapter 1

WORKHORSES OF THE AIR

Whenever there is a flood or cyclone at home, a tsunami in South-East Asia or a war in the Middle East, there is one aircraft of the Royal Australian Air Force that is almost always the first in and the last to leave: the C-130 Hercules.

The mighty Herc is the workhorse of the air force. Its distinctive stub nose and high tail have been beacons of relief for tens of thousands of people ravaged by natural disasters or political turmoil — and for countless soldiers. Built by US giant Lockheed Martin, the four-engine turboprop transport aircraft has been in continuous production for more than half a century. It is widely regarded as one of the safest and sturdiest military aircraft ever built.

Since entering service and their subsequent involvement in the Vietnam War, Australian Hercs have served from Cambodia to Somalia, Fiji to Afghanistan and the Solomon Islands to Sumatra. By 2011 they had flown more than 700,000 hours without a crash.

Even in VIP mode there is no doubt that the Herc's primary role is to carry cargo and troops into operations. The only concession to passenger status or comfort used to be a pod of forward-facing airline seats installed for very, very important passengers (VVIPs) such as prime ministers or heads of state. But with the frantic tempo of operations since 1999, the seat pods are rarely used nowadays. Everyone from prime ministers and generals now clambers up the rear ramps, between the cargo pallets and the aircraft's outer skin and perches on nylon-webbing seating strung in lines down the sides and along the centreline, strapped in by a quick-release safety belt.

Experienced Herc travellers know that the best chance of extra legroom is boarding last, otherwise you could be wedged in up front with your feet strategically placed between someone's legs. Down the back there might even be a chance to stretch out. The ever-present odour of aviation fuel and hydraulic fluid, and the exposed pipes and valves and numerous warning signs, particularly the one about 'Danger — Propeller', served as a constant reminder to thousands of civilian air travellers who travelled by C-130 on 'RAAF Air' during the 1989 domestic pilots' dispute that this was a military cargo plane and not an airliner.

A VVIP or senior military officer (VIP) might be offered a more comfortable spot up on the flight deck, but for everybody else it is a nylon-webbing seat, earplugs, loud noise and the ever-present hazards such as the floor rollers used to support the cargo pallets that are the bread and butter of these air-lifters. In days gone by some lucky passengers could snatch a kip on one of the crew rest stretchers slung above the plastic seats or even on top of the cargo. These days, strict occupational health and safety regulations enforced by unyielding loadmasters prohibit such luxuries, so it is the red nylon all the way.

Such is their workload that the aircraft are usually chock-a-block with cargo and people. Only those who can sleep sitting upright and ignore the constant high-pitched drone of the massive engines, each generating about 4600 shaft horsepower, stand any chance of sleep.

As well as its stub nose and upswept tail, it is the scream of the Herc's engines that distinguishes it from other aircraft. The sound can be a blessed relief for tsunami-hit villagers or strung-out diggers waiting for a flight home, but for civilian passengers the roar is deafening. Even foam hearing protectors only deaden a din that, like a dentist's drill, makes conversation impossible and concentration difficult. Not that much concentration is required; poor internal lighting makes reading virtually impossible unless you have scored a 'window' seat on a daylight run or have a good head torch.

Everything about the Herc shouts 'cargo' and the sometimes surly

RAAF loadmasters, who manage the back end of the plane and keep the load secure and the passengers safe, make it plain that cargo does not argue, ignore pre-flight safety briefings or stow its rifles incorrectly. Neither do boxes need to know how to correctly place a sealed plastic oxygen bag over their heads in a mid-air emergency. 'By the way, the rubber seal might become quite hot, so put it over your collar,' warns the pre-flight briefing.

Hours of drone and a 'numb bum' are part of the lure of military air travel that makes accessible exotic airports such as Diego Garcia, the Maldives, the Seychelles and the Cocos-Keeling Islands, not to mention the air bases across the Middle East.

On one trip to Somalia in the early 1990s a RAAF Herc carried members of the joint parliamentary defence committee and a couple of journalists from Port Hedland to Mogadishu in Somalia and back to RAAF Base Richmond in New South Wales. As the plane left Cocos Island on the outward leg the cabin filled with acrid smoke. After taxiing back to the terminal the crew phoned headquarters at Richmond seeking advice.

'Who have you got on board?' they were asked.

'A few pollies and a couple of journos.'

'In that case just keep going,' headquarters said.

The internal heating system was already on the blink so the freezing passengers — it gets cold at 25,000 feet — had the smell of smoke to keep them from drifting off into a teeth-chattering reverie, with nothing below except ocean. At least it broke the mind-numbing boredom of long, slow 324 knots (600 kilometres per hour) top speed stretches between small, isolated island fuel stops. Even the ice crystals forming on the inside of the aircraft's skin, just above the tiny metal box and tube of the urinal, made for a welcome distraction from staring at hydraulic lines and metal struts.

The Herc duly made it safely to Somalia and back to Richmond (some 24 hours' flying time) without missing a beat. The fact that the passengers had worn several millimetres off their teeth was of no consequence to the crew, whose flight-deck heating system and hot water urn had functioned perfectly throughout the long haul.

The flight deck on a C-130 is a spacious area where the two or three flight crew, depending on the model, work and rest in a much more comfortable environment than the loadmasters and passengers down the back. Climb the ladder into the 'office' and you are in a different world from the tiny portholes, exposed pipes, sharp edges and din of the cargo hold. The panoramic windows of the cockpit provide a remarkable view of the outside world.

During a flight between the Australian base at Camp Russell, near Tarin Kowt ('TK') in Afghanistan's Oruzgan province, back to Al Minhad Air Base in Dubai in April 2008, the lucky passengers, who included then Defence minister Joel Fitzgibbon, were treated to piping hot pizza and some breathtaking vistas of the mountains of southern Afghanistan, the incredible red desert south of Kandahar and one of the busiest chunks of airspace in the world.

Rumbling down the dirt runway at TK the crew are not only busy preparing to avoid the soaring peaks of the Hindu Kush but are ready to react to any ground threat at a moment's notice. Their hands never stray far from the electronic countermeasures switch, which controls the release of decoy flares. These are made of various metals which, when released into the air, burn in order to confuse a heat-seeking missile. After some steep turns and a rapid climb the pilots relax as they cruise out of range of any insurgent weapons, including many missiles dating back to the Mujahideen–Russian war of the 1980s.

Then there is all the other air traffic. Flying in and out of Afghanistan is a visual feast, but the workload for the flight crew is intense. The radio cackles incessantly and the pilots are on constant alert for fast jet fighters, surveillance planes, transports, air-to-air tankers and, at lower levels, even unmanned aerial vehicles (UAVs) or drones.

On the flight out of Tarin Kowt the Herc suddenly pitched left as the crew took evasive action following an alert from air traffic control. In a flash two American KC-135 tanker jets whizzed by slightly below and to the left of the RAAF plane — nothing to worry about, but proof of how congested this airspace is.

Flying by Herc into Baghdad International Airport presents even greater hazards. During one visit on Anzac Day 2006, then Prime Minister John Howard and his entourage were treated to some rollicking flying as the pilots used proven 'tac' (tactical) procedures to deliver their VVIP cargo safely into one of the most dangerous airports on earth, where the official party was greeted with a volley of AK-47 fire in the distance. Whether it involves steep turns just above treetop height or steep dives from 10,000 feet, 'tac' flying can be uncomfortable for civilian officials more used to the genteel surrounds of a RAAF VIP jet or a business class seat on a Qantas airliner.

There are few more effective platforms for projecting either hard or soft power than the Herc. More than 2300 have been built to serve 70 nations. In March 2010 the dozen H-model and dozen J-model Hercs from the Richmond-based 37 Squadron passed a significant milestone when they chalked up 20,000 hours of continuous service in the Middle East Area of Operations (MEAO) since February 2003. Three RAAF aircraft are based in the MEAO at Al Minhad Air Base in the United Arab Emirates.

The proud history of the C-130's service to Australia dates back to when the first A-model arrived at 36 Squadron's Richmond base in late 1958. In 1966 a dozen E-models were added. The H entered service in 1978 (replacing the A-models) and in 1999 the J replaced the E. Apart from being slightly longer than the H and having a six-blade propeller rather than a four, the J is operated by a crew of just three (two pilots and a loadmaster) compared with the H's five (two pilots, navigator, flight engineer and loadmaster).

The highly automated J uses 'glass cockpit' technology (including automated flight systems) and advances such as the head up display (HUD) that allows pilots to monitor all systems on a screen in front of their eyes. It does not require a flight engineer or navigator and can carry 30 per cent more cargo than its predecessor.

The C-130's ability to operate in virtually any environment — from short, rough dirt runways in the tropics to the icy wastes of Antarctica — makes it one of the most flexible and valuable medium transport aircraft in global military aviation.

The chief of staff at the Richmond-based Air Lift Group, Group Captain Paul Nicholas, describes it as the 'four-wheel drive' of the aeroplane world.

'It's not particularly fast or comfortable but it takes you to a whole lot of places not open to other people,' he says. 'You build a lot of camaraderie with a broad group of people.'

C-130 crew members are fiercely protective of the Herc and it is not hard to see why. Nicholas says the beauty is its simplicity. While the J is a highly technical aircraft, the basic design has not changed in decades and its ruggedness has not been compromised.

'It's got an undercarriage like a truck and a cargo compartment that can cope with a huge range of stuff and when they designed it they designed it around the back end, which was smart,' he says.

The designers started with an American cargo pallet and virtually built the aircraft around it. They gave it tremendous performance and good range, fitted rugged components and built it to operate from short, dirt airstrips. For the loyal Herc crew that is the essence of the aircraft. It is not glamorous, not even pretty, but when you spend years flying in and out of dangerous and exotic places, eating 'frozos' (frozen meals) from the tiny electric oven or drinking cold soft drink from a large ice box, it becomes almost part of the family.

Nicholas, an air combat officer (ACO), has flown Hercs to every corner of the globe, including Antarctica and the Arctic. He has also qualified in a range of tactical roles, including special operations, and greatly enjoyed working and training with a range of special forces.

'It gets your heart going; it's exciting, and professionally quite demanding,' he says. 'If you have very demanding customers, you extend yourself to meet their requirements, training needs and ultimately mission success.'

Nicholas has flown operational and disaster relief missions in Australia and overseas to places such as Somalia, Turkey, Timor, Bosnia, Papua New Guinea (PNG) and Croatia. Like many C-130 aircrew, he has also flown aeromedical evacuation (AME) flights, search and rescue (SAR) missions and urgent humanitarian flights, including to the tsunami on the north coast of PNG near Aitape in July 1998. He was on one of the early flights into that remote disaster zone, where more than 2,000 people died.

'You often have to re-role in flight,' he says. 'You could be flying passengers and cargo to, say, Malaysia, and air traffic control will call you up and say, "We heard a SAR beacon going off — can you go look for something?" So off you go and search for somebody.'

That happened when he was Commanding Officer of 37 Squadron in early 2007. Air Lift Group had a crew returning from Perth to Richmond on a training flight when the RAAF was asked whether it could search for a group of lost fishermen.

'They weren't all search and rescue qualified. Some of them were, so I gave them approval to conduct the search and they found the fishermen, who had lost their boat and were in a very bad situation off the Esperance coast,' Nicholas recalls. 'So that was a very rewarding day for all involved.'

Chapter 2

EAST TIMOR — THE AIR BRIDGE

Joint operational command had been in vogue at the Australian Defence Force for some time before East Timor erupted in 1999, but it had never been put to the test in a 'live' operation, let alone a large multinational mission led by Australia. East Timor saw the three services — navy, army and air force — operating together in a joint environment on a scale never before witnessed under the Australian joint model.

The then Major-General Peter Cosgrove would run the 22-nation International Assistance Force in East Timor (INTERFET), but he would rely heavily on RAAF and Royal Australian Navy assets. The mighty Hercules C-130 air lifter and its smaller cousin, the DHC-4 Caribou, would lead the way for Australia.

Before INTERFET was even constituted, the Hercs flew into Dili's Komoro International Airport under an operation code-named Spitfire to rescue hundreds of Australian, East Timorese and other nationals. They were fleeing the orgy of violence triggered by the overwhelming vote for independence in the historic ballot held on 30 August 1999.

After the vote, pro-Indonesian militias rampaged throughout the country, killing their opponents and terrorising and threatening foreigners. These included Australian and international journalists and unarmed United Nations staff from the large UN Mission to East Timor (UNAMET), among whom was a large contingent of unarmed Australian Federal Police officers, known as CIVPOL.

The Indonesian military, the TNI, were supposed to provide security but instead stayed in their barracks and watched as the militias, with names such as Aitarak (Thorn) and Besi Merah Putih (Red and White Iron), ran amok. Australian journalists witnessed TNI troops laughing and joking as pro-independence activists were hacked to death outside their barracks. The violence was so extreme that the United Nations ordered the evacuation of its entire mission.

Between 9 September and 14 September, an 'air bridge' was provided by RAAF Hercules aircraft to evacuate some 1500 people from Dili to the safety of Darwin.

Group Captain Paul Nicholas was lying in bed at home when he received the phone call telling him to get on an aeroplane and head north.

Nicholas, then a squadron leader and the flight commander with 36 Squadron at Richmond, was soon airborne with his C-130 crew on a 34 Squadron VIP aircraft heading to RAAF Base Tindal near Katherine in the Northern Territory to await further instructions. Before long they set off for East Timor to begin the evacuation.

'I remember when we landed there [in Dili] the first morning and I was thinking, "Gee, what is going to happen here?" It was a bit tense,' he recalls. 'We weren't sure what was going to happen, whether [the Indonesian troops] were going to be able to maintain airfield security, but they were. Over the next few days we progressively got all the people out and calmed everyone down.

'On these flights, it was common that within minutes of departure the back of the aircraft went very quiet. All the adults had fallen asleep and the children were still awake. Obviously the adults were exhausted from their ordeal. [They] just collapsed and went to sleep. We got them in, turned around and went back again. You felt that you had got them out of harm's way. You felt good about it.'

Air lift commander at Richmond, Air Commodore John Oddie, recalls a degree of trepidation among the Herc crews at Tindal on the eve of Operation Spitfire as they prepared to fly in to an uncertain and burning city to evacuate some very traumatised people.

'You don't quite know how things are going to pan out, so that was tough. In any battle environment or pre-operational environment the uncertainty is always a difficult aspect and I think at that stage we were just getting used to the notion of uncertainty,' Oddie says.

East Timor was a real eye-opener for chief loadmaster Warrant Officer Scott Willacott. He was on board the second Herc into Dili for Operation Spitfire, carrying only a security detail, and felt very nervous. 'We were all the junior guys and we were teamed up with the senior guys ... and not [having] been exposed to that sort of stuff before, yeah, I was a little bit on edge.'

He could feel the adrenaline pumping through his veins. 'But the guy that I was with said, "Oh mate, just chill, it's just like any other flight."'

Of course, everyone on the plane knew it was no ordinary flight and that things might go pear-shaped or not as expected.

'We were briefed on how to deal with those [situations]. I guess for guys like myself and guys around my era it was a bit of a combination and consolidation of all our training, all coming to a head at once,' he says.

The first Herc to land at Komoro International Airport, about 5 kilometres west of central Dili, had brought some air force staff to set up a passenger-processing system and Willacott's aircraft conducted two evacuation missions back to Darwin on the first day. Evacuees were ferried down the potholed main road in trucks, four-wheel drives and cars as enraged militia fighters watched and in some cases shouted abuse at the frightened tide of humanity.

He says, 'We were pulling East Timorese nationals out, we were pulling out Australian Federal Police, UN workers, all that sort of stuff — anyone that basically wanted to get out. The planes just kept going. It was pretty full on.'

Willacott had joined 37 Squadron in August 1998 after eight years in the RAAF, mostly in the maintenance world, and a year later found himself on his way to Dili. He had not been specifically trained to deal with a refugee situation during an 'operational stop' or 'op stop', where the engines 'turn and burn' (keep running) as the aircraft is unloaded and loaded, but his core training had covered the movement of passengers on board the C-130.

'What we were doing was just pretty much carrying passengers, albeit passengers under duress,' he says. 'We weren't necessarily trained to deal with the lack of security, but we had enough training to deal with the core elements of what we were doing. We had more than enough training under our belts to deal with that.'

Dealing with Customs and Quarantine back in Darwin also presented a few issues, but the gratitude of the East Timorese and other evacuees made it all worthwhile.

'I don't think there was one of them that didn't come up to myself and the other loadmaster and shake our hand and thank us — as big a big "thank you" as they could give us at the time — for getting them out of there,' Willacott says. 'Even though they were very, very long days, just that very small portion of it, at the end of the day, [for] someone you've never met before — he and his wife and four or five kids and they've got one plastic bag and that's all they've got left — to go, "Thanks very much"… was pretty rewarding.'

After five days spent transporting the passengers to safety under Operation Spitfire, Paul Nicholas thought that would be the end of it. But then the INTERFET peace-making mission was established and he found himself on the first aircraft carrying Australian troops into a conflict zone since the humanitarian mission to Somalia in east Africa in 1993. The mission, code-named Operation Warden, became the nation's biggest military operation since the Vietnam War.

It began less than a week after Spitfire ended. Cosgrove's INTERFET force was on its way to the smouldering city of Dili with the C-130s Hercules again leading the charge. At the peak of the operation more than 5500 Australian military personnel from all services were engaged in INTERFET and the RAAF's Herc fleet flew dozens of sorties between Darwin, Tindal, Dili and East Timor's largest airfield at Baucau in the east of the island. The Baucau strip has the longest runway in the country and had been its main airport until the Indonesian invasion in 1975.

Nicholas's first flight back into Komoro airfield for Operation Warden was nerve-racking because the airport status was uncertain and appeared not properly secured. There were people, including media, wandering around the flight aprons and taxiways. He became more concerned about shredding a journalist or local civilian than a confrontation with Indonesian soldiers.

'I was worried that a civilian might wander into the aircraft's path and get injured [because] there wasn't much security around there when we first got in there,' he says. 'We did engine-running off-loads, where we kept the engines running, because we wanted to maintain the flow and we didn't want any aircraft to break down. We were [also] doing combat off-loads, so just basically taxiing in with all four engines running, pushing pallets out, getting people out and trying to depart as quickly as possible. I was worried at the very beginning [that] if there wasn't security, people could get in the way, or be injured or hurt — killed at worst. Fortunately it was secured very rapidly.'

Once the Australian troops, including the RAAF Airfield Defence Guards, were established in and around the perimeter Nicholas felt confident that the aircraft would keep going with safety and the flow soon began to speed up. Things ran smoothly until day three when some aircraft began to feel the strain of the high operational tempo. An added complication was that the maintenance crews working on both of the East Timor operations were based in Darwin, Tindal or Townsville.

'On the third day we had a few maintenance issues. We had to run around and jiggle everything,' Nicholas says.

By that stage the big airport at Baucau had been re-opened and flights were landing frequently at both places.

'We got in, got out, people weren't getting hurt and there were no major incidents or confliction issues or airspace issues. They were things that occupied my mind the most,' he says. 'Once we had Australian forces in place, airfield security issues sort of went away and it really became the mechanics of making air flow work.'

Scott Willacott spent about 10 weeks working on both of the East

Timor missions and even after the first of the Australian troops had arrived and security had improved he felt uneasy whenever his Herc landed back at Komoro. Hearing reports of what the TNI had been accused of and seeing the smug attitude of some Indonesian troops, on top of the language barrier, made things quite tense.

To their great credit troops from both sides kept their cool and the Australians got on with their job and out of Dili quickly.

'You were always sort of looking around, keeping an eye on things,' he says. 'We were still operating with a small security detachment to look after us and the aircraft as well. Even they would make mention occasionally [that] it was not the best place to be at that point, but we had a job to do.'

The stress levels were boosted by the 'op stops'.

'You've got people that aren't familiar with operating in that environment, operating very, very close to your aircraft, so you are trying to get your aircraft unloaded and reloaded and keep an eye on everything that's going on and keep an eye on these people,' he says. 'By the end of the day you might have done a 14-, 15-, 16-hour day, but mentally you've probably done a 24-hour day.'

Despite the stresses the outcome was extremely rewarding. 'That just reaffirmed everything, just concreted everything: "Why didn't I do this sooner?" At the end of my 10 weeks flying to Timor, I felt that I had wasted seven years: "I should have done this seven years ago."'

Since then he has flown in the Solomon Islands and by mid-2008 had done five tours of the Middle East Area of Operations (MEAO).

Squadron Leader Peter 'Choady' Cseh had only been in the RAAF since the beginning of 1997 and at 37 Squadron for less than a year when the East Timor operations kicked off. The former North Queensland pizza shop owner was a raw co-pilot.

'The first flight I was on [was] the third aircraft with the Aussie troops down the back,' he recalls. 'I was young, you know, the heart's pumping a lot the first time you are going anywhere sort of half dangerous. I remember stopping on the runway and seeing all the Aussie grunts crouching in the bushes, in the long grass on the side of the runway. It looked kind of "war-y", I thought.

'We taxied to the end of the runway, turned around, and we were planning to take off in the same direction as the runway but there was a big Indonesian warship parked off that end of the airfield. So we elected to taxi down and turn around to avoid having to fly over the top of it. There was a guy in a hut — it must have been like their little guard post or something like that. He had a big heavy machine gun and he was just pointing it at the aeroplane the whole time as we were taxiing down the runway and turning around.'

Several weeks later Choady was back in Dili and this time the crew shut down the aircraft and wandered around Komoro airport, which had been transformed into a large refugee camp and very busy military airfield.

'A little Timorese boy and girl came up to me and grabbed my legs and gave me a big hug, like a "thank you" gesture. I really wished I had a better photo of that, that would have been cool, but I didn't have a digital camera,' he says. 'Some memorable times … very memorable times.'

As well as humanitarian evacuation, troop insertion and resupply, the C-130s undertook the vital job of food drops. People had begun to starve in some isolated mountainous regions. Air Commodore John Oddie, then chief of staff of Air Lift Group, says the method for the first food drop close to the West Timor border was engineered quickly at Richmond and used in Timor soon afterwards. Things came to a head after ABC News reported that the RAAF was preparing to drop food to starving villagers.

'I got to work very early that morning to find the air drop was a "go" that day and because of the pace of things we had to do something we hadn't planned to do. That involved establishing a container delivery system, which was basically four 44-gallon drums in a canvas bag with a plywood base to slide out the back with a parachute,' Oddie recalls.

Some areas where food was most needed were right against steep mountains so the aircrews had to come in low and slow, deploy the foodstuff and then fly away without hitting a mountain in low cloud and thick smoke haze. Unfortunately, a local boy was hit by one of the falling pallets and lost a leg but many Timorese people were saved from starvation by the RAAF food drops during September 1999.

During Operation Warden, the airfield at Baucau also became the base for a flight of Caribous from the Townsville-based 38 Squadron.

The Caribou, or 'bou', is a medium-sized twin-engine air lifter, smaller than the C-130 Hercules and capable of operating from very short airstrips, beaches or even paddocks. The then detachment commander, Squadron Leader Warren Schmitt, says his team started out with just two aircraft and 16 people and grew to five aircraft and 50 people. It was a hectic but rewarding time for the team and the now-retired Canadian-built de Havilland aircraft.

The first Caribous arrived in Dili to scenes of utter devastation.

'Nobody knew what to expect when we first went in there and we went in with guns loaded, live bullets,' Schmitt says. 'At that stage the Indonesian defence force was still on the ground, waiting to be moved out, and [it was a] fairly tense time. As it turned out it sort of blew over and there was no real trouble.'

The damage had been done in the days between Operation Spitfire and the arrival of INTERFET, when the Indonesian-backed militias had gone on their unchecked rampage. 'The place was on fire, there were basically no buildings left. What buildings were left were fairly wrecked, or already occupied by other people who got there before us. So we got a very small patch of dirt next to the airport!'

They set up their tents and some basic showering and toileting facilities and lived there for the next three weeks until they moved up to Baucau to free up space in Dili.

The 38 Squadron pilots had been trained on the high, humid and short dirt runways of Papua New Guinea's highlands and the mountains of Timor shared some physical similarities with Australia's nearest neighbour. They had expected a similar set-up but were pleasantly surprised.

'We got there and it was nowhere near as challenging as New Guinea. The terrain is nowhere near as big, the weather not as bad or unpredictable and the airfields we operated to, apart from Los Palos and Maliana, were quite large,' Schmitt says. 'The training we'd done in New Guinea had us in good stead so we could launch fairly junior PNG-trained crews on fairly complex tasks without having to worry about them. I knew if they could operate in PNG they could operate in East Timor without any trouble at all. That's why we continued to maintain the capability in New Guinea — if you can fly in New Guinea you can pretty much fly anywhere in the southern hemisphere.'

One junior captain 'blooded' in East Timor was Squadron Leader Ross Benson. He says the mission was a military pilot's dream. 'In six weeks I did 100 hours' flying and the most boring part was low level on the coast. It was just brilliant.'

Benson's logbook reads like a boy's own adventure, but his most powerful memories were generated by the humanitarian mission. In the peace-keeping section of the Australian War Memorial in Canberra there is an East Timor display that features video footage of a Caribou taxiing in at Suai airport. Benson is piloting that aircraft.

'As we pulled up and turned around this little girl was brought down on a stretcher covered with blankets,' he recalls. 'Her face had been badly damaged by a star picket, so we took her and her father to Dili for medical treatment, then a couple of weeks later took her back again, so that was good.'

In another more heart-rending case a Caribou crew flew a gravely ill baby to Dili with its father and a few days later returned the father with his baby in a box.

One of the more bizarre tasks was flying captured members of the militia around the country. For example, if militiamen were detained at Maliana in the west, the quickest method of transporting them back to Dili for interrogation was by air. So if a Caribou was heading in that direction then it was used to ferry the 'enemy' fighters.

In one case some arrested militia fighters came on board and literally began praying to Benson for mercy. 'As it was quite hot I asked for the rear cargo door to be opened to increase the airflow. Immediately after the door was opened the flight engineer beamed through on the intercom to advise me the the militia member had wet himself. What we didn't know was that the Indonesians had advised the militia, if captured, that the Australians would throw them out of their aircraft.'

When the aircraft landed in Dili the jittery militiaman kissed Benson's feet in thanks because he hadn't been thrown out of the plane.

What really struck the aircrews was how extensive and systematic the militia rampage had been. Even small, isolated villages on the top of mountains had been burnt and ransacked by the Jakarta-backed gangs.

'Everything had just been trashed, but when you flew over Dili there were still all these nice buildings. They were the Indonesian buildings. It was quite systematic, really, but it was great to fly up there. You are actually doing something positive. We all went in there with flak jackets on and you land and you pull up on the tarmac and they were playing cricket,' he says.

Benson had arrived in Dili as a raw, newly minted Caribou captain with a pregnant wife at home. He left two months later as an experienced operational pilot.

The Caribou light tactical air lifter was ideally suited to East Timor. Noted for the distinctive 'clunk' of its twin 1450 horsepower radial engines, the aircraft has almost mythical short take-off and landing performance. It was designed to clear a 15-metre-high object after a 300-metre take-off roll in zero wind or after 150 metres in 15 knots (28 kilometres per hour) of headwind. Many pilots claim much better performance than that.

Built for function rather than speed, the RAAF's 'bou' fleet chalked up more than 40 years of continuous service before they were retired in 2010 and in many situations it was the only fixed-wing aircraft able to do the job.

East Timor was bush flying at its best, whether moving people and boxes up into the mountains to Maliana or over the 'hump' to Suai on the south coast, or dropping SAS troops off in an obscure landing zone in the dead of night flying on night vision goggles. It was a wonderful mission for 38 Squadron.

The Australian Government had invested a lot of diplomatic energy and goodwill assuring the Indonesians that Australia's intentions were purely humanitarian.

The first RAAF aircraft to touch down in Dili before Operation Warden had even begun was a Falcon VIP jet from the Canberra-based Number 34 Squadron carrying senior military officers and diplomatic envoys sent by then Prime Minister John Howard to reassure the Indonesians.

Those reassurances were backed by the 'iron fist in a velvet glove' strategy that saw RAAF fighter jets, including long-range F-111 strike bombers, positioned at RAAF Base Tindal south of Darwin alongside F/A-18 Hornet fighters, fully 'bombed up' (armed with bombs and missiles) and on alert to move at short notice. The aircraft had arrived at Tindal during Operation Spitfire and stayed there for the early part of Operation Warden and the United Nations INTERFET mission.

Flying time from Tindal to Dili for an F-111 is less than an hour and the Indonesian generals were very aware of the jets' ability to carry a large payload and to strike with deadly precision.

The bombers and fighters provided a valuable back-up for both operations and acted as a blunt warning to Jakarta. Indonesia had long been aware of the ability of the 'pig', as the F-111 was fondly known, to fly from Australia to Jakarta, put a missile through any general's front window and fly home again, all on one tank of fuel. During the 1980s the then Defence minister Kim Beazley had provided Indonesian armed forces chief Benny Murdani with a comprehensive personal briefing about the jets' capabilities.

There was uncertainty about Indonesia's intentions in East Timor and the intelligence feeds coming from Australian officials in Jakarta and from electronic signals intelligence intercepts made it clear that it was not only possible, but also likely, that Indonesian forces might play rough regardless of orders from embattled President BJ Habibie calling for restraint. The Indonesian military had spilled a lot of blood and seen a lot of scarce national treasure poured into the former Portuguese colony, and many top officers, including the armed forces chief General Wiranto, were deeply opposed to what they saw as an 'Australian takeover' of an Indonesian province.

Cosgrove needed all his considerable diplomatic skills and contacts within the Indonesian high command to head off a confrontation. He was backed by exhaustive diplomacy from politicians, officers and diplomats in Canberra, Jakarta and at the United Nations in New York.

Geoff Shepherd (now a former Chief of Air Force) was at that time Chief of Staff at Headquarters Air Command. He had also taken out an insurance policy by making sure an F-111 flyer, Jeff Harland, was appointed to Cosgrove's headquarters staff in Dili as an air planner.

'If it ever got to that level of conflict there would be fast jet expertise in Cosgrove's air staff,' Shepherd says. Cosgrove was insistent that all Australian forces involved in the operation were 'loaded to bear' (fully armed) and prepared for the worst, and that included air assets.

Once INTERFET was established, Shepherd was sent to Jakarta with senior Defence official Shane Carmody to reassure the Habibie Government there would be no 'black' (secret) reconnaissance flights over Indonesian West Timor or anywhere else, and that there had not been any over the East while the Indonesians were there.

'We didn't put any flights in there until we had UN sanction and we'd taken over the airspace,' Shepherd says.

Shepherd was later also intimately involved in planning for the 2003 Solomon Islands intervention when Cosgrove was Chief of the Defence Force (CDF) and the same principles applied: carry a big stick just in case the carrot doesn't work.

'We did the initial plans for the Solomons fairly tooled up as well,' Shepherd says.

He emphasises that in 1999 the Australian Defence Force had no real plan for leading a major international operation. It would be another four years before the RAAF would bring out a targeting directive for the Iraq War. Meanwhile, some form of doctrine had to be developed for leading the INTERFET operation.

'It was up to us to do it, so I think the fact Cosgrove insisted that we go in there prepared for the worst saw us in good stead,' Shepherd says.

Paul Nicholas was born and mostly bred in Canberra and came to the air force late. Unsuited for the pilot stream, he became a navigator on Hercules transports. His regret about missing out was short-lived and he soon learnt that unless you let go of things in the military you don't progress.

'I've certainly done all the things I'm interested in doing,' he says. 'I was at the very end of, I guess, traditional navigation, where you do celestial sun shots and navigate by first principles, whereas now really the term "navigator" has gone by the by. Now they are systems operators and tacticians, they run defensive systems, they run radar systems, they run weapons, across the air force, and then they also apply their knowledge to make smart tactics and employ that platform. So the job is evolving rapidly. You can't hang onto stuff.'

By 2009 Nicholas had done everything in the Hercules world and was the chief of staff at Air Lift Group. He rates the East Timor mission as a high point.

'It was also a big deal in recent Australian military history. Obviously since then we've had Iraq and Afghanistan, which are probably another whole level again,' he says. 'I think it was probably the first time we'd led a force that size since I don't know when, but we didn't want to look like idiots.'

He was pleasantly surprised when both operations went so well. 'I was pretty confident it was all going to work. I was a little bit less confident with the evacuation because the whole place was less settled and I was thinking, "This could go one of two ways."'

The other pleasing aspect was the way the system got behind the crews doing the flying. 'Once the sausage machine starts rolling … a lot of the stuff you'd be fighting during your normal daytime job goes away.'

That 'can do' attitude, Nicholas says, came to the fore in the RAAF in 1999 and has remained ever since. John Oddie backs that analysis and regards East Timor as an early example of 'sustained endurance'.

'If there would be one thing that has really changed over the 15 years or so I've been here now, it would be the way we go about sustaining and enduring the support to operations,' says Oddie. 'It has become far more mature.'

Matt Hegarty had no idea just how important the politics strand of his Chemistry and Politics degree at ADFA would be when he graduated in 1990. In June 2009, Wing Commander Hegarty was the commanding officer of Number 37 Squadron at Richmond, not far from his old home turf at Epping in north-western Sydney. The former Epping Boys High student has not had much cause to use his knowledge of chemistry during the past 20 years, but his political acumen has come in handy.

'Politics is probably far more important for any officer these days than one would care to imagine,' he says.

Hegarty's first posting after completing flying training in 1992 was with 37 Squadron flying the E model Herc. He had joined the air force with fast jets in mind, but soon realised the macho world of the fighter pilot was not for him, which was fortuitous because that was also the view of the selection board.

'I can be determined, but I'm not comfortable with the overt aggressive pursuit and I worked out pretty quickly that I like working with other people,' he says. 'I have not one ounce of regret about the path that I took, not one ounce. It's been fabulous.'

Hegarty too believes the air force and the wider defence force underwent a metamorphosis during 1999. Before East Timor some people referred to the RAAF disparagingly as a 'flying club', although he believes that was unfair.

'Up until 1999 we did these things here and there, we went to Cambodia, there was always something going on in the Pacific somewhere,' he says. 'It was never terribly exciting, we weren't wrestling with body protection and armour, not many of the aircraft had self protection ... but in 1999 we realised, "Hang on, this is about conducting missions that we can't employ commercial operators to do because it carries a serious overhead of risk." We were prepared to a point, but we were not prepared structurally, physically. Literally, we just weren't ready.'

East Timor changed all that and the RAAF, like other branches of the Australian Defence Force, is now much better prepared.

RAAF historian Chris Clark says the RAAF passed a big test in East Timor, but it was a close run thing. 'I remember interviewing Air Marshal Neville McNamara. Now, he'd been retired for about a decade before we went into Timor, but he was very keen to make the point to me that we got away with it in Timor but only by the super-dedication of an awful lot of people,' Clark says. 'Can you always count on that challenge being met in the way you need it to be met? You are putting an awful lot of trust in a system that is almost begging to break and okay, we passed the test, but we did it at a huge personal cost. Is that the way to run an air force or an ADF at all? Because I don't think it was just us; the other services would have felt the strain of maintaining numbers of people.'

Former Chief of Air Force, Air Marshal Mark Binskin, who became Vice Chief of the Defence Force in July 2011, regards the success of the East Timor campaign as validation for a force restructure that saw the birth of combat support groups and brought more of an expeditionary focus to the RAAF.

The former navy and air force fighter pilot, who was in command of 77 Squadron at RAAF Base Williamtown in New South Wales in 1999, says the mission showed for the first time that the air force could go into a foreign country, establish an airfield quickly and then support it.

The air force already had an 'expeditionary' mindset within Australia with its remote bare bases at Curtin, Learmonth and Sherger, all more than 3000 kilometres from home bases such as Williamtown, Richmond, Amberley and Edinburgh. But East Timor had the added element of uncertainty and hostility.

'We have achieved a lot since 1999. We've been a more operations-focused air force, we've had to be, and except for air force training group, every force element group has deployed at one point or another,' Binskin says.

Chapter 3

JOHN ODDIE

Air Commodore John Oddie clearly recalls the day he decided to join the Royal Australian Air Force. He was driving a tractor on the family sheep farm at Skipton in western Victoria when two F-111 fighter-bombers whizzed over his head.

As an army reservist the young Victorian had already been for a flight in a helicopter.

'I was quite surprised the pilots actually got paid and got to sleep in far better places than I was as a soldier, and did apparently adventurous things,' he says. 'So I thought, "Well, they've made decisions that I haven't."'

He had two choices: to become an officer in the Army Reserve or to join the RAAF. He opted for the air force and away he went through pilot training.

It would be some years before he began flying C-130 Hercules and many more before he became Commander of the RAAF's Air Lift Group following the prolonged period of active service that began with the 1999 East Timor intervention.

Oddie, an intense man and a deep and lateral thinker, qualified as a helicopter pilot in the late 1970s when the air force was still running the nation's military helicopter fleet. He started flying Hueys, the iconic UH-1 Iroquois military chopper whose distinctive rotor blade 'thud' became an audio icon of the Vietnam War.

'I admit to being not an exceptional pilot, just pretty much your average, run-of-the-mill pilot, but it meant that there was the odd failure along the way and the odd bit of success,' he says. 'Success outweighed failure and I managed to get through the course and ended up learning to fly helicopters ... which was a great opportunity because I wanted to be a helicopter pilot.'

That ambition took him with the Hueys across to the peace-keeping mission in the Sinai Peninsula, whose sovereignty Israel handed back to Egypt on Anzac Day, 1982, following the historic 1978 Camp David Accords. As the United Nations was unable to set up a peace-keeping force, the three countries agreed to the establishment of a 'Multinational Force and Observers' to supervise implementation of the 1979 Israel-Egypt Peace Treaty's security provisions and try to prevent violations of its terms.

'We were moving the [civilian] observers around to inspection sites, which commonly meant you would fly a helicopter ... to a place. They would go and do the inspections and while we were there, we'd [often] sit and have a cup of tea with the Israeli army or Egyptian army and get to know their personal stories. That was the most delightful aspect of the whole thing, to sit down with these soldiers who commonly had very tough experiences, to sit down and understand them.'

They also did aeromedical evacuations, mostly of landmine victims in the Sinai desert. 'That [usually] meant we had to land in a mine field, so we had to think carefully about how we did that to pick up the people being evacuated.'

All casualties other than Egyptians were taken to Israel.

'We were taking Egyptians up ... well, I can't imagine taking Egyptians to Israel! Sometimes that was a bit tough because it was commonly at strange hours and crossing a military boundary in a strange aircraft in the middle of the night in that area of town wasn't the simplest job,' he recalls. 'The border at some places was 44-gallon drums painted white and placed on a line. Then we had to go along and map-read and say. "Well, that drum is not in the right place. It needs to move this way or that way" and we'd go back. The observers would check with us where the border was and we'd plot it down through visual navigation.'

They commonly flew at about 150 feet, checking ambiguous terrain features on the river valleys and small hills in the middle of the desert.

'There was the odd dangerous event, but mostly the only danger was operating at a level of performance of the helicopter where it was right on the maximum of performance,' he says. 'If you are landing on a hill, sometimes you didn't have the power to do anything other than just get there, and if anything went wrong you had to peel away and come back and have another go at it. Another 20 pounds less can make a difference, so you are riding on the performance envelope of the aircraft.'

Next, Oddie spent a couple of years flying Chinook heavy-lift helicopters in places such as PNG, mainly for training. He loved flying the 'chook', whose two engines and huge lifting capacity allowed it to undertake unique tasks in dangerous flying environments. In some cases the 'chook' shaved 12 months off humanitarian aid projects simply by air lifting whole tractors or other heavy loads directly into an isolated site. This was not always a straightforward proposition.

'I remember on a couple of occasions there we had to pick up a load that we didn't quite have the capacity to lift, so we basically just got it to the edge of the mountain and fell off the mountain with it until we had enough speed to fly. That was a rather exciting way of getting something airborne — to throw yourself at the valley,' says Oddie.

He adds dryly, 'We probably don't do things that way anymore.'

After the Australian Army assumed control of all battlefield helicopters in 1986, Oddie moved into a training role at the Officer Training School at RAAF Base Williams — Point Cook in Victoria — before returning to fixed wing, flying the Italian-built Aermacchi MB-326 ('Macchi') jet trainers at the Number 2 Flying Training School at RAAF Base Pearce, north of Perth.

'Going to be a Macchi instructor was exciting because that gave me a chance to establish myself professionally as a jet pilot and as an instructor, and to go somewhere a little bit quicker,' he says. 'You have to double the speed you think about things.'

He and wife Barbara, a former RAAF air traffic controller, also had their son Tatham in early 1988, so life was moving faster at home too. Later that year Oddie was posted to NATO in Germany on exchange with the Royal Air Force (RAF) to fly Chinooks. The posting also included an active deployment to the Middle East during the first Gulf War.

Returning home, Oddie spent a year at army staff college and then, with no flight time in a C-130 Hercules aircraft, was posted to Number 37 Squadron as the executive officer and given 12 months to become qualified on the aircraft.

'Having never flown a Herc before in my life, I got to be the number two in the Herc squadron,' he says.

Following his RAF experience, his focus — both in the squadron and later at Air Lift Group — was on combat operations. Life was still quite measured in Australia's post-Vietnam 'peace dividend' era. For most of the 1980s the Herc fleet had been flying humanitarian aid missions around the region. The famine relief mission to Somalia in 1993 was the beginning of the operational focus and the evacuation of Australians from the Cambodian capital, Phnom Penh, in 1997 signalled the start of more than a decade of virtually continuous operational flying for the transport team.

Oddie's time in the RAF stood him in good stead.

'Over there we didn't get just categorised,' he recalls. 'You became combat-ready or not combat-ready. If you weren't combat-ready you were sacked out of the unit; if you were combat-ready, well, "Get on with it!"'

His next job was staff officer operations at the Air Lift Group headquarters at Richmond. There he set about reshaping 86 Wing Headquarters, which directed the two Herc squadrons and the Townsville-based Caribou squadron, into a flying headquarters that could really drive military effects. The timing was exquisite, with the 1999 East Timor missions just around the corner.

'Timor went off pretty well, although I think it was pretty much maturing in the understanding of the wider defence organisation about how you go about hosting complex air lift systems into an operation while we have to do everything else,' he says. 'So our world was very much embracing a world of complexity and concurrency and that was what we were really discovering then.'

This complex and ambiguous operational environment has only become more demanding since 1999. After East Timor, Oddie was appointed commanding officer of Number 36 Squadron. His predecessor, Dave Harrison, had 're-set' the squadron to focus on military effects. The fleet was also undergoing a major upgrade, and complicating matters further was a string of difficult search and rescue missions including providing assistance to lone French sailor Isabelle Autissier in the Southern Ocean.

'Our search and rescue attempts in the Southern Ocean [involved] the toughest of flying, commonly down at 300 feet in the mist of the ocean waves, in the cloud coming down, making the aircraft drive near 100-foot waves,' he says.

In between the busy mission schedule Oddie built on his predecessor's work to mould the squadron into a combat-ready unit, modelled on his RAF experiences.

'I had no idea what was coming. I just thought, "Our job is to be the government's insurance agent; our job is to be combat-ready, so let's do it, let's do it properly, let's do it professionally,"' he says.

After two years as deputy commander of Northern Command (Norcom) in Darwin, Oddie returned to Richmond in 2004 as Officer Commanding 86 Wing in charge of heavy, medium and light air lift. His first impression was that risk was not being managed strategically.

He came up with a concept called 'battle worthiness' to cut through what he calls the 'sea of dynamic opinion' and produce tested, pragmatic and informed advice. He also used it to bridge the gap between pure military advice and advice that would be useful if the unthinkable happened and the RAAF lost a C-130 in Iraq.

'If we lost a Herc it was going to be a really bad thing nationally, a really bad thing,' he says. 'There would be all sorts of enquiries into it and if we didn't have our ducks in a row, then we were going to look pretty untidy. I also felt I didn't want to go round looking widows in the eyes and not be able to say, "I did the best for your hubby."'

Oddie strongly believed the chances of losing a Herc in Iraq were high and rising daily, the RAAF being one of the few operators never to lose one.

'If that happened we really needed to be ready for it,' he says. 'There had been some level of assumption in my own mind and maybe the minds of others that, "We've never lost a Herc; why would we lose a Herc?"'

His view was formed by the tragedy in October 1991 when a Boeing 707 jet crashed during training in Bass Strait. Five RAAF personnel were killed.

'There were two or three mates on board and I know the families, and I thought, "I don't want to see that happen on my watch,"' he says.

He learned it is vital not only to support the families but also to inform them properly. 'I also wanted to make sure families knew it was a tough business and while we are doing the best we could, it wasn't necessarily perfect.'

While building the dialogue process with families, Oddie was implementing a 'notion of tactical principles' that allows an aircraft captain to define the tactics and the higher command to define the principles.

'We brought battle risk management pragmatically to the table and as a team we started to balance risk. We invested not just in the gadgets but in the skills, the training, the education, the supply chain, the engineering, the maintenance of the day,' he says. 'We studied all that as a total system view, focused on the business of warfare. The fact we haven't yet dropped a Herc in these tough places, again has a modicum of luck in it, but I think we have made our luck to a large extent through tactics. We have had missiles go past aircraft and just miss … We might have a different world had we not invested back then.'

The end result, he believes, is a more flexible and more responsive air lift force. That has meant a fundamental shift from focusing just on aircraft, gadgets and methods to delivering the right support for the soldier, the airman or the humanitarian responder on the ground. Hence the Air Mobility mission: 'We fly important people and stuff to tough places on time.'

John Oddie finished his command of Air Lift Group in December 2010 and moved on to become Deputy Commander Joint Task Force 633 in the Middle East Area of Operations during 2011.

Chapter 4

BALI BOMBINGS

The scale of human devastation was the biggest shock for the first RAAF C-130 crews to hit the ground at Denpasar airport following the first Bali bombings in October 2002.

Early reports had indicated that just a few Australians had been killed and several more injured, but Operation Bali Assist would become the largest Australian aeromedical evacuation since the Vietnam War.

As the lumbering military transport planes droned northwards towards Darwin and then on to Bali's capital, it became apparent that the situation was very much worse than first imagined.

Terrorist bombers from the radical South-East Asian Islamic group Jemaah Islamiyah had struck where they could cause maximum destruction to innocent civilians and make a huge protest statement against western decadence — the crowded bars of Kuta's nightclub strip.

A trip to Bali was a rite of passage for many Australians and after sunset the bars, restaurants and shops were a magnet for Australian and other western visitors to Indonesia's tourist mecca and Hindu outpost.

Two bombs sliced through crowds of holidaymakers on the night of October 12, including a massive car bomb detonated outside the Sari Club. When the smoke cleared 202 people were dead, including 88 Australians, and dozens more were badly injured including many with shocking burns.

Sunday, 13 October 2002 dawned like any other for the then Darwin-based trainee surgeon Bruce Ashford. He was up and about quite early and he tuned into the ABC TV 'Insiders' program where host Barrie Cassidy was talking about a nightclub bombing in Bali and Australian casualties.

Ashford was due to go to work at Royal Darwin Hospital at midday for an overnight shift as junior surgical registrar. He was to be the only surgical registrar on duty that day and as he drove into work he got a call from his boss and fellow reservist David Read suggesting that he bring his gear with him, including his RAAF uniform. Darwin was going to be the main hub for Operation Bali Assist and it was unclear whether Ashford would be at the hospital or on a Herc heading for Denpasar.

Once it was confirmed that not just two people were dead and four injured as had been originally reported but the situation was much, much worse, the wards at Royal Darwin were cleared and disaster response plans activated to cope with an influx of gravely ill bombing victims.

'I got to work and Readie said, "Mate, I think this is going to hot up,"' Ashford says.

Read had arranged for himself and fellow reserve anaesthetist Sue Winter to get on the first C-130 that had left Richmond with an aeromedical team on board.

'I remember Sue Winter saying, "We need to put a big footprint on the ground here." So she was trying to get me on the first plane, but that didn't happen,' Ashford recalls.

He rang his wife Deanne, a former army officer, and asked, 'Can you just throw my cams in a bag and bring them in? I don't know what's happening, and I may be staying here but I may have to go to Bali.'

The first plane left about 4 p.m. At about 6 p.m. he received a phone call from a wing commander in Glenbrook.

'Bruce, how would you go managing ventilated patients?'

'Listen, I'll be fine. I'd be happy to,' replied Ashford, who had just completed an intensive care unit (ICU) term and felt ready to take on any mission.

'I think we'd like to have you on a plane going across,' she said, 'because our intensivist who was meant to be on the plane to go over and help with the ventilation missed the plane.'

They were moving people to Darwin on service transport.

'If they'd thought about it they probably would have moved everyone civvy air,' he says. 'But anyway I got my stuff together and got out to the RAAF base. There were a few of us going over. The plane arrived and we put an ambulance in the back and flew out of RAAF Base Darwin in uniform, not really knowing what we were heading over to at all.'

They left at about 11 p.m. and arrived at Denpasar around 2 a.m. Bruce Ashford will never forget the sight that met their eyes.

'The air movements apron, which was a covered area, [had] stretchers all over the place and wires strung up off the thing and bags hanging off them. I just got off the plane, and Readie or Sue — I don't know who it was — said "This is completely out of control. What's gone on here?" There were just people being delivered in by various means.'

Ashford began life as the son of a Methodist lay preacher and university bookshop manager in Perth but spent his formative years in rural Queensland near Dalby, where his father had purchased a pig farm. When he enrolled in dentistry at the University of Queensland in 1987, he was the first of 28 first cousins to undertake tertiary studies.

'During that time I was working in hardware stores and assisting in nursing homes and I thought, "There must be a better way forward." I heard of military undergraduate scholarships and figured that was going to be a good way of having money for not doing too much,' he says. 'My parents were of course disgusted that I would do that type of thing. They thought I was the least military person they would ever have met, but nonetheless I applied and was told during my officer selection interview that I was "verbose" — and did I know what that meant.'

In 1989 he joined the RAAF as a dental undergraduate and officer cadet. Between finishing dental school and his first posting to RAAF Base Williamtown he spent a month in India doing mission dental work. He excelled at officer training school at Point Cook before returning to Williamtown with his wife and new baby.

Former Chief of Air Force Air Marshal Geoff 'Shep' Shepherd became famous around the globe in 1988 for this dramatic take-off manoeuvre at East Sale when he was a young Squadron Leader and F-111 pilot. *PHOTO AL MEADOWS*

An army paratrooper jumps from the ramp of a RAAF C-130 during a training exercise. *PHOTO ADF*

A RAAF C-130 Hercules conducts airdrop training in a paddock near Richmond in NSW.
PHOTO RAAF

A RAAF C-130 disgorges its cargo of Australian troops at a dusty airstrip in the Middle East.
PHOTO ADF

A C-130 Hercules deploys its spectacular missile countermeasure flares that are designed to deflect heat-seeking missiles away from the aircraft. *PHOTO ADF*

A J-model C-130 Hercules departs from Tarin Kowt under the watchful gaze of a Bushmaster protected infantry vehicle and Airfield Defence Guards. *PHOTO ADF*

Senior loadmaster Warrant Officer Wayne Silverman oversees the loading of a yet another C-130 Hercules load of equipment bound for Australian forces in Afghanistan at the Al Minhad air base near Dubai. It is about a four-hour flight from Al Minhad into Kandahar. *PHOTO IAN McPHEDRAN*

Among the last RAAF flight crew to operate the legendary F-111 swing wing strike jet, Air Combat Officer Flying Officer Adele Merriman and F-111 pilot Flight Lieutenant Jasper McCaldin with a much loved 'pig' just before the aircraft retired in 2010. *PHOTO IAN McPHEDRAN*

Senior engineering officer (SENGO) Squadron Leader Pete O'Donnell believes the F-111 had a 'mystique'. *PHOTO IAN McPHEDRAN*

An Army Black Hawk helicopter makes a tight squeeze inside the cargo hold of a RAAF C-130 Hercules. *PHOTO ADF*

Two key hazards to aircraft operating in Papua New Guinea, including the DHC-4 Caribou, are clouds and high mountains. *PHOTO RAAF*

A familiar sight for 40 years at short bush airstrips throughout Papua New Guinea, a RAAF DHC-4 Caribou ready to take-off with the loadmaster up through the hatch to make sure the field is clear of hazards. *PHOTO RAAF*

Boxing kangaroo artwork on a blast wall at the C-130 detachment compound at an airbase in the Middle East. *PHOTO ADF*

Troops crammed into the cargo hold of a RAAF C-130 Hercules transport. *PHOTO ADF*

The legendary F-111 'pig' strike jet performs its signature move, the dump and burn, when fuel is dumped and ignited by the jet's after burners generating a long, fiery tail. *PHOTO ADF*

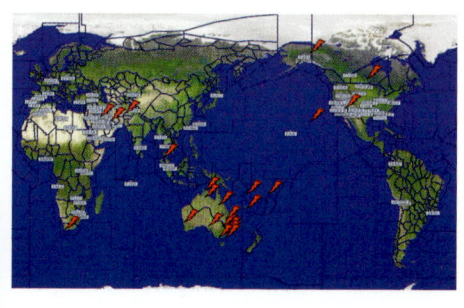

On any given day the RAAF will have aircraft and personnel scattered around the globe. The red arrows here mark RAAF deployments during 2010. *GRAPHIC RAAF*

A RAAF 'black hander' engine maintainer makes some delicate adjustments to a J-model Herc at Al Minhad air base near Dubai. *PHOTO ADF*

'It was a great place and as a dental officer in the RAAF it was fantastic, because you could provide the very best service without having to worry about the cash. You knew there was no cost imperative,' he says. 'We didn't do unnecessary things, but if someone needed a crown then they got a crown, if they needed a specialist consultation then they got that.'

By 1995 Ashford had developed other ambitions. By then the father of two sons, William and Baden, he left the full-time RAAF to become an oral surgeon. This meant a degree in medicine and further specialised post-graduate qualifications.

'I didn't want to stay in the permanent air force because I knew all I'd be doing would be the same things that medical officers do, essentially treating very fit people on a day-to-day basis,' he says.

Unlike the other services, the RAAF has a branch of specialist reserves where the service obligations are not arduous, but only very specialised people can get in. As such, Ashford was required only to serve for seven days a year, but to be available at all times.

After completing medicine in 1999 he decided to qualify as a general surgeon instead and see what happened. The family, now boosted by the arrival of daughter Eleanor, moved to Darwin so he could undertake basic surgical training at Royal Darwin Hospital. Deanne was back in the full-time army as a captain so life was hectic for the Ashford clan. Then came the Bali bombings.

Once the news got out in Bali that there was an Australian presence at Denpasar airport, people poured in by rickshaws, taxis or any other means possible.

Ashford says, 'We just hopped off the plane and walked off and said, "What do you want us to do?" There were 30 or so people; every one would have warranted a major trauma call in Liverpool or Westmead or Royal Brisbane. All of them were worthy of that because there was a high degree of burns and, you know, fractures.'

They got straight to work. They had no time to think about how overwhelming it all was. They just had to get into it, but they were desperately short of medical equipment and had to re-use much of it and improvise where they could.

'That was led by Sue and David and there was a few of us involved,' he recalls. 'We were all at the start of our careers and David and Sue were both qualified specialists, but again they were youngish.'

They were used to handling traumas at work every day but this was on a different scale. 'This was really, in hindsight, a major, major incident. It was very raw and it was not at all sophisticated on the ground.'

He recalls Read saying that they would have to load up the first plane because the pilots were almost running out of flying hours. 'We have to take this plane. There's another plane that's soon to leave Darwin but there are not going to be any other medical officers here for about four hours.'

Ashford says, 'There was myself and Squadron Leader Greg Wilson, the senior medical officer in Darwin at the time, so there was two of us, and there were other doctors around in outside areas, but only two of us at the place.'

Read then said, 'There are some really critically ill people in Denpasar [Sanglah] Hospital in the intensive care unit. We need to go and see what's going on with them. Who's going to go?'

'I want to go,' Ashford said.

'All right, well go and hop in that van, you go to Denspasar Hospital and suss it out. By the time you get back we are probably going to be gone.'

'Okay, thanks, see you.'

'So I hopped in this van with this [Australian] army reserve officer who, incredibly, turned out to be in the London bombings as well, three or four years later,' Ashford recalls. 'He came with me and I said, "Who are you?" He said, "I'm going with you to make sure everything is fine." We went in there. We weren't armed, we were foreign nationals in a country. We were there in uniform, it was completely bizarre and wouldn't be tolerated anywhere else, but it was completely out to lunch.'

The local Australian colonel and warrant officer who had been defence attachés in Indonesia were at the hospital.

'We sort of said, "This is who we are." And they showed me around various wards. There were people everywhere who were burnt and some in the process of dying. It was all over, everywhere you looked. There was a locals' ward [and] a white persons' ward — most of those [patients] were European, Australian or English.'

Then they were escorted to the intensive care unit. 'There was a young girl there; I won't forget it. She had very serious injuries, her blood pressure was really disastrous. She looked Australian, she looked like she was going to die.'

He called Di Stevens, the intensivist at Royal Darwin Hospital.

'Di, it's Bruce. I'm calling from intensive care at Denpasar. I'm going to tell you what's going on with this patient and I want you to tell me what's the right thing to do here.'

He told her the story.

'Bruce, anything you do will be an improvement on what is currently going on, so I need you to make the right decision based on what you can see and to be happy that that decision was the right one.'

So Ashford did as she suggested. 'We said to them, "We are taking this girl back to the airfield." So we put her in. They were a bit upset by that [but] I said, "What are they going to do?" We took her to the airfield and she didn't improve and despite all our efforts she died before she got on the plane. She was clearly a teenager and [it was] just a disaster. That was challenging and something you don't easily leave behind. You wonder whether it was the right decision but I think in hindsight it probably was; her injury was the main thing that dictated her death.'

They had no time to dwell on the sad fact of one teenage girl's premature and violent death. The situation was very similar to combat, where the medics have to try and save those who might live, given the limited amount of care and equipment available. Some people were going to die, but they knew they had to move on to the next patient, and then the next and the next.

'That's exactly how we were; it wasn't [just] any time,' Ashford says. 'We took her and within half an hour she had died, but all that time I was involved in her care, Greg [Wilson] was helping out with all these patients. The other plane had left with a lot of people, but the place was now full again. I remember Jason McCarthy, the [former] Collingwood footballer. We all [joked] to him, "You left Collingwood, so you're not going to get good care here, pal, because I go for Collingwood!" He was doing okay, but there were a lot of guys that weren't okay. The guy that was on the bed saying, "I'm all right, I'm all right" — the guy that was interviewed [Peter Hughes], common footage — we looked after him. There were a lot of people we took back, and subsequently it got close to morning. After we'd been run off our feet, another Hercules turned up and all these senior medical officers got off.'

They said to Ashford, 'We're four intensivists, what would you like us to do?'

'Okay, I need you to go there with those two girls that are badly burnt and one of them has lost her leg; I need you, sir, to go over here, there are these five people that need whatever,' Ashford recalls saying. 'So it was a matter of then just divvying up. From there it was only an hour or two [until], with two of the specialists, I took a plane of people home.'

Ashford had not done much aeromedical evacuation work and in this case it was all about medicine and damage control.

'So I took the plane home with two or three ventilated people, in a Hercules with about 20 people on the plane,' he says. 'We'd been up for a long time, we'd been awake for a long time, and this had been overnight and well into the next day. I think we got home late that afternoon and all those people were taken off the plane and taken to Royal Darwin Hospital. They sat us in the air movement area and said, "You know, you guys should go home for a sleep and then you come back and see us tomorrow."'

So he went home, remaining comatose from late afternoon until the next morning. Then he woke up and thought 'Well, I'm a doctor at Royal Darwin. I've got to go to work.'

He got up and did just that.

'We spent the next week operating on a lot of those people that we'd brought home, under the consultants there,' he says. 'That was a really fascinating experience, to see how Royal Darwin works: really experienced surgeons working with physicians and anaesthetists in a theatre setting. A lot of us were doing big surgery at a very junior level but there was always a surgeon around to pop in and say "Yeah, do this, do that, do this."'

For a young surgeon this was an amazing medical experience, albeit a disaster in terms of people's lives.

Ashford says, 'I am a bit fatalist with things like that. I think those things are sent to prepare you for what comes ahead. I think I was a much more adventurous and capable young surgical trainee as a result of it and I think it's probably helped me. I'm faced with people there in a hopeless situation and I think back to what we had, and say, "Guys, we just need to adapt and overcome."'

There is no doubt that they kept people alive who would otherwise have died on the ground in Denpasar.

'Absolutely,' he says, 'and to save limbs that wouldn't have been saved by splitting them with a knife, doing fasciotomies on them and giving people pain relief, giving people fluids they needed in an appropriate way. We had very little equipment and few resources because it all happened so quickly and the priority was getting them back to Darwin.

'And, in fact, it has brought about a bit of a change, because we had limited fluids. It's almost been a little bit of a paradigm shift in that we rarely use minimum volume resuscitation and these people probably did a lot better than they might have done. We didn't have enough fluid to give them, but we kept them alive until we got back to Royal Darwin.'

RAAF pilot Samantha Freebairn was on a day off when her boss called and told her she was going to Bali on a mission. The then 24-year-old flight lieutenant and C-130 co-pilot hadn't seen the news or heard about the mass murder at the Sari Club but as she and several mates drove to Richmond they heard news of the devastation.

'I just thought "Oh my God." I did not want to go to Bali,' she recalls. 'We didn't know whether they were going to target Australians.

Was the aircraft coming in going to be hit? There was very little information about it.'

She was on the second aircraft to arrive at Denpasar and she couldn't believe the scene on the ground.

'The tarmac was just a mass of people. Someone had got word the Aussies were coming and they were just sending everyone to the airport and a couple of doctors can only do so much,' she says.

Normally after landing, the pilots rest up and do their flight planning, but on this night it was all hands on deck and Freebairn was issued with gloves and told to help where she could.

'I love medical, the job they do is amazing, but they just needed all the hands they could and not many of us are good with blood.'

Once the Herc was loaded with 14 very sick patients it departed for Darwin and as Freebairn did not do the take-off, she was down the back for the first hour of the flight assisting the medical staff.

'We [went] around handing them earplugs,' she recalls. 'One guy yelled out, "Mate, I can't hear anything from the blast — what good are these things?" Fair enough! Another dude just grabbed my arm as I walked past and said, "My back is killing me, I've got to lie on my stomach," so he sat up and his whole back, the skin of his back just peeled off and I folded it over. He was swearing with the pain and I said, "It's just a scratch, harden up, don't be a girl, turn over" and the medical people were just phenomenal.'

Freebairn did conduct the landing back in Darwin and the airport apron was a sea of ambulances waiting to ferry the patients to Royal Darwin Hospital. After a psychological de-brief, which she says was well and truly needed, the crew had a well-earned rest and then met up to try to relax and talk about the experience.

Once she returned home to Sydney she opened up her backpack only to find that she had the wrong bag. One of the patients on the flight from Bali, a German girl, had exactly the same bag and it contained her belongings, including her passport.

'You couldn't get in touch with anyone for security reasons so it was almost impossible to get this girl her bag back,' Freebairn says. 'About six weeks later, after trying and trying, they confirmed she was in Concord hospital in Sydney so I went to visit her and I think that was really good for me. She was recovering, so she had skin growing back on her face and I visited her a couple of times. I think it was good closure to see her recovery, for me.'

These days Squadron Leader Dean Bolton flies C-17 cargo jets out of Amberley near Brisbane, but in October 2002 he was a C-130 pilot based at Richmond. On that terrible Sunday morning he was at home tuned into Channel Nine's 'Sunday' TV program when he got a call from his boss. He took a civilian flight to Darwin before flying a Herc to Denpasar.

Bolton had been to Bali for several holidays since the age of 12 and like many Australians had nothing but fond memories. Arriving in the dead of night during the nation's biggest aeromedical evacuation mission since the Vietnam War was a different story altogether.

The aircraft taxied to the casualty collection point near the fire station and his pleasant memories of smiling holiday makers with their plaited hair and Bali shirts were quickly replaced by grim scenes of people in pain, medics hard at work and a lot of bystanders watching on.

The flight crew had expected a speedy turnaround to get the patients back to Darwin as quickly as possible, but the gravely injured had to be stabilised before they could risk the four-hour flight. Once the aircraft was shut down and secured and all the checks completed, there was nothing for Bolton and his fellow crew members to do so they gave the medics a hand.

'I'm not very medically minded, so all I did was hold a drip for someone while they tried to put an IV drip into [a patient]. I'm a bit squeamish when it comes to blood so I was looking the other way, but I got a bit involved there, just talking to people. [You do] the best you can do to comfort people,' he says.

Normally pilots are isolated in their world at the pointy end of the aircraft, so this was a new experience for Bolton. 'You've got to help.

Obviously the medics are outnumbered by what they've got to do … so you just help out where you can. We just did what we could do, and helped stretcher-carry people onto the aeroplane. Just manual labour to help out.'

The Bali mission shattered Bolton's vision of the holiday island and left a sour taste in his mouth, but he found the job extremely satisfying.

'It felt really good to be helping people, because all too often we are doing what is seemingly mundane stuff — it is not necessarily so, but seemingly mundane. To be hands on and helping out, and in this case making a difference to someone's life, savings lives, hopefully, is what it was,' he says.

In a remarkable coincidence, John Oddie was in Denpasar on the night the bombs went off. He was deputy commander of Northern Command in Darwin at the time and had been in Bali on leave. He was waiting at Denpasar airport for the flight home when the terrorists attacked. His hotel was right where the big bomb was detonated and he should have been there checking out at about that time but had decided to go to dinner and then directly to the airport.

'I just got to the airport and as we walked in the door the lights went out and then people turned up with blood on them to get on flights out,' he says.

At first Oddie wasn't sure whether it had been a bomb or a gas explosion. 'There was a lack of certainty and I guess you don't tend to look for the worst,' he says. 'These days I have a slightly alternative view of things and assume the worst and hope for the best. I've sort of inverted my understanding since then.'

Oddie was not closely involved in the Bali mission but watched with interest the rapid process of coordination that took place at Norcom's Darwin headquarters.

'It was able to help synchronise the air force efforts, the wider defence efforts, the emergency service efforts in Darwin and the broader government and territory services up there and I think that worked out very well.'

The first Herc crews who flew into Bali did it pretty tough due to fatigue and uncertainty. Some were on the edge of their crew duty day when they arrived in Denpasar and supposed to rest for at least eight hours before flying again.

'There wasn't much that could be done about that,' Oddie says. 'We try not to go there and we've got some fairly tough rules about the way we treat fatigue and manage core duty, but we also know that sometimes jobs have to get done. The early crews that went on the ground there also went into an uncertain situation.'

According to Oddie, security was not clear cut. It was dark, there was confusion and people were making some big demands in terms of getting injured loved ones back to Australia. There was a great deal of uncertainty about patient priority, crew rest and fatigue, but the crews dealt with it and many remained on duty beyond their regulated limits.

'Eventually they ended up leaving without some people and they carried that burden with them when they left,' he says. 'They didn't know what they had left behind because they needed to get back. They were trained to get the people on board back, so they would have done it tough.'

Oddie pays particular tribute to the loadmasters and medical staff who kept many gravely injured people alive during the flights. 'The effort that goes on in flight by the doctors and nurses is amazing — tracheotomies, heart restarting, a lot of stuff going on. The crew aren't used to seeing what happens and some of them are not well; their lives are damaged due to their trauma experiences in those cases.'

Some aircrew suffered psychological damage and Oddie is not surprised.

'Many of our loadmasters — particularly the loadmasters, and sometimes the technicians we are carrying down the back, and the medical staff — they are the ones that really see the toughest end of things in these circumstances,' he says. 'The pilots and navigators and flight engineers primarily have to deal with making sure the mission gets delivered, so they are dealing with a different story.'

Chief loadmaster Warrant Officer Scott Willacott had only a minor involvement in the first Bali mission, but he was on the first Herc to touch down after the second wave of Bali bombings in Kuta and at Jimbaran Beach Resort on 1 October 2005, that claimed the lives of 20 people, including four Australians, and injured many others.

He says nothing can really prepare aircrew for a mission like that, when people are boarding the aircraft in various states of physical and mental trauma.

'You acknowledge the fact that, yeah, that's a guy on a stretcher, he's pretty well banged up and it's very, very touch and go, but right, I've got my job to do, the medicos have their job to do,' Willacott says. He had a talk to some of the medicos and the rest of the crew after the mission, but getting in there to get people out was the number one priority.

Willacott regards aeromedical evacuation (AME) missions — either wounded troops in the Middle East or civilians in Bali — as some of the most rewarding work he has done. 'Knowing you got someone out of somewhere that is either not a very nice place to be or somewhere that doesn't have the ability to care for them with the injuries they've got, to somewhere safe, and then they recover their quality of life to a certain extent, that's a pretty good feeling.'

His most rewarding evacuation flight was when two Perth families of about 10 people, who had been in the restaurant when the suicide bomber blew himself up, were flown out after suffering a variety of injuries from burst eardrums to shrapnel wounds. The crew told them they were going to get them safely back to Darwin and Willacott organised water and a hot meal for the group, who had not eaten all day. Once one of the fathers realised everyone would be safe his concern turned to 10 surfboards they had brought on holidays with them.

He said, 'Mate, I'm happy to give them away to the locals.'

Willacott replied, 'Don't you worry — just sit here with your family, look after the kids. I'll go and sort the surfboards out.'

By the time the families walked onto the aircraft the rear 6 metres of the Herc had been transformed into a surfboard rack. 'He thought that was the greatest thing since sliced bread,' Willacott recalls. 'Not only was his family getting back to Australia to a high level of medical care, but all his luggage and boards were coming as well. Just to see that weight being lifted off his shoulders initially, when we said, "Hey, we are going to take you home."

'Once he knew all the luggage and surfboards were going, an hour into the flight he virtually collapsed, he was that exhausted from worrying about things. Getting off the plane in Darwin, the federal coppers wanted to take him away to have a chat to him about what he witnessed and he turned around and shook my hand and said, "Thanks mate, that's awesome." That is up there with probably the most rewarding thing I've ever done.'

The American TV comedy 'MASH' was the inspiration behind Flight Sergeant Frank Alcantara's decision to become a military medic. He had wanted to be a fighter pilot but was too short. After three attempts he made it through and became a medic.

'It was the best thing I ever did. I love this job,' he says.

Alcantara has deployed to Rwanda, East Timor, Iraq and the Bali bombings. Rwanda was an incredible deployment for medical staff, who treated injuries and disease on a biblical scale. The Spanish-born medic, whose family immigrated to Australia during the 1960s, says nothing could top his eight and a half months in Rwanda, but Operation Bali Assist came close.

In October 2002 he was posted to Richmond for a three-year separated posting, away from his wife and kids who stayed in Townsville to minimise disruption. He was at a mate's place at Hornsby north of Sydney when Bali happened.

'I was woken up by my mate Ollie, and he said "Frank, I think you better have a look at this" I ran out of the bedroom and down the stairs — he had this really plush penthouse — and I ran to the TV and there was Bali in all its fury,' Alcantara says. 'Within seconds my mobile went off and it was my boss back at Richmond basically saying "Frank, you'd better get yourself over here." I had a quick shower, jumped in the car and what I remember most clearly is that from the time I got that call at Hornsby to the time we were wheels up at Richmond was exactly three hours.'

They called in at Darwin to pick up some ambulances that served as mobile morgues instead of patient transfer vehicles and flew on to Denpasar and the casualty clearing station set up at the fire station next to the main terminal.

'By that stage some of the bodies had already started coming in. We were aircraft number two that touched down,' he says.

Each C-130 aircraft could carry about 70 patients in litters, but in Bali they were restricted to six or seven due to the number of very serious burns victims. 'These people weren't just hurt, they were seriously burnt — 80 to 90 per cent of their body was burnt.'

They also carried a number of walking wounded and other less serious casualties and that is how it went for several days.

'Most of us probably didn't sleep for a good 76 hours before we got a wink,' he says. The stress was so intense that he even took up smoking again after a nine-year break. During his first five-minute break one of the nurses offered him a 'ciggie' so he took it and that triggered another six-year journey to give up the dreaded weed.

Alcantara had thought he would be ready for anything after witnessing the Rwanda genocide, but nothing had prepared him for the shock of seeing his own countrymen in such an appalling state.

'This was different; these were our people. I mean, there were a lot of Europeans there as well, lots of Germans, British backpackers, New Zealanders, the whole lot, but there were lots and lots of Australians,' he says. 'To see Australians going through that made me feel completely different. I had to slap myself around a couple of times to sort of focus on it. I remember Steve Cook, who was already on the ground, actually turned around at one stage and said, "For God's sake Frank, snap out of it!" And I thought, "Oh, yeah, sorry," and down I went, got to work.'

They were performing major procedures on the ground at the fire station, preparing critically ill patients for the flight back to Darwin.

'When the body fills up with pressure, particularly from burns, you've got to relieve [it] so you have to do surgical procedures,' Frank says. 'Those procedures can only be performed by doctors and intensive care personnel, so those people that were deemed to need further stabilisation had to be kept back. Once they were ready to fly, because you had to be fit to fly to go through the stresses of the flight, they were then placed on the aircraft.'

They were flown first to Darwin and then on to other cities such as Perth, Adelaide and Melbourne for specialised treatment. This went on for days and for the medical staff it meant grabbing a quick nap when they could and eating and drinking on the run.

Alcantara says the key lesson from Operation Bali Assist was to ensure that the right equipment was on board the aircraft.

'We had not transported that many people on a C-130 aircraft since Vietnam and even going back to Vietnam we hadn't transported that many people in one hit. This was just an absolute first,' he says. 'We had to rewrite the books really, but look the success rate is there, it's there now. People came back and are thankful for it.'

Many of the AME lessons learnt while using the C-130 during Bali Assist have been applied to the RAAF's new and much bigger C-17 Globemaster aircraft.

Alcantara was part of the transition team from the Hercs to the C-17 and now trains aircrew in how to deal with mass casualty incidents. He regards the C-17 as a quantum leap forward in AME capability.

'It is this humungous monster of a truck you could play football in. It's fluoro lit, all the oxygen is basically pumped into the aircraft so you don't need to take oxygen with you, the electrical system's already contained within the aircraft, it's comfortable, it's quiet and it's fast.'

The Boeing C-17 Globemaster is the first military aircraft purpose-built for carrying cargo and conducting AME. Not only is it a much more stable flying platform than the C-130 but it can be adapted easily to become a flying intensive care unit catering for fully ventilated patients.

If there were another Bali bombing today the evacuation, using C-17s, would take about half the time and half the number of aircraft. Gravely ill patients could be flown home almost immediately.

There was a great deal of personal and professional satisfaction for all the RAAF personnel involved in both Bali rescue missions. They helped save numerous lives and performed above and beyond the call of duty when their countrymen were in dire need of help. They saw shocking things and flew well outside their normal duty limits, but they did it because Australians were in trouble.

Frank Alcantara had another opportunity to help his fellow Australians with the evacuation of 173 patients from hospitals in Cairns ahead of Tropical Cyclone Yasi's arrival in Far North Queensland.

'I remember the date of the mission — 1 February 2011 — clearly, as this also happened to be my wife's birthday,' he says. 'In fact, when I rang her that afternoon she was expecting me to tell her I had finished work for the day, was on my way home and readying for our birthday dinner.'

Instead, as on many previous occasions, he greeted her with, 'Sorry babe, but I need you to take me home to grab my AME kit and bring me back to base ASAP.'

Alcantara did not know when he would be home again, so instead of presenting her with her birthday present of a diamond ring over a romantic Japanese dinner he simply gave it to her while he was packing his kit.

'The mission was fairly busy and arduous but professionally rewarding,' he says. 'We worked tirelessly through the night and much of the next morning loading [what seemed like] a never-ending stream of patients, and eventually took off from Cairns, destination back to Brisbane. The unload and transfer to Queensland Health was just as long and arduous, however once again very rewarding. I am proud to have been picked for the mission and more importantly to have been of assistance to the patients of Cairns hospitals during Cyclone Yasi.'

After working non-stop for 36 hours he came home, only to discover that his house in Townsville had been damaged by the cyclone. 'So instead of a few days' rest I was once again travelling north, this time to help clean up my house and property over the next five days.'

Chapter 5

LOADIES

The disruption of air force life impacts hardest on the people who work down at the back end of the aircraft. Pilots and navigators rotate in and out of squadrons in various guises, from aircrew to staff officers, but loadmasters are loadmasters and are on duty with the aircraft for years or even decades on end.

The job of the loadmaster or 'loady' is a complex mix of cargo management, aircraft safety, passenger liaison and strict disciplinarianism. It is not for everyone and the first requirement is a thick skin. Ask any diggers who have flown on a Herc into Afghanistan for their most lasting memory of the flight and most include a tale about a run-in with a grumpy loadmaster.

Some loadies have a reputation for being rude and intolerant and Australian Hercs are well known throughout the Middle East Area of Operations (MEAO) as the most strictly run flights of all the nations that fly troops and cargo around the region in Hercs. Jump on a British Herc and body armour and seat belts are seemingly optional, but board a RAAF C-130 and watch out if you do not stow your weapon correctly or try to remove your armour or helmet before the designated line of safety is crossed.

RAAF loadies take their safety responsibilities extremely seriously and some even appear to enjoy shouting at soldiers who equally enjoy ignoring their directions. They have lost only one passenger in the MEAO and no one wants to lose any more. That loss was an American civilian contractor, shot during a flight in Iraq. He was probably the unluckiest person in the world to be sitting in the seat where a 'one in a million' rogue shot from a lone gunman taking a bead on a fast-moving Herc on take-off from Baghdad International Airport penetrated the hull, hitting him in the neck.

Warrant Officer Wayne Silverman has been hauling cargo and passengers around the world in Hercs for 20 years. He joined the air force in 1975 as a raw 17-year-old in the supply department with air movements. His first job was to go to Darwin for the Cyclone Tracy relief mission when the northern capital was flattened by the violent tropical storm. His initial posting was to Williamtown and the work he did there, combined with what he had witnessed in Darwin, convinced him that aircrew was where he wanted to be.

His maiden flying job was with helicopters at Amberley as a loadmaster on the legendary UH-1 Iroquois 'Huey' helicopter. At that time the RAAF flew the nation's military rotary wing fleet and Silverman eventually moved on to Black Hawk helicopters before the political decision was taken in 1986 to move the entire rotary fleet over to navy and army control. Like most rotary wing loadies, he chose to transfer to Richmond to fly C-130 Hercules rather than swap his blue uniform for khaki to stay with the choppers.

'Because I had been in air movements, I'd worked a fair bit with the C-130s, so I had a lot of knowledge and experience with the aircraft. So the transition wasn't difficult for me to do,' he says.

In 1989 he became a Herc loadmaster and has been a loady ever since — one of the most experienced in the business. He has worked on the Boeing 707 tanker and VIP aircraft fleet as well as Hercs. He travelled the world with the 707s, flew into East Timor in 1999 and in 2009 was on his fifth rotation with C-130s in the MEAO. In between he has been pretty much everywhere the RAAF workhorses have gone, including the Solomon Islands, Papua New Guinea and throughout Asia.

The East Timor mission felt slightly strange to Silverman because he had been in Darwin in 1975 when the first group of Timorese refugees arrived after the Indonesian invasion.

'Twenty-five years later, there I was flying those people out again, evacuating them back out,' he says. 'Some of those people were probably children back in 1975.'

The wily veteran loady has experienced firsthand the angst that sometimes occurs between soldiers and aircrew and he believes the reason is quite simple.

On the new J-model Herc there is just one loadmaster and two pilots, who never leave the flight deck and so do not interact with passengers at all.

'The loadmaster is the face of the crew. No one else really gets seen,' he says. 'We are in their faces all the time, we are the ones telling them they can't do this or do that, we are the ones that have to keep enforcing the rules all the time, so that is why there is that angst. The pilots can't come down and tell them to put their seat belt on or that they can't sleep on the floor or to put the weapon under the seat.

'At the end of the day you just have to talk to people like you would expect to be spoken to — with some respect. We are only there to get them to where they want to go safely and if they do the right thing it makes our job easier.'

There is a good reason why the RAAF C-130 safety record is so exemplary and it is in the organisation's and the nation's best interests to keep it that way.

'We had that incident in Baghdad where unfortunately the civilian passenger was killed and that sparked the problem of everyone having to wear helmets,' Silverman says. 'A lot of countries here don't even wear body armour inside the aeroplanes but we are very safety conscious and it's important that the passengers we carry get to where they are going safely. If they are hurt because of something we've done in the back of the aeroplane they are no good to anybody.'

On the other hand, he believes that it is vital for passengers, especially soldiers, to be treated with compassion. The aircrew understands how tough it is for diggers who have to live rough and put their lives on the line while the flyers usually eat in a mess and sleep most nights in a bed with sheets.

'They get browbeaten and screamed at, whereas if we can put a little bit of compassion into our side of the house I think they will appreciate it,' Silverman says.

The older loadies have seen and experienced a lot and generally know how to treat people. They try to mentor the younger ones coming through. 'If we are setting a good example for them, then hopefully when we leave they'll have the same sort of outlook on things.'

Despite the negative view from diggers, Wayne Silverman understands just how uncomfortable it is sitting in the back of a C-130 for five hours with body armour on.

'We do what we can to get it off them if we have the space, give them that relief, and then once we cross over the fence they have to put it all back on again,' he says. 'Sometimes we can be really restricted in what we can do for people, but a lot of other times we can provide them with meals, hot coffee, stuff like that, to make them feel a bit more relaxed — try to show them you are human as well; you are not out just to carry boxes around the place.'

What soldiers might also fail to appreciate is that the Herc crews are in considerable danger every time they fly a mission into a hostile location where insurgents would like nothing more than to bring one down. A Herc taking off or coming in to land is a large and at times lumbering target.

Silverman has become hardened to the risks but he recalls the fear he felt during his first flight into Baghdad. As the aircraft descends below a 'safe' level all the crew are on watch for signs of enemy fire. The Australian Hercs are fitted with sophisticated and effective electronic countermeasures or ECM, but the 'mark-one eyeball' remains a crucial tool.

'I was a bit apprehensive about what was going to happen during our approach and [was] sort of looking out, and all of a sudden a thing flashed across the front of my face,' he says. 'I bloody shit myself at the time, [but] when I settled down I looked and it was a fly on the window of the actual airplane ... That was enough to just relax me and I go, "Well I'm over that now, nothing is going to come up and bite me."'

The fact that after more than 20,000 flying hours around the MEAO the Herc fleet and their crews were injury and accident free, apart from the unfortunate American passenger in Baghdad, underscores the hard-nosed approach of the RAAF loadies.

Silverman does admit to a rare negative thought but says, 'When you think about what other people are doing, you quickly turn it into a positive. There really is nothing negative about what we do. You know, you work long hours, it's hot, everything else, but at the end of the day we have the best office in the world and we really enjoy it.'

Motivation has never been an issue.

'I'm still having fun, I love doing what I do, I've been doing it for a long time now and I've been lucky enough throughout my career to keep having changes to keep me motivated all the time,' he says. 'If I'd been flying as a loadmaster for 35 years I might be over it by now.'

One of the vital issues for crews operating in and out of Afghanistan is the wild variation in climatic conditions. In summer the mercury can top 60 degrees Celsius on the ground in Kandahar and in winter Kabul can plummet to 20 below zero.

The aircraft's carrying capacity can vary by 5 or 6 tonnes depending on the heat and the humidity in Tarin Kowt, where the length and elevation of the runway restrict operations. It is worse for the older H-model than the more powerful J. Stress on humans also increases in hotter weather, especially in a Herc that has been sitting in 50-degree heat all day.

'If we have a transit leg up at 25,000 feet then the aircraft has a chance to cool down, but when you are on the ground and just jumping from base to base without getting to height, then there is no way it can cool down,' Silverman says. 'It is just heat soaked all day, [so] a lot of water gets drunk and we carry lots of boxes and Eskies and water in the back for passengers as well. The biggest thing for us is keeping an eye on each other, making sure the guys don't dehydrate and overheat.'

Sometimes the heat is so extreme that crewmembers can spend only 15 minutes outdoors before they must return inside for a rest and a long drink. 'You are just pumping bottles of water into you the whole time.

I think we've been very lucky; we've only had a couple of guys that have fallen over due to heat stroke and it wasn't too severe.'

Senior loadmaster Warrant Officer Scott Willacott, who was on his fifth rotation to the MEAO in mid-2008, says that if you were advertising for loadmasters in the newspaper the key requirements would be good communication skills, resourcefulness, flexibility, dedication and the ability to work well in a small team. 'They must be capable and able to operate in extremes of environment and under different types of stress and duress.'

No two flights are the same and no two arrivals or departures repeat any patterns. Some arrivals are at treetop height and some are steep descents from 10,000 feet.

'For obvious reasons we don't want to be predictable like the nine o'clock bus going the same way every time. We don't want to arrive at the same place at the exact same time every day to present an easier target for people,' Willacott says.

Initial loadmaster training takes between eight and 12 months and begins in the classroom. The theory and technical training is followed by about 200 hours of supervised flying before becoming qualified and endorsed. The endorsements include various stages of airdrop from paratroopers to lightweight loads, all the way up to 15 tonnes of cargo. As the weight increases so do the demands, procedures and qualifications required.

In the past, new loadies might have sat around for 12 months waiting to gain the experience needed to take on an operational deployment, but with the high tempo of operations it is not unusual for them to be on their way to the Middle East almost as soon as they are endorsed.

While a typical day for a C-130 crew is almost impossible to define, Willacott says some operational procedures never vary. They begin with the checklists that cover everything from cargo and passengers to aircraft balance. Then it is time for pre-start checks, beginning with a quick scan of the exterior, looking for oil leaks or anything out of the ordinary. Next the captain kicks off with all the checklists required before flight, on a 'challenge/response' basis, whereby the pilot or co-pilot makes a challenge and the appropriate crewmember responds.

Once the engines are started and the cabin secured, hydraulic systems are checked for leaks and pressures, control surfaces such as wing flaps and elevators are visually checked before a final scan of the cargo is made to confirm it is properly secured. The last thing anyone needs is tonnes of cargo flying around during tactical manoeuvres or turbulence.

Finally the pilot is given the all-clear and the aircraft is ready for take-off. Airborne, the checks continue with a visual scan outside, looking for unusual activity on the ground or other aircraft in the vicinity.

'We are looking for anything that is even remotely unusual, such as an unusually parked car, cars with people congregating at T-intersections or in laneways if you are in a heavily urban environment,' Willacott says. '[We look for] other aircraft — obviously with the frequency of air movements and the types of aircraft flying around, not everyone is the best aviator in the world, so we back the pilots and co-pilots up. They can't see too much past the wing tips so we back them up with a scan behind the aircraft.'

Once at altitude the pilots usually inform the loady of other aircraft and ask him or her to keep an eye out for the traffic.

The other important check is for any ground fire aimed at the aircraft. Loadies are trained to identify everything from small arms fire to missile launches, but the likelihood of seeing an incoming threat is rare. 'There is always that grey area between, "Is that aimed at us or is it just random stuff?" I've got no doubt there would be people around that have definitely had stuff aimed at them while they've been operating over there, but you do get that odd bit of stuff that is definitely in your general direction.'

Incoming rounds are most obvious when flying with night vision gear. 'Everything is a lot more obvious to us at night than it is during the day, so you pick up things very, very quickly. It is sensitive to light, plus one in every five rounds is a tracer round, so you are automatically drawn to that.'

Aircraft in Afghanistan are most vulnerable near airports and not just from hostile fire. Kabul is about 5800 feet above sea level and is surrounded by mountains that rise to 15,000 feet where blizzards are common in bad weather.

Willacott hails from a small town in Western Australia called Kwinana, south of Fremantle. His father, John, a Welshman, spent eight years as a signals operator in the Royal Air Force and encouraged his son to join the military. 'Dad said, "You can't go wrong joining the forces."'

His wife Alissa is a former RAAF dental assistant and understands the strains of airforce life but his family is not oblivious to the pressures. He says that whenever he has been deployed the family unit of four becomes a unit of three people for the duration.

'Someone has to fulfil the duties that either the husband or wife performs while they are away and that usually falls to the other partner,' he says. 'My family is in Perth and my wife's family is in Far North Queensland, and we're in Sydney, slap bang in between our support network. If anything does go pear-shaped while I'm away or whatever, my wife relies very, very heavily on our local support networks — our close friends or things like that.'

Fortunately 37 Squadron is a tight-knit bunch and are quick to respond to each other's needs. 'The pilots look out for other pilots, the co-pilots look out for other co-pilots, engineers look out for each other and loadies look out for other loadies,' Willacott says. 'Nothing is too much of a stretch for the guys to chip in and help out when it's required.'

Both their daughters are school-aged. Says Willacott, 'I know by looking at the type of work they bring home, especially my youngest girl, and speaking to her teacher. About two weeks before I go away, I'd go and pick her up from school and her teacher would come up to me in the playground and say, "You are about to go away on deployment aren't you? I can tell just by her behaviour." Then her schoolwork will dip quite significantly, her attitude at school will change dramatically, even her attitude at home will change, and then about two weeks before I'm due to come home it will pick up and then once I come home the change happens. I guess that is how they cope.'

In January 2009 Willacott was posted to a three-year desk job at Richmond and was home with the family every night and says, 'I'm very, very lucky in that respect. For the next three years I am what you call "surge capacity", so unless something drastic happens and the entire squadron gets called out, I won't have to deploy, so I've got a very nice, very rewarding Monday-to-Friday job.'

He acknowledges that his wife has effectively been a single mother for almost nine years. 'To have me there and for the kids to have a full-time dad for at least the next three years is a massive difference.'

Chapter 6

BYE BYE 'BOU'

The much-loved and idiosyncratic Caribou — or 'bou' — tactical air lifter was put out to pasture in 2009.

The guttural drone of the Canadian-built aircraft's twin 1450 horsepower Pratt and Whitney radial engines had brought comfort to flood-bound farmers, traumatised villagers and relieved diggers for 45 years, ever since an early batch of Caribous on delivery were diverted directly to the war in Vietnam in August 1964. The de Havilland DHC-4 Caribou provided a tactical capability unmatched by any other fixed-wing aircraft. It would shine from the high, hazardous mountains of Papua New Guinea to the flooded or drought-stricken plains of Australia.

Generations of RAAF pilots cut their teeth flying 'bous' around the PNG Highlands, landing and taking off from rough strips cut into mountainsides and navigating at treetop height to avoid the deadly cumulus clouds that can form and swallow an aircraft in seconds.

The Caribou is not pressurised, so must stay below 10,000 feet — not always easy in a country whose highest mountain, Mt Wilhelm, soars to 15,000 feet.

Just west of 38 Squadron's base at Townsville airport is the rugged High Range military training area. In November 2009 the squadron was preparing for the Caribou's last hurrah. Parades were practised, flypasts rehearsed and for the men and women of the squadron it was a time for reflection.

Squadron Leaders Warren Schmitt and Ross Benson had the honour of flying some of the final missions, and on 3 November they took Caribou number A4-195, delivered in September 1964, out to the range for a final burst of practice at two military airstrips called Puk Puk and Woolshed.

Despite a strong breeze and a degree of crosswind, the take-off and landing are straightforward for 'Schmitty' and 'Beno'. The 'bou' could take off and land several times along Puk Puk's 1000 metres of available runway. Woolshed is a different story. At just over 500 metres it is difficult to see the sliver of cleared bush from the air, let alone land on it. For these short-field veterans it is not a problem. The 'bou' touches down easily on the rough strip with plenty of runway to spare.

No other conventional fixed-wing aircraft can match this short-field performance while offering robust and simple systems that can be repaired or replaced on the run. The old engines might leak a bit of oil and make a strange and very loud noise, but when it comes to reliability and durability it is an amazing power plant. Nothing is automated; there is not even an automatic pilot, so the crew flies every hour by hand. That can mean many hours on the stick as the aircraft trudges along at a leisurely 150 knots (278 kilometres per hour). If it breaks down, it is up to the aircrew to fix it and fly it home.

Schmitt joined the RAAF from Adelaide in 1978 as an instrument fitter but was bitten by the flying bug when he saw an F-111 buzz the airfield at Wagga Wagga on his first day. 'I thought that looked pretty cool. I wanted to do that so I started working my way towards being a pilot. It took a few years but I got there eventually.'

'Schmitty' had his eye on fast jets, but soon realised he was not suited to the intense world of the fighter pilot. 'I didn't have the aptitude to do it and I just wouldn't have been able to hack the amount of time and study required.'

After qualifying as a RAAF pilot he was posted to 34 Squadron in Canberra and the VIP fleet to fly politicians and other dignitaries around before moving to Caribous to gain his captaincy.

'I'd flown with some people who had backgrounds in Caribou and they all told me to go and fly Caribous: "Best flying you'll ever do, best fun you'll ever have." And they were right,' he says. 'It is a great aeroplane to fly, brilliant aeroplane to teach basic skills to pilots in and fly around at low level, and doing stuff, particularly in New Guinea.'

It is also resilient, as he discovered in 2000 up at High Range. 'I stuck 20 foot of the wing tip through the trees doing a low-level training exercise. The wing tip was smashed to pieces but it kept flying and we brought it back and landed and a few days later I was flying again, so it's a very forgiving aeroplane in that regard — tough, built tough.'

The damaged wing occupies pride of place above the squadron bar at RAAF Base Townsville.

In Schmitt's early days the 'bou' had no satellite navigation systems so everything was done manually by dead reckoning. That meant looking out the window, holding a map, checking where you were heading and using physical features on the ground to stay on track. The aircraft also lacks the electronic warfare countermeasures required in modern warfare, so its days in military service had to end.

The thrill was not speed but the very high 'fun' factor. 'When you start doing what it's designed to do — landing on very short, semi-prepared strips — it's just an adrenaline rush.'

During the big drought of 1997 Schmitt was executive officer of 35 Squadron and led the push into PNG to fly relief missions, which were subsequently also supported by 38 Squadron.

'We went up there and spent the better part of six months doing drought relief around New Guinea. Now that was very, very rewarding, challenging flying,' he says. 'There was significant smoke haze, reducing visibility sometimes down to 3 or 4 kilometres, poking around in amongst big mountains with limited navigation equipment, limited ability to see where you are going. To get that aid to those people that really needed it made a big difference to their lives. We would like to think we saved a lot of people's lives doing that.'

Schmitt recalls his training flights there as a bit of a blur. Each

Caribou pilot flew about 150 hours — or four tours — across Torres Strait before being let loose as an aircraft captain.

'Here in Australia you've got 7000 feet lower safe heights, which a Caribou can do quite easily; it can maintain 7000 feet if you are reasonably light, even on one engine,' he says. 'So if you are poking around in cloud or above cloud and you have an engine failure, the chances of running into a hill in Australia are pretty low. Have an engine failure in New Guinea … there is every chance you are going to drift down into a mountain. So we tend not to go into cloud unless we have good escape options. You will be flying down a valley trying to maintain an escape route behind you; if it's raining then there is every chance that escape route could close on you in the next 15 or 20 minutes, so you need to always have a couple of different options … and that has caught plenty of people out.'

The RAAF crashed a few there in the early days but in the past couple of decades the Caribou maintained an enviable safety record in PNG.

Training new pilots to forget what they have learned about aircraft performance at sea level is one of the first jobs for instructing captains. According to 'Schmitty', trainers can warn about 'high-density altitude' (pressure altitude that can decrease in high humidity and reduce an aircraft's performance) a thousand times but it is only bitter experience that rams the message home.

One hazardous airfield is at a place called Kagi where the slope is up to 16 per cent over a 450-metre runway. Another, Woninara, has a 10 per cent slope over a 400-metre runway.

'You are committed quite a long way out. Once you get below a few hundred feet on finals, you are going to land on [Woninara] — there is no other option,' Schmitt says. 'You can't go around and try again, you have to land on it, so you want to make sure you get it right.'

Benson's abiding love of the Caribou is based not only on its performance but its 'cool' quirkiness.

'I just love how you can flick the window out and stick your arm and elbow out the window like you are driving a Chevy,' he says. 'Then putting an aircraft that's got nearly a hundred-foot wing span into these little dodgy airfields in PNG, is just phenomenal.'

Beno is a Townsville boy who joined the air force after a brief career as a design draughtsman. He had wanted to fly planes ever since his grandad took him to Townsville airport, aged six. A chatterbox who freely admits his 'gobby mouth' has got him into trouble at times, he has plenty of fond memories of places where airforce pilots will no longer fly now the 'bou' is retired.

It was the variety of missions that he expected to miss the most from his 2000 hours flying Caribous. He did a lot with Special Air Service (SAS) troops, driving out to an area dressed in civvies to survey landing sites and returning the next night flying on night-vision goggles to drop the specialist soldiers in a paddock in the middle of nowhere.

'I wouldn't drive my four-wheel drive on that bit of dirt. It's not an airfield, it's just a bit of dirt, and we throw this thing into it and for 45 years it's been doing it, so it's pretty cool actually,' Benson says.

Once he was flying the SAS 'bad guys' on an exercise to 'attack' a number of target airfields in the Northern Territory. They landed on one strip, only to be met by a Leopard tank and some irate soldiers. Beno had visions of himself strapped to an ant's nest but his co-pilot jumped out and told the major they were on a navigation exercise and had forgotten all about the army exercise. Could he please move his tank so they could be on their way? It worked, and they departed with a group of very anxious SAS troops in the back.

'They were the good days. As a tac [tactical] captain you would just survey and certify the airfield yourself, whereas now you don't do it,' he says.

During the same exercise he and another pilot drove out to the area and spoke to some soldiers, who told them where troops were deployed. So they chose a paddock well away from any positions and deposited the SAS boys and their quad bikes.

'They went out that night and took them all out, exactly where they were — it was a classic,' he says. 'It [took] about 60 seconds to get all their quad bikes out. We landed, stopped, took off and were gone. It's pretty cool to do that stuff. Everything is blacked out. We would turn our lights off, goggle up, get down on the deck and just head to where we were going so they never knew where we were. We'd fly down roads as well and they'd think you were a road train coming.'

While such tactical flying is professionally demanding and enjoyable, the humanitarian work was most rewarding. During one PNG flood mission the Caribous moved about 250,000 kilograms of aid supplies in 10 days. Unlike the chopper pilots, who remain strapped in and keep their machines turning and burning, 'bou' crews usually shut down, got out and got stuck in to help unload or refuel.

Its versatility came to the fore again after the crash of a civilian Twin Otter passenger plane near Kokoda in August 2009, with the loss of 13 lives including nine Australians. A Caribou dropped the search team and they hiked to the remote crash site, 1800 metres up a jungle-covered mountain, to prepare a landing zone for Black Hawk helicopters.

The 'bou' then dropped fuel supplies for the choppers so they could stay on task longer and carry heavier loads. As a result of the teamwork, driven largely by the Commanding Officer of 38 Squadron, Wing Commander Tony Thorpe, who has 2000 hours flying helicopters under his belt, the bodies were extracted in just four days.

'The Black Hawks were so happy because we were continually running supplies for them and kept them going so they got a lot done quite quickly,' Benson recalls. 'On the news it didn't look like it was done that quickly, but I actually went into that site on the back of the Black Hawk and it was devastating.'

Another unique aspect of the Caribou that pilots will miss is assisting with the repair of aircraft in the field. It is probably the last RAAF aircraft where pilots and flight engineers were allowed to swing on a spanner and get their hands dirty so their aircraft could be repaired and flown home.

The Caribou is a simple machine compared with modern aircraft and after it retired the days of pilots dabbling in repairs and maintenance ended.

'Things have become so reliable now that if they break, which is reasonably rare, you unbolt the whole thing and throw [it] away and then just bolt on a whole new engine or whatever,' Schmitt says.

It is a similar story with modern navigation.

'The days of looking out the window and holding a map and say "I'm flying over that road now, that's this road and in two minutes' time we'll be over this road", those days are pretty much gone,' Schmitt says. 'Now you need to be able to understand and monitor and drive the technology in the aeroplane. That is a quantum shift away from the Caribou. We had no technology to drive, we had the aeroplane to drive.'

Michael Burgess-Orton met the legendary World War II flying ace Sir Douglas 'Tin Legs' Bader as a young lad in his former homeland of Rhodesia (now Zimbabwe).

After that it was model aeroplanes and books about flying for the youngster, whose parents moved to the Queensland Gold Coast in 1982 when he was eight. His future was sealed during a summer holiday at Amberley: 'Being around F-111s and waking up on misty mornings and hearing an F-111's engines starting, all that sort of stuff really inspires a young kid to join the air force. There is nothing better actually — it is great.'

Burgess-Orton, known fondly as 'BO', graduated from the Australian Defence Force Academy (ADFA) in 1994 and was posted to flying school. During 30 hours of flying, with its associated aerobatics and spins, he suffered a major setback with the discovery that he suffered from chronic airsickness.

The result was a six-week tour of the dreaded 'vomitron' at RAAF Edinburgh in South Australia. It is really called the 'motion desensitise training course', designed to cure a pilot of airsickness. They are locked in a spinning box for five minutes every hour on the hour for 10 hours a day over six weeks.

'Gradually your level of tolerance for motion sickness rises so by the time I got back to 2FTS [Flight Training School] I was sitting in the back seat of PC-9s and all the instructors are doing aerobatic sequences and laying bets on whether BO would throw his guts, but I never did. Funnily enough I didn't get the money either,' he says.

By 1997 he finally graduated from the Cessna 172 pilots' course but his dreams of joining an F-111 squadron were not to be.

'I'm no Chuck Yeager [the first pilot to fly faster than the speed of sound]. I'm one of the pilots who has to work for everything, work my arse off, study my arse off and really work for it, but it's what you have to do; you have to be driven,' he says. 'Throughout my life I've been driven for most things and flying is one of them. It's a passion, not to be understated. When people have a passion they push hard for it.'

He was posted to Caribous with 38 Squadron, then at Amberley. He had wanted Hercs because they were 'bigger and better and faster' but his flight commander was a Hornet pilot who said, 'BO, you just won't fit in at Herc world, you'd be too stubborn. Go to Caribous — you'll love it, it's hand-and-stick flying and you'll really excel in it.'

His love affair with the 'bou' was clinched during his first short-field landing on Pad 9 at Amberley, a strip of grass right in front of the control tower.

'My heart was racing, the wheels hit the ground and the engines were going in reverse as we'd been taught — and pump the brakes, pump the shit out of the brakes as it's the first time — and everything stops,' says BO. 'You just go, "Wow, that was impressive!" This big aircraft stopped in less runway than a Cessna 172. It was just incredible.'

BO finished his tactical operations course in mid-December 1997 and two weeks later was off on his first operational job to drought-ravaged Papua New Guinea, flying food supplies up into the highlands.

He spent the first day standing between pilots to learn the procedures and terrain and on day two undertook his first mission into an infamous airfield called Tapini. The 900-metre-long runway with a 10 per cent slope — like a big ski ramp — had been the site of a RAAF Caribou crash in October 1968, so it had a certain aura.

'We landed at this airfield at all-up weight with a whole bunch of rice flour and oil in the back for people whose crops had failed for the second year running,' he recalls. 'It was a wonderful feeling to realise how appreciative the people were. They had smiles from ear to ear, so how could you not fall in love with an aircraft that does that to you so early on?'

BO, a 'bog rat' (junior pilot) flying under close supervision, learnt his first big lesson about PNG at an airstrip called Ononge, cut between two cliff faces. At the threshold the winds become very tricky, rapidly swinging between tail and cross.

He was flying with Schmitty on his first landing and everything was fine until he crossed the threshold of the 500-metre strip with a 7 per cent upslope, when he forgot his training and cut the power to idle too early during the flare.

'That is a big, big no-no and I know that now because I'm a PNG check and training captain, so I know what boggies can do when they get excited,' he says. 'I chopped the power, the lift dumped off the wing and it just slammed in pretty hard — from recollection it was about a 3.2 to 3.5 G-force landing. Very heavy.'

The left main landing gear bottomed out and was damaged and several panels suffered ripple damage from the force. They flew it back to Moresby for a full inspection and BO became famous for breaking aircraft 225. It was an early lesson and one he has never repeated.

Like many Caribou pilots he worked hard to stay at the squadron. Despite a posting to ADFA in Canberra he still got to East Timor and flew the mail runs from Baucau to Dili, Maliana and Suai. He also conducted numerous tactical missions, including the first reconnaissance flight to the Oecussi enclave, the small piece of East Timorese territory surrounded by Indonesian West Timor along the northern coast.

During Operation Warden access to the area was extremely sensitive. 'We had a diplomatic clearance to track to 12 miles off the coast of Timor to the Indonesian border and we were told, "As long as you stick by your diplomatic clearance you'll be okay,"' he says. BO was co-pilot to the commanding officer, Wing Commander Tony Bennett.

'Sure enough, at this little pinpoint 12 miles off the coast, at our turn point, was a little Indonesian fishing boat, a little sampan with a hood over the top of it, a little antenna coming out with an Indonesian flag on it,' he says. 'We went to Oecussi, did an aerial survey on the airfield there, could see it was workable, we could get in there. There were a couple of little structures around it but nothing the Caribou couldn't handle.'

The reason BO stuck with the 'bou' is that it could make a real difference to people's lives. 'How many people can say that about what they do?'

One of his most rewarding jobs was the Solomon Islands intervention in 2003. He was the lead planner for the Caribou force. By early June the squadron was asked to formulate a plan to deploy to Honiara to provide air support for a possible intervention. They realised that by placing aviation fuel at key points along the island chain, they could deliver up to 2 tonnes of cargo or troops at a time to the entire country.

At a formal planning conference with the army they were told the plan had to be worked up and ready to implement within 48 hours. During a coffee break BO fronted the operations officer from 2RAR and presented him with maps showing where the Caribous could operate.

He said, 'Sir, if you want to get around this archipelago you have to do it by air. Black Hawks are not available; Chinooks are in [the Middle East]. There are Caribous, and based on Honiara we can move 2 tonnes to everywhere in this rim. All the green circles you can see are airfields that Caribous can get to with 2 tonnes.'

That is how they came to deploy to the Solomon Islands, where between 15 and 20 airfields up and down the island country came into play. The mission showcased all the Caribou's capabilities. They flew multiple reconnaissance missions, intelligence-gathering flights, troop insertions and even maritime patrols.

The affection most pilots feel for the 'bou' was not always shared by the men and women charged with keeping them in the air. A 40-year-old radial engine attached to a 40-year-old airframe really tested the engineers and mechanics in the squadron's maintenance department.

Flight Sergeant Daryl Pead, 36, from Wauchope on the New South Wales mid-north coast moved to Townsville and the 'bous' from C-130s and 707 jets in 2005. The big difference was the frequency of the breakdowns. Simple things such as cast-iron exhaust pipes bolted onto aluminium cylinder heads can create nightmares for maintainers.

'The engine has a lot of vibration so that causes cracking in the exhaust pipes and exhaust components,' he says. 'The nature of the missions we do ... you get fairly rapid expansion and contraction of the metal. Throw in the fact the Caribou can reverse itself — it can throw propellers in reverse and back up — a lot of the cooling effect you get over the engine is lost when you reverse.' That is because, unlike a car engine that is water-cooled, Caribou engines are air-cooled.

Oil leaks from propellers were another problem. Despite exhaustive efforts, Caribou props just leak and that's the way it is.

'We did a lot of propeller changes,' Pead says.

The aircraft also has a very complex manual flight control system. With no autopilot, each tiny control surface has to be adjusted manually. Because the pilots fly hand and feet the whole time they notice even the slightest problem. Pead has lost count of the times he and his team put hours and hours into getting an aircraft ready to fly and watching it taxi out for take-off, only to turn around and come back in with something wrong.

'When you get it into a cycle of flying every day, it seems to come good for some strange reason,' he says. 'Whereas when they are on the ramp here in Townsville, particularly in wet season, you just seem to get more problems.'

Another regular culprit was 'liquid lock'. With a radial engine that has not been run for a while, oil sometimes leaks into the lowest cylinder, causing the propeller to stop during the compression stroke. 'We'd run out there with a bucket and pull out the spark plugs until we found the cylinder with the oil in it, drain the oil and away we would go.'

While modern engines use electronic diagnostics to find faults, on the Caribou fault finding and troubleshooting were more instinctive.

For young mechanics it was a good place to start because they learnt how to act intuitively.

As the aircraft runs on Avgas, reliable fuel supply was always an issue during deployments. The aircraft would often carry 200-litre drums of fuel and there was a regular competition to see who could pump a drum out in the shortest time. A guy called Zorba held the record of two minutes and 50 seconds and in PNG it became a macho thing with the locals to see who could wind the manual pump the fastest.

Pead has made numerous overseas trips with the 'bou' including several tours to PNG and one to Noumea. The most difficult was the recovery of a crashed aircraft from the Efogi airstrip. The entire machine had to be dismantled by hand by a team of a dozen maintenance staff who lived in huts near the airfield and spent every waking hour pulling it to pieces. Working 6 metres up on a rickety scaffold in pouring tropical rain to dismantle the rudder assembly and its 40-kilogram counterweight required significant teamwork.

'It was a real group effort, a family affair. The ideas and concepts for how we were going to do stuff safely were excellent,' Pead says. 'To get the undercarriage off we dug large ditches in front of the aircraft to pull it into. The aircraft settled on its belly so that we could then pull the undercarriage off.'

It took a dozen technicians a week to dismantle it and fly the bits out. Their work has been immortalised in an extraordinary time-lapse video.

Warrant Officer Rod Cairns is a senior flight engineer at 38 Squadron and worked with Caribous for more than 20 years. He and his wife Deidre have a son, Chris, who has followed his dad into the air force. Cairns joined the RAAF in 1978 as an apprentice airframe fitter and has worked on a variety of aircraft but says the Caribou gets into your blood.

'There is nothing automated; everything you do with this platform you have to work hard to get it to do. When the thing breaks down, inevitably in the middle of nowhere, you've got to sit down and think about it.'

The engineer on the Caribou doubles as loadmaster and Cairns says about 70 per cent of his 20 years on the aircraft was spent on loadmaster tasks.

The most 'interesting' incidents for him have been engine failures in flight, particularly at night.

'We had a spectacular one at night at Amberley one time; it was just like the *Memphis Belle* with flames coming out of the cowls,' he recalls. 'That was caused by a cylinder cracking down the middle … but our training and our procedures and everything dealt with that and we got the aircraft safely back on the ground.'

As he prepared one of the last two Caribous for its final flight to the RAAF museum at Point Cook, there was a lot of nostalgia in the squadron but also widespread agreement that the old girl had not only become unreliable and expensive but had also outlived her usefulness. The 'bou' couldn't even carry an army Land Rover in the back any more because the new models are wider and heavier than earlier ones.

'You are not going to win Bathurst in a 45-year-old car,' says Cairns.

Wing Commander Tony Thorpe was born in Sydney in May 1963, the month the government decided to buy Caribou aircraft. So it was ironic that he was the Commanding Officer of 38 Squadron and flew the very last RAAF 'bou', designated A4-140, to the Australian War Memorial in Canberra on 27 November 2009.

Thorpe loves the Caribou's 'dragster' sound and the hands-on flying. 'There is something about watching an aeroplane start and having all that smoke fly out. It coughs a bit and then it finally decides it wants to go. And then it will just keep going, just keep running and running,' he said. 'I'm sure the day will come where I'll get a chance to look at it in a museum and realise that I actually flew that.'

EYES ON THE TARGET

Chapter 7

AUSSIE ROULETTE

The cockpit of a Pilatus PC-9 tandem seat training aircraft is a tight squeeze for anyone weighing more than 80 kilograms.

The pre-flight briefing is very specific. In the event of an emergency ejection, if you don't squeeze in your elbows, push your backside into the rear of the seat and bring your thighs down hard before the pin is pulled, you might leave part of your anatomy behind. Or snap a femur as the ejection seat blasts you into space.

'We won't touch the handle now,' says pilot Flight Lieutenant Steve English through the intercom. 'But in [a] real [situation], the right hand will touch the handle, your left hand will grip your right wrist ... and tuck your elbows in as well.'

The thought of an arm or leg being torn off tends to focus the mind during a 45-minute flight in an RAAF PC-9 training aircraft that carries the famous 'R' of the Roulettes aerobatic team on its tail.

The low wing aircraft literally leaps into the air as the 1100 horsepower from the single Pratt and Whitney PT6A-62 turboprop engine sends it skywards at an impressive 4000 feet per minute.

The power-to-weight ratio of the PC-9 makes it an ideal training aircraft as well as a showy machine for the Roulettes. The RAAF operates the Swiss-designed and Australian-built trainer at its Central Flying School (CFS) at RAAF Base East Sale in Victoria, where pilots are trained as instructors, and at Number 2 Flying Training School (2FTS) at Pearce in Western Australia, where trainee pilots become fully fledged.

Flying over the Gippsland countryside and the small farming communities of Stratford and Maffra, English explains that due to poor weather the flight will be conducted in a low-level training area near the Victorian coast. Standard operating procedures limit the G-force loading on the PC-9 to 4.5Gs for training flights, although it is rated to 7Gs and the Roulettes often exceed six. The lower rating extends the airframe's life to about 20 years.

English will conduct a basic 'wingover' manoeuvre before each aerobatic routine. Not only does it allow him to ensure the airspace is clear of other aircraft, it also means he can regulate speed for the manoeuvre. During a right wingover, then a left, before a very smooth barrel roll, the local farmland and pine forests blur in and out of view. As the G force starts to rise, the G-suits we are wearing inflate and deflate in time with the Gs.

Having established that his large passenger is not filling his oxygen mask with his breakfast, he conducts a series of loops, steep turns and inverted passes to show what this mighty training plane is capable of. The loop generates the highest G-force of the flight with four times the force of gravity pressing down on the sweating body in the back seat.

The PC-9's turning ability is so good that it can outmanoeuvre a Hornet fighter jet. To demonstrate, English drops to 250 feet and follows the forest roads, tossing the aircraft like an airborne go-kart while talking his passenger through each and every move. 'Now I'm above all this cloud I'll find a hole to pop up, and rather than breaking up the aerobatics manoeuvres I'll do them all as one sequence. If at any time you are not 100 per cent just let me know. I'll knock it off at any stage. I will talk through each manoeuvre as I do it.'

Unable to find the words to explain that 100 per cent would be fantastic but how does 80 per cent sound, the next muffled briefing through the headphones really attracts the passenger's attention.

'There will be an inverted section, so you'll hang in the harness. Just resist the temptation to grab onto something or you might feel like you are falling out of the harness,' English says. 'That has happened before in other countries — they grab something and it is a handle and out they go, so don't do that. The harness is very secure. You won't fall out.'

It is time for the grand finale — a cocktail of aerobatic manoeuvres — before heading for home. His clear, authoritative voice soothes through the headset. 'The first manoeuvre is a vertical roll, so we'll pull up in vertical. I'll be looking at a left wing tip, basically putting the wing forward 90 degrees to the horizon. Once we are there, I'll check it, hold it there, I'll put a full left aileron in and we'll roll around, vertically rolling the aircraft, so basically spinning like a top,' he says.

Soon we are into what he describes as 'a nice, easy, simple barrel roll'.

'Look out [the] right-hand side, there is a rain shower [at] 90 deg to you so I'll try to miss that, inverted. Now we're just under a bit of cloud. I'll do a wingover to get us out from under that, here a roll inverted, just grab your harness on your shoulders if you feel uncomfortable. Aircraft nose down again, do a loop … Now we are pointing at the road that was on our left before, all parallel and that's a good mix of aerobatic manoeuvres that we normally do.'

Back on the ground at East Sale, the canopy opens. It's helmets off, ear plugs out —'Don't drop them because finding things in the cockpit of a PC-9 can be difficult' — and climb out of the snug space to reflect on an incredible 45 minutes.

The PC-9 is the backbone of air force pilot training and the public face of the RAAF, thanks to the Roulettes. The distinctive red livery of the screaming aircraft with their multiple smoke trails is a familiar sight at public events from Australia Day celebrations in Canberra to Anzac Day parades and small country shows in outback Australia.

The training school is divided into two flights: A and B. In late 2009 Squadron Leader Glen Canfield was the commanding officer of A flight before moving back into the Roulettes as the Roulette leader.

Any RAAF pilot can become a Roulette provided they are a qualified instructor. So the team might have Herc, AP-3C, Hornet and Caribou pilots. The Roulette posting is secondary to their jobs as instructors.

'The only requirement is they have to be an instructor. Typically, they've instructed at the schools and they come down here and pass the Roulette selection process,' Canfield says.

The first hurdle is a formation aerobatics course, learning to do two-ship (aircraft) formation flying before graduating to standard four-ship formations and finally the display-size six-ship routines.

'They basically start at 2000 feet and work their way down doing aerobatics to 500 feet in six-ship formation,' he says. 'It takes a month and a half to work the guys up, about 25 flights, to get where they need to be.'

Safety is the main priority so there are a lot of briefings, practice and repetition before the new team goes public. Flying at high speed, just 3 metres apart or less, there is no margin for error. Practice makes perfect and Canfield says there are specific reference points on the aircraft that are lined up and triangulated so pilots can maintain visual separation.

When the team does a spectacular dispersal move — when all the aircraft fly off in different directions — it is calculated to the second with pre-set headings, G-force levels and radio communications. The Roulette leader tells the team when to begin each manoeuvre.

'It is fantastic flying, some of the best flying you'll do,' says Canfield. 'As an instructor it is magnificent because you are actually flying for yourself most of the time.'

Of course the risks are very real and the team has suffered aircraft losses in training. Because they operate down to 200 feet and within 200 metres of large crowds at speeds up to 216 knots (400 kilometres per hour) and 6Gs, the Roulette pilots must be drilled to perfection.

'It's all part of the work-up process,' he says. 'Nothing is ever foolproof, I guess. That is why the training is there to make sure it doesn't happen when we are doing it for real.'

For the first two months the pilots train most days and once in the team they fly displays every second weekend. Every six months or so, two to three members rotate in and out of the Roulettes. The team is a secondary role for the flying school, but its high profile results in a lot of positive publicity for the air force.

Commanding Officer of the Central Flying School in 2009, Wing Commander Sean Bellenger, was the Roulette leader when the East Timor crisis broke out in 1999. He had been balancing the public relations demands with the core job of the flying training school when he was told to take the team to Singapore for a display in February 2000.

Flying single-engine aircraft over vast distances is difficult enough, but this flight also required transiting through Kupang in Indonesian West Timor while military tensions between Indonesia and Australia were running high.

The seven Roulette PC-9s arrived while, just across the border, RAAF C-130 Hercules were flying in and out of Komoro airport in Dili. The Indonesian military had a squadron of F5 jets parked at Kupang alongside several of their C-130s and a large number of troops. Unfortunately, the Roulettes's support C-130 had to land in Kupang on an unscheduled maintenance stop. The Indonesians detained the aircraft and crew while the Roulette pilots were at the terminal handing out stickers and posing for photos with the locals.

'We couldn't stick around too long because we had limited fuel,' Bellenger says. 'We had to leave early in the morning so we could get to places by lunch time, otherwise we wouldn't have the fuel to hold.'

That meant leaving the C-130 crew behind to argue their case with the Indonesians. They were held for a few hours as the Indonesians went through their paperwork with a fine-tooth comb, then released.

'By the time we got to Singapore, the Chief of Air Force was there, the Chief of the Indonesian Air Force was there and we were having lunch with them and having a bit of a laugh about how much political hot water this C-130 that landed at Kupang had caused,' he recalls. 'We said, "We know, we were there in the nice red-and-white aircraft handing out stickers to the locals. No one associated us with being a military force!"'

The East Sale facility is not just about pilot instructor training. Down the road is the RAAF's school of air warfare.

A nondescript series of buildings houses one of the air force's most advanced training bodies. It has undergone major change in the past 10 years from focusing on navigation training to mission command skills, so that the new generation air combat officer (ACO) can run an entire air campaign.

For Commanding Officer Wing Commander Jake Campbell that means providing ACOs with an in-depth understanding of air power and the application of air power before they are posted to active squadrons.

Campbell joined the RAAF 23 years ago from Lismore in northern New South Wales. His interest in flying had been sparked by family trips in his dad's Piper Cherokee but his eyesight was not up to pilot standard so he joined as a navigator on Orions. Before the posting to East Sale in 2008, Campbell was involved in the ACO implementation phase, where the air force rolled all air warfare categories, including navigator and air defence, into the one ACO role.

'We are starting to see some good results and we already have air combat officers who have graduated from here [over] in Afghanistan at the end of the radar there,' he says.

The school's flight commander, Squadron Leader Brett Mitchell, says they look for four key attributes in students: the capacity to collect and absorb information; the ability to maintain spatial awareness; the ability to process information; and the ability to prioritise duties.

'We are not trying to teach specialist officers from day one [but to] assess whether or not they have the right skill sets, the right capacity, the right sort of learning ability to subsequently pass an operational conversion unit,' Mitchell says.

The ACO course runs for 40 weeks. The first 30 are spent teaching basic skills that are then tested in air campaign planning and in intelligence, surveillance and reconnaissance (ISR). The move away from navigation focus does not mean those traditional skills are ignored. ACOs must know how to respond and navigate if their computer system suffers what Mitchell calls the 'blue screen of death'.

'It is more about managing information and managing crew, so crew resource management is a big player for us in the mission command phase as well as the ability to interpret and make real-time decisions,' he says.

The school trains about 60 students a year at a 65 per cent pass rate, but with 24 operational Super Hornets due in service by 2012, all with an ACO in the back seat, the numbers will increase.

The air force is not as brutal as it was in days gone by, when students who failed were simply shown the door and advised to seek a new career.

'We try to look for other employment in the air force or navy and quite often we can find them other work as intelligence officers or perhaps operations officers,' Jake Campbell says. 'Depending on why they've failed, they might be suitable to go and try [the] air traffic control course.'

A few are absolutely unsuited to a military career and are advised to try something else. 'When I did nav course, if you failed it was, "Pack your bag, jump in your car and go look for another job", but that's changed, which is good.'

About half the graduates follow the air battle management stream into the control and reporting units and the Wedgetail Airborne Early Warning and Control (AEWAC) aircraft with 2 Squadron at Williamtown. The rest go to operational squadrons such as the Orions or the Hercules, and a select few to the fast jet world at 82 Wing at Amberley in Queensland. The school also trains ACOs for the Royal Australian Navy.

The aim of the game is to teach students the limitations of aviation, the systems, general procedures and safety and mission command skills. Mission command skills are vital in the modern battle space when a vast amount of information flows to the mission commander.

'You have to filter that information, decide what's important and then what to do about it,' Campbell says.

The RAAF officers must be able to handle live control exercises with Hornet fighters by the end of their conversion course.

Campbell rates the ACO course as one of the most difficult in the air force. The ACO's job is right at the tip of the network-centric warfare spear with more information available than any human could possibly process.

'It is now more about information management than pure navigational skills or pure piloting skills. Those have become relatively easy,' he says. 'Information management is the difficult part of war fighting ... We are trying to develop those skills right from day one, rather than picking it up later. That is probably the biggest change.'

The officer commanding the air training wing in mid-2009, Group Captain Brian Edwards, gets a kick out of seeing a new batch of fresh-faced young trainees coming through the gates. 'It just reminds you of what you were like, and of course it makes you realise how old you are.'

He says the students receive excellent training and are given opportunities to fix any areas of underperformance. 'You sit them down and talk through and get their idea of how it went and find out if there is any underlying issue and work through it maturely and sensibly,' he says. 'If the underperformance is due to their ability to multi-task or think ahead, then you try to remediate that and work through it. It is their dream to do this and we've got to filter out whether they are able to do it or not. In the military we expect very high standards for the right reasons. That is the hard part of the job, the disappointment of telling someone, "We don't think you are going to make it."'

Motivation is not usually an issue but the air force makes it crystal clear very early that students who are not motivated are not welcome.

'BJ', as Edwards is known, was already a veteran operational jet fighter pilot when he joined the RAAF in 1990 as a qualified flying instructor from his native Zimbabwe. He has since served in numerous roles, including Commanding Officer of Number 77 Squadron flying Hornet fighters and Officer Commanding 78 Wing responsible for 'lead-in' (initial) fighter training.

He had flown a lot of operational missions for the then Rhodesian Air Force in close air support and strike roles but does not regard this as glamorous.

'I don't think you can say leaving school to go fight in a war is a healthy thing to do. I'm less complimentary of those things,' he says. 'It is not healthy for kids at morning assemblies to be hearing about ex-school mates who have either been maimed or lost their lives fighting an insurgency war, but that was the norm and you just became accustomed to it.'

The fact that he has flown operational missions and delivered weapons against people who were trying to kill him was a life-changing experience. The father of four says that while it validates the training it doesn't mean you need that experience to be a capable military aviator.

'When we sent the guys to Iraq they did a good job because we trained them so well,' he says. 'It is very interesting when you talk to young people now and quite a lot of them want to get involved in operations, so they want to fly the transport aircraft or the [Orions] because they are [more] involved in operations.

'I always wanted to fly fast jets and was lucky enough to do that, but there was also an element of me that wanted to do operations as a young guy. Now I am more mature I'm not itching to go do it, so when they went over to Iraq, I wasn't thinking, "I wish it was me they were taking over to do that."'

Squadron Leader Paul 'Simmo' Simmons knows what it is like to have a dream and what it takes to live it.

Growing up in the wilds of Papua New Guinea, he had his sights set on an air force flying career from a very early age. His dad, a former Royal New Zealand Air Force transport pilot, was a missionary and bush pilot in PNG. During the 11 years the family spent there, young Paul accompanied his dad above some of the most rugged flying terrain on earth. As a trained 'cargo boy' he was lugging 50-kilogram bags of coffee on and off aeroplanes from an early age.

When he was 16, his eyes firmly on the air force, the family moved to the Hunter Valley and took out Australian citizenship, essentially so Paul could join the Royal Australian Air Force.

Year 11 at Maitland Boys High School was pivotal. He was learning to fly part-time, washing cars and mowing lawns to fund the lessons. His dad matched his earnings dollar for dollar and his first solo flight was in a tiny Cessna 152 at the Royal Newcastle Aero Club.

'I remember flying around, looking at this empty seat, thinking, "I am too young to drive a car on my own and here I am flying around the countryside in an aircraft, solo." A very special day indeed.'

During a discussion about his dream of becoming a pilot, his father said, 'Son, I have pushed you and pushed you and you are not making the choice to work hard enough. Your marks aren't good enough and you need more fitness, but I'm not going to push you any more. I will provide you with whatever support you want, however you have to make the decision to do it.'

With only six months left to make the grade, if he did not work hard he would always have the question in his mind: 'Could I have done it?'

Simmons's Year 11 master was 100 per cent supportive but his physics teacher really laid it on the table. 'When he found out what I wanted to do he said, "Paul, you are too fat and too dumb." People think that is horrible, but it was the facts and the facts were, I wasn't working hard enough and I wasn't fit enough to get into the air force.'

The penny finally dropped.

'I had a mate who loved to run. I don't like to run, but he did, so we ran five nights a week,' he says. 'I asked for tutor support and I worked a lot harder so my marks went up about 25 per cent. I lost weight and got my fitness under control, so here I am. I say to kids, "You'll be very surprised. If you make the right choices, listen to the right people where you can, some of those dreams can come true."'

The dream for Simmo was a place in the direct-entry pilot course at Point Cook in July 1989 and an opportunity to become a RAAF fighter pilot. He graduated from the pilot's course in June 1991 and was selected to begin fighter training. He was posted to 76 Squadron at Williamtown for his introductory fighter course to learn the skills of a single-seat fighter pilot — dogfighting, bomb dropping and strafing techniques. After qualifying he stayed on at 76 Squadron for 18 months as a 'line driver', flying fleet support missions, working with the Royal New Zealand Air Force and its A-4 Skyhawks.

He moved across to Hornets in July 1993 and after graduating from the conversion course he was posted to 75 Squadron at Tindal in the Northern Territory.

'We arrived in a very desolate, hot place ... with my wife [Sandy] looking at me as if to say, "What the hell have you dragged me into?"'

Simmo spent the next two and a half years learning his trade in the wide-open spaces of the Territory with a passing parade of jets from North America and Asia. By this time he had set himself three goals: first, to become a fighter combat instructor (equivalent to the US navy's Top Gun); second, to go on exchange to the United States Air Force; and third, to become a Squadron executive officer or second-in-command.

He ticked off the first one at Number Two Operational Conversion Unit (2OCU) at Williamtown in June 1997 and was posted to 77 Squadron as the Fighter Combat Instructor (FCI) until December 1999, when he was selected for exchange in the US to fly F-15 Strike Eagles. His son Daniel had been born in 1998 so the family went off to the States for three years, where daughter Lea was born in 2001.

After three years of flying what he describes as the definitive multi-role strike fighter in the world, Simmo was put in charge of number 28 FCI course at Williamtown.

'That was the fiftieth anniversary of RAAF fighter combat instruction and really a "Top Gun" course, if you want to call it that,' he says. 'Australia has the longest standing dedicated fighter combat instructor course in the world based at 2OCU. We applied the lessons that were learnt from the Korean War where the pilots needed a focus on air combat tactics and air-to-ground tactics.'

Simmons was in Chicago at a conference when he got a call from home asking him to be the RAAF's F/A-18 Hornet demonstration pilot, leading up to the jet's twentieth anniversary.

'Normally when you are away you get shafted with all the bad jobs, but that was a brilliant one and I managed to do that for two and a half years,' he says. 'I flew that blue and white and red aircraft, that was painted up specifically, around the country to demonstrate it to the public, which was a great delight.'

The job also allowed him to indulge his hobby as an amateur photographer and he has had images shot from his unique perspective published in numerous magazines and books.

Simmons achieved his third goal in 2007 when he was appointed executive officer of Number 77 Squadron at Williamtown in what would be his final full-time job in the air force.

Part of his job as the Hornet demonstration pilot was talking to young people at air shows who were interested in a flying career. 'A big part of what I did with the air show is I wanted to be able to talk to those young kids and put a dream in their heart,' he says.

Most youngsters would immediately think they could never fly that big, powerful jet, so Simmo would look them in the eye and say, 'Man, if this is what you want to do, you work hard, you listen to your parents, you find out all the things you've got to do and you will be very surprised. You can do this.'

He says, 'I was nothing special; I am nothing special. I've just worked hard; I've been fortunate. I've got good eyesight and ears and all that stuff, but to see those kids go away thinking, "Maybe, just maybe I could do something like that," was pretty special ... To see the reaction of parents and especially mothers. I saw a few single mothers with their young kids. You know, to have someone encourage their kids, that really stands out to me.'

One day Simmo received a phone call from a lady whose son had met him at an air show at Amberley. She reminded him that he had taken the time to encourage the boy and write on his Hornet picture that he had put up in his room. Her son, who had just started flying training, had no idea she was contacting Simmons, asking him to phone the boy and encourage him some more. 'So I gave him a call and just said, "Hey dude, Simmo here" and I was able to communicate with him and mentor him a little bit through that two-week process. He has just been accepted to join the air force as a pilot.'

In 2006 a move up the chain, and probably to Canberra, was looming on Simmons's career horizon. Then he met a former air force pilot who was with the airlines and also worked part-time as a flying instructor with an organisation that managed kids with learning difficulties. Simmons and his wife Sandy had been thinking about something similar so he approached the RAAF with the idea of moving into the Reserves so he could pursue a second career as a youth worker. The RAAF didn't want to lose a top fighter combat instructor so they agreed. Simmo obtained his civilian instructor's rating and formed an organisation called LIFT (Learn Inspired Friendship and Trust).

'Our desire is for any young person that comes into contact with our program to learn key life skills, be inspired to achieve their God-given potential and actually understand true friendship and trust, no strings attached,' he says.

Getting inside the heads of troubled 15- to 18-year-old boys is not easy, but many young lads have a fascination with aircraft and flying.

'We found that when we took them to an aeroplane and gave them responsibility to check the aircraft down, to refuel the aircraft — all hands-on — and then we put them in the pilot's seat and allowed them to take the controls, it shattered their preconceived ideas of what they could do and couldn't do,' he says. 'We just saw kids coming alive, and more importantly start to listen to us ... and suddenly we were able to really communicate at a different level [and] develop a much stronger relationship very quickly.'

LIFT Youth Development Incorporated was up and running, with Simmons as president and a group of dedicated experts in aviation, accountancy, law and child psychology. They work with young people who are slightly off the rails or doing it tough through disadvantage, through to kids in the juvenile justice system; they have found that aerobatic flying really appeals to young offenders. In 2009 LIFT put about 100 youngsters through various programs, including one who has earned his pilot's licence and is now looking to join the air force.

Simmons says it is amazing to watch them grow when they are outside their comfort zone and all they have is each other.

'There are very few young people out there that actually want to be bad, so we really do our best to help them as long as they want to help themselves.'

He is the first RAAF fighter pilot to be employed under the part-time leave-without-pay category that was designed for pregnant women and working mothers.

'They had broadened it to a flexible employment contract and it was perfect for me, so I put in an application and was accepted,' he says. 'I am able to come back and teach on any F/A-18 course that the air force has, including the "Top Gun" or fighter combat instructor course.'

He works week on/week off, and in between instructing assists the Squadron executives, mentors younger instructors and does remedial instruction. 'I think it's a pretty good deal for the air force because they retain my 20 years of experience and they've also released me to be able to pursue a passion of mine, which is helping young people.'

Chapter 8

PIGS AND CATERPILLARS

Geoff Shepherd doesn't have a shed at his home, which is nestled on a hillside in the idyllic landscape of Eumundi behind Queensland's Sunshine Coast. Instead, the former Chief of Air Force has a basement full of memorabilia from his 38-year RAAF career.

'Shep', as he is known in flying circles, enjoys a reputation far and wide as a genuine character and a bit of a wag. Looking around his pilot's den it is not difficult to see why.

An extraordinary photograph of an F-111 strike jet dominates one wall of his workshop with its wingtip almost touching the ground as it struggles into the air. Not surprisingly, Shep was at the controls, and while it is not one of his finer flying moments it is a terrific conversation starter as he explains, still with some pride and embarrassment, what happened.

The year was 1988 and young Squadron Leader Shepherd was an F-111 display pilot for an air show at RAAF Base East Sale in Gippsland, Victoria. The day before the public show he was conducting a practice run for an audience of RAAF staff and their families.

'I was supposed to do a fancy take-off with a steep turn away, but I rolled before I pulled up,' he says.

Unfortunately for Shep, but fortunately for posterity, Warrant Officer Al Meadows was stationed about 800 metres along the runway with his camera at the ready. An F-111 normally needs at least 1400 metres to become airborne, but young Shep was only lightly loaded with fuel and managed to coax the jet off the ground just before reaching the brave photographer. Meadows shot off three quick frames before the jet almost took his head off. The first photo featured only half a plane, the second was the money shot, showing the F-111 staggering into the air with its starboard wing tip almost touching the runway, and the third was a blur as Meadows hit the deck.

Naturally enough, Shepherd copped an enormous metaphorical kick in the butt from then Air Vice-Marshal Alan Reed for his monumental 'cock-up'. He was told in no uncertain terms that he was a disgrace as he was presented with a 15 centimetre by 10 centimetre print of the infamous image. He was also informed that the incriminating negative would be destroyed, but when he returned from a diplomatic tour in Singapore he saw two-by-one-metre copies of the picture plastered all around the place, including on the wall at the Sacramento air force base in California where F-111 deep maintenance was carried out.

If the image neatly sums up Shepherd's approach to life then the door into his office says quite a bit about the man and the macho world of jet fighter pilots. It features the colourful image of a buxom woman and a pig carrying supplies of overproof Bundaberg rum along a beach.

The 'pig' is of course the nickname for the F-111 jet and the door has a history of its own because it was formerly attached to the crew room at Number 6 Squadron at Amberley. When Shep became commanding officer of the squadron the door was plain yellow so he told the squadron's youngest pilot officer, Terry Deeth, now a wing commander at Amberley, to do something about decorating it. Young Deeth commissioned Corporal Mick Kelly, a former signwriter, to come up with an appropriate image. Shep loved it and the door became an integral part of Number 6 Squadron.

Several years later he was back at Amberley as Officer Commanding 82 Wing when 6 Squadron was moving to new premises and the door had been classified as excess to requirements.

'They didn't want it so I knocked it off,' he says. 'I bought a replacement and took the door home because it was part of our history.'

Fighter pilots are regarded as the elite of the RAAF and the competition is extreme. Of the thousands of young Australians who apply to join the Australian Defence Force every year, 5.73 per cent want to be pilots. Defence Force Recruiting sifts through the applications and presents about 500 candidates to the ADF Pilot Selection Agency. The agency then selects some 275 for screening as potential pilots across the three services.

Of that pool, the air force picks around 70 to undertake the pilot course at the Basic Flying Training School in Tamworth. Of them, only 45 will graduate from Number 2 Flying Training School at Pearce with their RAAF pilot wings.

Just 15 of the 45 will be identified as displaying the potential to become a fighter pilot. They proceed to the Introductory Fighter Course at Number 79 Squadron at Pearce and then Number 76 Squadron at Williamtown.

Three-quarters of them are then chosen to undertake Classic Hornet or Super Hornet operational conversion courses (previously the F-111). Not all will make it. The bottom line is that only about 10 will survive the comprehensive, four-year training to graduate as qualified RAAF fighter pilots.

Shepherd himself didn't harbour any real ambition to be a pilot or even to join the RAAF when he was growing up in Queensland. He saw some recruitment material about the RAAF academy at Point Cook and thought it looked interesting.

'I had never really built a model aeroplane and never had a great passion for flying, but I saw the air force academy and thought that would be all right and started the process and away I went. That was January 1971,' he says.

Throughout his career he always regarded the flying part of his job as secondary to operating the weapons systems.

'You don't fly in the air force, you operate a weapon system to achieve a military outcome; we happen to do it with air vehicles,' he says. 'I'm not that interested in flying, frankly. I like operating a weapons system, thinking about tactics, enemy tactics, radar, when we get next refuelling, the whole complex activity that goes into a military flight, rather than flying a Cessna waving at cows and clouds. I enjoy that whole sense of operating the aeroplane in a military system.'

Part of that experience is the rare marvel, such as the sunrise over the Pacific while flying at high altitude or surviving a mission through a thunderstorm flying at 480 knots (890 kilometres per hour) and 230 feet above the ground using the F-111's terrain-following radar. 'Not very high, but tough little mountains in northern New South Wales, [are] very scary, but when you get back and you pat yourself down and you are still alive, [it feels] very exhilarating.'

Shep followed a well-worn career path through the RAAF including a tour as deputy defence attaché in Singapore, Commanding Officer of Number 6 (F-111) Squadron, Officer Commanding 82 Wing (all F-111s), Director General Joint Operations, Air Commander Australia and finally in 2005 he was promoted to a three-star and appointed Chief of Air Force, retiring in 2008 to the family seat at Eumundi.

'I just fell into the air force and I often wonder why I went that way. I had long hair and a motorbike and I used to go surfing all the time. You fall into certain things and if you stick at it, it all turns out okay,' he says.

Becoming chief means that things really did turn out 'okay' for the optimistic and cheerful Shepherd. He admits he never had a plan to run the RAAF but also concedes that if you get in and work hard, put your head down, bum up and do good work, you get your just rewards.

'You need an element of luck. I think my career was probably dead in the water a couple of times, no fault of my own, but obviously every one-star can't get promoted to two-star and so on,' he says.

Shepherd was as surprised as anyone when he got the call to leapfrog several other more senior two-star officers to become the chief. 'I certainly wasn't the classic Canberra warrior; I've only had three tours in Canberra in total. I came from an operational background to Chief of Air Force and I wasn't one of the senior two-stars, but then neither [was] Mark Binskin.'

The Australian Defence Force had been trying to break the nexus of seniority in its top ranks for some time. Shepherd was among the first to jump the 'seniority' queue and Mark Binskin and the former navy chief, Vice-Admiral Russ Crane, followed him.

Shepherd's philosophy is remarkably simple and is summed up in three core pillars — work hard, play hard and keep your nose clean.

'I still think in the modern military, certainly in the modern air force, we have a need for characters. We have a need for people to enjoy themselves,' he says. 'It's a bloody fun job, we are doing important work [but] it's a fun job. We should bloody well get out there and enjoy it. I always believe in play hard, work hard.'

His favourite aircraft is and will always remain the F-111. He logged nearly 2500 hours on his beloved 'pig' from four flying tours and he regards the jet as an icon of strike aircraft.

'It has been a wonderful aircraft … until the last minute,' he says. 'It was a great buy for Australia and the fact that we've never had to use it in anger is good for the nation. I suppose as an airman you always wish you'd been out there and had a go in operations. I know that sounds naive and silly because you don't want to be out there dropping bombs and killing people, but as a professional airman you'd like to see your capabilities and weapons system put to the test.'

He also has great admiration for the first jet fighter he flew, the French-built Dassault Mirage. He says it was a wonderful aeroplane to fly, but difficult to land because it landed very fast.

'We used it on relatively short 8000-foot runways in Malaysia without any heavy winds to assist you in braking,' he says. 'We used to land a Mirage at 175 knots [324 kilometres per hour] minimum, but a bit of fuel onboard would put that up to 195. The parachute wouldn't work over 150 and the brakes wouldn't work over 120 knots. Therefore, the challenge in the tropics operating from short strips was always excessive speed and how to wash it off.'

The Mirages also had a habit of breaking and ultimately one would almost kill Shepherd and provide him with membership to some very exclusive clubs.

It happened on his eighth ride in the dual-seat trainer jet at Williamtown in August 1976. He had gone solo on flight number six and was learning formation flying with instructor Bruce 'Poodle' Wood in the back seat. The pair arrived back in the circuit with minimal fuel left in the tank and a serious problem with the undercarriage. The left wheel was not showing up on cockpit indicators as being locked down at all.

'We had someone come and do an airborne check and they said, "No, it looks fine," so we came into land at a slightly higher speed, about 200 knots [370 kilometres per hour], thinking that if the undercarriage collapsed, we could race and pick up the wing with aerodynamic controls and fly away,' he says. 'When the wheel did collapse, the wing hit the ground very quickly and very hard, and the jet skidded off the runway doing about 200-plus knots and almost hit the rescue helicopter hovering nearby.'

After that it just missed the control tower and some temporary buildings before making an uncontrolled beeline for the hangars. It had landed with about 30 gallons (136 litres) of fuel and was now on full afterburner, chewing through a gallon a second as it careered across the base, shredding its left wing fuel tank as it went.

'It could have snuffed out at any time,' he says.

Shep gratefully acknowledges that Wood was the real hero of the piece, as Poodle fought to control the damaged jet. 'I remember very clearly thinking we were going to hit all the hangars. There were people jumping out of the hangar windows and running away, people jumping out of Mirages, there were guys strapped into the Mirages who were trying to unstrap and hurry to get out of the way. We were going to clean up the whole RAAF Australian-based fighter force!

'I remember seeing this in very slow time — the brain is pumping, adrenaline is pumping, thinking, "Oh, we are going to hit those hangars and we are going to die and that's going to be a bit of a problem" but it was all very calm and happening in slow time.'

According to Shep (although he says Poodle Wood disputes this version of events) the jet hit a raised roadway and literally bounced back into the air.

'Now Poodle says that he did that; that's when he pulled back on the controls. He is correct, of course, because he was pilot in command at the time,' he says. 'I was sitting there as the student enjoying the ride. We literally, and I say again — Poodle doesn't like this description but that's what it seemed like to me — "bounced" over the hangars and over Number Two Operational Conversion Unit, and Poodle told me to eject straight away. We were very low, had literally no fuel and were missing bits of the left wing. How we didn't just spin, how it had enough aerodynamic surface to fly vaguely in a straight direction, I'm not sure.'

Shep ejected first, which was unusual because normally the back seat goes out first, but as the student he was happy to obey orders and go first.

'We were so close to the base, the canopy landed where the ADF Warfare Centre is now, which was then just bushland,' he says. 'I remember hanging in the parachute straps there waving at all the guys in the 2OCU car park, [and them] waving at me, literally 200 metres from the car park. Just as I banged out I looked over and saw the aeroplane. It had flamed out at that stage, it ran out of fuel. I saw Poodle come out — he was over bushland on the other side of the back gate — and there we were. It was a big day, big day.'

He adds, 'I remember checking the old family jewels as I was hanging out of the parachute to make sure they were still intact from all the straps. Hadn't had any kids then. Thankfully they still worked.'

Ejections were not unusual in the RAAF back in the 1970s and he recalls that his was number four or five for the year from Mirages and it was still only August.

Fortunately, both men sustained only minor injuries and for their efforts they were granted membership of two very exclusive clubs: the Martin Baker Club, named after the manufacturer of the ejector seat, and the Caterpillar Club, formed in Britain during World War II to honour aircrew that successfully escaped terminally damaged aircraft. In those days parachutes were made of silk and silk comes from caterpillars (more commonly known as silkworms).

The Caterpillar Club never meets, has no officers or any formal organisation, but membership is strictly supervised and only open to those airmen who have been saved by an Irvin-brand parachute. They receive a distinctive caterpillar pin and can wear the caterpillar tie that is only available from a particular men's outfitter on The Strand in London.

Famous members of the club include the former astronaut John Glenn, record-breaking aviation pioneer Charles Lindbergh and legendary World War II American flying ace General James 'Jimmy' Doolittle, who led the daring first bombing raid against Japan's home islands using B-25 Mitchell bombers that flew off the aircraft carrier USS *Hornet*. The bombers could not land back on the carrier and lifted off with orders to drop their bombs, head for China and take their chances. The story was most recently immortalised in the 2001 film, *Pearl Harbor*, starring Alec Baldwin as Doolittle.

Despite the crashes and near misses with the Mirage fleet, Shep says the fighter served the RAAF very well.

'We used that aeroplane probably grossly away from its intended design criteria as a high-level interceptor,' he admits. 'We used it for air-to-ground, low-level navigation at night — used it for lots of things — and we all held it in high regard. But a serious air force, and the RAAF is exactly that, needs to refresh not only our platforms, but also our doctrine, our way of doing our business. That's occurred in the decades since, and reminiscences from old buggers like me are best kept for around the bar.'

Chapter 9

PIGS DID FLY

Friday, 3 December 2010 marked the end of another era for the Royal Australian Air Force. That was the day the venerable F-111 'Aardvark' strike aircraft made its final flight at its home base at Amberley, west of Brisbane. As the only air force on the globe still operating the jet, it was also an event of world significance and a large contingent of international media was on hand to record the final operational moments of a remarkable military aircraft.

For several generations of pilots, navigators and ground crew the day was a solemn reminder that all good things must pass and as they watched the final landing through misty eyes they reflected on what a unique war bird the 'pig' was. Its nickname was derived from its designation as an aardvark, which means 'ground pig' in Afrikaans, and the fact that it flies low and fast 'down in the weeds'.

'Fun' is the most common description used by the men and women who had the privilege of flying the General Dynamics F-111 swing-wing aircraft.

After a controversial start in Australian colours following some early crashes, the jet became an icon and a much-loved symbol of air power for the public who witnessed the famous 'dump and burn' routine at countless air displays during its 42-year reign.

It will always occupy a special place in the hearts of men such as Air Vice-Marshal John Harvey, who served as a navigator and weapons operator on the F-111.

'I remember doing the old ANZAC Day fly past. You'd fly over about a dozen towns in Queensland,' he recalls. 'And I remember flying around low level in winter in Brisbane. You fly low level at night, plugged into [terrain-following radar]. There's a full moon with fog in the valleys, you fly towards the mountain and you hear 'dit dit dit' [of the radar] and over the top and over the back of you, you just see this sea of light, this brilliant moon. And all of a sudden, whoosh, you are into the fog and it's all white around. You pop up out of the black with the moon up there again. It's amazing.'

One of the last to fly a RAAF F-111 was Flight Lieutenant Jasper McCaldin. Like many air force pilots he learned to fly before he could drive, bitten by the aviation bug at an early age listening to tales of his father's flying adventures in Africa.

The 27-year-old's love affair with the 'pig' was much shorter than most but no less intense, as one of the lucky few who have flown at almost two-and-half times the speed of sound at 50,000 feet and at 648 knots (1200 kilometres per hour) just 400 feet above the ground in heavy rain at night.

The first test the keen 'bog rat' faced when he arrived at Amberley in January 2008 was to pass the F-111 conversion course. It would be the last course ever conducted.

'It's a very demanding course and you still saw people who had made it as far as I had and still didn't quite pass at the end, so that was where my attention was,' he says.

The first obvious thing about the aircraft is its size. It is much bigger than any other fighter jet and as he approached the cockpit for the first time McCaldin was amazed. 'Climbing up that ladder felt pretty awesome,' he says.

Inside the broad, two-seat side-by-side cockpit was a 40-year-old set-up with dials and knobs, instead of touch screens and head up displays (HUD) of the modern, narrow, tandem-seat fighters.

'Taxiing out you realise how high off the ground you are and how big the machine is,' he says. 'The moment I really knew that I was in a pretty awesome aircraft was when I pushed the throttles forward and put them into afterburner and the acceleration was just amazing. The speed, range and endurance is the biggest difference. It's just incredible, flying around at 550 knots on a training sortie, whereas in the Hawk and other aircraft it was 420 [knots].'

On McCaldin's first night training sortie using the terrain-following radar, the target was a simulated army barracks near Tamworth in New South Wales. The weather was appalling, with showers and thunderstorms all the way.

'I remember just flying through the rain at 600 knots,' he says. 'We couldn't see anything outside, just hearing the rain, and we still managed to hit the target despite the weather at low level at night. That was when I realised it was a pretty special aircraft.'

By 'low level' he means about 400 feet (130 metres) above the ground regardless of the topography. Flying along a narrow line, the jet can zip through a valley where the surrounding terrain towers high above the aircraft or power over a mountain where the peak is 130 metres below. A 'hard flying' setting allows it to fly even closer to the ground at higher 'G' levels.

In the past, the crew saw only occasional flashes of light or the moon, but with night vision goggles they can watch the terrain flashing by below them and the mountains looming up ahead.

'It makes quite a big difference as well, being able to see the mountains as opposed to just light flashing by above you,' he says.

Despite its age the F-111 proved time and again that it could hold its own against even the most modern fighters and ground defence systems. During Exercise Red Flag in the Nevada desert outside Las Vegas in 2009, RAAF F-111 crew were put through their paces in a simulated war.

'It's pretty much the most realistic training you can get in a non-wartime environment that I've seen,' McCaldin says. 'It's just amazing having a whole other aggressor air force out there to try and get you, along with simulated threat systems on the ground giving us indications in the cockpit, and even seeing launches. Sometimes you felt like you were in the real thing. That was definitely the best flying I've done and the best training. The progress you make in that three weeks was just tremendous.'

McCaldin had no 'kills' recorded against his aircraft and they hit all their targets. 'It was a good feeling knowing that we could go out there with the world's best air forces and still hold our own.'

Flying low at night, using what is known as 'terrain masking', the old jets were able to evade attack.

'We were the only people over there who could do that at night, thanks to our training and the radar. I remember coming through into the target area and we were getting engaged by multiple threat systems, doing defensive reactions, defeating those shots,' he says. 'We managed to hit the target within our "time on target" window, so we hit our target and then just pointed back towards the friendly zone, put the wings back, put the afterburners in and kind of ran away at Mach 1.7 [2000 kilometres per hour]. There are not many fighters that can chase you down when you are doing that, so that was definitely pretty cool.'

After one exercise, F-111 pilots were chatting with some British Tornado pilots and watching a replay on the big screen. They could see the four F-111s egressing the target area and one of the Tornado pilots asked what ground speed the F-111s were doing.

'They said "800 knots", which is about Mach 1.2 [1500 kilometres per hour] low level and apparently everyone started clapping. I've spoken to a lot of American pilots … and they all like hearing more stories about how fast it can go down low,' McCaldin says.

He also loved regaling his Hornet mates with tales of flying a three-and-a-half-hour mission from Amberley to Puckapunyal in Victoria, completing the job and then flying straight home to Amberley in time for dinner. A Hornet might go one way without refuelling.

Despite his personal attachment to the jet and the aviation milestones he achieved while flying it, such as breaking the sound barrier at low level over water or reaching Mach 2.4 (3000 kilometres per hour) at 49,000 feet, he realised it was time for it to retire. After all, the 'pig' was flying in Australian colours 13 years before he was born.

As he prepared to be one of the last pilots to fly an F-111, McCaldin felt honoured. 'Knowing all the people that have flown before me on the aircraft and how they love it, and knowing all the things it's done for Australia for such a long period, the last flight is going to be a pretty special day I think — not a sad day, a special day.'

The RAAF's Director of Operations, Group Captain David 'Doc' Millar, was first posted to the F-111s in 1987 as a navigator, at Number 6 Squadron at Amberley.

'It was fairly daunting getting posted to F-111s because we'd lost a crew in 1986 and a crew in 1987 and at that stage there was about a 5 per cent mortality rate, which is a little bit eye-watering,' he says. 'That is one of the great changes you've seen in air forces — the improved safety culture. I had been to 20 funerals by the time I was 30 years of age.'

Millar was selected to be part of the team to buy 15 'G' model F-111s from the Americans. The planes were stored at the famous aircraft 'boneyard' at Davis-Monthan Air Force Base in Arizona. The best 15 were flown to Sacramento where they were readied for the long over-water ferry flight to Australia.

'We bought those aeroplanes on what you would call in Australia, an "as is, where is" basis,' he says. 'You could either ship them out on container ships and spend years putting them back together again after the sea voyage or do a base-level inspection and fly them out.'

After five hours or so of test flying it was off to Australia via Hawaii, Pago Pago, the Marshall Islands then Amberley. 'They were checked out by the Americans at Sacramento but they weren't pulled apart. I was flying Aircraft 281 with a guy called Andy Seaton and we felt this dull vibration through the airframe.'

The aircraft's fin was moving a metre from side to side in the breeze.

'Above about 350 knots indicated [648 kilometres per hour], this thing would flap,' Millar says. 'It wasn't until we took it back to Australia and ran the full major service on it we found that only one of the primary bolts that hold the fin on was actually there.'

Back in Australia they also discovered major faults with the ejection system. Fortunately, it had not been required during the trans-Pacific delivery flights.

No aircraft were lost during the ferry flights and apart from a pelican strike that killed the crew off Evans Head in New South Wales in 1977, all other RAAF F-111 fatalities were controlled flight into terrain and mostly at night. The last F-111 flying fatality occurred in 1999 at Palau Aur in Malaysia.

Flying Officer Adele Merriman, 24, wanted to be an air force pilot from a very young age. As an eight-year-old living at Dubbo in western New South Wales, she travelled overseas with her family and was bitten by the flying bug. In her early teens she began to read air force literature to find out what she would need to do to realise her dream. She worked hard at school and achieved the marks needed to apply for Officer Training School where she enrolled in August 2005. Her dream of being a pilot was shattered early when she was told she was not suitable, so she became a navigator instead.

'I still got to fly. It just wasn't the hands and feet, but I still got to do what I wanted to do,' she says.

Merriman was resigned to going to AP-3C Orions when she was given a late opportunity to train as an F-111 air combat officer (ACO).

'I did the tactical training on King Airs at Sale [Central Flying School] in Victoria and was judged suitable to come up here [Amberley]. So I was absolutely rapt because it was what I wanted to do. The maximum speed of a King Air is about 260 knots [482 kilometres per hour] and we rarely get down to that speed in an F-111, so it's a big step.'

Having grown up with two brothers and no sisters meant the macho world of fighter squadrons did not intimidate her at all. There have been six women aircrew posted to 82 Wing and the F-111s, but in 2010 Merriman was on her own.

'At the squadron you don't get segregated, you don't notice that I'm female and they are all males,' she says. 'I can do my job just as well as any of them and that's what it comes down to. I'm just another member of the squadron, I'm just another crew member. If I can sit in the seat and do the same job as the guys then that's all they care about … I've never felt it's been an issue because of my gender.

'They are a really good bunch of guys here, so I have no issues hanging out with them on weekends and going away with them. I have my fair share of girlfriends outside of the military as well, so I get the best of both worlds really.'

As a two-seater, the F-111 demands high intensity workloads from both the pilot and the ACO.

'A lot of the time we are cross-checking the pilot, just monitoring what he's doing, but in the target area essentially it's our job to get the bombs on target,' Merriman says. 'The pilot will press the pickle button to release the weapons but it is up to us to ensure that the bombs get to where they need to be. We are there to provide an extra set of eyes [and an] extra set of ears; to know what is going on in the bigger picture threat-wise; to provide updates to the pilot on what's out there; and make sure the jet is going generally in the right direction.'

With the side-by-side cockpit configuration the ACO is also responsible for 'clearing' the right-hand side of the jet to make sure there are no 'bad guys' coming up or mountains in the way. 'You do place a lot of trust in each other to get through a sortie so, you know, that trust has to be there.'

After another stint training she hopes to transition to the back seat of a Super Hornet. That will mostly spell the end of flying at 330 feet above the ground at 810 knots (1500 kilometres per hour).

Merriman loves flying and wants to continue for many years. She does not regard herself as any sort of pioneer for women and regards women flying fast jets as a perfectly natural thing to do. She believes it will not be long before the RAAF has its first female fast jet pilot.

'If you think about the number of females that apply in comparison to the number of males that apply, percentage wise, you know, it's probably similar,' she says. 'We may only get 10 per cent of guys through a year going to Hornets and the number of females that come through pilots' course a year is not very high, so percentage wise it might take a few years to get one through. But we'll get one through eventually. I've done some recruiting and [girls] are just not aware that it's a job that is available to them. Recruiting is putting a lot of efforts [into attracting] females for fast jet positions but not many young girls want to come and fly jets in the air force. It's not something that is a common interest in young women.'

Despite all the talk about being just another member of a gender-neutral team, the reality is that there is still some novelty value in Australia when a petite young woman emerges from the cockpit of a loud and fast jet-powered killing machine.

'The public awareness of it is not that great, so they always think it's a male orientated job and they are not aware that females are just as capable and can just as easily do it. So sometimes you get a bit of a reaction,' Merriman says.

That reaction is usually one of quiet shock although women are usually quite impressed and greet her with 'Go girl!' comments. The men are more muted.

'No one has ever said, "You are a female, you shouldn't be able to do it." I've never heard anything like that,' she says.

The Officer Commanding 82 Wing until his own retirement in early 2010 was Group Captain Pete Lloyd. His successor, Group Captain 'Zed' Roberton, took over the job of retiring the aircraft and mopping up a lot of tears.

A former Townsville boy and 32-year RAAF veteran navigator, Lloyd chalked up several stints at Amberley including one as an instructor with the F-111s at Number 6 Squadron and another as Commanding Officer of Number 1 Squadron. Despite the early hiccups he regards the F-111 as the mainstay of Australia's strike deterrence role for more than three decades.

'It was born in controversy and we have some cartoons up on the wall of our tea room that clearly illustrate the low esteem in which it was held when we first got it,' he says. 'There is the flying opera house, gold studded, gold plated, way too expensive. One shows the wings falling off, which actually happened, but since the problems were remediated it has done an outstanding job.'

As the jet was the first to feature variable geometry or 'swing-wings', and the first to use terrain-following radar, many say it was a wonder there were not more problems.

Lloyd says the F-111 could easily have been purpose-built for Australian conditions with its long-range capabilities, large payload, strong undercarriage and big brakes. During a recent exercise it had dropped almost 10 tonnes of bombs on the range in a single pass. He says the reason that it was only ever operated by the US and Australia was that few countries in the 1960s had the engineering capabilities and financial backing to support such a complex aircraft.

That support was not without a cost and a number of maintenance staff have mounted legal action against the Commonwealth for the damage they suffered conducting 'deseal/reseal' work to repair the jet's massive fuel tanks. The 400 or more men were not provided with adequate protective clothing and equipment and a number have died from cancer or other illnesses associated with the toxic chemicals that were used. The government has offered two compensation packages following a scathing board of inquiry and a later parliamentary report but some of the legal actions are continuing.

Lloyd says the aircraft has provided enormous strategic value for the nation throughout the region. While it never fired a shot in anger, he has no doubt that during the East Timor crisis the presence of the 'bombed up' F-111s at Tindal had a strategic impact. 'Walk softly and carry a big stick,' he says.

He too has been amazed by the public's attachment to the 'pig'.

'I was standing on a hill in Brisbane about 5 kilometres from the CBD a couple of years ago watching the fireworks and the F-111 went over doing a "dump and burn" and people just stood up and applauded spontaneously, which I was quite surprised about,' he says. 'The other thing is it looks like a war plane. It looks like it's going flat out even when it's standing still — it has that lean-and-hungry look.

'We call it the Cadillac of the skies. It's big, it's fast and it's comfortable; it doesn't turn too well but it has an enormous capacity for speed. You can feel it leap forward when you sweep the wings back and light the burners. It truly is built for the low-level environment. It gives you a very comfortable ride.'

Lloyd did, however, agree that it was time to retire the fleet. It had become too expensive to keep in the air and he believed the new Super Hornet would fill the gap before the F-35 Joint Strike Fighter arrived.

'Every hour of flight requires 180 hours of maintenance, whereas with the Super Hornet you are looking at in the order of 20 to 30. The level of expertise and skill required to support that airframe is truly remarkable.'

Those experts were senior engineering officer (SENGO) Squadron Leader Peter 'Stan' O'Donnell and his team of hardworking maintenance staff. It had become a daily challenge to keep the aircraft flying, but the team was up for it because many had grown up with the 'pig' and were desperate to keep it going until the very last day.

A flying buff from a very early age, O'Donnell, who hails from the Murray River region of southern New South Wales, regards the SENGO job with the F-111s as the pinnacle of his career.

'The jet has a mystique. It's a huge part of the air force's aviation history,' he says. 'We've been operating aircraft since 1972 and the first F-111 flew in July 1968 and I was born in 1964, so it has been a part of my whole aviation life.'

But inevitably, as the F-111 did its last dump and burn in southern Queensland, the RAAF had already turned its face towards new icons in the futuristic era of stealth.

Chapter 10

SURVIVAL

Military flyers usually prefer a comfortable bed and a hot shower to sleeping rough in the bush, but if they are forced down behind enemy lines their combat survival training can mean the difference between life and death.

Learning how to get water from the sun, start a fire with sticks, butcher an animal or eat plants that sustain rather than kill you are vital skills.

For aircrew regularly flying over hostile insurgent territory in southern Afghanistan, the methods and tactics taught at the RAAF's Combat Survival Training School (CSTS) in Townsville are never far from their thoughts. Being marooned in Taliban country is not something they dwell on, but each one knows that if they come down they will need every ounce of their training to survive the harsh Afghan environment and to outwit an enemy that treats the Geneva conventions with contempt.

Squadron Leader Col Evers is the commanding officer of CSTS. The unit and its staff of 17 have the job of ensuring that all navy, army and RAAF aircrew are equipped to deal with any survival scenario they might face, including evading the enemy and defending a position. The laid-back and cheerful Queenslander relishes challenging his charges and ensuring that when they graduate from his course they can not only survive but also thrive if stranded far from help.

Born and bred in Mackay in central Queensland, Evers and his wife of 30 years, Therese, have four adult children, two of them also in the military. A navigator, Evers joined the RAAF after stints in the Queensland Police Force and as a civil design draughtsman. Most of his flying has been in AP-3C Orion maritime patrol aircraft, apart from a five-year stint as an instructor at the school of navigation at East Sale and the obligatory desk job at air force headquarters in Canberra.

In 2006 he applied for and won the job as CO of the CSTS and so, after 23 years away, he was able to return to his beloved north Queensland. As a country boy who had spent a lot of his youth bush-bashing and messing around in creeks, running a bush survival course was a natural fit. He had completed the course when he was aircrew and like all graduates has never forgotten it.

'It is one of the hardest tactical courses any aircrew ever does, and at stages through it you hate it,' he says. 'But at the end it's after one of those courses that you can really sit back and say you've done something totally out of the box, you've stretched yourself, your mental and physical capacity has been stretched to 110 per cent.'

The primary aim of the course is to take people who spend most of their time operating high-tech equipment on the ground or in an aircraft out of their comfort zone. Following a serious heat stroke issue some years ago the course was reviewed and modified slightly so as not to expose pilots — a very expensive taxpayer funded resource — to undue risk of injury. It was split into two (one for peacetime and one for wartime) and still lasts for 21 days. In Col Evers's opinion it remains 'hard and practical'.

'You come out at the end of it able to light fires anywhere and everywhere without matches and cigarette lighters, able to build things, adapt the environment to suit yourself to stay there for as long as you need to in peacetime and wartime, so it's a real sense of achievement ... These guys are used to sitting in nice comfy seats with a flat tarmac to walk across. The hardest thing they do is walk up the stairs carrying their bag,' he says.

As soon as they arrive in Townsville, the participants, who come from all over the country, are fitness-assessed with some early morning beach runs and scrambles up Townsville's dreaded Castle Hill wearing flying boots.

'You remember those, and one of the earliest memories of my Castle Hill runs was [that] on about my second or third run, the soles fell off my boots — just totally unused to that sort of environment,' Evers says.

The physical activities are not designed to make people fit, but rather to acclimatise them to the brutal north Queensland heat and humidity.

Next, it is into the classroom to learn skills as diverse as tying knots and building a shelter. In the environmental course, a lot of time is spent teaching basic survival skills such as how to find and purify water, light fires in dry and wet environments and how to decide whether food is safe to eat.

Survival priorities are reinforced over and over again so that by the end the students know how to observe insects and birds that can lead you to water, how to get water from trees and how to recognise what parts of a tree you can eat, as well as how to build snares to trap animals and prepare those animals for the pot. The key is convincing students that it is about nutrition and not what part of the animal you are eating.

'You've got to survive — strangle a chicken, if you like — and there are various ways you can prepare that to eat,' he says.

Survival is not about three meals a day. In fact, for the first couple of weeks food is a lower priority than water. Evers says the students' minds have to be shifted from, 'It's morning tea time so I've got to eat' to, 'It's morning tea time; I don't really need to eat but I've got to get some form of water production going, otherwise I'm toasted.'

Mind games play a crucial role in the training, but what really tests them are the physical stresses. Many experience hunger and dehydration for the first time as they learn how food and water deprivation can affect thoughts and actions.

'We put them under physical and mental stresses in a controlled way just so they can experience what it's like to be slightly hungry; experience what it's like to be dehydrated and how that affects their actions,' Evers says.

Once the classroom work is finished they are treated to their first practical experience of a life raft at sea. For those from multi-crew aircraft such as C-130s or AP-3C Orions it is a night spent in an 11-person life raft and for fast jet flyers a single-person life raft. Following their very uncomfortable night in the cramped and bobbing vessels they are dumped on Herald Island, north of Townsville, and provided with some supplies that might have survived an aircraft crash. Unfortunately, food is one item that didn't 'make it'.

Evers says it is fascinating to watch how some students get out and start to find food such as oysters or mussels while others sit back.

Bodily functions are another indicator of how people will cope with a real life-or-death situation. They have to build latrines so their camp is not contaminated and after a night in a life raft this can be an urgent requirement for those who are too modest to hang over the side of a raft in front of 10 new friends.

The students spend just a day and a night on the island, then return to the barracks for a short break before the final phase in a more barren environment.

'We take them out and demonstrate how to light fires using just your flints, and how to kill a chicken rather than other birds,' Evers says. 'We used to have a goat, but we had to give that up. It is not kosher to kill goats out in the bush in case you are distressing the goat — and some of the students.'

Navigation is a vital component, as students learn that navigating on the ground at walking pace is a far different proposition from navigating an aircraft travelling at 190 knots (350 kilometres per hour) using GPS and other gizmos.

'They have to be able to learn how to walk from here to there, to where the rest of the party will pick them up, using grid references. We teach them to navigate through the bush, how to measure distances and all that sort of stuff, how to read maps on the ground rather than in the air, and set them loose [to] do a day navex [navigation exercise] and a night navex,' Evers says.

During the night exercise they are guided to a spot where their aircraft 'crashed' and they have to build shelters, find water and food and signal a rescue aircraft into their position. Just when they think it is time to head back to the base for a shower, a cold drink and a warm bed they are taken into a jungle environment where the groups continue to be steadily reduced from the original 10 members so that each member is forced to get involved in every aspect of the training.

'They spend two nights in the jungle where it is often wet, so if they don't build things correctly it can be very miserable,' Evers says. If they create good shelters they find that the jungle environment can be quite comfortable, with creeks full of fish and yabbies. After mastering that environment as a group, they are 'rescued' but as part of the scenario they 'crash' and find themselves as the sole survivor, along with a limited amount of gear for the ultimate solo survival test.

'We give them two nights to get themselves and their stuff sorted, their shelter made, get their fire going and get into their routine,' he says.

Evers is amazed by what some achieve in just a few hours in the bush.

'By the next afternoon some of them will have even made little chairs out of bamboo,' he says.

An important part of the training is observing how modern individuals cope with boredom and being away from television, iPods and mobile phones. They go from the full suite of communication devices to absolutely nothing but silence and something rustling in the grass.

For some the two-day individual phase can be a nightmare — literally. The staff visit regularly to make sure they are not going off the deep end, but the 48-hour solo exercise is a huge test for many.

'They have to be able to prove that they can do it on their own and when they've done that, they've achieved the aim and are extracted,' Evers says.

After passing the bush survival skills section the students have a brief break back at RAAF Townsville before they are immersed in the wartime-focused combat survival training element of the course.

Because the RAAF has people operating in conflict zones, the survival training is particularly important. The skills they are learning might be needed to save their lives. Unlike the straight peacetime survival training, where the crews might stay put for some time awaiting rescue and so can fill time by making themselves as comfortable as possible, in a combat situation they must keep moving. They learn how to contact friendly forces without compromising their position.

'You've got to have the smarts to know when to stay close to your downed aircraft and when to run, and whichever one the situation dictates, how and why and when,' Evers says.

They are taught how to hide, how to move through treelines and across fences and be unobtrusive in an urban environment. The final part of the course involves evasion exercises in both urban and bush environments with a hostile enemy in hot pursuit. The urban section is conducted on the base where students are dressed in 'enemy' clothing so they can't blend in, and told to evade capture.

On the final weekend they go into the bush and their skills are pitted against infantry soldiers who don't need much motivation to 'hunt and capture' a bunch of 'Raafies'. The students might be told on their radios to go to a secure location for extraction and when they arrive find it is a trap, and the 'enemy' waiting for them.

'It compromises them and there is lots of shooting [blanks] and carrying on and they run away and go to another point,' Evers says. 'Then we show them how in some war situations it will be friendly civilians that will provide assistance to get you out and how to know the good civilians in a foreign land from ones who might not be so good.'

They also learn how to best approach friendly troops who are trying to rescue them in such a way that they don't shoot them.

'That really spoils your rescue,' he says.

SAS soldiers take years to master these skills so nobody is expected to be perfect after a one-week course, but there is a standard and those who do not meet it must repeat the course until they do.

Before deploying to a combat zone aircrew are immersed in an intense combat-survival course that includes classified elements such as techniques for resisting interrogation and the all-important secret code words to identify friend from foe.

They do not suffer the same physical and mental deprivations as SAS soldiers being trained to resist torture, but the course is intense and focused.

Commander Air Combat Group, Air Commodore Mel Hupfeld, who led the Australian F/A-18 Hornet fighter contingent during the 2003 Iraq War, said the first thing a pilot focused on would be surviving the catastrophic failure of the aircraft.

'If that required ejection, [it is] then to survive the parachuting into the hostile environment and then what to do when you got on the ground,' Hupfeld says.

'We had refreshers on that before we went [to Iraq] and then when we were on the ground there was lots of discussion and what-if'ing, I guess, and some planning for that combat environment.'

Hupfeld flew 16 combat missions over Iraq and during his pre-deployment training was bombarded with stories about the fate of hostages and prisoners of war and the effects of electrodes connected to male genitals. During each mission those lessons were never far from his thoughts. Everyone had read *Bravo Two Zero*, about a British SAS patrol captured during the first Gulf War, and they knew to expect some harsh treatment from the Iraqis if they were captured.

'We were given some information on how to deal with these sorts of issues and what you could expect, how best to respond and how you take care of yourself if you are under that sort of extreme captured environment,' he says. 'I was quite confident that all of my aircrew were well prepared if that dreadful outcome did occur. That certainly makes you very focused on being prepared for the mission.'

The first step was physical fitness and the ability to be able to run long distances.

'If I was going to end up on the ground and had to run, I was going to run pretty quick and for a long time,' Hupfeld says. Fortunately, it did not happen and the training was never tested.

The RAAF survival school also runs a two-day snow survival course in August each year at Mount Hotham in the Victorian Alps. For aircrew flying over the Hindu Kush in the depths of an Afghan winter, knowing how to build a snow cave or how to avoid capture in the snow and ice are very important skills.

Col Evers says most students emerge from the environmental and combat survival courses between 5 and 8 kilograms lighter, but mentally much tougher than before.

'They've pushed barriers they never thought they could push through and have been able to keep going without falling in a heap,' he says. 'The mental barriers are tough — things like the extra night out solo in the jungle, the running away in the field knowing there are people out there shooting and dogs yapping at their heels — and the priority is not being caught. You end up with a real sense of achievement and a job well done at the end of it.'

The combat survival training school is a treasure trove of survival gear, and improvised shelters and amazing tales of people staying alive because of their training. The school runs seven courses a year for all Australian aircrew, ranging from fighter pilots to crew attendants on the VIP fleet.

Aircrew carry a kit that contains matches, a sewing kit, fishing kits (including lures and gill nets), snare wire, torch, sharpening stone, candle and lip balm. Some special forces soldiers have been known to eat the lip balm when supplies of food have run down to dangerous levels. The kits also contain chocolate, muesli bars, instant coffee, sugar and water purification tablets. The fishing gear is considered extremely valuable in case you come down near a productive stream.

Evers says that looking after survival gear is vitally important because once something is broken it is broken and there are no shops to nip down to for a replacement.

In the corridor between classrooms back at the school in Townsville there are cabinets displaying survival kits and actual bush survival equipment built by enterprising survivors and students from earlier courses. The displays include improvised items such as a bush mallet, lots of different animal traps, bows and arrows, knives, fish traps, lights, a bush axe and spears as well as repair kits and even a ball and a dice to relieve boredom. There are also photographs and descriptions of bush tucker plants that might look appetising but can kill you.

One cabinet contains a signal fire and instructions on how to build a good smoking fire that will be seen from miles around, using nice dry wood and green leaves. 'This all ties together. You can put the wood over a camp fire to keep it dry in a wet environment, so you can take it out quickly when you need it, so [that] it's nice and dry and ready to go,' he says.

Another cabinet features classic makeshift coastal and jungle survival camps for peacetime operations, including one with cupboards made in the bush. The most common piece of equipment is the animal trap. Clearly students fantasise about living off the land on a diet of reptiles or marsupials, but the reality, according to Evers, is that catching animals in the wild is extremely difficult. 'Not too many are very good at it and they don't catch much.'

At the back of the training school is an open area where shelters and camps have been set up to demonstrate what is possible in various environments, including beaches, deserts and swamps, where the shelter is built up in the trees to avoid moisture.

Some of the survival stories from previous generations of POWs and those who have survived crash landings behind enemy lines are quite remote from the current generation of military flyers.

'Just because it hasn't happened to the Australian military in the last few years doesn't mean it is never going to happen,' he warns. 'So my advice is, take it seriously because this stuff can save your bacon.'

Rivalry between the army and air force can be intense. So when a seasoned army warrant officer gets the chance to teach basic infantry skills to a bunch of flyers who, soldiers say, are 'rarely available after five' (RAAF), it is an opportunity to show the boys and girls in blue what real bush survival skills are all about.

117

Warrant Officer First Class Wayne Harper is the army training officer at the survival school. From Tweed Heads in New South Wales, Harper joined up straight from school and after basic training was posted to the Army Aviation Regiment. After a stint as a ground crewman he transferred to aircrew and has been an aircrewman/loadmaster since 1997.

His job is to teach students what 'combat recovery' means and what the job entails, so that if they are ever on the receiving end they will know exactly what the combat recovery crew, whether air-, sea- or land-borne, will be doing to try and recover the downed aircrew.

Like all the teachers at the school, Harper instructs on both the environmental and combat survival courses. On the environmental course he focuses on location aids and survival radio as well as camp structures. On the combat survival course he focuses on helicopter rescue and defensive tactics.

'For the army guys it's a boring lesson because they are revisiting a lot of stuff they've already done, but for the air force, and particularly for the navy people, their eyes are like dinner plates,' Harper says. 'They really don't touch on this sort of stuff, and unfortunately we don't have the time to really expand on it as we would like to.'

His class in infantry tactics takes about one and a half hours to cover what is taught over three days at the army school of infantry. Most students pay close attention and any who feel that it could never happen to them usually tune in after a few of the real-life stories of aircraft coming down are told.

In Afghanistan, for example, the Townsville-based Australian Army Chinooks are regularly under fire and occasionally even hit by a stray round from an AK-47 assault rifle. In Iraq there was the death of the American contractor on a Hercules.

Slow-flying helicopters are in constant danger from ground fire and other hazards such as 'brown out' (caused when dust is thrown up by the rotor blades) and three Australian special forces soldiers were killed when a US Black Hawk chopper crashed at night in Afghanistan in 2010.

Harper agrees that the most important thing about survival training is getting people out of their comfort zones. For navy sailors, that usually means a stint in the bush and for soldiers it could mean a dunking in the ocean.

'The motto is "adapt and return" so we try to get them out of their comfort zone although some of them go to their comfort zone on every phase,' he says. 'The whole idea is for them to be able to fill the newsreels inside their heads so if they get put in a similar situation again, they [will] be able to fall back on some type of experience that got them out of there.'

He says the most telling part of the course is always the lone survival exercise. 'You've got to be able to change your routine and the way you are as a person when you get into a survival situation,' he says. 'It's not about getting up in the morning and brushing your teeth, having breakfast and driving to work. Out there in a survival situation they have to think about every particular thing they are doing because if they do something wrong, potentially it could kill them. It may not kill them outright but if they were in a solo survival situation that mistake may end up killing them down the track, through illness, injury, whatever.'

The four priorities for survival are protection, location, water then food. Harper says fire is the nuts and bolts of survival. 'It helps you with first aid, shelter and drying clothing. Fire is pretty much it.'

He has noticed a stark difference between older and younger students and between those from the country and those from the city. Generation Y students struggle the hardest and question the most.

'If they come from the country they've generally got some survival skills, but if they are from the city and have grown up pretty much getting what they want and doing what they want, then no, they don't,' he says.

Younger students often struggle with the fitness aspects as well.

'I used to ride 5 kilometres every afternoon to go surfing, so I was naturally fit and strong, but you've got young guys who come on this course that can't run 2.5 kilometres under 14 minutes. That's just because of the way they've been brought up, and it is unfortunately a fact of Defence today,' he says. 'In Defence you are expected to be a little bit sharper and fitter than the average civilian, but unfortunately we get people on the course who aren't and they are found wanting. If they don't meet the required standard they are removed from the course for their own safety. We can't allow them to go out in the bush and cause injury to themselves or someone else.'

Students who excel in some aspects of the course after he expected them to fail often surprise him pleasantly. He has also been amazed by the tenacity of some female students. In one case a young woman was injured and had to leave the course. She returned and injured herself again but did not tell the instructors. Despite a serious and painful lower back injury she made it through and passed.

'On another course we had a bunch of guys whinging, saying it was all too hard so one of the instructors told them about what she did and all of a sudden they shut up.'

At the end of the day, Harper says, it is individual personalities that determine the outcome for most students.

'We put them into a situation where they have no idea what's coming next because in a survival situation they wouldn't and they just have to be able to adapt,' he says. 'We try and work on the idea of routine. In your normal life at home you are in a routine so the sooner you can change that routine into a survival routine the better your chances are of surviving.'

Some cope well with being alone in a strange environment while others suffer considerable mental trauma. 'You walk in and some are curled up in the foetal position and others are absolutely killing it. It's just up to them.'

IRAQ

Chapter 11

BAGHDAD OR BUST

All the while the US-led coalition commanders were marshalling their forces against Saddam Hussein, they had no compelling evidence of the extent of Iraq's air power.

American forces had mounted a huge information operation to convince the remnants of the Iraqi air force that any attempt to resist the coalition invasion in March 2003 would result in their certain demise. Despite this and a wealth of human and electronic intelligence, US-led coalition forces were in the dark as to exactly how many Iraqi fighter jets had survived the war with Iran and years of United Nations sanctions. Neither did they know whether Iraqi Air Force pilots would be crazy-brave enough to launch even if they could muster some workable airframes.

This uncertainty played briefly on the mind of then Flight Lieutenant John Haly as he lined up his F/A-18 Hornet fighter on the runway for his first combat mission.

In the early days of the war the RAAF Hornets were engaged in what is known as defensive counter-air (DCA) missions. That means protecting high-value assets, such as airborne warning and control aircraft or fuel tankers, from any enemy aircraft.

Haly was flying as a wingman in a 'two ship' sortie and he felt a mixture of excitement and fear as his jet bucked forward and lifted him off to war.

'It was exciting but it was also one of those weird moments where you don't really know what to think, so you just cut straight to your job,' he says.

After a few days of war it was apparent that Saddam's pilots had listened to the message and the focus of the air war shifted to ground strikes.

Haly's first strike mission was just north of Basra to attack a column of eight enemy tanks. A US air force A-10 Thunderbolt (or Warthog Tank Killer) was monitoring the target, having expended all of its munitions, and was running low on fuel.

'He gave us the coordinates and basically handed off the target area to us before he ran out of fuel and had to go home,' Haly says. 'My lead and I proceeded to then go on and deploy ordnance on the tanks.'

Armed with 250-kilogram laser-guided bombs, Haly managed to take out two Iraqi tanks before turning for home.

'We were a little concerned about surface-to-air fire so it was ... get in and do the job and get out of harm's way,' he says. 'Flying back from the mission I thought, "I can't really believe I just did that." That was the first time I've ever done that in my fighter flying career, employed real ordnance in anger in a real conflict. It was a mixture of surprise and pride and also satisfaction that we had done it and got home.'

The coalition uncertainty about the extent of Saddam's air power was justified when Australian SAS soldiers captured the vast Al Asad air base in the western desert of Iraq. The troops from SAS Number 1 Squadron uncovered a veritable Aladdin's cave of weaponry, including dozens of aircraft that the intelligence reports had said did not exist. The reports had said there would be just two MiG fighters at the base that covered an area measuring 14 by 7 kilometres.

Much to their surprise — and that of everybody up the chain of command — the diggers literally unearthed three Russian MiG-25 Foxbats, a MiG-29, dozens of MiG-21s, helicopters, 100 surface-to-air-missile systems and almost 8 million kilograms of high explosives. In total there were 57 Iraqi aircraft at the base and despite numerous coalition air strikes several were virtually ready to fly.

The SAS men had the satisfaction of calling in Australian Hornets as they moved to secure the area and two of the jet fighters would provide a flypast during the Anzac Day service at Al Asad on 25 April 2003.

The icing on the cake for Australia's biggest trophy of the war came when a RAAF C-130 from 36 Squadron at Richmond became the first coalition aircraft to land on the Al Asad runway after its bomb craters had been repaired by the SAS boys, using hot-wired equipment from the base and earth-moving gear borrowed from the nearby Kubaysah cement works that the diggers had secured a few days before.

One of John Haly's most satisfying missions was providing close air support for his own countrymen when he was called in by the SAS during a major firefight against Iraqi fighters in sports utility vehicles. The SAS men were going from area to area basically securing anti-aircraft ammunition because they weren't allowed to destroy military hardware. It was to be kept intact for Iraqi forces once Saddam's regime had been neutralised.

'While that was happening they were being attacked by a bunch of people in pick-up trucks,' Haly recalls. 'We were up above talking to the guys on the ground telling them where the enemy vehicles were and what they were doing and hearing the fight going on in the background as we were talking on the radio. We were an information platform with a God's eye view.'

The other tactic employed with great effect by the SAS troops was to call in the jets for a low and fast pass over civilians to show who was in charge. 'We would just go screaming over at high speed, very low, right over the top, almost a "Hey, we are here, we see you" kind of a thing and I think that was fairly effective on a number of occasions. It is not a conventional use of fighter aircraft but it is very effective.'

The SAS spends a great deal of time conducting close air support training with 75 Squadron around Tindal and many of the well-tried unconventional tactics developed in Iraq are now embedded in the training manual. In the future, with platforms such as the Joint Strike Fighter and the Super Hornet, on-board sensors will be able to be utilised in ways not yet imagined.

'These days the guys on the ground are carrying rover kits so the capability exists for guys fighting out in the Middle East to have a US navy Super Hornet over the top with the infrared pod looking at something. The image is transferred down to the man on the ground holding his little hand-held kit and he can physically confirm, yes that's right, that is the target,' Haly says. 'That real, two-way kind of streaming is amazing. It's just getting more and more efficient and extending the length of the kill chain.'

It was September 2002 when then Group Captain Geoff Brown arrived at the Shaw Air Force Base in South Carolina to begin planning for war. The base is the home of United States Air Force Central, or Central Command Air Forces as it was known, and Brown's job was to integrate RAAF aircraft into coalition war plans should an invasion of Iraq take place.

The Howard government had already decided that if there was a war it would offer up Hornet fighter jets, C-130 Hercules transport planes and AP-3C Orion reconnaissance aircraft as a major part of Australia's contribution, but Brown's riding instructions were clear: 'Do not make any specific commitments.'

Brown, or 'Dog Biscuit' as he is known around the air force, was the commander of 82 Wing at Amberley and he was pulled out of that strike and reconnaissance role to lead the nation's air power contribution for both the planning and operational phases of the Iraq war. A larger-than-life character with a renowned sense of humour, his first task was to win the trust of the American commander, General Michael 'Buzz' Moseley. Fortunately, the two men hit it off immediately.

'General Moseley was really quite a magnanimous US general officer and he took me under his wing and pretty much gave us a bit of open slather as to how we would operate the air force,' Brown recalls.

Despite the relatively tiny scale of Australia's planned contribution to what would be a massive air war, Brown and his small team of planners were given the same status at Moseley's planning table as the British team that was offering a much larger air combat and transport force.

'The UK guy was one side, [Moseley] was in the middle and I was on the other side,' Brown says. 'I hadn't realised what a powerful effect that is in the American system. It basically told all his colonels that I had a direct line to Moseley, so that's a good way to start. We just planned where we might use the F/A-18s and how we could use the C-130s and the bases, and we went through all the targeting, collateral estimations and civilian considerations. So there was a fair bit of work during that time to try to harmonise how we would fit in, if the government decided we go.'

Considering that RAAF aircraft had not dropped a bomb in anger since the Vietnam War more than 30 years before, the Australians had to go to school on what the Americans had been doing, especially in the area of targeting and collateral damage.

'We took a lot of what they'd done and used that as a basis for all our targeting directives,' Brown says. 'I had the same sort of decision power on collateral damage effects that General Moseley did, so when he had to go to the President, I had to come back [to Canberra] pretty much along the same lines.'

Brown joined the RAAF in 1980 as a Chinook helicopter pilot, but the former Queenslander has also flown F/A-18 Hornet fighters and F-111 strike aircraft. His first solo flight was at the age of 15 in a glider and he still pilots a glider for sport and fun at weekends when he has time. After studying for an engineering degree, the 21-year-old decided the air force was for him and he signed up as a direct-entry pilot officer. There was no flying tradition in his family but many of his gliding instructors had been ex-wartime pilots who told tales of combat missions in Lancaster bombers and Spitfires.

Flying is his passion and he is happiest with some distance between himself and the ground. That passion has generated some 5000 flying hours on military aircraft and almost 2000 in gliders.

The now Air Marshal Geoff Brown took over from Mark Binskin as Chief of Air Force. Reflecting on his 30-year career, he said the biggest change had been the coming of age of the truly joint operational model for the Australian Defence Force.

'There is always a hard-edge rivalry between the three services, but I think these days there is a fairly strong view that each of them does a good job in their own environment,' he says. 'You see that now, especially in the [joint] headquarters where the sort of inter-service fights that used to go on don't happen to the same extent. I think everybody has a pretty deep respect for what the other guy does.'

Brown believes the high operational tempo post-East Timor has enhanced the joint operations process and deepened the respect. He says the defence organisation works best when it is focused and it has been very focused since 1999 and that there is nothing like high operational tempo to make people appreciate support elements that would otherwise barely rate a second thought, such as intelligence officers, lawyers and logistics specialists.

As war clouds loomed, Brown and his team deployed to Moseley's headquarters in the Middle East. Despite Australia's very small contribution, Brown and his team were always made to feel valued by Moseley. At one meeting of senior officers, the US commander asked Brown how much of the RAAF's fighter force was deployed. When he replied that it was about one-third, the Americans appreciated just how significant a contribution it was. When the RAAF contribution was lined up with the SAS in the western desert, and many SAS air support missions were coordinated through the CAOC, it was clear that Australia was well and truly pulling its weight.

One of Brown's personal highlights — the photograph hangs prominently on his office wall — was sitting beside Moseley and General Tommy Franks during a video conference with President George W. Bush and his national security team hours before war was declared.

'Initially they could hear us but we could not hear what the President was saying,' Brown recalls. 'Finally Tommy Franks realised what the problem was and turned up the volume knob on the control panel! He tells the president that there had been a technical glitch but contact had been re-established. As quick as a flash [Bush] came back and said, "Well Tommy, lucky you are surrounded by three fighter pilots to keep you under control." That's the story I always tell, especially with an army audience. That was a pretty historic day.'

As it happened, Brown had almost missed the most important video-conference of his career. Live video hook-ups were commonplace and no one had explained the significance of this particular one, so he adopted his usual practice of leaving his arrival until the last minute.

'I turned up with a minute and a half to go before it was due to start and these three gentlemen were already sitting down, having left a bit more time because it was going to be with the President of the United States,' he says. 'I walked in as the cool Australian, but they didn't know I hadn't read the video conference notes well enough to know who was on the other end. I think they were getting a bit worried as to whether I was going to turn up at all!'

As the war progressed it was apparent that the Iraqi air force was not going to fly so the Australians decided to load Advanced Medium-Range Air-to-Air Missiles (AMRAAMs) and laser-guided bombs so they could be employed against 'time-sensitive targets' if necessary. One RAAF patrol was called upon to mount a strike against a 'senior' Iraqi target. That turned out to be 'Chemical Ali', but the slippery character fled the trap. The tactical change proved so effective that the US navy decided to follow suit.

'We did get called on to some time-sensitive targets after that, and then we moved into strike operations where the missions were planned,' Brown says.

The extent of the RAAF's bombing missions in Iraq has been played down for political reasons, but when the sorties are plotted on a map they amount to a lot of high explosives. Geoff Brown is not happy that much of the good work done by Australian aircraft during the war has been left under the radar as far as public perceptions are concerned.

'There were some big surface air missile engagement zones that the guys had to go through and some of the crap you have to read from people about not having the right kit, it is just bullshit,' he says. 'Some of the later RAAF raids were even supporting the American special forces.'

* * *

Then Squadron Leader Terry Van Haren was Executive Officer with 75 Squadron when war was declared against Iraq. He had deployed with the Hornets from 77 Squadron to the US air base on Diego Garcia in the middle of the Indian Ocean between November 2001 and February 2002 and was fulfilling a boyhood dream when he flew to the Middle East in 2003.

In 2009 Van Haren, who grew up on Sydney's northern beaches dreaming of flying jet fighters, was serving as Commanding Officer of 3 Squadron at RAAF Williamtown. The father of three boys was infatuated with flying from an early age. He joined the RAAF as a direct-entry pilot officer in 1986 and, ironically, the young man with a passion for speed was posted to the slowest aeroplanes in the air force — Caribous. It was three years before he managed to roll over to the fast jet world but by 1993 he was a very contented, fully operational Hornet pilot.

Diego Garcia is a vital strategic base for US forces on the tiny British Indian Ocean Territory outpost literally in the middle of nowhere about 3000 kilometres east of Africa and 2000 kilometres south of India. The atoll is strictly off limits to all but military personnel. It houses top-secret US ship, submarine, aircraft and space facilities and is rumoured to include an arsenal of US nuclear warheads.

'Diego Garcia was like a police action. We were there to protect the island if any sort of threat would come to it,' Van Haren says. 'It was characterised by a long time on alert; we had armed jets on standby to fly 24/7. We flew a couple of times a week for training and a few times in response to things that occurred around the island which were suspicious, but nothing that ended up having any combat action involved.'

If Diego Garcia was a dream come true for the wide-eyed former plane spotter then Iraq was nirvana.

Van Haren flew 15 combat missions over Iraq during Operation Falconer in 2003. They included the air combat patrols around the Baghdad area just in case Saddam decided to send aloft any MiGs or

Sukhois to try and bag a coalition aircraft and pilot. Such missions lasted between seven and nine hours and involved numerous air-to-air refuelling hook-ups with US tanker planes. The weather also played a role and some Australian Hornets were diverted to other bases when they couldn't get home because of sandstorms.

'Once we got into the groove, it was a sort of integration exercise working with US and the UK forces, and I think they really appreciated us being there,' he says. 'If we had any comms issues we just put on an American twang to what we were saying and they seemed to go away! You were just another player in the operation over there. It worked very well and was fairly seamless for us — and sobering, I suppose, that after a bunch of years of not being involved in that sort of operation we could walk into it and work well. The only real issue was that being a long way from home some of the spares took a little bit longer than they should have to get to us, but once we got some more priority for critical spares, we recovered.'

He says the Hornets performed very well and the main concern was some of the targeting pod technology. The aircraft were fitted with fairly rudimentary early generation infrared pods that the pilots use to identify and verify targets. At times the pilots found it difficult to confirm a target, so they had to reduce height to get a reliable picture.

'Sometimes our pod maintenance guys were rebuilding those things every night,' he says. 'We'd get home and they'd pull it off the aircraft and totally rebuild it and put it back on the aircraft and off we'd go again. They would work 24 hours rebuilding pods, breaking one pod down, breaking two pods down to make a good pod.'

That was the catalyst for an upgrade program that led to the much more effective LITENING AT pod being fitted to all RAAF Hornets, providing a much clearer picture and far greater reliability.

According to Van Haren, the Iraq mission proved that a fighter unit that 'trained like it fought' would 'fight like it trained'.

'Once we got into it, it felt very much like a major exercise we'd normally do,' he says. 'The attitude was, "Okay, it's another mission and

I've done these sort of missions before in a training sense. Now I'm going to do it in an operational sense; the only real change is that people are going to fight back."... Once we jumped on the aircraft and off we went away, it very much felt like another training mission.'

As the Australian Hornet fighter pilots were preparing to 'cross the wire' into Iraq, a group of anxious senior officers were virtually living in the basement command centre at Russell Offices in Canberra.

Monitoring the first use of Australian fighters since Vietnam and the first stand-alone RAAF fighting force sent overseas since the Korean War, the then Air Commodore Geoff Shepherd admits to feeling slightly nervous.

No one knew precisely what Saddam had up his sleeve, but as the strategic headquarters staff bunkered down and their number swelled from 30 to more than 100, the daily air tasking order issued by the Combined Air Operations Centre (CAOC) in the Middle East became the bible.

'The order runs in a 24-hour cycle so, "Tomorrow all these missions are going to happen." We knew what our guys were going to bomb and we had maps and imagery ... so we could verify the order against the target directive,' Shepherd recalls. 'You weren't ... watching in real time like in the movies, but as near as you can in real life.'

One of the first missions the Australians were given was a pinpoint strike on a target where Saddam Hussein himself was said to be hiding out. Unfortunately, the intelligence was not accurate.

The target directive contained the intent of the American commander, Moseley. The then Australian Chief of the Defence Force (CDF), General Peter Cosgrove, placed few restrictions on the RAAF Hornets. Australian aircraft were under US command but still had to meet national legal obligations under Australian rules of engagement.

Shepherd says there was never a specific order given for RAAF planes to stay away from downtown Baghdad and urban targets.

'I admire General Cosgrove for this,' Shepherd says. 'He could have put restrictions on what we were allowed to do. He could have said, "I don't want our Hornets bombing inside an 80-kilometre ring around Baghdad", but he never did. Our 14 Hornets didn't play a decisive part in any battle. We didn't start any bombings until day three or four because our Hornets were the best air-to-air platforms we had so we kept them on air-to-air duties in case Saddam decided to get airborne and make a fight of it.'

When it became clear that he wasn't going to do that, then the Hornets rolled into the air-to-ground role.

'The targets we attacked were probably good, standard middle-of-the-road military targets,' Shepherd says. 'We weren't looking for some adventure or to break new military doctrine out there in the leading edge of military experimentalism. We were going to stay in the mainstream and Geoff Brown made sure we did a good job of getting those targets, and our guys performed very well.'

While the war was not being run from Canberra, there was a national command structure that gave Australia a veto card. The real power for the Australian commander was the ability to say, 'Australia is not going to do this.'

'We had to develop a target directive,' Shepherd says. 'We certainly didn't have one in Vietnam — we bombed what the Yanks told us to bomb. We bombed what the Brits told us to in World War II and we bombed what they told us to in Malaya, but we signed different protocols with the Americans in Iraq. We wouldn't bomb just American targets. Every target they had — and they had thousands of them, of course — we had to vet and make sure our laws weren't in conflict and a lot didn't [comply].'

At times that meant some complicated legal manoeuvres and Shepherd says Australian military lawyers did a great job ensuring that all bombing raids were conducted to the letter of the law. Occasionally that meant obtaining an exemption under Australian law. For example, if a pilot destroyed an Iraqi tank it was a good military outcome, but in fact he was breaking Australian environmental law.

'Australian environmental law is applied to all Australians wherever you are in the world,' he says.

The RAAF pilots followed a six-step process before being authorised to release their bombs. The most important was positive target identification.

'On a couple of occasions they didn't drop because they couldn't get through their six steps in the correct way and they said that wasn't a valid target for us,' Shepherd says. 'This is an example of how we did exercise our sovereignty over there. We didn't just sort of sell our arse to Mr America and do what he told us to, we exercised our sovereign control under our legal and international obligations.'

Chapter 12

TOP GUN

Australian Flight Lieutenant Matt Hall received a US Air Medal (First Oak Leaf Cluster) for meritorious achievement in aerial flight for his part in destroying the Medina Republican Guard headquarters in south-east Baghdad on 22 March, 2003.

But the Australian fighter pilot almost didn't make it to war at all.

He was posted to the United States on exchange in December 2001 to fly USAF F-15 Strike Eagle aircraft. For his conversion and instructor training, he was posted to the Seymour Johnson Air Base in North Carolina. The work was a little frustrating for a pilot with 2000 hours on fast jets, including 1500 on the RAAF's F/A-18 Hornets and Hall admits he found the experience a little underwhelming.

The one positive was that he managed to take almost every weekend off so he could travel around the States, and, for the first time in his air force career, not just work all the time.

'It was the first time that I gained a social life and had weekends off. I'd worked every single weekend of my entire life in the RAAF,' Hall says. 'I always worked a full day on Sunday preparing for the next week of flying, whereas when you fly the F-15, it was a conversion for me, just learning different systems, but it was still just a fast jet, similar tactics to the Hornet and I could learn everything I needed quite comfortably with a couple of hours' work a day.'

The USAF had elements stationed in Afghanistan during 2002 but as the year progressed America's attention shifted from the wild mountains of the Hindu Kush and the hunt for Osama bin Laden to the deserts and waterways of Iraq and its notorious dictator Saddam Hussein. A new concept known as 'regime change' was born.

Hall had been at home in Newcastle when he heard the news about the 9/11 attacks on the World Trade Center in 2001. As he went for a run along Merewether beach on September 12, he knew the world had changed. 'I remember running past people who were walking back towards me. I was just very emotional. I thought, "This is going to change my life — this event will change my life."'

At work that day he received some very serious briefings.

'At that point I'd already been selected to go to the US on an exchange program to fly the F-15,' Hall says. 'I didn't know if that was still going to occur or Australia was going to go and do anything about it. So my future, all of a sudden, was not very clear at all. Really it just came down to living in the moment, continue to do what I was doing, continue to just prepare for going to live in the US but being very aware anything might change.'

And change it did for the 30-year-old whose personal life was in a state of flux.

'My whole world was a mess — my marriage was failing, I was supposed to be leaving the country to live in another country to fly a different aircraft with a different air force. A stake had been put through the heart of the free world and it was up to people like me to stop it bleeding … That particular event for me was massive.'

As the invasion of Iraq loomed large on the US military's radar, Hall, by now in the US, was dealing with some unique and frustrating issues. After being briefed, along with his American colleagues, that the invasion was likely to happen and that if or when it did, then their base would be intimately involved in the air war, Hall wondered what his role might be.

It was clear that the last thing the Howard government would want would be an Australian fighter pilot shot down over Iraq and paraded on TV. During one briefing the American base commander looked at the Australian flight lieutenant and said, 'Unfortunately, Matt, you are probably going to be sitting on a bench.'

Hall says, 'That was very disappointing to me. Once again, I was trained, I was ready to go, I was probably one of the more experienced people on that base.'

Adding to his frustration, at about this time an Australian wing commander visited Hall at his home in the US. The wing commander was there on a planning mission for the possible involvement of a RAAF squadron in the air war. This was not good news for Hall, one of Australia's most experienced and highly rated fighter pilots who was seemingly stuck in the US on an instructor's course.

Two F-15 squadrons had already deployed, including one at 3 a.m. when Hall was lying, wide awake, listening to jet after jet after jet take off from the base bound for the Middle East. Later that week he met the wife of his good friend, a US officer, Mark 'Grace' Kelly, who had been on exchange in Australia. Kelly was by then the director of operations with the 'Rockets' fighter squadron in the Middle East.

'She told me that she had been talking to Grace and he had told her he'd bumped into the Australians there and they were at the same base. That was like a stake through the heart: "Yep, they are all there in the Middle East and I'm here not even flying any more. This is terrible,"' Hall says. 'I was going to be a cheerleader, sitting on the bench doing nothing and that was quite depressing to me. But there was nothing I could do. It was well above my pay grade to try to make any decisions, but I voiced my opinion.'

He felt that the powers-that-be were making a huge mistake leaving one of the best pilots from either air force out of the fight. He went away for the weekend feeling very angry and spent the break dwelling on it. He thought the situation was completely crazy.

'I wasn't having a good time,' Hall says. 'I went to work on Monday, [all] wound up, and I went into the boss's office and laid it all out, quite aggressively.'

He said, 'I'm being treated unprofessionally. I am an asset to the Royal Australian Air Force, I am one of their most highly trained pilots and you are treating me in this way, which demonstrates you see no reward for anything I'm doing. I'm actually a hindrance to you and the best thing you can do with me is shove me in a corner because you don't want to worry about me. If you are going to treat me like that I want out of here.'

Rather than do nothing, he would prefer to return to Australia where he might help his RAAF comrades with their war.

The American officer listened to his tirade. Then he said, 'Accepted, understood; I now have something to say back to you.'

'I thought, "Here it comes." I thought I was about to be dressed down like you wouldn't believe.'

But the American officer simply said that 'Grace' Kelly had specifically requested that Hall be sent to the Middle East to work as a weapons tactician to assist him with tactics development, as part of building up the strength of his squadron. It would require clearance at the highest level but the process was already under way.

'If it all comes back positively, are you willing to deploy?'

'Yes!'

'Right, go home. We need a copy of your will, a copy of your power of attorney ... Go and start getting yourself ready, turn up at force prep tomorrow morning at 9 a.m. and if it all turns out, you will deploying within the next two weeks. Okay?'

Hall thought, 'Wow, off we go.'

Even though he knew it was still touch and go as to whether he might deploy, he could barely contain his excitement as he raced home to begin the long list of pre-deployment administrative chores.

The clearance came, and then the Australian pilot found himself in the bizarre situation of preparing to go to war with a foreign country's forces but still being considered an alien and therefore a possible security risk. Military forces are reluctant to give any foreign citizen, even those from close allies with top-level security clearances, access to the most sensitive information at their disposal and there is nothing more sensitive than a war plan.

The matter came to a head during a pre-deployment briefing where everyone who was travelling to the Middle East had to be told how, when, where and what their journey would involve. The information included what airline they would catch, the timings and who would meet and look after them at the other end.

The female officer who was conducting the briefing suddenly spotted Hall in his RAAF uniform and stopped dead in her tracks.

'What are you doing here?' she asked.

'I'm deploying'.

All his American mates said the same thing: 'He is one of us. He's wearing different uniform but he's one of us, he's going.'

Hall explained that he was cleared to Top Secret level, so could be privy to very high-level government secrets, but this cut no ice with the briefing officer, who asked him to leave. She did not want to jeopardise national security and her career by telling a foreign officer her country's war plans or even where the US forces would be based.

Hall's pilot mates did not take kindly to her request. 'You are saying we are sending him, but you can't tell him where we are sending him?'

'That's correct,' she said.

The situation was becoming tense and Hall could see his deployment evaporating before his eyes, so he left the room.

'I walked out just to calm the situation down and they have a briefing about where I was going,' he recalls. 'At the end of the brief, they then gave me my airline ticket which said where I was going!'

A few days later he and his American mates were on a flight bound for the Middle East via Amsterdam. After a couple of days of intensive pre-war briefings at a base in Saudi Arabia, they finally arrived at their operational base in a friendly Gulf state at three o'clock in the morning, just four days before 'Shock and Awe' was due to kick off.

As a line pilot and weapons instructor, Hall knew he was in for a hectic time. But he was seized by feelings of a different kind when he arrived at his allocated tent, only to find it was pitched right next door to one that was flying an Australian flag with a magpie on it.

'I grabbed my flashlight and went into the tent and there, asleep, are all my mates from Australia. It was absolutely amazing,' Hall says.

Unable to contain his excitement, he kicked a few of the boys awake to announce his arrival. 'The last time I saw them I was waving goodbye to them to go away for three years to America, "See you in three years." But it was really only about 14 or 15 months later and here we were in the Middle East meeting up again. It was absolutely bizarre that out of all of the thousands and thousands and thousands of people deployed to this base, here we were in the tent next door.'

Despite the early hour his comrades were pleased to see him and to chat about the mission ahead.

During the next couple of days it became apparent that USAF 336 Squadron, with whom Hall was flying, would be at the very pointy end of 'Shock and Awe', including flying bombing missions over the Super MEZ. The Australians would be conducting slightly less hazardous missions away from the Super MEZ and its alleged layers of strategic and tactical missiles.

Says Hall: 'I was briefed as soon as we got there that we, as a squadron, and most of the guys in the room, would fly on day one in one form or another and go inside the Super MEZ to drop bombs in and around Baghdad.'

The orders were simple: 'Go straight into the heart and prick it, get that all suppressed and then support the ground forces.'

During the next couple of days, Hall and his American comrades were provided with a mountain of briefs in the lead-up to war.

'We got a heap more briefs — tactical briefs, strategic briefs, intel briefs, system briefs — because we were carrying a few new systems as well that had been brought in specifically onto the aircraft,' he says. 'So we actually had to learn a few things about the planes.'

He also had to go through quite a process with the rules of engagement because he was operating under American rules of engagement but with the limitations set by the Australian Government. 'So I had my own specific set of rules of engagement of what I could do in combat.'

Those limitations were largely to do with political and legal issues and how it might be viewed back in Australia if a RAAF pilot was allowed to operate 100 per cent as an American warrior.

'There was one type of weapon that I couldn't deploy and the Americans could, and there was one offensive form of attack that I wasn't allowed to do that the Americans could,' he says.

The war came into stark focus for Hall and his fellow pilots after the first 'pin prick' strikes to try to take out Saddam and his notorious sons, Qusay and Uday. Had that objective been achieved, a full-scale invasion might have been avoided. The job was given to a couple of F-117 stealth fighters from the same base.

Hall was sitting in the bar (they were allowed one beer each a night) watching TV when suddenly there were images on the screen of bombs striking the outer suburbs of Baghdad. TV crews stationed on the roof of the Palestine Hotel had captured the first strike of 'Shock and Awe'. Two hours later he was sitting in the same bar when four pilots who had dropped the bombs in Baghdad came in for a drink.

Hall recalls, 'That was my first personal touch of combat. Sitting at the table next to me are the guys who dropped the bombs in Baghdad. Wow!'

He was due to fly the next night so the fact that the F-117s had made it back safely was reassuring. At this point no one really knew how effective the Super MEZ would be or even whether the remnants of Saddam's air force might take to the skies to confront the invader.

'All the indications were that they would fight and fight hard,' Hall says. 'They had the Super MEZ ready to shoot us down and they had jet fighters ready to scramble. Iraq was ready, we were ready — yep, "We are going to take some losses. There are going to be guys shot down tomorrow night."'

As he left the bar he ran into 'Grace' Kelly, who would be leading the first bombing mission. He asked Hall how he was going and whether he was ready.

'After all, he was taking a risk having an Aussie pilot with just 60 hours flying time on the F-15 jet as part of his team,' Hall says.

Kelly offered a few bits of advice on who to trust, who to be wary of and who might let him down when he needed them to perform.

'So [it was] a very close conversation, actually,' Hall says.

Then Kelly said, 'I wonder if anyone will bag a MiG tonight.'

Hall thought, 'This is serious.'

Sleep is always difficult in a tent at a busy air base where jets are coming and going 24/7, so to ensure they were rested up for their first mission Hall and his wisso had both popped sleeping pills.

As the war got under way Saddam responded to the early raids on his capital by slinging some Scud missiles down range. When Hall and his mate emerged from their bunks at 3 a.m. everyone was talking about the missile warnings, donning their gas masks and chemical suits and rushing to the bunkers. Neither Hall nor his wisso has any memory of the air-raid warning

'"Oh shit!" For some reason, we were the only guys trying to get sleep for that mission,' Hall says. 'Everybody else in our tent was either already at work or in the next wave and had got up and run while we were in the security of our tent, during a Scud attack.'

Hall's first mission was to be a 'four-ship' — four F-15 'bomb trucks' operating together — and he was to fly as deputy lead or number three in the formation with his wingman. His job was to assume the lead if anything happened to the number one. They could also operate as two-ship formations. Their target was a cluster of buildings just to the southeast of Baghdad that housed elements of Saddam's Republican Guard. The guard had fallen back to the capital to protect the President and it was Hall's job to hit them at sunrise as they were getting out of bed.

'We were to hit them really hard. This was my first taste of combat and I knew these were not storage warehouses, but you try not to think about what is inside.'

For the mission the F-15 was armed with five GBU-12 227 kilogram laser-guided bombs and six Mark 82 227 kilogram 'dumb' bombs. These were carried in case of sandstorms that can render laser-guided weapons ineffective.

As he began his pre-flight inspection of the jet, Hall couldn't believe how many bombs it was carrying. 'This was the first time I'd seen bombs on an F-15 and I was trying to pre-flight the bombs. You've got to pre-flight the lugs and the cartridges that deploy the bomb when you press the button. So, I'm under the jet wondering, where are the cartridges?'

Hall couldn't identify the cartridges so he handed over to his wisso. 'I said, "Mate, I've got to be honest with you, I've never even seen a bomb on an F-15, can you pre-flight these bombs and make sure we've got carts in every single bomb to get them off the jet?"'

The irony was not lost on Hall. 'I had spent 10, 11 years in the air force, worked every single weekend, did every course I could, got great results, was one of the highest trained fighter pilots in Australia and could build a Hornet with my eyes closed with a meccano set. Now I am going to get shot at and drop real bombs in an aircraft that I've got 60 hours on and I didn't work a single weekend to do it. What an idiot!'

His route took him above the North Arabian Gulf, where a fleet of aircraft carriers was parked, over Kuwait City, across northern Saudi Arabia to rendezvous with the tankers for an air-to-air refuel while they waited to see how the battle ahead was going.

Grace Kelly's initial sortie had been flown without incident so headquarters decided to get on with it while the going was good. The F-15s refuelled one at a time and after numbers one and two had filled up they set off for Baghdad. 'So there I am, Mr 60 Hours, getting refuelled in an F-15. It's just me and my wingman here now, no one else around. A bit lonely.'

The feeling of isolation was soon replaced by adrenaline as Hall's two-ship formation — 'his' formation — headed off to war. As they flew through a clear sky over hazy ground, with the sun up and a bright, white light all around, Hall glanced at his wingman in his large, dark grey jet and recalls thinking, 'You are a sitting duck out there.'

In a flash he realised his offsider was looking back at him and probably thinking exactly the same thing.

The two F-15s were about 160 kilometres behind the lead formation and thanks to their sophisticated data links they could monitor every move of the lead flight.

'You see a line from each aircraft, in front of it; they are now getting designated targets and they are about 10 or 12 minutes in front of us and then I get indications that they have actually dropped a bomb. This is real — they've dropped bombs. They go round and I'm only 10 minutes away myself. It was exactly the same for us, [when] we came in. It was eerie,' Hall says.

The flyers were now totally focused on the mission as their training kicked in automatically. As they approached the Super MEZ, the aircraft's global positioning system (GPS) suddenly stopped working because the Iraqis were using GPS jammers.

'Okay, switching to manual systems now, radars go in there, start doing pre-emptive defensive manoeuvring, not flying straight line just in case somebody takes a pot shot at us, very aware that we are now in the Super MEZ, very aware that the initial wave has gone. They've done their bit and gone out, stirred up the hornet's nest but nothing's come out to get us yet. When are they coming? Putting radars down, mapping the target area, finding the environment. There is the building we are looking at … then wisso says "Target captured, confirmed, cleared to release"; look up … Still jinking around, 10 seconds, whoosh, clean her up, boom, bombs gone, go off and watch it hit. That was probably the most surreal one.'

Hall's formation never hooked up physically with the two lead jets again throughout the initial mission. They were the only coalition aircraft in the area at the time so they concentrated on looking after each other's backs. 'He was going out in one direction and sweeping with his radars and defensive systems while I was attacking, and then he'd turn around and start attacking.'

All the time the pilots and wissos were glued to their sensors making sure that no Iraqi air force MiG fighters were sneaking up on them. The extent of the destruction of the Iraqi forces was not yet clear, so in addition to missiles the Americans were wary of a secret stash of MiGs suddenly swooping in on them.

Laser-guided bombs contain 'seekers' that home in on a target that displays a laser target designator. The laser beam is set to a pulse rate that matches the seeker on the bomb so that it will not be distracted by other laser beams in the area. The target designator, commonly an infrared beam that is invisible to the enemy, is deployed on to the target either by forces on the ground or by a targeting aircraft.

Having deployed his five GBU-12 laser-guided bombs it was time for Hall to deploy his six Mark 82 'dumb' bombs. The weapon does not contain a guidance system so their accuracy or otherwise depends entirely on the skill of the pilot.

The F-15 crew gets a clear view of just how accurate their aim is via a targeting pod fitted to the aircraft. The most common of these is the Israeli-developed LITENING, featuring a high-resolution, forward-looking infrared (FLIR) sensor that displays an infrared image of the target to the crew. The pod also includes a camera, laser designator and laser range-finder.

On his first pass, Hall's dumb bombs flew wide of their target so he decided to fly a steeper, more accurate approach for the next bombing run. The 'hard deck' was set at 12,000 feet so the first bombs were released at about 15,000 feet.

'The way to get more accurate with dumb bombs, the closer you are to target the more accurate you become; the steeper the dive, the more accurate they become,' he says.

His plan of action was to roll out at 20,000 feet in a much steeper angle of attack. The wisso would designate the target in the pod and Hall would confirm it through the 'head up display' (HUD) projected on his screen. This was the mission that gave Hall his first taste of anti-aircraft artillery.

'He led his element into the heavily defended target area, found the headquarters buildings, and executed a crippling series of attacks on the main facility,' the official US Air Medal citation says. 'HIFI 21 flight successfully dropped 16 GBU-12s and 18 Mark-82 bombs destroying five buildings, eight targets, two artillery pieces, and two armoured personnel carriers. During his last attack, Lieutenant Hall was targeted by anti-aircraft artillery and forced to execute defensive reactions. The professional skill and airmanship displayed by Lieutenant Hall reflect great credit upon himself, the Royal Australian Air Force, and the United States Air Force.'

Hall flew 16 combat missions during his month-long combat tour to the Middle East. Some planes in his squadron were hitting the downtown area of Baghdad, including Saddam's palaces and other high-value targets, but Hall mostly worked elsewhere, down in the south-east of the country where the British marines were involved in some firefights, and up towards the Syrian border in the north-west of Iraq.

On some days he flew two missions in a row, simply jumping out of one jet, taking a drink of water and strapping into another that was 'bombed up' and ready to roll. Thanks to his night vision goggles, the RAAF pilot could see and evade most of the anti-aircraft rounds that he encountered.

'I spent most of my time flying at night and I started to get used to being shot at by [anti-aircraft artillery (AAA)],' he says. 'With night vision goggles you can see the AAA in the air; you see the traces, the heat sources in flight. So you can see the flight of the AAA then you can roughly make an assessment if it's going to be close or no threat at all.'

Hall likens the sensation to playing football when someone kicks a ball or, in cricket, hits the ball to you. 'It's coming my way and then it takes another second or two to go, "Yep, I'm heading to the right spot to catch this." So you see the initial shot and you go "Aha!" And then you rapidly see the line of sight and whether it is going to be effective or not.'

After a while Hall developed his own method of calculating how close anti-aircraft fire would come to his jet.

'If it's going to hit you, it will stop just before it hits you,' he says. 'If it's going to go in front of you, it never stops, it keeps moving forwards and just goes forwards across the front of the canopy. If it is going to go behind you it will come up, look like it stops and then turn and look like it goes rapidly back the other way as you go past it. If it stops its motion a long way from you then you know it's not even going to get close. If it stops its motion very close to you, you know it is going to be very close.

'There were a few times you had rounds coming up, they stop somewhere near you ... "This one is going to be close!" You are still manoeuvring aggressively at the time, and they go past.'

The most frightening thing for coalition pilots operating over Iraq in 2003 was Saddam's stocks of surface-to-air missiles known as SAMs. Hall had three close encounters with SAMs and he rates the one missile attack he saw — the others were called in by his comrades — as the most frightening thing that happened to him throughout his deployment.

The first occurred in south-east Iraq when they were flying missions in support of American and British ground troops. His wisso called it and Hall immediately broke off his attack run, launched his electronic countermeasures and heat-sensitive 'chaff' (a stream of small metal strips designed to confuse a missile). The missile flew harmlessly in front of the F-15.

The second attack was called by his wingman. 'My wingman was behind me; they were doing some bombing and I was just about to roll in to drop bombs. It was night-time and he saw the missile get shot straight at me. He called for me to break. I didn't see that one either, I just reacted with the countermeasures and tactics and he said, "No, it's missed" as it went past me, behind me.'

The third one was the closest shave of all. On this occasion, Hall saw the SAM launch and watched the missile as it headed towards him.

'I saw it with my own eyes coming to get me. That was scary. That was in fact the scariest thing that happened to me the entire trip.'

Ironically, he wasn't even dropping bombs at that time but was transiting the Super MEZ, about 10 days into the war, just to the south-east of Baghdad en route to a mission close to the Syrian border. It was at night once again. He had just come off the tanker, heavily loaded up with fuel and ordinance, and was flying below some bad weather.

'We actually wanted to stay visual for a number of reasons and we were just skirting the south, to the south-west of Baghdad, heading to the north-west and the aircraft were flying fairly sluggishly because of the weight. I typically didn't fly straight at any particular time. My lead at that time, he was just flying straight and we were trying to conserve fuel and I was getting a bit frustrated.

'I should have listened to my gut feeling. I was feeling exposed and I was jinking, not aggressively jinking but just slowly manoeuvring backwards and forwards. I was in a right-hand turn at the time. I had my night-vision goggles on so I could see very clearly what was going on. I could see the city, all lit up as a glow, but really I was looking for those AAA being fired. There were quite a few missiles getting shot around. I could see them being shot but they were quite a way off, so lots of action, lots to look at.

'I just happened to look straight down below me — typically what is going to hit you is straight down below you. Looked down and there was a very bright light, almost like looking at someone with a welder, this very intense light source straight below me which caught my attention. It was there for about a second, then it moves aggressively forwards and I could tell it's a plume. It now has a big long flame hanging out the back and it just accelerates extremely fast, forwards, but in my direction of flight. So there is a missile launch. I call on the radio and I start my first tactic, to test it, and to test it I'll change my flight path. If it's guiding on me it will react to me, so I test it, still not really thinking, "Yes."

'I've now seen a lot of missile launches, not necessarily on me. That one is damn close, and I pull, and as I turn, it turned with me. It's like "Ohhh, that's a very bad thing. This thing is very close to me already; it's launched very close to me and it's on me." So straight away — everything: react the jet to it; heap of dispensables go out; I reverse; I go for my next tactic; it is still coming at me — this is probably about two and a half seconds after launch now — and because it's such a close launch, I go straight into my last-ditch manoeuvre. I go to jettison stores at the time

— my bombs and my tanks — and I take my hand off the throttle to get rid of them and I don't. I'm not sure why I didn't. The only thing I can think of was [that] the jet was flying okay and it was either going to miss or it wasn't, and getting rid of that wasn't going to help because it was such a quick reaction. So I didn't get rid of them, I pulled back — my final reaction as I was doing that — and I lost sight; I couldn't see it any more and that was the scariest part.

'It was like the shark is chasing you and now you don't know where it is. It is a horror movie situation. Now everything has gone really quiet, and you know there is something out there that's trying to kill you and so all I did was [a] pre-emptive last-ditch manoeuvre … did that regardless. I came out of that, nothing, fly away. So I don't know how close it came. It would have been bloody close because it was guiding on me. It was still guiding on me after two turns and the whole engagement would have been five seconds, so somewhere in the last two seconds it came off me.

'The conversation was quite bizarre between my lead and myself, because I called, "SAM launch!" and reacted, and he was about a mile and a half, two miles in front of me at the time and I finished the reaction and it was gone. I was just sitting there, my wisso is not talking and I'm not talking. We are just wired, looking around, and my lead says, "Did you see that?" That was about all that was said.'

They continued on their way towards the Syrian border.

'We went out and did some work to the north-west. That was hard to come home [from], that one, because to come home you had to go through the same area and the chances of being shot at again were no more [or less] than anyone else. I kind of felt like I was on a second life at that point and all this superstitious stuff started bouncing up. I was like, "You idiot, you survived it" and now, once again, it was like a horror movie — "Don't go back in the room, you are still alive!" — It was exactly all those thoughts [that] were running through me — "Don't go back" — but I had to because that was the way home. That was hard work going back into that area.'

He did not see his lead again until he was refuelling for the homeward leg. 'There he was waiting for me on the tanker when I rocked up. He came sliding in, got some fuel and we went home as a four-ship again.'

He saw virtually nothing of the city of Baghdad on this or any other mission in the skies over Iraq. 'I probably could have if I looked. That's what I found from my whole time in combat. People talk about seeing this or seeing that, or seeing beautiful countryside here and there. I guess probably because I was so focused, I didn't see. I was within 15 to 20 miles of downtown Baghdad. People said they saw it; I didn't. I guess it was wasted time to look at it. I was only looking at where I knew I had to look.'

On the homeward leg Hall began to reflect on the near miss. 'Once you get out of Iraq, you cross into Kuwait. It is the first time you start to relax [and think] "I've made it home." From memory it is about a 45-minute flight down the north Arabian Gulf and that was just a domestic transit, making sure there were highways in the sky, there were fighters going in and out all the time, so making sure you are following the correct highway.

'It is pretty quiet in the cockpit when you are thinking about it. Your first thoughts are, "Did I mess up, did I make a mistake, did I bomb on target, am I happy that I did everything correctly, is something going to reach out and grab me and torment me for the rest of my life that I've bombed something I shouldn't have?" You replay every bomb very carefully in your head, then you just start to think, "Okay, what was interesting on that flight? What could have gone wrong?"

'And then you have a lot of official de-briefs. First thing, you land, guys come and grab your tapes off you to show the intel officers, you get back to squadron and de-brief the intel officer in person there and then. You de-brief with your flight — what went wrong, what went right, what we'd do differently next time, write a quick summary, submit it, then you review every single pass.

'You get your tapes back from intel [and] log all the parameters of every single bomb, just so you can track, for history's sake and for future development, what bomb parameters we used, what the target was, what the effectiveness was of the bombs, so for future planning you know there was an overkill, or not enough angle, not enough speed, whatever. Then, yeah, that is the end of a 12-hour day — you go home and go to bed.'

Chapter 13

BOMBS AND BABIES

Wing Commander Mel Hupfeld was a worried man. It was March 2003 and the commanding officer of the Australian fighter detachment in the Middle East was about to order a new generation of RAAF fighter pilots to undertake Australia's first bombing raid since the Vietnam War.

The pilot who would lead the air strike against Saddam's forces deep inside Iraq would be 75 Squadron's fighter combat instructor (FCI), Flight Lieutenant Ray 'Homer' Simpson. His wife, Heidi, was seven months pregnant with their first child.

'I didn't want to have to imagine coming home without him when his wife was about to have their first child,' Hupfeld says. 'I wouldn't say it was pressure; it was just one of those things that goes through your mind. It focuses you very much at the job at hand.'

As the commanding officer of 75 Squadron based at Tindal, Mel Hupfeld also commanded the RAAF's detachment of 14 F/A-18 Hornet fighters and more than 150 personnel deployed by the Australian Government to the war under Operation Falconer.

'There was no doubt what we were out there to do and we were going to be the best at doing it to make sure no one was lost,' he says. 'I was determined that would be the case.'

The RAAF's 14 Hornets were part of an overall coalition force of 2000 aircraft, including 250 F/A-18 fighters from the US navy and US marines as well as the RAAF. Hupfeld flew his Hornet into the air base in the Middle East at the head of the Australian detachment on Valentine's Day. When the war started in March, Hupfeld was the first Australian pilot to 'cross the wire', leading the first combat air patrol in support of coalition platforms such as Airborne Early Warning and Control (AEWAC) and tanker aircraft.

The coalition mounted three of these patrols that had to be in the air constantly throughout the war just in case the Iraqi air force got off the ground. The flying was tough and the patrols often lasted up to nine hours locked in a cramped cockpit.

'The first mission I flew across the wire, I came back and every Australian aeroplane was airborne,' Hupfeld recalls. 'I was the first one out and the first one to come back and there was not a plane on the floor. After that, most of the time we flew 12 out of 14 planes every day.'

Altogether Hupfeld flew 17 sorties over Iraq during Operation Falconer.

'It's pretty much a 16-hour flying day for us,' he says. 'We covered initially about an eight-hour window for an air patrol, but you've got a few hours either end of that transiting out and back and starting up and shutting down and moving aeroplanes around, so the main sort of activity was over a fairly long period.'

At the peak of the air campaign, coalition forces were flying up to 3300 sorties a day.

'It's kind of remarkable,' Hupfeld says.

After several days of combat air patrols it was time for the Australian detachment's first bombing run inside Saddam's feared Super MEZ. The Australians would operate flights of two aircraft, consisting of a lead pilot and a second less-experienced flyer known as a 'wingman'.

Hupfeld and his wingman, Flight Lieutenant Allan Hagstrom, were due to set off a couple of hours after 'Homer' Simpson and his wingman, Flight Lieutenant Tim McDowell.

'When I got my mission intelligence brief there was some discussion about the surface-to-air-missile threat,' Hupfeld recalls. 'There was an Iraqi general who was well renowned for mounting effective surface-to-air engagement against allied aircraft. His tactic was pretty much hit and run, where he'd go in under his own defensive engagement zone [with] a big umbrella of missiles to protect him. He would occasionally run a missile launcher out into an area where there hadn't previously been one, set it up and then wait for someone to come through and take a strike. Then, [he would] pack up quickly so he could be gone before anyone could find him and destroy his surface-to-air missile site.'

The threat from surface-to-air-missiles and the fact that no one was 100 per cent certain about the state or fate of the Iraqi air force fighter fleet kept Hupfeld and his team intensely focused on the job at hand.

After the 1991 Persian Gulf War, Iraq's fighter fleet was reduced to a handful of French Mirage, Russian MiG-23 and Sukhoi Su-22 jets. But as the massive coalition military machine rolled into place on the countdown to invade Iraq in March 2003, no one on the coalition side could say with certainty exactly how many Iraqi fighter jets might be squirrelled away waiting to attack invading aircraft.

As the squadron's FCI and key tactician, Homer Simpson was, in the gung-ho world of fighter pilots, the squadron's 'top dog' and the natural choice to lead Australia's first bombing mission since Vietnam. His sortie would take him and his wingman deep into Iraq's Super MEZ to strike a deliberate ground target. For that particular sortie the coalition air commander had appointed Simpson the mission boss for a larger package of coalition aircraft that included strike and jamming aircraft and tankers.

Mel Hupfeld, waiting for news of Simpson and McDowell, was focused on his own imminent take-off, but he couldn't help feeling apprehensive about the father-to-be's safe return.

'I was very confident of him being able to do that effectively, to get in and out and bring his wingman home with him, but it still didn't stop me from being concerned,' Hupfeld says.

It was before the break of dawn when he and his wingman, Hagstrom, took off. Soon after becoming airborne, Hupfeld's radar transponder picked up the signal from Simpson's flight.

There was still a lot of civilian air traffic flying across the Middle East and the fighter pilots had to stay well clear of jumbo jets full of travellers criss-crossing the busy airspace, but there on his cluttered radar screen was the coded signal from the jets of both Simpson and his wingman.

'I knew what codes identified him and his wingman and as I took off I saw that well down range I had a hit with his code on it. So I knew he was okay and he was on the way home, which was pretty neat,' Hupfeld says.

As the Australian aircraft transited the fighter corridor between the Gulf and the Iraqi border, Hupfeld found himself flying almost directly underneath Simpson's Hornet as he was returning.

'He knew it was me and as he went over he just did this really big wing rock and I could see that he had no bombs on,' he says. 'There were two of them and I could assume that they'd achieved their mission so that was a pretty good feeling.'

On that first Australian bombing mission, British GR4 Tornados, American F-16s and a US navy Prowler electronic warfare aircraft joined Simpson and McDowell. The target for their 1000-kilogram laser-guided bombs was a military facility in a well-defended satellite city not far from Baghdad.

'We'd practised it heaps of times. There was nothing different except that the targets were real. In a lot of instances real targets are easier than training ones because they are actually there and it is not just a piece of dirt simulating something,' Simpson says.

The attack was adjusted due to fuel issues and his own awareness levels were boosted considerably when he found his Hornet being 'lit up' several times by enemy surface-to-air missile radars. On that occasion the defensive counter-air weapons were only 'looking' and no missiles were fired at the RAAF jets.

'If they shoot, then they know they are going to get shot at,' he says. 'So it's a bit of cat and mouse game of, "How hard do they want to fight really?"'

Nevertheless, once their bombs had gone the Aussie pilots skedaddled as fast as they could.

Simpson says he felt no fear on the first bombing mission; he just wanted to do a good job.

'I felt very alert. I was taking a lot of care and looking at my wingman and making sure nothing was coming up from underneath us. The main threat for us was a surface-to-air system. If the Iraqis launch [fighter jets], well so be it. I thought we were pretty well prepared to deal with that, but the surface-to-air missile is something you can't control very much from where we sit. So, yeah, I just felt alert.'

Simpson was acutely aware of what the enemy was capable of doing if they captured a coalition airman. Like all his colleagues, he had received comprehensive survival and counter-interrogation training prior to going to war. Each Australian fighter pilot carried a cloth with an Australian flag and a note in Arabic advising any person who assisted them that they would be handsomely rewarded.

'I had more than one option with any of the Bedouins out there so if I got shot down I could try to buy my way out,' he says.

The alternative to escape and evade was to be captured and in the context of Saddam's forces, stories about torture and the appalling treatment of prisoners were well known. No pilot was allowed to carry any family photos or references to home because that is the first thing a trained interrogator would use to weaken their resolve.

During training back in Australia the 'enemy interrogators' first try to build a picture of their victim and focus on any weak spots. The pilots are deprived of their liberty and tested to limits that none had experienced before.

Recalling the counter-interrogation training that occurred just before they deployed to the Middle East, Simpson says, 'It's funny, all the thoughts that go through your head. All I could think of was, "They [his fellow pilots] are all cold and wet; they are going to get sick, and I've only got two weeks to train them [before we deploy]."

'In the end I just got pissed off. I was [thinking], "I'm still sitting here in the same position," and I started looking at the "guards", thinking, "If I ever see you, mate, I'm going to sort you out", taking snapshots in my head. You end up feeling like a captive. I found for me that was a good thing. I embraced it and shut down and they could do whatever they wanted — "I don't care, I'm getting out of this." You never got into the full scenario, but your reaction to it, I think, is what I took away from it: "I can deal with it somewhat."'

Simpson also found the course a strong motivating factor to do the job well.

'We are at high risk of capture because we fly well beyond our line of troops on deep strike missions, where there are only bad guys out there. That's why you have to do this training but that's also why we didn't fight fair. We weren't given this great aircraft and all this intel to try to fight fair. We were flying as high and fast as we could and staying the hell away from them … We were good enough to bring those assets to bear and bring them home again, so you don't need to be stupid to be brave.'

The Iraq war mission was a dream come true for Simpson despite having deep pangs of guilt about leaving a heavily pregnant wife behind to deal with her first born far from their family support networks at RAAF Base Tindal.

The couple was living in Katherine, Heidi's family was from Perth and his was in Sydney. They had discussed the issue at length when it looked as if 75 Squadron and its 'top gun' FCI would be in line to go to war.

Knowing his personal circumstances, Hupfeld had offered Simpson an 'exit' strategy, but being a typical male he took the soft option of handing responsibility for the decision over to his wife.

'I just said, "Hey look, this is the situation. If you don't want me to go, I won't go." She had a think about it and came back and said, "You need to go." That was the hardest thing she ever had to say.'

Simpson had seen hundreds of Australian pilots go through an entire air force career and never be given the opportunity to fire a shot in anger. As an air force wife who had been with him since he was on his pilot's course 10 years earlier at Pearce near Perth, Heidi had lived and breathed what it had taken for him to get to that point.

'I've got a lot of admiration for her for that,' he says. 'It was a tough decision; a very unselfish decision. She said, "You train the guys. How would it look if you didn't go?" I don't know how she did it. I think if the coin was turned over I don't know what I'd say.'

As the war drew near a communications blackout was imposed across all coalition military bases. That meant the regular emails and phone calls home had to cease. However, when Heidi went into labour in Australia the restrictions were relaxed briefly and Simpson could talk to her and follow the progress of her labour.

'That's the modern marvel,' he says. 'I always think back to the poor old guys in previous conflicts when they only had snail mail that might or might not get there.'

Baby Skye Simpson arrived safely in the world on 1 April 2003, soon after her dad had started dropping bombs on Saddam's forces.

'Being able to talk was a big relief,' says Simpson, 'especially once I knew the baby was well.'

As it turned out, in typical air force fashion, the entire Tindal community came together and supported Heidi. Her mother flew up from Perth for the birth, but supporters surrounded her and her birthing suite was filled with teddy bears and flowers, and the house was awash with meals cooked by friends. Even Liz Houston, the wife of then Chief of Air Force, Angus Houston, phoned to check up on her fellow teacher.

'People look at Tindal and think it's going to be really tough in the middle of nowhere, but that worked in our favour because it is a very small community and everyone rallied around her,' Simpson says.

While the support at home was strong, the backup in the detachment was also good and the squadron's second FCI, Steve Chappell, took on a lot of the day-to-day load.

'I feel guilty in some ways because Steve was awesome and he did a lot of work on the mission-planning front and that let me keep my head out of the sand,' Simpson says. 'I was just watching the guys execute [their flying missions] and picking things up on the go. It's quite ironic because the FCI in normal squadron life is flat out, but over there all I was doing was executing [my missions] and watching and adjusting tactics as we went and then watching guys execute.'

Apart from flying his own sorties, the most awesome aspect of the mission for Simpson was the size and scale of the air war. He had been sent to a war fighters' conference hosted by General Moseley and was astonished by the size of the planned coalition air operation. When Simpson arrived back at the base there was a stunned silence as he explained to his fellow pilots just how many coalition airframes would be flying around the Gulf region once hostilities commenced. It was beyond anything they could have imagined.

'America copped a lot of bad press, but Moseley impressed me with his very simple plan,' he says. 'The objectives he set as component commander, from my point of view as a tactical guy at the end of the chain, were clear and you can't ask for more than that. The plan was precise regarding what we needed to do as far as the air component went.'

After a few days of ground-strike missions the Australians moved into defensive counter-air and close air support for coalition ground forces, including Australian SAS troops operating in the western desert area.

The war was a defining moment for Simpson, a boy from Sylvania Waters in the Sutherland Shire, south of Sydney, who dreamed of flying as he grew up watching airliners descend over Botany Bay into Kingsford Smith Airport. The clincher came when, at the age of 12, he was returning to Sydney from the Sunshine Coast on a Fokker F27 and he was invited to sit in the jump seat between the two pilots.

'The guys took me past the harbour going into runway 16 and there is the Opera House, there is Sydney Harbour. The pilots were talking pretty casually about how good the job was and I thought "That's it. I need to go flying for a job."'

After being knocked back twice by the RAAF, Simpson took on several part-time jobs while at university to pay his way through flying school, where he earned a commercial pilot's licence and planned to join the airlines.

One of his instructors was an ex-RAAF officer and a former commander of the Central Flying School who was impressed with his work and encouraged him to give the military another try. So, on his third attempt and at the age of 22, Ray Simpson made it through the door to become a trainee air force jet pilot.

Being both motivated and mature meant that he breezed through the various courses and just three years after he joined up he was flying Hornets. He went on to break all records and just six years after his RAAF career began Ray Simpson was a fully-fledged fighter combat instructor.

'I made up for time lost, I guess, not through any prowess, just more by being in the right place at the right time. But it was a steep learning curve and I kept my head down,' he says modestly.

He was posted to 75 Squadron and their first mission after 9/11 was Operation Guardian for the Commonwealth Heads of Government Meeting (CHOGM) in Queensland in 2002.

'The first thing I had to do as an FCI in the squadron was to think about how to shoot down civilian airliners and minimise collateral damage on the ground,' Simpson says. 'You get the right tools to do that sort of stuff, but thankfully nothing came of it.'

Soon afterwards planning began for the possible Iraq mission and things became very busy out at Tindal.

Ray 'Homer' Simpson's war had been going for just three months, 16 missions and 80 hours flying over Iraq, when suddenly he found himself in the back of a C-130 Hercules bound for home.

'I had no idea, so the boys packed my room up [and] packed my bags. I lost a few things as you can imagine, but I was quite happy and next thing I was sitting on the Herc on my way home,' he says.

The flight landed at Port Hedland in Western Australia and Simpson convinced the Herc captain to drop him off at Tindal on the way back to Amberley.

'He was good enough to do an ops drop so they just dropped the ramp and pushed me out the back and it was quite strange. Literally 24 hours before, I was up overhead Iraq and suddenly I am in air movements at Tindal with a sergeant asking me what I was doing.'

Simpson replied, 'I've just come back from the Gulf.'

'Oh, okay, welcome back.'

'That was it, nothing crazy,' Simpson recalls. 'And then I see my wife in the car and my little baby was in the back seat and that was the first time I ever saw her and I just had been pushed out of the back of a Herc. It was very surreal and it was so quiet. It was just me and my wife and my child — and that was kind of nice.'

Chapter 14

FIGHTER PILOTS — THE AFTERMATH

By 2007 it was apparent that Ray 'Homer' Simpson's flying days with the air force were numbered if he were to be promoted. So rather than 'fly a desk' in Canberra he left the full-time service with about 3000 flying hours in his log book and joined Qantas to fly 747 jumbo jets.

The airlines are a popular option for RAAF pilots approaching their 40s with many years of family disruption and removalist vans under their belts. As a reservist he kept his hand in by instructing young pilots on the Hawk trainer and at Qantas he trained to become a Boeing 747 second officer.

In 2009 Qantas was experiencing a slight downturn and the RAAF was keen to get Simpson back, so an arrangement was made. He would take a two-year leave of absence from the airline and go back into the RAAF as a flight lieutenant with number two Operational Conversion Unit (OCU) at RAAF Williamtown, on the Hornet.

'I've got two years in air force, then at the 18-month point I'll make a decision whether I want to go back in and I'll go back to being a squadron leader again, or I might get an extension on my specialist contract. Or I could go back to airlines and do the reserve thing,' he says. 'If my body could hold up and I could keep flying these things until they kick me out, I'll do it.'

Flying a jumbo jet is about as far removed from flying a fighter as any two airborne jobs could be. The 747 is designed for fuel efficiency and high altitude and it doesn't want to slow down. Cruising along at 36,000 feet with 400 souls down the back is a lifetime away from dropping high explosives on enemy targets in Iraq.

Matt Hall remembers the exact moment he knew he would become an air force fighter pilot. Aged 18, he had graduated at the top of his school but had decided to take time off to earn money for professional flying training. So he took a job in the public service.

'I had committed myself — non committedly, I guess I have to say — into getting my commercial licence to be an airline pilot, but not with any passion,' he says.

Six months later he had his private pilot's licence and was building up his flying hours when his father had a sudden heart attack, culminating in open-heart surgery. At the hospital, Hall sat waiting with other family members, including an uncle of his father's.

'They were all sitting there talking about, "Matt, yeah, he's going to be a commercial pilot and fly with the airlines." And I remember them saying how good I'll look in an airline uniform … and I was thinking, "Yeah, that's not what I want, to look good in an airline uniform. I want to go and enjoy life."'

Then someone mentioned that his dad's uncle had been a fighter pilot during World War II, flying legendary Spitfires. Hall was instantly enthralled. 'I was just amazed by this stuff. I'd never met a fighter pilot before.'

Hall said, 'Wow, you are a normal person and you were a real fighter pilot!'

'I only have one regret — that I'm not your age right now so I can do it all again,' the older man said.

Hall went home. Standing in the shower, he thought, 'There is an old man who has lived his life, who would trade it all in to have the opportunity I have right now. I've got to do it, I can't hand up the opportunity that I have. There are people willing to hand over all their life experiences to be what I am now and I'm just letting it go away. I have to do it.'

He had stepped into the shower thinking it had been an interesting day and stepped out determined to join the air force.

The application process took six months. Of 16,000 applicants nationally for the pilots' course only 16 could get in. 'I went down there thinking, "This is going to be easy, they'll love me, I'm a superstar teenage pilot that flies everything" to "Ooohhh there are pretty smart young kids here who are also flying planes."'

Back at the office, a work colleague said, 'Just get over it now. You are just a Newcastle guy. You are not going to get to fly in the air force — you are a public servant.'

It was a sobering moment. Later, the phone rang. 'You've got a letter,' his father said. 'Do you want to wait until you get home?'

'You've got to open it.'

Then, 'Congratulations.'

The day Hall went to Sydney to sign up, a senior officer in a blue uniform stood up and said to the assembled recruits and parents, 'I just want to inform you that America has just started bombing Iraq, about an hour ago.'

It was 17 January 1991 and the first Gulf War had just begun.

Going in as direct entry meant 12 weeks at Point Cook before proceeding to pilot training.

'I'd never met such a group of motivated and intelligent people my age,' Hall says. 'I was like top of my school … and I kind of did really feel, without sounding arrogant, I had better things left for me. When I joined the air force, for the first time I felt average because there was a bunch of really smart and motivated people. So when I started the training I thought, "I just want to be an average air force pilot; I just want to pass."'

He graduated from Number 1 Flying Training School (1FTS) at Point Cook as dux but says, 'It was a massive surprise to me. "Wow, how did that happen?" So I had not expected that at all. That motivated me that maybe I am better than average.'

So he set off for Number 2 Flying Training School at Pearce (2FTS) with a more determined attitude to do really well. Trainees who made it to Phase 5 got their wings and graduated as air force pilots but Hall was absolutely focused on becoming a fighter pilot.

'That was the exciting flying that I was looking for, just like I think 90 per cent of guys that join the air force. A lot of people change their mind during their training ... but I did join to fly fighters and that was one of my motivators,' he says.

His instructors told him, 'You want to fly fighters, that's great, but you need to dux your course. We are only going to take one guy from the course and you need to be number one.'

So he did. Next he joined 25 Squadron for 18 months and then 76 Squadron at Williamtown, flying Macchis while he waited in line to learn how to fly — and, later, to instruct other fighter pilots to fly — the supersonic, all-weather, multi-role F/A-18 Hornet fighter jet. All the time in the back of his mind was the thought of operational flying, of going to war and using the aircraft for what it was ultimately designed to do. 'It's your job and it's like being trained as a thoroughbred but never getting the chance to run on a racecourse. You just know if action happens, you want in.'

Looking back, he says, 'I have to say in hindsight — because at the time I did find it frustrating — what I was doing was the most professional thing of any aviation fraternity. Training your replacement and training them well is the most respected thing you can do.'

Hall did not only fly pre-planned ground attacks in Iraq. On most missions he was supporting ground troops in offensive air support (OAS) or strike coordination and reconnaissance (SCAR).

'That's where I'm not a forward air controller [FAC] but I am locating targets for other fighters that have come on to the scene. So I'm taking control of a kill box and I'm using my bombs to mark targets, and guiding other fighters into those areas and staying airborne for a long time to manage this area. The last two forms I did was close air support for mainly marines and I was also a bomb truck for someone else doing SCAR mission, typically an A-10 that was out wandering around as a FAC, locating targets and pulling me in to hit those targets.'

One close air support mission remains vividly in his mind. 'I was working with marines. They were in a firefight, and just the emotion in that man's voice of wanting me to do something, that was probably the most satisfying mission I did. You could tell they were in trouble and they needed us to help. It was night-time, I could see shooting — I could see lots of shooting on the ground, just like I could see AAA coming up. I could see all sorts of stuff going on, on the ground.'

He could hear the marine saying, 'Thank God you are here! We are under fire, we need support.'

Hall says, 'That was the first time I'd had that response. I'd often had the response, "Yeah, I've got targets for you, report when you are ready for information", but that was a "We need you, we are under fire."'

The marine was yelling on the radio, 'You are clear of friendlies, clear to engage, clear to engage!'

'We already had the weapon in flight,' says Hall, 'In fact there are about five seconds until impact and he's yelling, "Clear of friendlies! Engage, engage!" Yeah, in that particular moment, that particular bomb took out a truck that was shooting. And just the relief in his voice… I felt I helped. That was the first time I actually helped somebody as opposed to inflicting.'

About halfway through the conflict some dark thoughts had begun to emerge.

'I started having a few emotional thoughts like, "What have I done?" And you start thinking from the other man's perspective: he was just in his barracks getting up to do what his boss was telling him to do and I put a bomb through his building. You can't, unfortunately, help thinking like that, but if you continued thinking like that you'd go crazy; a lot of people in history have. So that was probably a small voice in my head, while it was still the other man's perspective [that] I was definitely helping someone else live in the immediate future. They were under threat of not living and I helped.'

He also tried, wherever he could, to pass on useful encrypted information to Australian pilots in the area about targets that he had already vetted.

'There was an exchange of information airborne a number of times

— it is not only what coalition is about, but it at least made me feel better that I was helping my buds out,' he says. 'I specifically remember going through that process [twice] and there were a number of other times I suggested it through a third party, "Hey, we're leaving, here's some targets, can you pass those to the Australians on board?"'

So far as he knows, they were never used, but at least he tried.

Back on the base Hall kept his darker thoughts to himself. 'You need to talk about it afterwards, but in the environment itself, you don't really want to be going there because you just don't know how you are going to react and it's not productive to what you are trying to achieve.'

Mel Hupfeld, who instructed Hall as a trainee pilot, remembers him as one of those students who learned almost in spite of their instructors.

'He was exceptional, even at that stage,' he recalls.

Hupfeld views the relationships between exchange officers and their hosts as a very important part of creating links with coalition partners.

Hall, of course, was flying F-15s with the Americans and staying on the same base as the Australian F/A-18 Hornet pilots, and Hupfeld had one American navy and one marine exchange officer in his squadron.

'And indeed the executive officer or what do they call it? the 'ops' officer of Matt's squadron was a guy that was on exchange in Australia flying F/A-18s about three years before this,' Hupfeld says. 'So those interactions are there; they got the relationships established, everyone in the squadron knows about the Australians, so friendships form very easily. And aircrew is aircrew the world over.'

Geoff Shepherd agrees wholeheartedly about the importance of the exchanges and the relationships and the information exchange that they foster.

'You know, there are all official exchanges of information at the senior level, all intelligence levels, all the interactions you have, but when it comes down to people knowing people, that's when it really comes down — having friends that are passing information.'

★ ★ ★

After five weeks in the Middle East, Hall arrived back in North Carolina and it felt quite surreal.

'Good job, take two days off, then turn up to squadron and keep training instructors how to fly their F-15. And I think for the US air force it was just another day, almost. They'd done that so much themselves — gone to war — but for an Australian, that was the first time Australian fighter pilots had been used since Vietnam. I had two or three days off, turned up to work again wearing my green flying suit instead of my desert flying suit, went out to the practice bombing range with the students, taught them how to drop bombs and that was about the end of it.'

But it wasn't really the end.

'Unfortunately, it was one of those conflicts where there became doubt as to whether it was the right or wrong thing to do. And then the media … it all gets political, the opposition use it as a lever to overthrow the current government, all those little things start to pop up.

'As a military pilot, I did what I was told to do and I had information at hand that most media and general population didn't have as to why I was doing what I was doing. But still, when it is bombarded upon you every day in the general press, [that] what you were doing might not have been the required thing, that does have a bad effect upon anyone that was there, guaranteed. Because while you still believe in yourself, you start to [think] one day, "Was I doing the right thing?"

'I also think once you've been to war there are not many people around that want to go back to war. I am very proud of what I did and if there is a conflict that involves the defence of Australia or defence of the free world, if terrorism threatens the free world, I'm going to be the first person to rejoin the military and say, "Give me an F/A-18 full of bombs and missiles and I'm going to go out there and stop this." But to tell you the truth, I really don't want to go back into a war environment unless it is absolutely necessary.

'I've seen it. It's not pleasant, and it does bring out even unpleasant emotions and thoughts as well. I had thoughts and emotions and said things that I am really disappointed in myself for thinking or saying. Even just when a bomb explodes on the ground, having that feeling of enjoyment and satisfaction of doing your job right — and then, in hindsight, you think of that, and the consequence of that. So yeah, you have to come to terms with how you viewed it. But, yeah, it did change the way I've progressed in life and it probably was one of the factors that had me start thinking about what I wanted to do when I grew up.'

His superior officers told him he could go as far as he wanted in his career; good fighter pilots with combat experience can rise to the top of the military.

'People who have been to combat understand the defence force better just through the fact that they've dealt with those emotions and know how it works,' he says.

But it was not to be.

'In the end I got out of the air force, as did quite a few people who went to war, and I think it's a little bit of, "I've done it and I don't necessarily want to do that again"; [and] some of it [is], "What else is there to do in life? I've been to war, dropped bombs, now being in the air force is almost boring." You know, a huge amount of different thoughts to it. It definitely was a life-changing event.'

The then Wing Commander Hall took time off to pursue a career as a Red Bull air race pilot and ultimately resigned his commission with the RAAF in January 2009.

'Maybe I'll spend these next couple of years outside the air force and [then] go, "You know what, I love the air force." I'm sure I'll probably rejoin if I want to, back into my same position. I am still young enough to do something like that, but at the time there were a few conflicting thoughts in my head and possibly some hypocritical thoughts as well,' he says.

Hall was an instant hit in the Formula 1 of the flying world and while he says that flying close to the ground and hitting objects is counterintuitive for an air force pilot, who is trained to avoid rather than court peril, he soon adapted to the concept of racing fast along a set course just a few metres off the ground, pulling high 'G' half-Cuban turns that would render most mortals unconscious.

In his rookie Red Bull year in 2009 he finished an incredible third and after a second place finish in Perth in 2010 was looking for an even better outcome when near disaster struck and he hit the water during the Canadian event. Other pilots put his split-second recovery and survival down to his air force training.

Of his former student pilot, Mel Hupfeld says, 'He is very disciplined and capable, so he has a great knack of using those attributes. With his military background, it's helped him a lot [but] it still takes a lot of individual talent to do what he is doing.'

Hupfeld, now an air commodore and Commander Air Combat Group, has stayed in the air force and in 2011 is rapidly rising in the ranks.

Asked to compare the flying in Iraq with what he had previously done in his career, he says, 'Well, you always wonder whether you'd make the grade when all you have been doing is a lot of training [and] you are never going to face a threat. So that was the feeling we had before we went there — a kind of strange emotion, I guess. And we found the threats we faced weren't as complex as we'd prepared for, thankfully.

'Now I feel very confident [that] if the threats had been realised … we would have been well able and capable of dealing with them, but I think it might have been a little hair-raising! Even so, it meant we had to be well on our game and focused on every mission we flew.'

As the then junior wingman Grant Burr headed out on his first strike mission on a ground target, a building complex containing one arm of the Iraqi security forces, he felt naturally nervous.

'I was quite apprehensive about whether I was going to be able to perform and survive, I guess. I was solely focused on that, and I guess that not wanting to stuff up is a big part of it,' he says.

But he felt absolutely no qualms about the job ahead. 'I was quite comfortable with that, I guess because the intel behind who this group was and what they were doing didn't paint a particularly good picture. So I didn't have any moral objections to it.'

In fact, he felt comfortable throughout his time in Iraq. 'There was a very heavy focus on all the aircrew, that we understood the legal background behind each mission we were going on — what we could and couldn't target. So I think it was made pretty clear and very practical, airborne, how to apply the rules of engagement. And we were given pretty strict instructions that if we were in doubt we wouldn't attack.'

Reflecting on his own Iraq experience, Ray 'Homer' Simpson says the strange thing about the military pilot's job is that they are personally divorced from the consequences of their actions.

'In a lot of instances you are looking through a targeting pod, which is just a TV screen on the left-hand side, and it's quiet in the jet, it's comfortable in the jet, it's air-conditioned, so you are very removed from it,' he says. '[But] I don't think that removes you from the responsibility of what you are doing. For me personally, yeah, I think about that, but then again that's the game, isn't it? If you are in the military that is the job, so I'm confident of what our target list was and that it was valid. We dropped only on valid targets out there and we were very careful with our collateral damage responsibilities and I was really proud of all the guys for the way they did it.'

There were several missions flown where no bombs were dropped at all because the Australian pilots were not 100 per cent sure of the targeting information.

Simpson is certain that some of the targets he destroyed had enemy fighters in them but that is not something he dwells on.

'It's not something you are necessarily proud of, in that sense, but that was your job. You were assigned it so if you didn't execute it someone else was going to,' he says. 'In reverse, they are trying to remove you from the air. That's the game. War is a terrible thing, but we don't get an option if the country asks us to do it. The best thing we can do is execute the mission as well as we can and get out of it as quick as we can.'

The now Air Marshal Geoff Brown admits to having had a few sleepless nights early on during the 2003 air war in Iraq.

'I'd been part of that fighter community for the last 13 years, and I knew most of the guys we sent out there. That's a pretty interesting feeling,' he says.

The most satisfying element for Brown was how the Australian pilots and support staff conducted themselves.

'We had the most potential to damage Australia's overall engagement there,' he says. 'If we put a bomb in the wrong spot we could have undone a fair bit of work quite quickly. It was a responsibility carried by all the guys who flew those missions.

We've got tapes where they just directed the bombs off to a clear area because they weren't absolutely sure where the target was. The overall professionalism of the force and the way they executed the mission is the most satisfying thing for me.'

In 2004, seven years before coming Chief of Air Force, Brown was awarded the United States Legion of Merit (Degree of Legionnaire) for exceptionally meritorious service.

EYES IN THE SKY

Chapter 15

OPERATION RESOLUTE — OCEAN HUNTER

Setting off for a routine surveillance mission in June 2009, a RAAF AP-3C Orion maritime patrol aircraft taxis out in the early morning for a daylong mission over the Timor Sea.

Under the command of veteran captain Wing Commander Terry Mackinnon, the aircraft from 292 Squadron leaves the lush gardens and tropical buildings of RAAF Darwin behind as it heads north over a calm, tropical sea. With trainee pilot Flying Officer Justin Clarke at the controls, Mackinnon watching like a hawk from the right-hand seat and Tactical Coordinator (TACCO) Flight Lieutenant Brian Brown plotting the mission, the AP-3C Orion flies past Melville Island.

Cruising at about 216 knots (400 kilometres per hour), the sensor operators begin picking up radar blips representing vessels some 120 kilometres away. Large contacts such as freighters or tankers are immediately discarded as the focus turns to dozens of smaller vessels crisscrossing the ocean below. Soon the Orion's radar screens resemble dot paintings as the highly skilled TACCO, airborne electronic analysts and the navigator decide which targets warrant closer inspection. On the screen the targets appear in different colours: red means hostile, yellow indicates that the vessel is known and blue means unknown.

Once identified, blues transform to yellows. The TACCO guides the aircrew onto the suspect vessel for a closer look using the powerful electro-optical camera. From many kilometres away, and well outside the vessel's visual range, the sensor provides a crystal-clear image of the boat

175

and its crew. The aircraft does not have to 'buzz' each contact and, once identified, every vessel can be monitored electronically for the duration of the mission.

As the aircraft flies closer the image becomes even more remarkable, revealing the smallest details on the deck. You can almost tell the eye colour of the people on board. The infrared sensors scan the vessel, searching for any hidden heat signatures such as people hiding under tarpaulins.

During this mission most of the flying is above 1000 feet moving at about 135 knots (250 kilometres per hour), but when a suspect vessel is identified the 60-tonne, four-engined machine descends to as low as 165 feet above the water to fly past for a closer look. As the aircraft swoops in, seemingly just above the waves, its four huge Allison 4600 shaft horsepower turbo-prop engines screaming, a crew member armed with a Canon digital camera and telephoto lens snaps the vessel through a panoramic porthole just behind the captain's seat. The view through the round convex windows is incredible and allows the operators to maintain an unhindered lookout on the sea below and the skies around the aircraft. The images can be instantly transmitted to the mainland for identification.

The seven-hour mission covers a vast swathe of ocean from Melville Island almost to Timor and down to the Kimberley coast. On this particular day most of the vessels are fishing legally in international waters, some are transiting the 'zone' and others appear to be doing not much at all. None are regarded as 'suspected irregular entry vessels' or SIEVs, as the government now calls them.

It is another long day on Operation Resolute with nothing to show for it except some valuable training for the rookie crew members who are on board.

This mission is another step along navigator/communicator (NAVCOM) Flying Officer Trish Kelly's two-and-a-half-year journey from civilian to an operational squadron and a posting to the Middle East. The 24-year-old from Rockhampton in Queensland, who studied Biomedical Sciences but joined the RAAF in search of 'something different', loves the travel and the team environment on the Orion, as well as the fact that she never quite knows what that day's job will be.

Women are widely regarded as superior to men at multi-tasking, a vital skill. 'There is always something different happening. You plan for one thing and then half an hour later something different comes up,' she says during a tea break in the galley at the back of the aircraft. 'The negative is the long days, but we stick together as a team and it is much better than an office or a lab job.'

Her next step, she hopes, will be up to the 'complicated' TACCO position.

Another trainee Orion pilot who is on board is 24-year-old Pilot Officer Daniel Vern, from Lilydale in Victoria. Buzzing suspect vessels in the Timor Sea is a long way from the economics department at Melbourne's Swinburne Institute but much more fun, he says..

His father works in business and Vern was destined to follow suit until he decided to try something completely different. Munching on a toasted sandwich in the crew rest area during a break, he says he knew nothing about Orions when he enrolled at officer training school at Point Cook. He wanted to be aircrew and was aiming to be a TACCO before being bitten by the flying bug and joining the pilot stream.

'It is a pretty cool job for a single bloke. I am away for eight months of the year and we have a lot of fun,' he says.

After about six hours 'on station', rocking and rolling around the tropical sky at between 330 and 1600 feet, it is clear that the people smugglers and their desperate human cargoes are not trying to run the gauntlet from Indonesian to Australian waters on this day. Turning for home as the storm clouds build over the tepid sea, the Orion climbs to a comfortable cruising altitude and most of the crew start to relax.

Vern has to fly the aircraft on the return to Darwin and then try for a perfectly smooth landing under the watchful eye of Terry Mackinnon and the rest of the crew. The operators down the back use the transit as an opportunity to relax, gather their thoughts, have a coffee and prepare for the de-brief on the ground.

Back at RAAF Darwin the de-brief is straightforward and fast, giving the crew time to go home for a shower, meal and a sleep before they return in the pre-dawn hours for another long day to fly their aircraft back home to RAAF Edinburgh near Adelaide.

The 11-hour mission represented another successful day in Mackinnon's long and distinguished flying career. The former South African joined the RAAF in 1982 and by 1984 was flying Orions. He became a pilot in South Africa after receiving an invitation from the president of the Republic to undertake national service.

'There was no RSVP on that. You just had to go and do it and after that I joined the air force, where I was for five years,' he says.

During his time as a fighter pilot and instructor on Macchi jet trainers, he took a holiday to Europe where he met his Australian wife Jan, a nurse from Adelaide. 'It was the most expensive holiday I ever paid for, because I'm still paying for it 27 years later.'

The couple has two children, Tom and Kate, and after stints at RAAF bases around the country they are now happily settled back in Adelaide, the Orion fleet's home town. Mackinnon says that apart from Jan he was attracted to Australia by its stability. He was opposed to apartheid but leaving his homeland was still a difficult decision. The final factor was that his maternal grandfather was an Australian who fought in the Boer War. His grandmother followed her beau out to Australia and they were married for 57 years, both living until 94 years of age.

As an instructor and mentor of young pilots, Mackinnon brings an easygoing and humorous approach. Quick with a joke, he felt a little nervous having civilians lurking behind him in the cockpit of the Orion because he once had the misfortune of having someone vomit down the back of his neck during a turbulent flight.

He says young pilots today are under a lot of pressure from technology, which he views as being there to help rather than to make human beings somehow infallible.

'I say to the guys, "Hey, if you make a mistake, that's good. Learn from it — it proves you are a human being and if you do it again we will have a chat. Do it a third time and you are going to get a fat ear.'"

Spending weeks on end in Darwin away from their families searching for boat people or illegal fishermen is not exactly what most of the flyers imagined themselves doing when they signed up. But sign up they did and they must do whatever the government and their superiors tell them to do. In 2009 and 2010 that meant covering vast areas of ocean to the continent's north in pursuit of illegal vessels, or up to two flights a day of about nine hours each.

The RAAF's AP-3C Orion maritime patrol aircraft is built for comfort as well as function, unlike the Hercules C-130 transport plane. With up to 13 crew working for 15 hours at a time inside a cramped three-metre high by four-metre wide metal tube, some little luxuries are catered for.

Down the back of the 35-metre long, 20- to 30-year-old four-engine C model aircraft is a well-equipped galley with an oven to heat up 'frozos' or frozen meals, power outlets for sandwich makers, boiling water and a fridge full of soft drinks. There is a proper flushing toilet, crew rest station with bunks and a table and benches where the crew can eat and chat.

Forward of the galley are the sonar tubes for deploying anti-submarine listening devices known as sonobuoys and two observer stations with large, protruding, circular, convex windows providing panoramic 180-degree views. These are vital for search and rescue missions. Further forward on the left (starboard) side are the crew stations or the tactical rail ('tac rail'), where airborne electronic analysts sit monitoring screens in semi-darkness collecting and analysing data being sucked up by the aircraft's powerful sensors, including radars, electro-optical systems and infrared sensor suites.

Like the C-130, the Orion is built by Lockheed Martin. It has been in service around the globe since 1962 and its primary roles are anti-submarine and anti-surface warfare and maritime surveillance, including search and rescue.

RAAF Orions are also on permanent standby for six months each year under Australia's global maritime search-and-rescue obligations. When they find a distressed sailor, they might drop an air-sea rescue kit containing a life raft, radio and provisions. Hitting the spot precisely in high winds and rough seas requires a great deal of practice.

Following the fatal explosion and fire on an illegal entry vessel near Ashmore Reef in April 2009 that claimed five lives, an Orion crew dropped 80 'heli' boxes of critical medical supplies to assist the 35 burns victims rescued by navy patrol boats.

The boxes have four wing vanes that rotate like helicopter blades to help deliver the contents accurately and undamaged. The crew drops a smoke canister into the water to estimate the wind at sea level before three operators strap themselves to the floor and open a rear door. The aircraft comes in at about 230 feet above the water, flying at about 135 knots (250 kilometres per hour), and the pilots provide a countdown to the drop master, who signals when the package should be literally kicked out of the open door. The boxes are dropped one at a time and the crew can usually land them on a five-cent piece.

During the 2003 Iraq campaign Australian Orions flew land surveillance missions over Iraq and the aircraft also patrol the skies above landlocked Afghanistan in support of coalition operations. The dozen or so crew members can spend hours at a time concentrating on their screens, not missing a square inch of the sea or ground below. The mission can be anything from searching for refugee boats or illegal fishermen in the Timor Sea to overseeing a vehicle convoy in Afghanistan, scouring the Arabian Sea for pirates or the Southern Ocean for a lost yachtsman or poachers chasing lucrative Patagonian toothfish.

In full-blown war, the planes would be hunting enemy submarines and managing a payload that could include 9000 kilograms of bombs, torpedoes, sea mines or missiles. As the Taliban doesn't have a navy, in Afghanistan the aircraft's high-tech 'eyes' scan for insurgents and roadside bombs rather than periscopes or hostile ships.

Overseeing the four airborne electronic analysts (AEAs), who man the radar, camera and infrared screens, is the sensor employment manager or SEM. The SEM ensures the data is being interpreted correctly and processed in a timely and effective manner for the mission commander, the TACCO, who sits at a station just behind the aircraft captain and opposite the navigator's work station. The TACCO manages the mission and decides which 'targets' to investigate or monitor; where the aircraft flies; and at what level and how long it remains on station. If a target requires detailed investigation the TACCO directs the aircraft and its sensors and has the final say on what the target is, for example an illegal vessel or just a fishing boat.

The NAVCOM sits on the starboard or right-hand side behind the co-pilot and plots the aircraft's course, working closely with the TACCO and the flight crew to optimise flight times and endurance, and maintain safe flying heights. He or she also manages the secure communications and most missions carry two NAVCOMs who rotate in and out of the nav station and the tactical situation display or electronic warfare station that manages the classified side of any Orion mission.

The Orion also carries two flight engineers. One is always on duty, sitting just behind the two pilots. The 'flight eng' monitors all aircraft systems and ensures they are working efficiently. In such an ageing platform, troubleshooting is a key aspect of the flight engineer's job and during a 10-hour mission both engineers are usually kept very busy. The aircraft captain and co-pilot fly the plane based on the plan compiled by the TACCO, but the captain has the final say on all aspects, including time on station. However, it is very much a team aeroplane.

Although the AP-3C Orion is primarily a war-fighting plane designed for anti-submarine warfare, in modern Australia the focus is on people smuggling and poachers or insurgents.

During 2009 three Orions from Number 92 Wing, based at Edinburgh in South Australia, were on permanent watch for boat people and illegal fishing in Operation Resolute above the waters off northern Australia. Covering a vast area of sea from Thursday Island to North West Cape and Christmas Island up to Cocos-Keeling, they are on the frontline of the government campaign against illegal maritime activity run by the Border Protection Command. The planes are tasked by the military's Joint Operations Command, based near Bungendore, outside Canberra.

On any day Australia's vast northern approaches are patrolled by two AP-3C Orions and up to eight Dash 8 aircraft from Customs/Coastwatch.

Detachment Commander Squadron Leader Steve Parsons is posted to Darwin for three years and has his wife and three of their four children with him. Parsons regards the northern surveillance mission under Operation Resolute as a piece of cake compared with the high-intensity anti-submarine and anti-surface warfare flying that is the Orion's bread and butter.

The Sydney Boys' High graduate and former Hurstville boy describes it as the government's 'forward eyes' in the battle against people smugglers, drug smugglers and illegal fishermen.

'When the contact density is high the work is very interesting, but some of the patrols can just be long and arduous because of the areas we need to cover,' he says. 'A crew in any deployment would probably get a good mixture of very challenging flying and then not-so-challenging flying.'

The biggest difficulty is determining which contacts are of interest.

'If we are after an Indonesian fishing boat and there are 100 Indonesian fishing boats, the challenge would be working out the 99 that are fishing and the one that is not,' Parsons says. 'If it is apparent that they are fishing and they are in known fishing grounds, then we can discount them. Anything outside that, then we have a closer look.'

Often the toughest aspect of a mission out of Darwin will be the fickle tropical weather.

By far the most difficult and demanding flying is anti-submarine warfare.

Navigator Flight Lieutenant Brian Brown regards hunting submarines as the pinnacle for any AP-3C flyer. Brown hails from Queenstown on Tasmania's rugged west coast and joined the RAAF as an avionics mechanic. He transferred to ADFA to study for a Bachelor of

A regular sight in the Middle East Area of Operations, a massive dust storm engulfs a coalition air base. PHOTO ADF

The first RAAF C-17 Globemaster cargo jet to fly into the Australian base at Tarin Kowt, in Afghanistan, lands on the unsealed airstrip. PHOTO ADF

Then Group Captain Geoff Brown (far left) at the big table in the Middle East on 20 March, 2003 just hours before the bombing of Baghdad began in earnest. With Brown are US Supreme Commander General Tommy Franks, US Air Force General Michael Moseley and British Air Vice-Marshal Glenn Torpy. On the other end of the video was US President George W Bush and his national security team. *PHOTO COURTESY GEOFF BROWN*

Then Chief of the Defence Force, Air Chief Marshal Angus Houston, discusses the campaign against terrorism with RAAF personnel at their base in the Middle East. *PHOTO ADF*

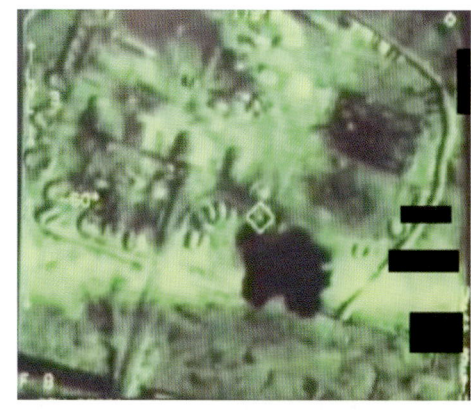

These are the first bomb camera images from the Iraq War ever released by the RAAF. The first shot features Republican Guard strongholds before the RAAF bomb hits and the second shows the weapon striking the target. *PHOTO ADF*

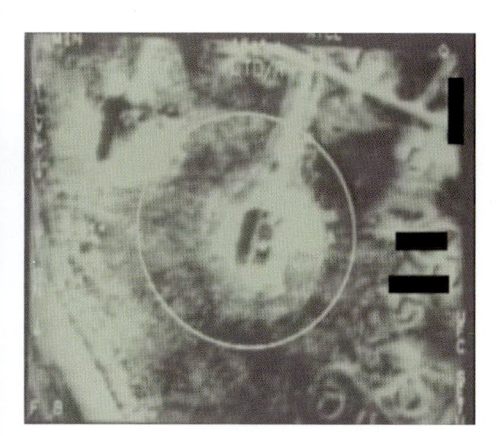

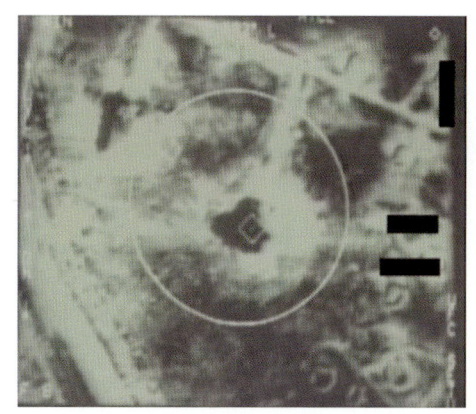

An Iraqi army tank before and after it is hit by a missile fired by a RAAF F/A-18 Hornet in Iraq, in March/April 2003. *PHOTO ADF*

Sensor employment manager Squadron Leader Matt Basedow (right) glued to his screen with airborne electronic analysts providing top cover surveillance for a convoy in Afghanistan.
PHOTO IAN McPHEDRAN

An Australian flag flying at half mast at Al Minhad air base near Dubai as a RAAF AP-3C Orion aircraft is loaded in the background, signifying yet another coalition casualty in Afghanistan.
PHOTO IAN McPHEDRAN

The crew of an AP-3C Orion maritime patrol aircraft safely back at Al Minhad following a convoy protection mission over Afghanistan. They are pilot Flight Lieutenant Lachie Hazeldine, TACCO Flight Lieutenant Mick McGreevy, Sensor employment manager Flight Lieutenant Matt Basedow, co-pilot Flying Officer Matt Jones, Navigator Flight Lieutenant Carl Godwin, Engineers Warrant Officers Lex Glasby and Greg Kerr, Sensor Operators Sergeants Colin Renten, Nick O'Brien and Dwayne Helbig, Flight Sergeant Stephen Pryce and Warrant Officers Alex Vanderwijngaart, Peter Doyle and Todd Desroche. PHOTO IAN McPHEDRAN

Then Chief of Air Force (now Vice Chief of the Defence Force) former fighter pilot Mark Binskin at the Iraqi air force boneyard at Tallil air base in central Iraq. PHOTO RAAF

Former fighter pilot and Red Bull aerobatic pilot Matt Hall flying his highly manoeuvrable Giles aerobatic aircraft. *PHOTO COURTESY MATT HALL*

RAAF fighter pilot and commanding officer of 3 Squadron at Williamtown in NSW, Wing Commander Terry Van Haren, in the cockpit of his F/A-18 Hornet jet. Van Haren flew missions over Iraq during the 2003 war. *PHOTO IAN McPHEDRAN*

C-130 technicians or 'black handers' with 37 Squadron Leading Aircraftswoman Jade Evans from Melbourne and Corporal Danny Laver from Toukley, NSW. *PHOTO IAN McPHEDRAN*

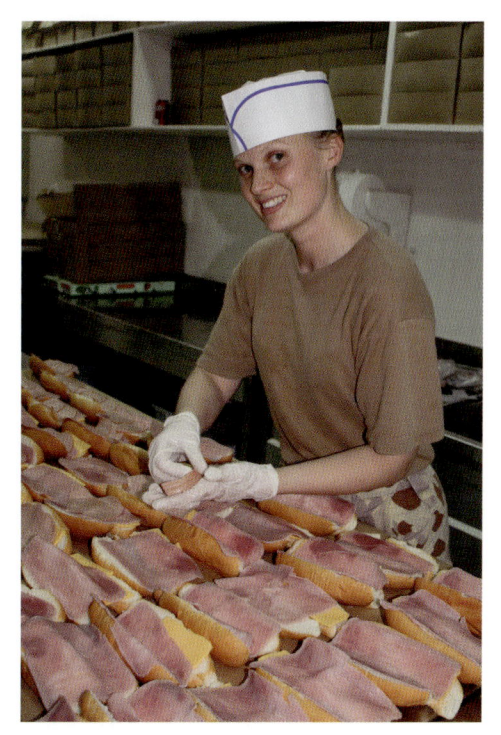

Leading Aircraftswoman Kina Noble, a cook, preparing lunch for coalition aircrew at Al Minhad Air Base near Dubai, in November 2009. *PHOTO IAN McPHEDRAN*

C-17 loadmaster Sergeant Paula Ivanovic and pilot Flight Lieutenant Sam Freebairn in the cavernous cargo hold of the giant jet. *PHOTO IAN McPHEDRAN*

AP-3C Orion maritime patrol aircraft captain Squadron Leader Lachie Hazeldine flies a surveillance mission over Afghanistan. *PHOTO IAN McPHEDRAN*

F/A-18 Hornet fighter pilot and Iraq-war veteran Squadron Leader Ray 'Homer' Simpson with his wife Heidi and daughters Skye, Bronte and Eden. Skye was born while her dad was flying combat missions over Baghdad during the 2003 Iraq War. *PHOTO COURTESY SQUADRON LEADER RAY SIMPSON*

Science before becoming a AP-3C navigator, and has also spent time on F-111s.

He and his wife Lindy, from Queensland, have two young children and live in Adelaide.

The Operation Resolute missions present significant tasks for navigators, including establishing where oil rigs or islands are located and looking after all communications into and out of the aircraft. But it is the anti-submarine missions that really test the crew. Brian Brown describes it as a giant game of underwater chess.

'You are trying to outsmart the submarine captain and he's trying to outsmart you,' he says.

Submarines can use their sonars or periscopes to detect the aircraft, which in turn can deploy passive and active sonobuoys and powerful image sensors to detect either a sub under the water or its periscope slicing through the water. The passive buoys detect a submarine's noise and the active ones emit a soundwave that reflects off the submarine to the aircraft. Using active sonar means the submarine commander will definitely know that the hunter is there, whereas the passive sensor can lull him into a false sense of security where he might bring the sub to the surface. The AP-3C's radar will then pinpoint it in an instant and the aircraft can position itself for an attack using torpedoes, mines or missiles.

'For me that is the most challenging and most rewarding sort of stuff, when we go out there and we search and then conduct an "attack" on the submarine,' Brown says.

Fighting submarines requires the most concentration and teamwork from the whole crew. The AP-3C is also employed in the anti-ship warfare role and can be armed with Harpoon air-to-surface missiles for that task.

'The challenge is being able to identify what the target is so that if we release a harpoon ... then we don't get it wrong,' he says. 'The harpoon is an indiscriminate weapon, so once you release it, that's it. You don't have any further control over it, so you really want to get the identification of the surface contact right prior to releasing it.'

For the crews from the operational 10 (Strike First) and 11 (Shepherd or Destroy) Squadrons and the 292 (Beware the Hunter) Training Squadron, border protection is the job they enjoy the least, but do it they must.

The incredible capacity of the AP-3C Orion to remain airborne for up to 15 hours, flying on just two or three of its four engines in 'loitering' mode, and to see and identify even the smallest of targets on water or land, makes it the ideal weapon against smugglers and poachers. No one in the squadrons wants to see the aircraft retire, but retire they must.

Chapter 16

AFGHANISTAN — THE CONVOY

The convoy winds around the twisting mountain road like a worm, stretching out and bunching up again as two Apache helicopters buzz up and down the 6-kilometre long line of trucks like anxious wagtails fussing over their young.

Australian Light Armoured Vehicles (ASLAV) from the Mentoring and Reconstruction Task Force, based at Camp Russell near Tarin Kowt (TK), rove up and down the column to keep the trucks moving at optimum pace.

From high in the air the scene is remote and slightly surreal but on the ground the dangers are real and potentially lurking around every bend on the long and winding road between Kandahar and TK. The dull browns and greys of the mountains and desert are in stark contrast to the thin strips of green in the narrow fertile river valleys.

There are 100 trucks and numerous Australian army vehicles in the Australian-led convoy heading north to TK. The show of strength is designed to inform the locals and the insurgents that the coalition has freedom of movement along a major supply route that has been badly disrupted by insurgents.

For one of the RAAF AP-3C Orion crews, Thursday, 19 November 2009 began at 3 a.m. Departure from the Al Minhad Air Base on the outskirts of Dubai was scheduled for 5.45 a.m. with Squadron Leader Lochie Hazeldine in command, Flight Lieutenant Mick McGreevy running the mission as tactical coordinator (TACCO) and Flight Lieutenant Matt Basedow in the sensor employment manager's (SEM) seat.

At the pre-flight briefing in a windowless office at the Australian headquarters, detachment commander Squadron Leader Roy Philpott emphasises the importance of the mission.

'The convoy stretches out for 6 kilometres so there are a lot of vehicles in there to provide overwatch for,' he says.

Philpott, a former Canadian air force navigator who joined the RAAF in 1997, reminds the crew that the Taliban's weapon of choice, the improvised explosive device (IED), will quite often not detonate until several vehicles have passed by.

'It will go off somewhere in the middle to cause disruption throughout and it's normally a multi-pronged attack, so they will stop a vehicle with an IED and then they'll use RPGs [rocket propelled grenades] and guns to finish off,' he says.

The AP-3C's job is to sanitise the route between 1.5 and 3 kilometres ahead of the convoy and to liaise with the two Apache helicopters and the convoy guards. A small, unmanned aerial vehicle known as a Scan Eagle will also be operating above the vehicle column, feeding signals to the troops on the ground and the headquarters in TK.

'Our job is to look for things that are suspect — vehicles parked on the side of the road, containers, people that are where they shouldn't be,' Philpott says. 'We normally look at bridges under construction; we can't really clear them because we don't have that capability, so we will say, "Use caution when approaching this area because that is a potential hot spot for you."'

After a spectacular 6.15 a.m. departure from Al Minhad, flying directly over the world's tallest building, Dubai's 828 metre Burj Khalifa, the crew sets course for the 'boulevarde', a narrow strip of airspace between Iran and Pakistan that coalition aircraft transit into Afghanistan.

Breakfast is eaten en route and the flyers consume toasted chicken wraps and ham and cheese sandwiches, tea, coffee and even cereal. The larder is stocked with enough snacks, including soft drinks, bottled water, chocolate bars and chips, to keep a dozen hungry aircrew and passengers topped up throughout the 10-hour mission.

After two hours' flying over the Arabian Gulf and a US aircraft carrier, the plane alters course to the north to fly over the lower reaches of the Hindu Kush mountain range before crossing the spectacular red desert south of Kandahar. Soon after flying over Kandahar airfield and Kajaki dam to the north and three hours into the mission, the crew commences four and three-quarter hours of overwatch duty above the convoy.

It is just after 9 a.m. and the visibility is perfect. From the safety of the air, the Afghan scenery looks incredible with distant snow-capped peaks framed by folded foothills that appear like dominoes resting on their sides with desert in between. The distance from Kandahar to TK is about 120 kilometres and it will take the convoy about 17 hours to make the journey.

The AP-3C's high-definition Star Safire electro-optical cameras and infrared sensors begin to scan the convoy and the road ahead as the crew concentrates on identifying anything out of the ordinary or anything that doesn't quite tally with the 'normal pattern of life'.

'Patterns of life in Afghanistan, especially in this region, are not what we expect to see as westerners, as Australians,' Philpott says. 'It's not something we are used to, so our determination of what a "normal pattern of life" is takes a bit of banter on the aircraft: "Does that look normal? Does this look suspect?"'

If something is regarded as 'suspect', the crew notifies the guys on the ground or in the choppers, urging caution.

The aircraft's cameras provide an incredibly detailed image of what is going on far below. With the infrared sensors combing every drain and parked vehicle for hidden heat sources, the electro-optical cameras feed in images of such clarity that you can almost tell what the people are eating.

Matt Basedow constantly oversees and monitors the sensors and the operators throughout the mission. Like McGreevy, he rarely leaves his seat during the mission. Basedow has control of the sensor suite and manages the movement of the sensors inside their turrets mounted on the bottom of the fuselage. The turrets are driven by motors and can scan left or right.

Another feature of the advanced reconnaissance system is called 'slewing'. That allows Basedow to pick a spot on his display and click on it to focus the sensor directly on that point. The system is linked with the aircraft's navigation systems so it can fly to the exact position.

Such is the effectiveness of the sensors that when he was training as a sensor operator for the overland intelligence, surveillance and reconnaissance (ISR) role, Basedow was watching a guy on the ground, using infrared, and his hands were literally glowing. For maritime operators used to scanning the oceans, observing people on land was very different. 'I didn't understand why this guy's hands were glowing. What was he doing?'

As it turned out he was having a cigarette.

'When he finished his smoke he flicked it and I watched the cigarette cartwheel and explode on the ground,' he says.

As a trained maritime observer he had never seen anything like it.

'I had never been trained to look at something like that and I was watching it on the EO in amazement. The detail you can get out of this kit is quite astonishing,' he says. 'That is why we use IR (infrared) and EO (electro-optical) because quite often when people are trying to camouflage themselves or wearing clothes that blend into the environment, you switch over to IR and "hello", there are arms and legs and a person lying on the ground. It is very, very visually distinctive.'

Meanwhile the convoy has spread out over about 6 kilometres and the AP-3C is clearing the route out to about 3 kilometres ahead of the lead vehicles. At one point the aircraft spends 15 minutes orbiting around a suspicious-looking truck and car parked by the roadside some distance ahead of the convoy. There are two men on the back of the truck so the crew directs an Apache helicopter to make a closer inspection.

The two-person Apache crew judges that there is nothing abnormal with the two vehicles so the aircraft resumes the clearing mission. For tactical coordinator Mick McGreevy the main threats to the convoy are roadside bombs and coordinated ambushes.

'They usually start with IEDs and then once they've disrupted the freedom of manoeuvre or retreat or tactical advantage of the convoy they employ small arms, heavy machine guns and RPGs and they have a position of significant tactical advantage,' he says. 'So when we overfly those roads we are looking for anything that fits the profile of an IED or suspicious activity — digging on or around the roads, thermal anomalies, any sentry behaviour, people observing the convoy from a distance, tailing the convoy or moving ahead of the convoy from point to point, people always looking over their shoulder, people standing in OPs [observation posts], either on mountains or roofs of houses — looking more suspicious than what we deem to be normal.'

Another strong indicator that something might be brewing is when the local people move to higher ground or react when a chopper flies overhead.

'When someone sees a chopper and runs for the hills it's a reasonable indication, not a foolproof indication, but a reasonable indication they have a reason to fear or to try to disappear.'

The stretch of road between Kandahar and Tarin Kowt is notorious for Taliban bomb attacks and ambushes so the crew must be particularly alert for any activity. Even places where bombs have previously gone off cannot be treated lightly.

'Just because there is a hole in the road already doesn't mean they won't use it. They will use it a second time. If they've blown up a place already they will wait until it is filled in and then use it again,' McGreevy says.

Any sort of vehicle qualifies for special attention from the AP-3C crew and their sensors.

'There have been several instances of people pretending to fix a car in broad daylight just so they can get underneath to dig in an IED and then drive off,' he explains. 'Anyone that looks like they have a broken-down car ... could be up to no good. You have to be suspicious of everyone, really. Most of the vehicles we saw were there when we travelled south the other day, but it still doesn't mean that they are safe by any means. The Apache reported that a passenger of one of the vehicles was digging on the side of the road, which was of significant interest. As it turned out, by the time we left, that vehicle was still hanging around and nothing significant happened, but stranger things have happened.'

Because the convoy is moving at a reasonable pace the AP-3C crew cannot inspect every square metre of ground so they must prioritise their searching. Apart from vehicles and people, or a lack of people, the most dangerous places are narrow cuttings, drains or waterways. Straight stretches of road with flat land either side are low risk and the crew does not waste valuable time on such areas.

If they pick up something suspect, such as men loading a long tube onto a vehicle, they can stream the imagery directly to the troops on the ground. In many cases, that has allowed the troops to avoid an attack and eliminate a threat.

Despite the heavy workload Mick McGreevy regards the mission as fairly routine and 'low tempo'. He says things get much busier during a TIC (troops in contact) but it is during anti-submarine missions, working for a navy task group, that his head can be 'on fire'.

It is 1.30 p.m. and the mission has been running for four and a half hours without incident. The convoy has safely passed a pre-arranged point known as 'Juliet' and the AP-3C's job is done. It is time to turn south for the long flight back to Al Minhad and the schedule is tight because the Dubai Air Show is on and there is a lot of air traffic in the area. Visibility deteriorates over the Gulf and Dubai where the air is thick with dust and smoke making the city and its sky-piercing towers virtually invisible.

Safely back on terra firma the Orion crew assembles in the headquarters building for a post-mission de-brief. Aircraft captain Squadron Leader Lochie Hazeldine provides an overview and asks for any questions from the floor. He declares the sortie a success and apart from some frustrating communications shortcomings he says it ran 'fairly smoothly'.

'Radios throughout the day were fairly hectic … Kandahar's radar was down so [air traffic control] was an absolute nightmare,' Hazeldine says. 'The big one that came out today was priorities and making up our minds, given we were running the sortie ourselves.'

Mick McGreevy follows the captain and voices some frustration on behalf of the crew. Due to good pre-flight planning and liaison the mission was a success, but because they could not talk directly to the joint terminal air controller (JTAC) inside the convoy he could not directly task the aircraft for his own needs.

'I felt like I wasn't being used on the high-priority tasks and being the most efficient or adding the most value to the sortie,' McGreevy says. 'Now, there are a couple of facets to my frustrations. First one is we have been spoilt in the last two weeks where we've had JTACs who have given us the highest priority task …

'We've come back down to an operation that had real limitations based on the self-protection suite of the convoy. As much as it felt like we were being under-utilised in the first instance, I'd rather be under-utilised and have a quiet day and have everything go as planned. We had a mission success, we escorted them from Gulf to Juliet unscathed without incident, which is a mission success. I'd rather have that than be dynamically tasked on an incident that could possibly cost lives or injuries to our guys. Procedurally, it was sound and a significant improvement on our last flight, so well done,' he tells the crew.

Matt Basedow praises the team for its use of communications and the effective way the aircraft spoke to the helicopters operating over the convoy. 'There was good use of the helos to investigate stuff that we couldn't, and I was really happy with the way we did that today.'

Basedow's job is to oversee all the sensors and the operators, and that means monitoring the screens for the entire sortie. 'The operators rotate through and they tend not to be fully aware of the surroundings, so quite often I'm the first guy to see stuff and will direct them onto it.'

His primary focus is the electro-optical camera. 'You get a feel for what's normal and you talk to the guys on the ground and they'll tell you what's normal, and you are looking for things that are out of the ordinary,' he says. 'Quite often it can be something as simple as a hot spot on the road, or a cold spot on the road, or it could be a ditch that you might not have seen in previous missions.'

The detachment boss, Roy Philpott, a veteran of Bosnia and Iraq, says the successful conclusion of every mission is a great relief. His biggest frustration is not being able to fly many missions himself. In three months at Al Minhad he had flown just four sorties.

During one of those, a convoy overwatch, he was the tactical commander when his observer called a large dust cloud or possible explosion right in the middle of the convoy. 'The instant thought that goes through your head is, "What have I missed? Have I stuffed this up?" The next thing you are thinking about is, "Are the guys on the ground, are any of the vehicles destroyed, is anybody hurt in any of the vehicles, what have I done wrong?" You are putting yourself in their position, you are clearing it as aggressively as you can, thinking that if I was in that convoy, how secure do I want this road to be?'

Fortunately the dust cloud was just a helicopter taking off. 'Everyone on the aircraft was just relieved, it was a win: "Phew! I've done my job; I haven't missed anything."'

One of the most satisfying aspects of the job for them all is being directly involved in assisting ground forces during a troops in contact (TIC). During one incident US Marines were under fire with the AP-3C overhead providing support. The troops had found some opium oil and a cache of weapons and were holding several prisoners. Philpott was speaking directly with a marine who was running into combat.

'I could hear him running, hear his breath as he's running across the paddock,' he says. 'These guys have been hit with rounds and they are fine, they are pressing forward to try to get the aggressors.'

This was no chance encounter. The AP-3C crew had spent days liasing with the marine unit through its JTAC, who told them what they could do to assist, to align radio frequencies and so on.

'We get a picture before we get there and when we come on task the first thing we do is establish radio communications and build that picture again, just to make sure what we are expecting is what we are seeing,' Philpott says.

The Australians used their powerful optics to identify suspects fleeing the scene of the battle.

'We did pick up one individual who looked like he fled the scene carrying a long tube which, although we made no assessment, the guys on the ground believed could have been a mortar kit,' he says. 'So their direction then was, "Stay eyes on that guy until we intercept him and take whatever he's got off him."'

Philpott, who is married to an Adelaide girl and has three children, says the most pleasing part of his job is greeting the crew at the end of the mission and receiving positive feedback from their 'clients'.

'We get the feedback from the guys in the field to say, "Great work" and that's a big puffy-chest thing,' he says. 'I guess I inherit some of that pride from the fact it's some of my guys flying it. The two crews that are here are my crews and my flight. I'm their flight commander. I guess if you make sure the guys do the right things and they all come home safely, that's another day.'

Not everything goes to plan and during his tour Philpott did have cause to take disciplinary action against one crewmember.

'You do some soul-searching. You look back at all the things you've told them,' he says. 'I'm all about individuals accepting responsibility for their actions and making decisions. If you don't blatantly disregard any of the rules and regulation and you've just made a wrong choice or a mistake you get 110 per cent of my support. But if you blatantly disregard one of the rules and regulations you basically cut me off at the knees because I still have to abide by those and I will not have the flexibility to support you.

'We have had one minor incident that is currently going through some disciplinary stuff. Now that is probably the only disappointing time I've had in my tenure here, and that's it, that's pretty good.'

★ ★ ★

Matt Basedow is also married to an Adelaide girl, Kylie, and they have four children. He grew up on a farm near the small town of Cobar in central New South Wales.

'The army used to come through all the time on exercises,' he recalls. 'The convoy would come in and they would camp just outside of town in their little tents and all of us kids would go straight over to the army boys and they'd give out bits of their ration packs and horrible chocolate, which we just thought was awesome. And every year without fail the recruiting people would drive their cars into town, set up their displays, give their presentations, and it was always of interest to me.'

After starting an education degree he realised the military was for him and he chose the RAAF with the specific intention of becoming an airborne electronic analyst. He began as an avionics technician but soon transferred to the AEA stream and the Orion mustering. In September 2008 the former warrant officer took a commission and became a SEM.

'It is very, very competitive because there are only limited spots, one or two spots a year, and quite a few guys will go for it,' he says. 'You have to steer yourself into being competitive, so I did a lot of extra study.'

To give himself an edge, Basedow enrolled in a master's degree in IT and undertook management and leadership courses and he was successful.

'It is a very dynamic job which takes you to all corners of the globe,' he says. 'I am on my third passport because I filled my first two with stamps from different countries I'd been to since 1994. You are always challenged mentally. It's very demanding and you have to study, and I like that. I like the competitive nature of it as well … You don't get people who are just willing to cruise and do the bare minimum. Everyone wants to excel.'

A most frustrating aspect is watching the action on the ground from high above on a screen.

'I can't stand being up there when there is a TIC. If I could open a door and throw a parachute out and jump I would because I'd rather be down there,' he says. 'I think it's just every military person's way — they'd rather be in there helping, risking a lot, than sitting back. It's all about that

Australian mateship. You don't want to see your boys shot at. It's horrible.'

The thought that he is helping to keep his fellow Australians safe is all the motivation Basedow needs to maintain 100 per cent focus. He says he never gets tired until the mission is complete.

'You've got your Aussie soldier on the ground who is actually at risk and taking fire. They are in trouble — how could you not be switched on? How could you look at this screen without the intent of finding something harmful for those guys? Sure I get tired but do I switch off at all? I don't think so.'

In addition to the ISR patrols over Afghanistan, the AP-3C detachment has been tasked to assist with anti-piracy patrols off the coast of Somalia and around the Horn of Africa. Unlike the so-called war against terrorism, the war against piracy has almost universal support and even China and Russia have devoted assets to combating the Somali pirate gangs who have the potential to severely disrupt global trade.

Roy Philpott views it as being more about piracy observation than stopping them. He flew on board the second RAAF mission into the pirate zone down along the coast of Somalia to observe the pirate camps and their booty.

'We can't really counter anything and unless there is a surface unit there supporting us there is not a whole lot that we would be able to do,' he says.

The pirate camps resemble small fishing villages with high-speed skiffs beached on the shoreline and several large captured vessels anchored offshore. Some of the pirated ships still have crews living on board so Philpott believes the AP-3C sorties have a valuable role in lifting the spirits of the captives.

'When they hear us go by there is a level of comfort because I think they believe that they haven't been forgotten and that we are still there. Whether they see us or not, they'll hear us.'

Despite the high priority of the anti-piracy role there is a limit to what can be achieved unless they are caught red-handed. Some have been, and the United States Navy has taken a strong approach when any of its citizens have been captured and held for enormous ransom.

Philpott says that unless the flyers witness an actual pirate attack there is nothing to distinguish the pirate enclave from anywhere else along the poverty-stricken African coastline. 'It comes down to the ability to police it, and who has the authority to do it in that part of the world?'

Ships plying the Horn of Africa route are taking extreme security precautions, to the extent of hiring armed ex-special forces mercenaries and lining their decks with nets and razor wire to prevent pirate attacks. A big concern is that one of the hijacked supertankers might be scuttled deliberately or run aground by pirates, causing enormous environmental damage.

'Their agendas and their respect for life and the environment are far different [from] anything we would be used to,' Philpott says.

Matt Basedow says that piracy has fundamentally altered shipping patterns around the Horn of Africa. 'A while ago you would look on a map and see the "iron highway" through the canals and a massive number of merchant vessels heading in all directions. Now they are all compacted and escorted and skip off almost due east. They don't go anywhere near Somalia.'

The Australian patrols continued into late 2010 as the crews monitored merchant vessels in the area and observed the 'patterns of life' along the remote coastline. With no place for the AP-3C to land in the region, they are limited by fuel to just a few hours on station before making the long flight around the Arabian Gulf and back to Al Minhad.

Chapter 17

THE BUZZ

Out in the suburbs of Seattle in Washington State, a group of young scientists and engineers from the Boeing Corporation are working in a nondescript warehouse creating what they are certain is the future of aviation.

As their Boeing colleagues toil away in some of the world's most spectacular production lines on the other side of town producing an airliner a day, this small warehouse has been converted into an unmanned aerial vehicle (UAV) laboratory.

Swarms of tiny pre-programmed UAVs buzz around without slamming into each other.

What makes watching these model aircraft circle, land and fly pre-programmed flight paths so fascinating is that no one is providing any control inputs. There are no remote joysticks being operated by the fresh-faced nerds in their jeans and T-shirts. They simply sit back and watch their autonomous flying machines going about their business, after programming in pre-determined routes, tracks, altitudes and collision avoidance mechanisms using advanced algorithms that could spell the end of piloted aircraft. It is an eerie experience.

The project's aim is to build mathematical models to allow unmanned aircraft to fly safely in controlled airspace. The algorithms developed in the lab have been tested over Kingaroy in Queensland in the world's first trial of unmanned aircraft inside controlled airspace. Airspace authorities in the US and Australia, wary of having pilotless drones near airliners carrying hundreds of passengers, require 100 per cent guarantees before they will allow the two to mix.

Ask most pilots what they think about UAVs, remotely piloted vehicles (RPVs) or unmanned aerial systems (UASs) and they say that of course they have an important role, but that humans will never be totally removed from the cockpit.

That natural instinct for career self-preservation is being slowly overcome in the US where highly qualified fighter pilots now sit in boxes at air force bases across the country flying UAVs via satellite on combat missions in Iraq, Afghanistan, Pakistan and Yemen. UAVs have become so important to US forces that many air strikes launched against high-value al Qaeda or Taliban targets are conducted by drones armed with air-to-surface missiles.

Intelligence about enemy activity is filmed or recorded by hundreds of UAVs criss-crossing the airspace every hour of every day. The airfields at Kandahar and Bagram are alive with UAVs taking off and landing, including a fleet of Israeli-made Herons operated by the RAAF.

The Heron is a medium-altitude long-endurance aircraft with high-resolution intelligence, surveillance and reconnaissance capability. It can conduct operations longer than 24 hours, with a maximum speed of more than 100 knots (180 kilometres per hour) and at altitudes of up to 33,000 feet. It has a wingspan of 16.6 metres, a length of 8.5 metres and a maximum take-off weight of more than 1 tonne. It navigates using a GPS with a backup capability for GPS-denied environments.

Since the Iraq campaign in 2003, Australian special forces and infantry patrols have received live video feeds from unmanned reconnaissance aircraft called Scan Eagles. They know exactly what lies over the next hill before they even make a move.

In the future, Australian troops in Afghanistan will be protected by a fleet of 18 RQ-7B Shadow UAVs valued at $175 million to be operated by the army, under a $1.1 billion troop protection deal announced by the Rudd government in 2010.

At night-time near a forward operating base called Mashal in Oruzgan Province in Afghanistan the deep, dark silence is broken by the soft, distant lawn-mower-like buzz of a UAV as it flies overhead, completely unlit. Its infrared sensors seek out the 'bad guys' who use the cover of darkness to plant the improvised explosive devices that dominate the insurgents' arsenal.

RAAF Wing Commander Lyle Holt says it is precisely the noise you want to hear as you nod off to sleep. 'That is what force protection is. It's looking after the guys on the ground so they are in a better position to do their jobs. Sometimes it's as simple as letting them sleep.'

Holt commands the RAAF's Number 5 Flight, which manages the Heron UAV capability and has spent the last few years developing operations for them. He gained a very clear understanding of the future of military aviation in 2000 when he was at Palmdale in California being briefed by senior staff from Boeing and Lockheed Martin. Both companies were vying for the contract to build the F-35 Joint Strike Fighter (JSF) and each told the delegation separately that the new stealth fighter would probably be the last manned fighter they would ever design.

Holt, a former F-111 navigator and electronic warfare expert, was completing his masters' thesis on employing UAVs in electronic warfare at the time.

'UAV is almost a misnomer,' he says. 'It gives the impression that there is no human in the loop, but I would argue that you would always want a human in the loop. A more accurate term would be 'remotely piloted aircraft'. You will always have that person there and Kosovo was a classic example. You had airlines flying up and over and lots of airspace users in the one piece of sky, so you need to have a level of confidence that these things are operating as you would expect them to operate.'

Apart from pilot safety, a strong argument in favour of unmanned systems back in 1999–2000 was that taking the person out of the airframe resulted in huge weight savings (no ejection seats or oxygen systems) and vastly extended endurance.

Since then, there has been a technological revolution. Nano-technology has been used to develop tiny, silent UAVs that sneak around like insects, filming or targeting unsuspecting humans and feeding the data back to their masters in a control room half a planet away.

'In 2000 there were real estate agents doing the same thing with remotely piloted helicopters that you buy from Toys'R'Us,' Holt says. 'They strapped a little lipstick camera to it and flew around over the house they were trying to sell to get that perspective and it was much cheaper than hiring a helicopter for an hour. People have been doing this sort of thing for ages.'

What has changed dramatically is the number and variety coming onto the market. Air shows around the world are dominated by displays of unmanned systems, ranging from model aeroplanes to huge jet-powered surveillance platforms such as Northrop Grumman's $120 million Global Hawk. It can soar to 66,000 feet and remain airborne for more than 24 hours monitoring 100,000 square kilometres of land or ocean a day. It uses the latest synthetic aperture radar that can penetrate cloud cover, smoke haze or sandstorms and advanced electro-optical cameras and infrared sensors for around-the-clock surveillance.

Australia was due to purchase the system for a mainly maritime surveillance role, but the Rudd Government decided to delay it indefinitely.

Rotary-wing UAVs such as Northrop's Fire Scout, Boeing's Hummingbird or European machines from Thales UK and EADS are being developed for use on navy ships, to carry missiles and supplies onto the battlefield and even to bring wounded soldiers out of harm's way.

For the time being, however, Australia's focus will remain on surveillance and reconnaissance rather than weapons delivery and force support.

The Boeing Scan Eagle has been the mainstay of Australian UAV operations in Iraq and Afghanistan and in 2009 the government agreed to a similar lease deal with the Canadian military and its UAV supplier, MacDonald, Dettwiler and Associates Ltd, to use the Israeli-built and Canadian-owned Heron aircraft at the hectic Kandahar base, where the Canadians already had a large footprint. So the RAAF was able to slot into their infrastructure with a team of 28 Australian and New Zealand Defence Force operators.

'In essence, our insertion as a capability into Afghanistan was actually reasonably small. We weren't asking for time and space; we weren't asking to build a new hangar for our aeroplanes,' Holt says.

The RAAF is leasing a service rather than a set number of aircraft. It is up to the contractor to meet the required hours per month.

'He could provide one aircraft and put all his eggs in that one basket and if it goes down he is contractually liable for not providing the service, or he can provide 20 and totally take away that risk but at his own financial cost, so that's his game to play,' he says.

The primary role of the Australian Herons is to support Australian ground forces operating across southern Afghanistan.

'We are new in this game so we are learning what we can do. The approach we are taking is we will try anything we need to protect the guys on the ground,' Holt says.

The 'birds' are also used to protect other International Security Assistance Force (ISAF) troops and local Afghan forces and people.

Very early on they had an experience where an aircraft in transit to its next job flew past a 'facility of interest' that had already been earmarked for an air strike. As the Heron flew over, the operators noticed women and children in the vicinity.

'This hadn't made its way into the intelligence system,' says Holt, 'so they fed it in, acknowledged that we were going to strike this thing shortly — "Be aware there are women and children in the area" — and the strike was called off.'

The Heron is flown by a two-person crew consisting of a pilot or air vehicle operator and a payload operator with other imagery and sensor experts in support. The two sit in a small container with a bank of computer screens and unlike an aircraft cockpit the pilot sits on the right-hand side with the payload operator on the left. At the other end of an intercom in an adjoining container is the 'back end crew' of imagery and sensor specialists.

Other countries operate the Heron with a three-person crew in the one room, but the RAAF is seeking to add more value to the information from the UAV so has added a couple of extra analysts.

Holt says that because the environment in Afghanistan is so dynamic they are looking to deploy 'higher end' pilots as UAV operators. Fast jet pilots are ideal because they have a greater situational awareness of the dynamic environment.

'You are talking to the guy on the ground, you are talking to air traffic control, airspace is popping up all the time. We are setting ourselves up to win in our selection process,' he says. 'We do have predominantly fast jet guys, both F-111 and F/A-18 and [AP-3C].'

There has also been a VIP jet pilot, but generally they look for pilots with close air-support experience with the army because they are used to talking to ground forces and dealing with the information.

'There might be times when you talk to these guys and they are under significant duress, they are under fire or whatever, and you need to stay calm, keep doing what you are doing and provide them the best possible service to allow them to win.'

The RAAF began operating Herons in Afghanistan in January 2010 and by year's end four groups of trainees had been through the Canadian system.

'In our last round a greater number of people put up their hand for selection. It's now a little bit better known and the interest has been sparked,' Holt says.

The father of two has no doubt that UAVs will dominate the future military aviation landscape. By late 2010, after just one year of operation, the appetite for Heron missions was already insatiable and yet it had not been anticipated in the Defence Capability Plan (DCP) in 2009.

'We need to take the lessons we learnt from Heron and apply them to whatever we buy down the track, recognising that we are learning all the time.'

Wing Commander Jake Campbell has absolutely no doubt that unmanned systems will one day dominate the military airspace.

In July 2009 Campbell was the commanding officer of the air combat training school at RAAF Base East Sale and to the former Orion navigator the rise of unmanned aircraft was part of the evolution of air power. He has no problem at all with the prospect that the JSF may be the last manned fighter aircraft in the RAAF.

Campbell predicts that the demand for pilot skills will wane during the next few years and the skills of the air combat officer (ACO) will be more highly sought after. As a member of the Air 7000 project team looking at the replacement for the AP-3C Orion and unmanned systems, he said that when they asked the question, 'Who would be operating the UAV?' they found that it was the air combat skills that were needed.

'It is keyboard and mouse and it's point and click where you want the aeroplane to go, which is exactly what a mission commander does — he directs the aeroplane and fights the mission so the pilot skills of hands-and-feet flying aren't required,' he says.

'In my view, and I am biased, the ACO category will have a growth path as we move to a more unmanned kind of fleet and I'd say pilots will probably start to decline.'

Campbell went to Beale Air Force Base near Sacramento in California during 2003 to meet the guys flying the Global Hawk over Iraq. 'They were directing fighters onto targets and at the end of the shift they would get out of the box and drive home to the wife and kids and then get up and do it again the next day — just incredible technology.'

Wing Commander Terry Van Haren, Commanding Officer Number 3 Squadron at Williamtown, has every confidence that the fighter pilot is not an endangered species.

He believes passionately that there has to be a human in the combat environment to make the correct decisions. With a vast amount of information collected and processed in the modern battle space, Van Haren argues that only a human can process it and arrive at the correct decision.

'The pilot will have to take all that information, plus what he can see and smell, and he'll be in the best position to make decisions about using lethal force,' he says. 'You can't do that from a remote station because the risk is you don't always get that right, because you don't always see what's going on.'

Van Haren says there are numerous combat situations where 'eyes on' is vital for making the right decision.

'Some things, such as pre-planned strikes on buildings, things that are fixed, you can deal with those remotely. They are not going to move, not going to change and something unexpected is not going to happen.'

However, in a dynamic environment where things are changing by the second, he maintains that sensors cannot replace the judgement call of a human being.

'If you can get the decision maker up closer to the target I think they can make a better decision than someone who is further away. The only reason to take a pilot out of the cockpit is if there is a threat to the pilot. The threat is reduced with stealth so the pilot can get onto the scene and make a better decision. Having eyes-on is always best in a combat environment, on the ground and in the air. And I don't think that's ever changed.'

As an experienced pilot, the former Chief of the Defence Force, Angus Houston, has a very firm view that humans will be in the air warfare loop for a long time to come. He has no doubt about the value of unmanned aerial systems, but he believes that for a country of 21 million people, 'multi-role' platforms are the key and will need to be driven by humans for the foreseeable future.

'We don't have unlimited resources so we are probably going to go for the multi-role manned aircraft because it is more flexible,' he says. 'Unmanned systems tend to be very specialised, and for the high-altitude, long-endurance persistence role, we will get them for that; for the surveillance role in support of the commander on the ground, we already use them for that. We will probably get into unmanned aircraft that can do strike, but I don't see that in the immediate future. I think [that] because we need flexibility and we need to do other things, JSF air combat aircraft — or manned air-combat aircraft — will be around for quite a while yet.

'As soon as you get into air combat [or] any sort of competitive environment, the manned aircraft retains superiority for the foreseeable future.'

ON THE JOB

Chapter 18

BLACK HANDERS, HEAT STROKE AND CURRY

When the mercury nudges 55 degrees Celsius and the reflected temperature can be as high as 72, the last thing air force technicians want is to don gloves to prevent their skin burning off as they fix a broken C-130 or AP-3C Orion.

In summer in the Middle East an aeroplane's metal skin is too hot to touch, but for the men and women who keep them flying there is often no choice — the mission must go on.

At a maintenance bay not far from the runway at Al Minhad Air Base near Dubai, RAAF crews work around the clock on 12-hour shifts to keep three Australian Hercules transports and two Orion surveillance planes on task. That sometimes means toiling in the open in extreme heat wearing an ice vest and drinking litres of iced water to stave off heat stroke. An hour of labour is the most a human can stand before taking a 30-minute break from the brutal desert heat to rehydrate and recover.

By early 2010 an air-conditioned maintenance hangar had been built for the Australian contingent, but before that all work was conducted in the open or in hotbox hangars.

Warrant Officer Paul Martin is the maintenance boss for the C-130s in the Middle East. He is responsible for the discipline, morale and wellbeing of his 35 maintainers as well as for having serviceable aircraft on the flight line ready to meet a demanding mission schedule, in which the H and J models bear the brunt of the load.

Martin's workforce is split between aircraft technicians ('black handers') and avionics technicians, with a few specialists such as life support fitters and a metal worker. The three Hercs based at Al Minhad fly up to 60 hours a week between them and most days one or two are away in Afghanistan or Iraq. On many missions, particularly those involving overnight stays away, maintenance staff accompany the aircraft.

A 20-year RAAF veteran, Martin says it is vital to rotate the aircraft through the flying schedule.

'As soon as you let them rest they start leaking oil and everything else, [so] you get yourself into trouble,' he says. 'I rotate the aircraft consistently to ensure that each aircraft is equally utilised. That also manages the fatigue issues of the aircraft as well.'

In addition to dust and dirt the Hercs are often heavily loaded and subjected to aggressive flight manoeuvres when approaching dangerous or dusty operational fields.

'It is fair to say that they cop a flogging,' he says. 'They are treated brutally and they show little wear for the actual flogging that they cop. They are definitely a good machine.'

Martin, who celebrated his thirty-eighth birthday during the 2009 deployment, cringes every time he sees a spectacular image of a Herc emerging from a massive dust cloud after landing on the unsealed strip at Tarin Kowt.

'We do a lot of additional maintenance just simply because of the environment,' he says. 'It takes a lot of our workforce away, but it's the only way we can present a reasonably reliable airframe and without it we would get ourselves into trouble.'

All external moving parts are lubricated and as he puts it, 'dirt and dust sticks to lubricants like shit to a blanket'.

'As soon as you have that coagulated sort of dust–oil arrangement you start to increase the wear on your components,' he says. 'It gets in the flap system, all the internals of the engine, the undercarriage, it's everywhere, so we are consistently lubricating the systems.'

Managing heat stress during the brutal summer is a huge issue.

'From about 9 a.m. to 5 p.m. they are simply unable to work,' Martin says. 'If they do have to go and work they wear ice vests, they are drinking constantly and can only work outside for about half an hour. We go through our people very quickly when we have to do these activities. The problem is that we don't have enough people to do them, so our heavy maintenance is done at night because we do not have the capability to do it through the day.'

Repairing frontline military aircraft in the Middle East is a long way from fixing cars in Corporal Ben Luke's hometown of Galong in south-west New South Wales. He has done four tours to the MEAO, including a dreaded summer stint in 2008.

'It's hard work, the plane is hot to touch, it will burn you, so it makes it really hard to work in the engines at that temperature. You just can't cool down,' he says.

Keeping the fluids up is vital so Luke takes an esky full of ice and water and as soon as he feels too hot or notices one of his crew getting too hot they retreat to the shade and air-conditioning.

'Everyone wants to get the job done, so a lot of time they put their own comfort aside and push through,' he says.

Yet the maintenance staff reckon their job is more enjoyable than back at home.

'It's a lot easier than back in Australia and there is not as much politics. You just get in and fix whatever is broken,' Luke says. 'Everyone gets in and gets the job done. At home you are knocking off for smoko every couple of hours and lunch whereas here you just break when you need to and get the job done.'

The work is also satisfying because they are part of a tightly knit team.

'In Australia you don't really see what goes on — you fix it and it goes away,' he says. 'Here it comes back to you and you hear what they've done or you fly away with the airframe and see what it is doing, so there is a real purpose behind the job.'

Sergeant Garreth McKnight is on his fourth tour of duty to the Middle East and one of the biggest challenges for the former pizza shop manager from Cooma in the New South Wales Snowy Mountains is getting spare parts.

'Over here you have to justify why you are ordering every part and it has to go through so many more levels of control before it gets approved,' he says. 'And then there is a whole time delay getting parts from Australia to here, through whatever means ... We might go through a period where we use one particular component at a fairly high rate and we'll burn through all our spares, and a month later we won't be doing anything with that component and we'll have a full stock. So it's hard to judge.' As a senior maintenance supervisor it is also his job to monitor his crew to ensure they are not affected by heat stroke. The 30-year-old Sergeant McKnight watches his staff like a hawk.

'Towards the end of their shifts we closely monitor fatigue levels and if they start making little mistakes, we pull them off a job and give them a break,' he says. 'The last thing we want to be doing is making mistakes because you can't pull an aeroplane over on the side of the road at 30,000 feet.'

Some are more prone to heat stress than others and as a redhead McKnight is acutely aware of the impact. One of the toughest jobs of his four tours was a midsummer C-130 engine change at Kandahar.

'There was a whole swag of logistical problems with that,' he says. 'We had to get cranes in and organise tooling and scaffolding to get up to the height of the engine.'

After 10 years in the RAAF, McKnight says jobs like that provide the maintainers with great satisfaction.

Risk mitigation is a key role for Paul Martin. The risks are often at their peak during VIP visits when two airframes are engaged in carting ministers or defence chiefs around the area of operations. With only three aircraft in the detachment, that leaves little margin for error and it places an enormous strain on the maintenance team.

Martin says that due to the delays in obtaining spare parts, maintainers often have to 'cannibalise' other aircraft. If an aircraft is needed for a high-demand task such as a VIP visit or a rescue repatriation flight they just have to deliver a working Herc.

'It is incredibly inefficient but you have to do it to present the frames,' says Martin.

Lower tempo flying days provide the opportunity to pull an aircraft offline for deeper maintenance. That luxury is not often available and the team often has to fix a plane that arrives at 2 a.m. and is due out again at 6 a.m.

'We have just four hours to fix it and that is unreasonable. It's very difficult to do that, considering the guys are fatigued out,' Martin says.

Many of the maintenance team have been deployed to the MEAO five or six times and he worries that the strain is beginning to show.

'It's a long time to be away from home and it's a fairly big chunk of their lives,' he says. 'They very much enjoy coming here but you can see the strain caused by being away from home, their partners [and] kids. It certainly takes its toll. As their boss I'm almost like their bloody father, mother and whatever else, but you have to look out because there are no second chances in this business, so you've got to get it right.'

Most aircraft accidents are caused by 'human error'. For Martin that means being eternally vigilant in looking for sub-standard maintenance practices due to exhaustion, anxiety, homesickness or other human factors.

'It's very difficult to do that, especially when you feel the same way yourself,' he says. 'The biggest challenge … for the four months I am here is managing my workforce. The aircraft will look after themselves and they will be fixed. You worry about your people first and the rest will come.'

He tries to spend at least 10 minutes a day with each person in his team. That takes a lot of time but he believes it is vital to know how they are feeling and to head off any issues before they fester.

'Once I build that relationship with those guys then hopefully they will come to me if there is something wrong,' he says.

★ ★ ★

About 100 metres along the airport apron from the Herc maintenance area, two RAAF AP-3C Orion aircraft sit on the tarmac as maintenance teams battle age as well as heat and dust to keep the high-tech spy planes operating. The RAAF's Orions first entered service in 1968 and the current fleet from Number 92 Wing, based at Edinburgh near Adelaide, were upgraded to AP-3C models in 2002.

The senior engineering officer (SENGO), Squadron Leader Phil Telfer, who was on his first operational deployment during November 2009, really enjoyed working at Al Minhad.

'Sometimes I walk around the flight line at night and look up at the aircraft and just think, "Yeah, we are here, we are doing it, this is real stuff." So it provides a good sense of satisfaction,' he says.

Unlike Hercs, the AP-3Cs do not get down and dirty on rough unsealed strips but the high-tech equipment and sensors are ultra-sensitive to heat and dust. So in addition to keeping an ageing airframe and its four engines in the air, technicians devote many hours to ensuring that the high-tech gear is serviceable.

Telfer, who is married with two children and hails from Renmark in South Australia, says each of the two AP-3Cs flies a heavy schedule so the demands on his two 17-person maintenance crews are quite intense. They work up to 14 hours a day and are rostered on 12-hour shifts, seven days a week.

The 19-year RAAF veteran says managing the workforce is a balancing act.

'We did a survey across 92 Wing to determine factors that make people enjoy the work and dislike it,' he says. 'The top reason why people liked working in 92 Wing was that they got to go on deployments. The main thing people didn't like was that they went on too many deployments.'

The strain on some specialised trades such as structural fitters or life-support technicians is much greater than on aviation technicians, where the pool is larger.

Between Operation Resolute in Darwin and the MEAO

deployment, some technicians are away from home a lot and many are on their fifth or sixth mission to the Middle East.

'It stops them from joining into perhaps what you might consider a normal life,' Telfer says.

Sport is one example. 'They can't always make training, or the days when they play, they can't join particular clubs because they might be on late shift or they might be deployed and that's when it really does start to hit them.'

Warrant Officer Gary Bridge followed his dad into the RAAF and 32 years later has worked on a list of aircraft as long as your arm including Canberra bombers, Dakotas, Caribous, Iroquois helicopters, F-111s and F/A-18 Hornet fighters.

'The only ones I haven't worked on in my time were Hercs, 707s and HS748s,' he says.

After three months at Al Minhad, his maintenance teams had kept the two Orions flying for 100 per cent of their missions. Given their age and the vintage of the avionics, this is a significant achievement.

Bridge, who is responsible for the performance and morale of the maintainers, says that has more to do with his team than the aircraft.

'I wouldn't say the aeroplane was reliable, I'd say the workforce is reliable to meet the times,' he says. 'They put the effort in and there is [a] reward at the end of it when you walk away and there is at least one serviceable bomber sitting on the deck out there. The two crews that we've got here now are golden. They are all go-getters. They are keen.'

One of the busiest Australians at the Al Minhad Air Base in November 2009 was Wing Commander Peter Davis.

The affable father of four from Foster in Victoria had spent eight months at the base as commanding officer of the Combat Support Unit (CSU), responsible for more than 115 of the 400 RAAF personnel charged with keeping the place running during a period of rapid expansion. He ran everything from the food supply and mail to physical security and ensuring that the toilets worked.

The CSU had only been formed in April 2009, so his deployment flew by as he also managed all the policy and plans associated with establishing a brand new outfit.

Al Minhad is a coalition base owned by the government of the United Arab Emirates and used by a number of other nations. It is located between the desert and the vast coastal city of Dubai on the Arabian Gulf. In late 2009 the Australians were sharing Al Minhad with a number of coalition countries and the base was set to become the main Australian staging post for the MEAO. It would house up to 1000 people, including the RAAF's C-130 Hercules and AP-C3 Orion detachments. Peter Davis was responsible for every tradesman, fire fighter, security officer and all external contractors working on the expansion program.

Running a busy air base is nothing new to Davis, in 2009 the Commanding Officer of 381 Expeditionary Combat Support Squadron at Williamtown, but this one is 10,000 kilometres from home, belongs to a Middle Eastern government and the external contractors don't speak English.

'The general supply chain here works differently to back home,' Davis says. 'It's not just a matter of ringing a local provider and saying "I need this delivered tomorrow." It just doesn't happen that quickly.'

The weather also has a major effect. Then there is the daily inter-service friction that comes from working under army command.

'I've been told a few times by army logistics officers that I was trying to run this place as an air base, which I thought it was,' he says. 'We agree to disagree on that one! I mean there are very subtle differences between an air base and an army logistics unit, but all in all we just get down and do the job. There are things all of us don't agree with from time to time but in the end you have your say. If your word doesn't get heard, you just get on and do the job; if it falls apart later on, well, you say, "I told you so."'

His operation is divided into a number of 'flights' including the administration and force protection flights, the command element, logistics, general maintenance, air movements, health flights and an operations room that is manned around the clock.

'I get a daily briefing from them to let me know the status of all our equipment, personnel, where aircraft depart, what the refuelling situation is, everything I need to know to … keep the base running along,' Davis says. 'I've also got a fire section within the ops squad as well. They work alongside Dutch, Canadian and British fire fighters to provide a Category 8 fire service to the base and all coalition aircraft.'

The logistics flight looks after warehousing, procurement, stock and even catering.

'At the moment I have six cooks in the Canadian mess and they will transition to the newly built Australian Mess when that opens,' he says. 'From an engineering perspective, I have a mechanical engineering workshop, which basically services all the equipment used to support the aircraft, all the ground support equipment … and alongside them in the same flight I have an airfield engineering team — a carpenter, plumber, electrician and a works supervisor — that does a lot of the day to day maintenance.'

More routine work is done by contractors but if something goes wrong overnight, his team gets involved.

'A couple of hours ago we lost water on the base here,' he says. 'We just put it back on again, so fairly seamless. Most people probably didn't know, unless they went to use the toilet and no water came out, but it's all fixed again now.'

Unlike other force elements, the combat support unit literally never stops.

'There will always be a group of people that have to be working, whether it is the firies because they are embedded with other coalition forces, the refuellers refuelling coalition aircraft, cooks working in the mess, ops room or the guards — somebody has to keep guard on the place regardless. So there are always going to be combat support unit staff working at any time,' Davis says.

He says staff in the CSU probably work 20 hours per week more than the other units. It doesn't seem to bother anyone, especially the first timers such as Leading Aircraftswoman Kina Noble, a cook.

The 28-year-old from Adelaide joined the RAAF in 2006 as a cook. Her posting to Al Minhad was her first overseas job and first time out of Australia. She was always a keen cook but the most daunting thing about her new career was the number of mouths she had to feed.

'It's amazing, the organisational skills you pick up when you have to feed several hundred people,' she says. 'At first it is, "Oh my goodness, how am I going to do this?" But the skills come along and that's quite surprising. In the military you can't panic, because if you do, things don't get done. You have to fall back on your training [and] the skills you have learnt.'

Working in the Canadian-run mess has been an eye-opener for Noble, who is convinced that Australians have a much healthier diet than most other westerners.

Making rolls for the Canadians with three different kinds of meats and cheese and serving up lots of sweet things was a cultural shock for the young cook.

'Australians tend to like things a bit more natural and not so much of the processed stuff,' she says. 'We like fresh, we do like fruits. I know our guys would prefer carrot sticks to a chocolate bar. If you give them too many sweets they'll start asking for healthy stuff, so [it's] just different tastes. A lot of people have goals they want to achieve before they get home. They have a time limit and I think healthy eating, being healthy, being fit is one. You want to get home looking good for your wife or husband.'

The cooks have two main jobs at Al Minhad: cooking for the mess and 'flight feeding', where they prepare meals for aircrew.

'Different countries want different things and we are all working out of the same mess,' Noble says. 'Your focus generally is on the extra thing that the different countries want, apart from what is on the servery.'

She was one of six Australian cooks at Al Minhad in late 2009. The curry nights became one of the most popular culinary attractions in the MEAO. She also works with Arabs, Indians, Sri Lankans and other nationalities.

'They are great and they are more than happy to teach you as well.

Their curries are amazing,' she says. 'I'm actually getting really sick of them, but they taste amazing and they make fresh roti bread and it is fantastic. That's been the most enjoyable part for me, working and learning the different cultures. I've even got one of the cooks learning the Hindi language because that is the universal language we use; he's learnt heaps of it. The other nationalities are more than happy to teach and interact and get to know you.'

Corporal Rod Craigie is one of those irrepressible characters that make life interesting and keep morale up on a military base.

In 2009, the 42-year-old electrician had been in the RAAF for seven years after a brief four-year career with the Royal Australian Navy. In between, he had drifted around for a while before deciding to give the RAAF a go.

'For a bloke my age it gets harder and harder to get work outside; they all want spring chickens. It's not what you know or how good you do it, it's all about speed,' he says. 'This is not a bad life — you keep fit and it doesn't matter how bad things go, you are always going to get fed.'

Travel has been another bonus for the rough diamond, who was born in Shepparton and raised in Melbourne

'I joined in 2003 then worked over in Learmonth in Western Australia for a couple of months and that was bloody shit-hot,' he says. 'We did a convoy across the top of Oz and it was just one of those sort of jobs — 20, 30 of us and everyone got on really well ... and had a few laughs.'

His next deployment was to the MEAO for four and half months in 2004 before he spent three years as the bare base 'sparky' at Curtin Air Base in north-west Australia. His next posting was Townsville, which in 2009 was still home although he had spent only eight months there in the previous two years.

Craigie is in a good position to judge the worth of a job and he regards the air force fairly highly on his workplace scale.

'Sure, I haven't had a day off and I work seven days a week, 12 hours a day plus call-outs, but it's different. You don't know what is going to get thrown at you from time to time and then, bang, you have to deal with it and work through it.'

In a climate where temperatures regularly climb above 50 degrees Celsius and the dust menace is constant, sensitive electrical equipment tends to degrade at a much faster rate than normal. Apart from reactive maintenance work and making sure that the lights and power at the base stay on, Craigie was involved with the commissioning of the new base power plant.

'Not many people get the opportunity to be involved in the handover of a new power station and then be part of the formulation of procedures, so from a work perspective that's been absolutely red-hot; something to hang my hat onto.'

Chapter 19

SOLDIERS OF THE AIR

Ever since he was a boy growing up in England, Sergeant Eddie Westney wanted to join the military. His grandfather and great-grandfather served as Royal Engineers in the two world wars and he spent a lot of his childhood accompanying his dad to air shows and military displays. He had a fascination for aircraft and air forces but his real interest was soldiering, so after his family moved to Australia and he completed his Higher School Certificate he inquired about a career with the RAAF's Airfield Defence Guard (ADG).

Not many people outside the military are aware of the existence of the guards, nor would be able to distinguish them from infantry soldiers unless they were wearing their blue air-force dress uniform.

The ADG is a small group of specialist airmen whose job is to protect aircrew, aircraft and bases where there are Australian air assets. The job, which has a primary function of defending rather than taking and holding ground, can entail patrolling into well outside the wire to keep enemy forces at bay.

The idea of blending specialised combat skills in an air force environment was a compelling mixture for Westney.

'If you join up in the army to do an infantry-type role, you are just another fish, whereas the air force offers a similar type of job but you are a lot more specialised,' he says. 'There are only [400] ADGs in the air force so it's quite a small, tight-knit community. You are doing the same sort of job but you are with the air force and we thought we'd get looked after a little bit better.'

The RAAF has two integrated squadrons of guards — Number 1 and Number 2 Airfield Defence Squadrons based at Amberley. Both have a mix of permanent and high-readiness reserve personnel who can deploy at short notice to protect air force and Australian Defence Force aviation assets.

After recruit training the guards are sent on a three-and-a-half month specialised course at the RAAF Security and Fire school at Amberley. The training includes weapons skills, physical fitness, bushcraft, patrolling and communications and introduces them to the unique operating environment of an air base and how they can best protect the assets it contains. They are then posted to the squadrons and continue their training to learn advanced communication skills, advanced first-aid, self-defence, aircraft security operations and how to operate other specialist weapons and equipment.

The role of the ADG is split between guarding aircraft and airfields, providing close personal protection, instructing the rest of the air force in weapons handling and defensive tactics and managing all RAAF armouries around the nation and overseas. They must be ready to support missions at short notice.

'You hear the term "guard" and it is a bit deceptive,' Westney says. 'You think of someone standing at the front gate with a rifle, but it is not that at all. Anything done inside the wire is normally left up to security guards or the military police. ADGs work outside the wire; we work up to 10 kilometres or more out from the strip. We'll provide screening operations, deny enemy movement into the base and we have a quick reaction force with Bushmaster-protected mobility vehicles. We've got our own gun buggies, we'll carry out counter-recons and counter-sniper operations to try to defeat the enemy coming in.'

The ADG doctrine is based on the fact that it is unlikely for an enemy to use a large, conventional force to attack an airfield. It is more likely to be a small, specialised reconnaissance or special forces unit so a great deal of ADG training is devoted to defeating such enemy forces and aggressively dominating the ground.

'We have to organise ourselves to combat those guys to reduce their effectiveness in carrying out the mission,' Westney says. 'It's easy just to say "Oh, it's very similar to the army" but it's not. The army takes ground, we defend ground, and therefore our tactics have evolved from looking at what they are going to do against us.'

Because they exclusively dominate the approaches to an airbase, their tactics, developed over 30 years, are very different from infantry tactics. Depending on the task, the guards operate in various size groups, from a team of four or five to sections of about 10 men and rifle flights of up to 30. Patrolling an airfield involves covering a lot of ground and the force will be broken down into small teams that are trained to 'swarm' if a contact takes place. This means that lots of small groups would converge from all directions to harass the enemy.

'We will try to travel fairly light but be heavily armed,' Westney says. 'It's our airfield; we know the ground, we will engage them as much as we can, as well as calling in other fighters, including vehicle-mounted rapid-reaction troops to provide support. Within 20 minutes you can have 30 guys done up to the max with machine guns, grenade launchers, the whole works and jerks.'

The ADGs are issued with the Australian-made Steyr assault rifle supplemented by specialised weapons such as the MAG 58 7.62mm and F89 Minimi machine guns, and Bushmaster vehicles with three heavy guns mounted on top.

'There is nothing like a couple of medium machine guns to put a dent in an attack,' Westney says.

Corporal Geoffrey Bell describes the guards as 'hunters'. The 10-year ADG veteran is a Brisbane boy, born and bred, and he followed his older brother into the unit. He always wanted a military career, and a family member, who served in the SAS for his entire career, suggested the air force was the way to go.

'He said that the air force treated its members better — nothing against the army, of course — but he said you get the best of both worlds in the airfield defence guard mustering. You get the same sort of roles as the army [but] you are more specialised and you are treated better,' he says.

Bell thrives on the specialised nature of the job and loves nothing more than pitting his skills against those of his army rivals. 'We don't try to be special forces, but we try to understand who they are and what they are trying to achieve so we can stop what they are doing.'

They test themselves against their specialised army mates whenever they can.

'They are busy boys, so when we are lucky enough to have them involved on an exercise we thrive on the opportunity to go and learn from them or work against them,' Bell says. 'It's a very big thing for them if they get caught or spotted by us because then the rest of their boys will never let them live it down. There have been exercises where they have caught a couple and the guys will say it was "sheer dumb luck". We hunt, we are constantly mobile, we are very rarely static and remain as mobile as we can in small groups to saturate the area and never give them a chance to move.'

Several ADGs have successfully completed special forces selection and joined the SAS, Commandos or become joint tactical air controllers (JTACs).

The guards use whatever assets they need to track down and defeat an enemy and that includes dog teams, ground sensors, roving foot patrols, vehicle-mounted reaction patrols — anything at all to win the day.

The last time an ADG squadron was deployed in any strength was to East Timor in 1999 and, as for the rest of the Australian Defence Force, East Timor marked a turning point for the unit. Before 1999 there had been a push to replace them with army soldiers, but since then the ADG has grown and is equipped with the latest equipment, including the Bushmasters, armour, night vision gear and hand-held thermal imaging equipment.

'Since Timor the whole of the ADF has been a lot more operationally focused,' Eddie Westney says. 'The funding and support we've received for the airfield defence squadrons has gone through the roof and we are getting all the new kit we've been asking for. We've got proper armour, we are getting remote gun stations, the funding is there and it's all coming to us, which is good.'

The ADG focus is very much on the region and where RAAF assets dominate, and the guards have deployed to the Solomon Islands, East Timor, Pakistan and Aceh. They have supported operations in the MEAO continuously as security elements at bases where RAAF assets are deployed.

In November 2009 Westney was deployed with the RAAF contingent to the Al Minhad Air Base near Dubai in the United Arab Emirates to train and certify all air force personnel on the base in small arms use.

Every deployed member of the Australian Defence Force — from the cook and the pay clerk to the commanding officer — has to meet a minimum standard of marksmanship. In addition to weapons training, the guards are responsible for security-awareness training. Complacency can be a major security risk.

'It's all very well to say, "Why didn't you go off to Kandahar and do one of the tours over there, securing the base?" But there are just not enough RAAF assets there,' Westney says, sipping a coffee in the recreation area at Al Minhad. 'If everything [that is] here at this base was [in Afghanistan], in a more threatening environment, then there would be a need for us to go there.'

A team of ADGs supports the International Security Assistance Force (ISAF) to assist with coalition aircraft security operations, both flight-line and airborne security. If an aircraft is transporting 'undesirables' such as prisoners or suspect locals during an evacuation, guards will be positioned on board to prevent any inflight interference to the crew or the aircraft itself and are armed with specialised weapons and ammunition designed to cause minimal damage to the aircraft.

'Obviously, if we get into some sort of battle and we cause as much damage [to the aircraft] as the enemy then there is no real point having us around,' says Westney. 'We are pretty mindful of where and how we are going to do stuff around the airframes.'

A small team of about 10 ADGs trained in close personal protection (CPP) are deployed as bodyguards for VIPs. Special forces units such as the SAS have primary carriage of CPP but the RAAF guards, who are trained to the same standards and graduate from the army-run course, are used to supplement the requirement. They have been used to protect the Chief of Air Force and Chief of Army during their visits to the MEAO.

Like frontline army infantry units, membership of the ADG has been specifically denied to women but change is on the way. The Gillard government announced in April 2011 that it would open up all roles in the ADF to women, including combat roles, with determination for suitability to be based on physical and intellectual ability, not gender.

One aspect that is unlikely to change is the intense rivalry with army diggers. Whenever an ADG element is deployed alongside soldiers they suffer the derision of being tagged 'Raffies' and the usual barbs such as 'Time to spare, go by air', but when push comes to shove the two forces operate in professional harmony.

'There is obviously rivalry between us and the infantry [because], on face value, we do a fairly sort of similar role,' Westney says. 'They think we are useless and vice versa but it's all good natured stuff, so any time you get to work with them is really good because we usually come away shaking hands saying "Good job, guys." I did a three-month trip to Malaysia with part of the rifle company that is based there along with some permanent army and reserve army units. By the end of it they'd learnt a thing or two,' he adds with a straight face.

Leading aircraftsman Lachlan Pegg experienced the friendly rivalry firsthand during a deployment to Baghdad with the Australian embassy security detail (SECDET) during 2008. The former Rockhampton boy says the Iraq job taught him there wasn't much difference at all between the army and the ADG. He was attached to an infantry platoon.

'They were kind of stand-offish to start, but once they learnt we were pretty much the same as them, they warmed to us,' he says.

Geoffrey Bell has been deployed to East Timor and the Middle East and he says the job doesn't really change much, just the faces and customs.

'The main focus is always people, that is the Australians that are going over there to help, and of course, the locals. Assets can always be replaced, planes can be rebuilt but the priority is always people. There is nothing worse than sending someone home in a body bag, so everything we do is about the safety of the Australians on the ground and anyone else we are tasked to look after.'

Chapter 20

VERY HEAVY AIR LIFT

One of the few female pilots in the RAAF, Flight Lieutenant Samantha Freebairn is deeply aware of the responsibility the air force shoulders in support of Australian troops deployed overseas.

As a pilot, whether she is repatriating a casket and bringing a fallen digger home to his family, saving lives or transporting the latest piece of kit into Afghanistan to make the soldiers a little safer, her focus is always on the outcome.

'I've done a few repatriations, sadly, and I find them very hard to do, but at the same time it is important to get them home to their families and loved ones as soon as we can,' she says.

The 33-year-old is one of the first generation of RAAF pilots to fly its biggest aircraft, the Boeing C-17 Globemaster, but not the only woman to do so.

Purchased under a 'rapid acquisition' contract by the Howard government, it was a textbook example of how defence equipment should be acquired. It took just nine months after the decision to purchase for the first aircraft to arrive in Australia from Boeing's factory in Long Beach, California, in December 2006. It was another female pilot, Wing Commander Linda Corbould, who flew the first of the C-17s to Australia in 2006. All four planes arrived on time and on budget in the best performed purchasing project since the navy's Australian-built Anzac frigates.

The four-engine jet aircraft represented a huge step up in the nation's strategic air lift capability. They can carry about 77 tonnes of cargo or two and a half times the load of a C-130 Hercules in a 26-metre hold, and can fly from eastern Australia to the Middle East at 454 knots (840 kilometres per hour), cutting the flight time in half and with fewer refuelling stops. The huge C-17 is designed to operate into dirt airstrips just over 1000 metres in length. High-powered thrust reversers that can be deployed in flight for rapid descent during tactical operations also mean that the aircraft can be reversed, so it can turn on the most rudimentary of airstrips.

The arrival of the C-17 meant that the Hercs were no longer required to do the long, slow intercontinental strategic lift flights and could concentrate on shorter, tactical hops around the Middle East or the Pacific. A smaller target than the C-17, the Herc was designed to fly into rougher airstrips closer to the front line.

Freebairn grew up in the small Victorian town of Drysdale near Geelong and her love of flying began at the age of nine during a family holiday to Fiji when she was invited onto the flight deck of the airliner.

'The sun was setting but there was certainly light and clouds and I was just mesmerised, and I guess that sparked my interest in aviation,' she says.

She began private flying lessons at Bacchus Marsh School of Aviation but soon realised that her after-school job at the supermarket wasn't going to fund a career as a pilot. By the time Year 12 came around she was on the path to applying for the Australian Defence Force Academy (ADFA) in Canberra.

Like most budding air force pilots, her aim was to fly fast jets and, like many before and after her, she was judged unsuitable for single-seat flying. So after completing a science degree and pilot training she was posted to Hercules and the world of crewed aircraft.

In early 2001 she was posted to Number 36 Squadron at Richmond to fly the 'H' model C-130 Hercules. After flying to Bali for the bombing evacuations in October 2002, she was in the Middle East in 2003 and 2004, flying missions in and out of Iraq. The mandatory Canberra desk job came along in 2006 but in 2008 she was lucky enough to be selected to go to C-17s and the new 36 Squadron at Amberley.

Freebairn has a soft spot for the Herc because it can get in and out of places that other aircraft can't and therefore gets closer to the troops or disaster victims on the ground. She also loved the tactical flying, especially flying VIPs into places such as Baghdad, a roller-coaster of a ride to avoid missiles and bullets.

She had not really been looking for a change of flying jobs when the C-17 opportunity came along. 'I liked the Herc and I definitely liked the role, but this has four jet engines and it's new and the best thing about it is that it has a toilet with a door, not a little bucket with a curtain! Little things like that become very important as you get older.'

In addition to comfort and speed, the C-17 is also used for tactical missions and the crews are trained to do air drop, troop drop, to fly on night-vision goggles and conduct air-to-air refuelling. A powerful computer and just two pilots and a loadmaster control the entire package.

'The computer does help you a lot, but you still have to have a basic understanding and when something goes wrong you do really need to know what to do,' she says.

The biggest difference between flying a Herc and flying a C-17 is responsiveness. With its single joystick and fly-by-wire controls the C-17 is extremely agile for a huge aircraft.

'It's a very manoeuvrable responsive aircraft, but at the same time it has a load of inertia and you have to think ahead,' she says. 'The Herc is very responsive but it also responds quickly, whereas with the C-17 you have to kind of predict that you are going to need to get over there a little bit earlier. It forces you to maintain a disciplined scan and be able to project the flight path, more than in the Herc.

'In the Herc you just react, "Oh, I want to go there", or "I want to go here, let's go over there now", whereas on the C-17 you think, "In order to get over there I need to be here at this point and this point", so it's a little more demanding mentally.'

But she loves the C-17's power and says, 'Because you can put the engines into reverse thrust while airborne [a definite no-no in most large jets] you know you can just drop out of the sky. The rates of descent and the rates of climb it has are just great.'

With her new marriage and house to manage, Freebairn knew in 2009 that she was approaching 'crunch time' in her RAAF career.

'Do I want to stay in the air force, do I want to leave, do I want to pursue a military career, do I want to pursue a civil flying career? They are questions I need to ask myself,' she says. 'I'd like to start a family in the next few years and I could see that flying would be quite difficult then. You are away a lot from home. You're not away on deployments — we don't do the deployments like the Herc does. We resupply, come home, resupply, come home, but it's still a fairly fluid lifestyle.'

She sees what a struggle it can be once children arrive and describes as 'phenomenal' the wives and partners who support the flyers so that they can keep doing the job that they love but still be an active member of their family. In the meantime, it's on with the flying and piloting the RAAF's biggest aircraft around the globe, carrying massive loads to where they are most needed.

The young pilot strains to link up with the fuel hose from the KC-30 tanker aircraft, as it bobs up and down in the wind and turbulence 23,000 feet above the ground. After several aborted attempts he finally links up and can relax a little as his C-17 is pumped full of fuel at the most dangerous bowser on the planet.

This operation takes place inside a large box at the Amberley air force base. The full-motion C-17 simulator is one of the most advanced pieces of simulation technology in the world, allowing instructors to expose trainees to every conceivable inflight scenario. Flying modern simulators is so realistic that in some cases pilots can go straight from the computer-generated environment and into the cockpit in a seamless transition.

Before the C-17 'sim' was installed, RAAF pilots used to travel to the Boeing plant in St Louis, Missouri, to undertake simulation training.

Simulation is a key part of the syllabus for future pilots and for qualified pilots to maintain their currency. Some pilots spend more time in the 'sim' than in the cockpit.

Loadmasters also use simulation technology to keep up with the complexities of running the back of the plane. With just a single 'loady' required to manage the cavernous cargo bay, simulation is important — but nothing substitutes for hands-on experience.

Sergeant Paula Ivanovic joined the RAAF in 1991 after completing her secondary studies and trained as a communications operator. She switched from her former job as a communications information system controller (CISCON) to loadmaster in 2005. The 20-year air force veteran was prompted to change careers after a stint manning the high frequency radio set in the air operations centre. That involved talking to aircrew and logging the calls. In 1999 she was selected to provide communications support for a C-130 Hercules during the Bougainville peace talks, which involved establishing a communications link between two 'H' model Hercs and working closely with the crew.

'I got to work with the crew and their dynamics, saw the way they worked and how much reward there was in achieving what they did,' she says. 'I did some familiarisation flights in 1999 with the intent to [become] loadmaster, but was then deployed to Timor, Afghanistan and Iraq, providing communications networks.'

Between 1999 and 2005 she was too busy as a CISCON to make the move, but every time she saw or heard a Herc flying around she felt the pull to aircrew. She finally put in her application for what was an unusual move in the RAAF, made even more unusual by the fact that she is female. But she made it and did her initial loadmaster conversion on 'H' model C-130s. Soon afterwards, she was lucky enough to be selected for C-17 conversion and was posted to her home state of Queensland, although she says that she would have gone anywhere to join the C-17 crew.

Diversity is the name of the game and since she joined the squadron Ivanovic has flown to Sumatra for Operation Padang Assist, ferrying emergency supplies into Padang airport following the devastating earthquake in October 2009. She has been to Papua New Guinea, made several sorties to the Middle East and picked up loads in Scotland, France and the United States. She is also qualified to conduct heavy air drops and during training has dropped 1500 kilogram loads from the rear of the flying C-17.

She says air dropping is an inherently risky business where a lot can go wrong. 'There is a lot … you need to do and you really need to be following your checklist, ticking off what needs to be done at a certain time,' she says. 'You've only got a certain drop-zone time-frame to drop your load so everything needs to run smoothly. It's pretty exciting. We need to make sure the deployment parachute is rigged correctly and everything is rigged to the floor with certain types of knots.

'Then you have to rig it to the extraction link and the extraction chute. So there's a whole lot of checks and balances in place that you need to do. Everything has a checklist, everything has a tick, everything is signed for, so everything is accountable.'

The 'loady' cannot afford to make a mistake because people's lives are often on the line. The main game is knowing the aircraft's limitations.

'Our training means that we know how the cargo compartment is put together, we know where we can put vehicles, what weights can go where, what heights can go where, so it's all a matter of putting a box inside a box and restraining it correctly,' she says. 'If you are carrying five ASLAVs [Australian Light Armoured Vehicles] you have to look at your axle limitations and maybe you need to offset them so you don't break floor limitations and weight limitations.

'I've carried helicopters — Black Hawks, Seahawks and Chinooks. I was also part of the Abrams tank load trial. We even brought back an LR5 rescue submarine from the Scotland trip [and] an MRH 90 helicopter from France, so we do deal with a lot of outsized cargo.'

When a new, large piece of cargo is to be carried for the first time, specialists from Richmond are called in to conduct detailed weight and balance calculations.

'They make all the calculations. The engineer then sits down to work out exactly what needs to go where and what we need to restrain it with and they come up with a load plan.'

Ivanovic loves her job and says satisfaction levels are very high. 'The capability of this aircraft is fantastic,' she says. 'Where it might take a Herc three trips to provide a particular load, we can do it in one, so it has definitely broadened our scope. We can do it quicker as well, but I feel quite lucky that I've experienced both aircraft.'

There was no let-up in the workload in early 2011. As loadmaster, Ivanovic took part in the responses to the Queensland floods, Tropical Cyclone Yasi and the earthquake in Christchurch, New Zealand. 'In Op Yasi we had the youngest AME passenger ever carried of 5 hours old and the oldest of 90 years,' she says.

Like most people who join the RAAF to fly aeroplanes, Flight Lieutenant Dean Bolton wanted to be a fast jet pilot, but instead found himself flying C-130s in a war zone while his fast jet mates were still at home on conversion course.

He had observed several flights in RAAF 'H' model Hercs and British 'J' models before he took the controls for his first sortie 'over the fence'.

After numerous deployments with the Hercs to the Middle East, Afghanistan, the Pacific and Asia, Bolton was due for a stint as an instructor or a ground job when the C-17 acquisition occurred.

The first group of C-17 pilot trainees were virtually 'stolen in the night' but Bolton felt very lucky to be in the right place at the right time when the recruiters came knocking for a second time.

'I was a captain at that stage with 400 to 500 captain hours and I was also an air drop, NVG [night vision goggles] airborne operations captain as well, so I had the high end of C-130J skill set,' he says. It was not a huge leap for Bolton, who had been flying the very latest technology, including the head up display in the 'J' model Herc. In fact the 'J' was probably a few years ahead of the Globemaster, whose cockpit hasn't changed much since they entered service in the mid-1990s. For pilots from the older C-130 'H' model Herc the step up is much more significant.

Bolton had to move from 37 to 36 Squadron to fly the big jet. 'For them it was just "a new aeroplane but same squadron" whereas I had to build new relationships in a new squadron,' he says.

Being a 'fly-by-wire' aircraft means that when the pilot moves the joystick it talks to four computers that decide if the move is safe and achievable. If so, the computers order the hydraulics to move the control surface.

'That makes the aeroplane more responsive at slower air speeds,' Bolton says. 'In a Herc, if you wanted to turn you really had to give it a boot full of aileron and rudder to get it around. This thing here, if you are slow and say "I want to turn as quick as I can", it responds, "Okay, I can do this for you" and that begins a complex flight-control reaction. Therefore, instead of just the aileron moving, maybe the spoilers will pop up and a whole lot of things will move out the back.

'Essentially it's a really sporty jet with big roll rates. Sometimes you forget you're flying around in something the size of a blocks of flats — you can be in low level and crack into a turn and away you go. It's quite manoeuvrable. That means pilots need to keep account of the 50 metre wingspan so if [they are] flying just 100 metres off the deck in a steep turn, they are 25 metres closer to the ground on one side. I've not flown any other heavy jets, so I'm not sure what they are like, but I think this is particularly sporty for a heavy jet.'

Bolton had the honour of flying as captain of the first RAAF C-17 to land at the Australian base near Tarin Kowt (TK) in Afghanistan. As well as two experienced pilots flying the aircraft, another two were on the flight deck for the heavily laden sortie into the 1800 metre runway located 1500 metres above sea level.

'We had a lot of airspace to deal with. It was a busy day up there in Afghanistan and this aeroplane descends really quickly compared to a C-130. We can really come down like a space shuttle — it's really, really good,' he says. 'So we came smoking down the hill, rolled out on finals there and it was probably then that I remembered that it was a dirt strip.

'I'd forgotten about the whole gravel [and] dirt thing. You are so stressed about the airspace and de-confliction and the threat environment, and all these other things rattling through your head, like "Oh, that's right, it's dirt and an up-sloping runway as well." You've got to sort of flare more than you normally would as well. Anyway, we pulled it off and it was pretty exciting. Your heart starts beating when you are up the other end and you've pulled off the runway, you've got the ramp on the ground, park brakes are on, "Ah, breathe again." I don't think I breathed too many times between [the] top of descent and actually pulling up on the runway.'

Also on the flight deck that day was the man who had run the C-17 transition office for the RAAF, Group Captain Gary Martin. The former Zimbabwean air force pilot was Australian air component commander in the Middle East in November 2009 following 18 months spent running air lift at 86 Wing at Richmond.

The extent to which the C-17 Globemaster has changed the game for Australia is most evident in an operational environment and particularly in Afghanistan.

'The aeroplane doesn't carry any more persons than a C-130, but it carries a huge amount of cargo,' Martin says. 'If we go in there with three Bushmaster vehicles plus a couple of pallets of gear [and] a few people, which is a standard load, we are moving 93,500 pounds [45,000 kilograms] of cargo in one hit.

'The vehicles don't fit in a C-130, so they simply could not have been lifted by us. We would have had to have gone to coalition support. The only other aircraft that is going to land there is a US air force C-17. USAF forces are heavily committed now, so our ability to get a hold of them on a moment's notice is few and far between. Standing up our own horsepower [by] having the C-17 fleet has been essential. If we'd planned the time, we couldn't have done it better.'

Most importantly, it cuts down on the number of flights into the hostile environment. By hostile, he means weather and terrain as well as threats.

'To get a 90,000 pound [41,000 kilogram] payload in C-130s I need five aircraft — that is five approaches, five departures, five chances of somebody having a mess-up somewhere around there,' he says. 'Doing it just once is a huge bonus.'

There was some talk of basing a C-17 at Al Minhad in Dubai with the rest of the air component but 36 Squadron is not really structured for that and Martin says it is easier to fly an aircraft in from Australia fully loaded, utilise it in theatre for several days and then send it home fully loaded.

'When you deal with exceptionally busy airfields such as Kandahar that has the same air traffic flow as Gatwick International [in the UK], but with just one runway and not four, getting airplanes on the ground, parking points, service and so on becomes more and more difficult,' Martin says. 'For the C-17 to have the reach to go from here to there, to a couple of other places in Afghanistan and not have to worry about fuel or any other requirements — just load and off-load — is an exceptional advantage for us.'

The C-17's advantages in heavy air lift were on display closer to home in early 2011. The earthquake in New Zealand hit on 22 February and Operation Christchurch Assist was the Australian Defence Force's contribution to the Australian Government response.

Over the month of the operation, RAAF C-17s and Hercules aircraft conducted a range of heavy air lift and transportation tasks between Australia and Christchurch, carrying emergency services personnel and equipment including an entire 75-person field hospital, a disaster victim identification trailer and a water desalination plant. Altogether, RAAF aircraft transported nearly 500 passengers and 290,000 pounds (132 tonnes) of cargo.

Next came the Japanese earthquake and tsunami of 11 March. As part of Operation Pacific Assist, an RAAF C-17 flew the Australian emergency services task force to Yokota Air Base in Japan and remained in Japan for two weeks undertaking 23 sorties, providing air lift of vital stores and equipment for the humanitarian effort. The C-17 and its crew moved more than a million pounds (450 tonnes) of cargo including 41 vehicles, as well as 135 passengers. Two more C-17s carried a remotely-operated water cannon system to help containment operations at the stricken Fukushima Number One nuclear power plant.

In March 2011 it was announced that the Australian Government was buying a fifth C-17 Globemaster for the RAAF.

EYES ON THE MIDDLE EAST

Chapter 21

THE NERVE CENTRE

The US air force's B-1B Lancer bombers blast into the air like rocket ships with their twin dual afterburners streaking red and blue into the inky night sky.

The noise from the General Electric turbofan engines is deafening as each one winds up to its maximum 30,000 pounds of thrust on full afterburner and the swing-wing bomber uses a large chunk of the 5000 metre runway to free itself of the bonds of gravity and carry 20 tonnes of high explosives on yet another sortie over Afghanistan.

The flight line at the massive air base in a friendly Middle Eastern country is a plane spotter's paradise, but access to the very secure American-operated base is a rare privilege. The only hint that you are nearing one of the biggest air bases in the Middle East is a sign that says 'Army Camp'. Security is so tight it takes almost an hour just to get through the main vehicle checkpoint.

Apart from rows of elegant Lancers, there are fighter jets, giant C-17 Globemaster transport planes, KC-35 air tankers, C-130s — virtually every type of military aircraft required to mount a modern air war.

During 2009 the base was being transformed from a temporary coalition war fighting facility into a much more permanent base with solid new brick accommodation blocks, dining facilities and recreation areas replacing temporary structures favoured by visiting military forces.

In the centre of the vast grey and flat, sandy construction site is a windowless building known as the Combined Air Operations Centre or CAOC. This is the nerve centre of the air war in the Middle East and it comes under the direct control of United States Central Command in Florida. The day-to-day, hour-by-hour movement of hundreds of military aircraft is managed from this building, which looks more like a large warehouse than the brain space for an air war.

At the heart of the CAOC is the operations centre where the movements of all military aircraft operating across Iraq and Afghanistan are plotted on four huge video screens. The screens provide a big-picture view of the main assets and concentration of aircraft. Two screens cover Iraq and two Afghanistan. Another two smaller screens give the location of dozens of unmanned aerial vehicles (UAVs) that typically fly at lower altitudes, but whose position is crucial when plotting the direct path for a fast jet scrambling to support troops under fire.

The screens tell the operations staff precisely where every coalition fighter, transport plane and tanker is located, their altitude and what they are doing. They also carry information on the unmanned fleet but often the purpose of those missions is so top secret that it is not disclosed even to the security-cleared screen warriors.

Projected on another wall are the individual aeroplanes so if there are troops in contact or a B1 is about to launch weapons, the operations staff can bring the picture up. It shows live, full-motion video of what the aircraft sensor is seeing on the ground. This might include vehicles driving down a road or an individual running along a track.

Around the main floor are individual operators who are responsible for their own small pieces of this vast aerial puzzle.

The CAOC director and his team of battle managers virtually run the air war across the Middle East Area of Operations (MEAO) from a space called the 'battle cab' that sits above the cube-shaped CAOC floor. That vital position is rotated between America, Australia and the UK. The director's chair has been occupied by very senior RAAF officers, including Air Marshal Mark Binskin.

Binskin was on Hornet refresher course prior to taking command of the Air Combat Group in September 2003 when he got the call to become the first RAAF CAOC director. The rotation concept had been the brainchild of US air force Major General Bob Elder and then RAAF Air Commodore John Kindler, who had met at a Pitch Black exercise in Darwin when Kindler was commander of the Tactical Fighter Group.

Elder was deputy coalition air component commander and he was determined to make sure the CAOC ran as a true coalition operation. As well as the rotating director its 300 staff were drawn from the US, UK and Australia.

'I got back from one of my F/A-18 refresher flights and one of those notes you never want to see was written on the whiteboard, "Binny, ring Air Commander at two o'clock",' Binskin recalls. 'I got on the phone and he basically said "The job is ours. We want you to go and I need you to be over there in about three weeks." So I came off Hornet refresher, went down and started doing all the force preparation and ended up over there middle of November.'

Having been on exchanges with US forces and worked with them on numerous exercises, Binskin slotted into the job quite smoothly.

'Culturally it wasn't that much of a step to go into, because I knew how the US worked and predominantly the coalition at that stage was still the US, Australia and UK,' he says.

The most difficult part was the ongoing stress of operations and the brutally long days locked in a windowless building.

During his 120-day deployment Binskin slept just a few metres from the nerve centre where he usually worked from 6.30 a.m. The days began with briefings about current operations that had been running during the night. Then there were strategic sessions about missions coming up in the next few days, more detailed decisions for two days' time and a high level of detail for missions to be conducted in the next 24 hours.

'I would knock off about 10 or 11 at night, then if there was something time-sensitive — such as weapons targeting or troops in contact [TIC] during the night, or [during] the hours I wasn't physically in the battle cab — that was going to require a bomb to be dropped, then I had to be up there,' he says.

Bombing sorties had to be authorised by a one-star officer or above and there were only two on staff.

'So chances were I was going to get a disturbed sleep pattern and I think that was the biggest challenge,' Binskin says.

The one period of respite sometimes happened in mid-afternoon when he could adjourn to the gym with his mobile phone for some much needed exercise.

Whenever a 'troops in contact' (TIC) is reported, the CAOC staff respond instantly to get close air support above the soldiers as fast as possible. They must identify suitable aircraft with enough fuel and prioritise their movement across the airspace to the battle site. This is adrenaline-pumping work for coalition airspace management and air movements experts.

In November 2009 Wing Commander Jack Foley was Australia's senior national representative within the CAOC. The 28-year RAAF veteran from Mackay in Queensland joined up because he loved planes and travel and here he was in an exotic location surrounded by hundreds of military aircraft.

Like many 10-year-old boys young Foley was smitten with commando comics and a glossy-brochure view of the air force. As the youngest of five sons of a sugar farmer he understood that he was unlikely to inherit the family farm. When F-111s flew low and loud passes over the farm, young Jack's future was set — he was going to be a fast jet pilot. But Mother Nature had other ideas and he became an engineer and ultimately a navigator on C-130s.

He was on his second tour of the CAOC, having spent several months there in 2005 in a job one rung down the ladder. As detachment commander his role was to coordinate and facilitate Australia's contribution to the CAOC team and to guard closely the RAAF's reputation.

Foley says the Americans go out of their way to include their coalition partners in all aspects of the centre's running. Despite having most of the people and planes engaged in the campaign, he says they are genuinely committed to an inclusive coalition.

'We all do get a reasonable voice in how things are done,' Foley says. 'Having a job like CAOC director occasionally reinforces that beautifully well, but people do get on very well with our coalition folks and we make a conscious effort to make that work.'

The CAOC looks after the strategic level assets such as transport planes, strike aircraft, tankers and fighters, but not the day-to-day missions of lower level air assets such as helicopters and the growing fleet of UAVs. On any day there are hundreds of intelligence, surveillance and reconnaissance (ISR), strike, air lift and tanker flights across the MEAO, operating from major and minor airfields as diverse as Bagram in Afghanistan and Baghdad in Iraq and from US carriers steaming in the Gulf.

'This base is physically further back, so it tends to have more of the bigger, longer-range assets and as you get closer to the front line, if I can call it that, you've got more of your smaller stuff such as fighter planes, RC-12 King Air intelligence aircraft and big choppers,' Foley says. 'If you look at it on a big screen, if you look at a map of Afghanistan, each individual aircraft comes up as a little label. Things like fighters are normally in pairs — there are labels over the top of each other and you can't figure anything out. You really need to drill down to a level where you just concentrate on your little block. It might be 100 miles square for example, and a cube of airspace up to 25,000 feet, so you concentrate on that and who is in that airspace and who is doing what. And there are reserve chunks of airspace for all sorts of activity, everything from "I want my Predator to sit over the top of me" to "That's an area I want to be able to fire back with my howitzer." So if you need to use that airspace, if you want someone to fly through it, you have to ask their permission.'

When a TIC occurs the battle director has to get the relevant assets overhead as fast as possible while ensuring that tankers are positioned to refuel the fighters so they can get back to base.

The battle director, whose position is also rotated through coalition partners, runs the tactical aspect of the operation and has a variety of people assisting real-time decision-making, such as a RAAF C-130 expert, a USAF tanker specialist, a British bomber pilot, weather experts and air traffic people. A massive effort goes into ensuring all air assets are set up to achieve a 'checkmate' situation.

'Whatever the enemy does, you have an air power response ready,' Foley says. 'That means having all the ducks in a row so that when it happens we can get a camera on that spot, we can throw a weapon on it, we can throw a helicopter over the top, whatever it might be.'

The CAOC works closely with the regional commands in Afghanistan to establish where the weight of effort needs to be and what is practical, particularly for bigger strategic aircraft that can undertake multiple missions in a single flight.

'There are lots of army commanders all through Afghanistan and they all want their own personal F-15 Strike Eagle package and a B-1, but that is just not doable,' Foley says. 'In fact, it's a very inefficient way to use what are extremely expensive assets so it's a matter of trying to divvy those up [and] take into account the risk and effect you are trying to achieve.'

By 2009 the focus of the air war had shifted from using 'kinetic effect' (bombs) to operating more reconnaissance aircraft, monitoring the enemy and directing ground forces.

'These days we spend more time looking and trying to understand the situation and less time in a physical, kinetic response,' Foley says.

High explosives are not always the best solution, as Mark Binskin found out on a cold Boxing Day in 2003. At about 11 p.m. the CAOC received a call for help from a commander running a small protection force for a provincial reconstruction team at a town south-west of Kabul. It was snowing there, the food had been ordinary and his itinerant workers were starting to revolt. Was there was anything the CAOC could do to help?

'All we had was a B1 airborne up around Kabul at the time so we said, "Tell you what, we'll be there in about 20 minutes or so." About 20 minutes later as he was trying to quell the revolting workers a B1 swooped in supersonic at 3000 feet with its four afterburners lit up and it achieved the desired effect. They had never seen anything like that back then. The tactic really boosted the spirits of the coalition forces out in the boondocks in the freezing cold. They knew we were there to support whenever needed. We got a phone call from him about 10 minutes later saying "Thanks, they'll be good for another month."'

Binskin says that if there was a way to solve an issue without dropping bombs they endeavoured to achieve it.

'At the end of the day there are real people on the ground, and those real people want to get on with life. In the middle of it all you've got the small pockets of insurgents, whether it's Iraq or Afghanistan,' he says. 'You want to make sure you keep the general population on side and let them get on with their lives and keep rebuilding the country.'

During his second tour of the CAOC in 2009 Foley found the mission focus completely different from his first tour in 2005, when Afghanistan was on the backburner and the main game was strategic air lift in and out of Iraq.

'Now it's more of a coordination and facilitation role, I suppose, and to a degree a kind of reputation role.'

That included managing more than 100 Australians who were living on the base before the C-130 detachment moved to Al Minhad in Dubai in 2009. Life for Australians living on the huge but isolated American base meant eating American food, listening to American music, watching American sports on the batteries of flat screen TVs. It also meant having to sit back and sip Coca Cola while watching, to their chagrin, their American colleagues consume a daily ration of two icy cold (Fosters) beers after a hot day in the desert, because all uniformed Australians in the Middle East were banned from consuming alcohol.

Air Commodore Jim Brown was CAOC director in late 2008. The Commander of RAAF Surveillance and Response Group at Williamtown was Director General of Operations when he was appointed to the CAOC job.

He describes the role as the pinnacle of air operations anywhere in the world. With about 1000 staff, and 300 on duty at any one time, it is on a scale most RAAF officers will never experience.

'First of all, it's a great privilege for Australia to be offered that position and to be responsible for running the headquarters that runs that air campaign,' Brown says. 'In terms of responsibility, nothing really surpasses it in the Australian environment as you bring together the sheer extent of the air operations.'

When he was in charge, the CAOC was running up to 75 KC-35 tanker missions a day, a couple of hundred air lift sorties, several hundred air support fast jet missions and a large number of ISR missions. The aircraft came from the US, UK, Germany, France, Italy, Australia and many other nations. 'Insurgency doesn't operate to schedule, so you've got to be able to respond to emergency situations. It's a very dynamic space,' Brown says. 'It is the scale, the magnitude, the breadth that really is the key difference.'

The job gave him a clear view of Australia's overall contribution. 'The feedback you get was certainly [that] the job our people were doing was on par with anything that anyone else could do. It was certainly satisfying being an Australian over there.'

In November 2009, Flight Lieutenant Jim Ewart was a watchkeeper in the CAOC. The former Rockhampton boy, who has flown Boeing 707s, King Airs and Caribous, was on his second tour at the CAOC. His job was to ensure the movement of Australian aircraft was integrated into the massive CAOC machine and that the RAAF plan folded seamlessly into the bigger picture.

'I'll make sure [it] gets entered into the system, we get the necessary approval to land at various airfields and also act as a central communication point,' Ewart says. 'We man 24 hours, so we get calls from Australia any time of the day or night. We also act as liaison officers so if any of the other nations want to get passengers and cargoes onto [RAAF] aircraft they come to us. So we have a central point always available.'

His workstation has access to four separate computer systems and he must ensure he has the relevant data to enable air movements staff to get an accurate picture of the air war. His time is spent amending mission schedules, talking to the C-130 mission planners and making sure they have all the information they need.

'A lot of it is just sitting there waiting. It is one of those jobs where you can have periods of inactivity, then all of a sudden something happens and it's quite busy for the next two or three hours or so,' Ewart says. 'If an aircraft decides they may need to add another fuelling stop we've got to coordinate that and it might be while the mission is going on,' he says. 'Obviously in this kind of environment ... there is a fairly rigorous process to go through before you can go and fly to a particular airfield.'

If an aircraft needs to divert to pick someone up or refuel, that creates a massive amount of work for Ewart and the team.

'We have to make sure there is somewhere for it to land, a parking spot for it, somebody to refuel it, somebody to unload it, the new path it wants to fly to ... The whole pack of cards.'

There are also occupational health and safety considerations for aircrews and operational limits on different airframes such as the size of a load, weather and winds.

'All this changes the amount of fuel you need to carry,' Ewart says.

Squadron Leader Steve Henry is the conduit between the C-130 detachment and the joint movements section of the CAOC. His job is to ensure the smooth transition of information between the Herc operational staff and the CAOC as well as the joint operations staff. For example, if a load is too heavy for a route, the aircraft has to be rescheduled to stop at several airfields to re-fuel or lighten the load.

'It really is a big puzzle they put together,' Henry says.

The priority is always what is required to support Australian troops but a couple of days a week the Australians offer an aircraft for coalition tasking. The two RAAF AP-3C Orion maritime patrol aircraft based alongside the Hercs at Al Minhad are constantly on coalition tasking but the Hercs move in and out of the coalition stream.

Moving civilian aircraft in and out of airports is a complicated task based on 'slots' when an aircraft must land and be parked. In a war zone the complications are multiplied by several factors so people like Ewart and Henry must be problem solvers as well as experts in their chosen fields.

'All resources in theatre are finite — that includes parking at an airfield — so if we make a change to something like that it can have fairly significant consequences,' Henry says. 'You might say, "Look guys, we need to come into that airfield an hour later." They say. "Well, you can't. We physically don't have the space on that airfield." Then you need to consider, "Do we go to another airfield, do we cut the mission and do it tomorrow when we can get a slot?" You might be carrying guys into theatre, it might be guys coming out that need to get on an aircraft, so the follow-ons are always significant. Any time there is a change … you have to start looking several days out. If that aircraft doesn't make that, what are we going to do? What's on board? Where does it need to get to? How important is it? There is always something going on, bringing a band in or the PM, [as] we had recently. It's not a bus schedule.'

Chapter 22

CALLING IN AIR

Whenever soldiers on the ground need bombs or a low-flying supersonic jet fighter to turn the tide, the person they turn to for help is their joint terminal air controller or 'JTAC'.

The JTAC accompanies ground troops on patrol and is the direct link to air support, calling in air strikes or any other aircraft that are needed, often in the heat of battle. They are highly specialised individuals who need to pull their weight in a commando section while bringing a detailed knowledge of complex aerial warfare to the battle space.

This is hard and dangerous work and JTACs must be trained to rough it for days or weeks on end, fight hard in the event of a contact and share the load with the grunts. The role is fairly new in the RAAF. During the 2003 Iraq war, Australian SAS troops were supported on the ground by American JTACs from the USAF Special Tactics Squadron who worked as integral members of their patrols.

Nowadays, Australian JTACs are more likely to accompany the commandos, who conduct more overt operations and require close air support, since the SAS have (in Afghanistan) resumed more of their traditional covert long-range reconnaissance and surveillance patrols behind enemy lines. They tend to call in air only as a last resort.

Flight Lieutenant William Powell is a special tactics officer based at RAAF Base Williamtown and has served as a JTAC in Afghanistan.

From Beaudesert in Queensland, he joined the air force in 2002 as a direct-entry trainee officer following a gap year after completing Year 12 at Beaudesert State School. His first job was a ground defence officer with the Airfield Defence Guards. Powell's grandfather had served in the air force during World War II and after meeting some airfield defence guards (ADGs) from the Vietnam War, Powell knew that was the career he wanted.

He spent 18 months doing the general services officer training course at the Royal Military College, Duntroon, and then returned to the RAAF. After several years as an ADG the 27-year-old wanted a new challenge. He even contemplated leaving the air force but when the opportunity to move into special tactics came along he joined the initial intake in 2007.

Gaining entry is no mean feat. It first involves passing the commando selection course and the same reinforcement training cycles that the army special forces troops must complete before being posted to their regiments.

'It just enables us to work alongside those guys in the field, you know, look after ourselves and integrate with them in terms of operating on the ground,' he says. 'Our primary function is to coordinate the air effects and the air support such as aerial resupply.'

However, if there is no aerial element then Powell is just considered another gun fighter in the section and must be able to perform to the standard. The JTAC forms part of the platoon or patrol headquarters, depending whether they are working for commandos or SAS, but most of their work is with the commandos.

Once he finished commando training Powell was posted to Number 4 Special Tactics Squadron at Williamtown. His first deployment was to Afghanistan in early 2009.

The two main missions of the JTAC — aerial resupply and close air support — require very different skills and training. Resupply might be carried out by a fixed-wing aircraft dropping boxes or a helicopter landing where the troops are.

'We would just find an area that was suitable and just go through the procedures of coordinating how much of what type of supplies we need,' he says. 'We then send the request back through the channels, via radio or whatever. That then gets coordinated and planned and then we get notified of the time for the resupply. We then just secure the area we've chosen for it to happen and stand by for the aircraft to come and then we'll make radio contact and coordinate the final approach and set-down.'

Coordinating close air support and air strikes is taught during a special course run by 4 Squadron that qualifies graduates to coordinate close air support.

'If a situation develops and you need air support then the JTAC on the ground, or special-tactics guy, will start planning what effects are required and then calls for that support on the radio,' he says. 'The requirement then goes into the command chain and they will find the suitable asset to send to us. We just establish radio communication and talk directly to the aircrew and brief them on what we need. There are a number of procedures that we might use to direct the effects onto the right target.

'When the aircraft turns up we explain what the situation is, what the effects are that we want. We'll get information off the aircraft as to what type of aircraft it is and what he's carrying to support us then we brief him on how we want the attack to occur. Once you've met all their requirements, ensuring everything has been briefed correctly, you proceed with the engagement and it's our decision on the ground as to whether or not the engagement will occur.'

During his deployment Powell called in air support from numerous types of aircraft including F/A-18s, F-15s, F-16s, Apache helicopters, C-130 Spectre gunships and his favourite, the A-10 Thunderbolts (or Warthogs).

'They can all be pretty impressive in their own right, depending on what the target is, but an A-10 rolling in with a 30 millimetre cannon blasting, that is very impressive.'

To manage this complex and dangerous mix, a JTAC must have an intimate knowledge of aircraft type — their speeds, weapons, the effect of various weapons — and the difference between a 200 kilogram and a 1000 kilogram bomb and the performance of a dumb bomb compared

253

with a laser-guided weapon. Most importantly, they need to know how far humans need to be away from an air strike to be safe.

'There are often times when the strike can be reasonably close and there is a risk there you need to manage, in terms of the safety of friendly troops on the ground,' Powell says.

As well as the qualified JTACs in 4 Squadron, the army commando and SAS regiments have their own fully qualified JTACs (mostly from the RAAF).

'We can be the point of contact for the planning and execution of any air-related support they might need in the field,' he says.

Speed and good communication skills are crucial for a JTAC who might be on the radio to pilots or battle managers from numerous nationalities.

'It is often a contact situation on the ground so it's pretty busy and quite hectic and once the decision is taken that we need air support, you don't have a long time to think about it,' he says. 'Afterwards it's a good feeling to know that your training prepared you well and that you were able to successfully conduct the mission but I don't think anyone really stops to think about it at the time.'

Once the decision is made the JTAC has to assess the situation, order the effect and then talk the pilot down onto the target, often while he and his mates are under intense fire from enemy fighters.

'We have to understand how long it is going to take a given platform to make it to our area or how far out a weapon will be released given the type of platform,' Powell says. 'We have common procedures so you know in terms of how you brief, it's standard, so everyone expects the same information to be passed off in the same order. It can be a challenge at times, but I didn't find that any language difficulties complicated any engagements.'

Avoiding civilian casualties is a top priority for JTACs as well as aircrew operating in a place such as Afghanistan.

'You have to build situational awareness and be familiar with the area you are operating in,' he says. 'You get a feel for the pattern of life in the area, talk to people as you move through the area. It's a level of experience that you develop as you work closely with the ground commander and make sure you draw in all the information from everyone.'

Powell says he didn't get involved in missions that were very complicated and certainly never had a situation where there was any ambiguity about what the target was, or whether it was inside the rules of engagement.

'We certainly didn't have anything that was questionable. It was pretty straightforward.'

While air transport is crucial, air battle management is the life and death side of the house at the Combined Air Operations Centre (CAOC).

Squadron Leader Steve Masden was the RAAF officer posted to the battle space command and control 'pyramid' in late 2009. Because there was no air-to-air combat during the war his job was to get fast jet close air support to troops on the ground in the shortest possible time.

An air force veteran of 30 years, the father of two is a former fighter combat controller and staff officer with 41 Wing at Williamtown and was on his first five-month tour in the Middle East. The battle space management 'pyramid' is run by the USAF's 71st expeditionary air control centre.

'Our primary role is to make sure fighter jets and close air support [get to] any troops in contact and then, once there, we make sure they get the fuel they need and then get follow-on support,' Masden says.

He mostly works with tanker aircraft and is only interested in the next two hours. 'I'm managing those tankers to make sure the jets get the fuel they need to make sure they can do their job — and in the case of navy, get home to the boat.'

The CAOC produces a spreadsheet each day setting out the tasks for each tanker.

'The reality is it never goes 100 per cent to plan and if a tanker breaks or jets don't get airborne we end up with more gas [fuel],' Masden says. 'We don't like sending tankers home with gas in their bellies. We want to keep them in theatre, so if they have finished their assignment and ... have

255

to go home with 50,000 pounds of gas, I'll find another tanker I can plug in, to take that gas away. So it's a bit of a dance.'

On any given day there are dozens of tankers in the battle space. Masden works on three computer consoles with the two outside displays running chat rooms and the centre a traditional radar display featuring the airspace above Afghanistan. He has up to 18 chat rooms open at any one time and 80 per cent of his time is spent in those windows talking to JTACs on the ground, the CAOC, the tanker boss, the fast jet boss and air traffic controllers up and down the country including terminal controllers in Kandahar, Bagram or Kabul.

'Someone asks me a question, or gives me a piece of information and I then have to feed that to the right person, either an aircraft or controller sitting beside me,' he says.

The radar display allows the battle managers to ensure aircraft are 'altitude deconflicted' and inside tactical working areas or 'boxes' of airspace. 'Once they get in [the box] they talk to the JTAC on the ground and he gives them coordination to prosecute targets they are looking for.'

Without the coordination he provides, troops on the ground might be left without the close air support they need.

'We try to get guys moving towards troops in contact within two minutes, but sometimes that can be quite difficult. They are flying around at low level, talking to someone else so we spend a lot of time talking to the JTAC. We give [the fighter pilots] words they need for the next task, we get them there expeditiously, make sure there is a tanker there to give them fuel, either on the way or when they are ready.'

Often a JTAC requests a specific aircraft type but if that is unavailable Masden sends a closer one. Safety is top priority but 'troops in contact' (TIC) is not far behind. Deconfliction of air traffic is a job for air traffic control and he has controllers sitting beside him. He can get up to 10 or more troops in contact calls per shift.

The Afghanistan campaign is a very different war from the one most military officers trained for.

'We've trained for a long time for air defence, so fighter against fighter, and the strike role is something that doesn't apply in your home territory, so we were mostly defending against an attack,' he says. 'Here it's all about getting bombs — well, not necessarily bombs, but getting fast jets over the troops in contact so they can either show their presence, show a force by flying low over the area just to scatter whoever is in contact or, if necessary, engage with weapons. The biggest challenge though is getting used to doing everything in a chat room which is something we [RAAF] don't use a lot.'

The 12-hour shifts can become tiring but the operators are trained to maintain a scan pattern throughout.

'You have to look at a screen and it is like looking at your car indicator panels — you know what is normal or what you saw last, so you are looking for differences,' he says. 'There are certain windows that are more important so as I get busier and busier I drop looking at certain patterns [and] boxes, and just concentrate on key chat areas — the CAOC, the tanker guy over here, what's happening on the ground.'

They are dealing with aircraft from at least seven nations plus the US air force, navy and marines.

'Every country has their own rules of engagement so there are certain tasks for which I will look for a US asset as opposed to just anyone. It doesn't happen often but it can happen. But in terms of engaging with weapons, each pilot is responsible for when he releases his weapon so he follows his rules and that's between him and the [JTAC] he is working with.'

Masden has spent 30 years training and operating some of the most advanced military aviation systems in the world, including the RAAF's new Wedgetail airborne early warning and control planes.

'You never know how you are going to perform until you get into the real thing,' he says. 'Like most military people I don't wish for combat, but when it happens you want to go and exercise your skills and make sure you are as effective as possible. If I make a mistake and a jet doesn't get there as expeditiously as possible, people on the ground can die. I watch the news every night like everyone else, and when I see certain news footage of guys that were in contact yesterday or two days ago, often I can say, "Gee, those are the guys we supported with that asset," and "Did I do everything right?"

'Most of the time the answer is "yes".'

Chapter 23

IN A BOX AT KANDAHAR

Kandahar airfield in Afghanistan is a vast, dusty military base. It houses thousands of coalition military personnel and the busiest single runway airport on the planet.

On the southern side is the main camp with boardwalk cafes and shops, huge American and British dining facilities, PX (Post Exchange) stores, accommodation blocks, gymnasiums and even a hairdressing salon.

The northern side underwent a major redevelopment during 2009 to cope with the 'surge' of tens of thousands of extra US troops and the associated support structure, including extra air assets. Before that, the northern side of the base was largely an empty wasteland framed by a spectacular mountain range in the distance. Apart from the fuel dump the only other facility was a series of tents and two large shipping containers grouped in a makeshift compound.

This was the Control and Reporting Centre (CRC). For two years it was the turn of RAAF air battle managers to coordinate the air war in Afghanistan from these isolated and very exposed steel boxes. Coping with up to 3000 military air movements a day is complex enough, but throw in 45 languages, dozens of aircraft types, long shifts, 55-degree heat and dust like talcum powder and the challenges become astronomical.

Mounting the CRC in August 2007 was a huge job for the RAAF's Number 41 Wing, based at Williamtown in New South Wales.

Wing Commander Richard Pizzuto was CRC detachment commander from October 2008 until February 2009. It was his job to ensure the CRC was operating properly and that its 70 or so staff were as well protected as possible from enemy threats. The most dangerous and sinister threats were random rocket attacks against the base. The CRC was never hit but there were some close shaves.

For the former Perth boy and 23-year RAAF veteran the job was the pinnacle of his career. While he had been well briefed before he hit the ground in Kandahar it still came as a shock.

'I knew what to expect visually when I got off the plane … I knew there would be a mountain range in the background,' he says. 'Still, it was a little bit daunting. I knew it wasn't the safest place in the world.'

When he arrived the CRC was virtually alone on the far side of the airfield, closer to the fence line than most other places on the base. This turned out to be a blessing in disguise because the enemy rocket attacks, while largely uncontrolled, mostly targeted the main base on the southern side.

'We had a few instances where we felt a little bit alone and afraid but that is why we took our force protection very seriously,' he says. 'We knew we were a little bit more exposed on the northern side of the runway, both to rocket attacks and to other issues as well, so that was always on my mind.'

Rocket attacks occurred several times a week and on occasions the insurgent Katyusha weapons landed close to the RAAF detachment, generating plenty of noise and activity as everybody hit the deck. The Australian unit did not include any formal force protection so security was built into the structure of the CRC. There were two teams — one active and one passive — drawn from members of the unit who received extra training in ground defence, first aid and weapons handling. They were the initial responders to any threat.

'Everybody over there was fully qualified in weapons and we all carried weapons with us. That was par for the course,' Pizzuto says.

Given the strong perimeter security and the various camps within it, a full-scale massed enemy attack was unlikely and multi-national quick-response teams stood by with armoured vehicles and large weapons to quell any trouble.

As well as the shipping containers, the CRC camp comprised air-conditioned accommodation tents, a dining facility, gym, chapel, a recreation area and a logistics area. There was no kitchen, so all meals were delivered in hot boxes from the southern end of the airfield. Finally, there was a sports field with its own concrete cricket pitch laid by the RAAF.

'When I was there we had a Boxing Day test, which the Australians luckily won and I have a T-shirt to prove it,' he says.

So on one side of the airstrip about 15,000 people lived in reasonable comfort and on the other side 75 Australians lived in tents and worked in steel boxes. They took every opportunity to make the journey to 'the other side' and 'civilisation'.

'Most of the guys, when they had time off, would hop in the car and get over to the other side for a coffee and a bit of respite, I suppose, from the daily rigmarole of the CRC,' Pizzuto says. 'It was about a 15-minute drive, or in the rain or mud it could take 35.'

Squadron Leader Clinton Morris was a mission commander at the CRC. He spent most of his shift inside one of the steel cabins alongside a force marshaller, physically running the air war over Afghanistan. Next door were the surveillance team and the technicians who maintained the equipment, taking the total team per shift to about 12 people. The 32-year-old Morris, an air battle manager and Iraq War veteran, was also the direct liaison point back into the Combined Air Operations Centre (CAOC).

'I would implement their plan for the day, managing the tanking plan, talk to other agencies on the ground and make sure my force marshaller sitting beside me was sending the aircraft to the right locations and getting the job done,' he says.

The force marshaller talked to aircraft and looked at the immediate picture whereas the mission commander focused literally on the big picture, projecting up to two hours ahead to ensure there was enough fuel in the tankers and that air support assets were in the right position to affect the ground battle.

Morris was not surprised by the working conditions at Kandahar because the cabins were exactly the same as those used by the RAAF's mobile control and reporting units in Darwin and Williamtown. What was different was the volume of air traffic. A 'troops in contact' (TIC) was the busiest time. Morris would be notified of a TIC via the secure computer system and would work with the headquarters to move an asset to support the troops. Their response time was quick and the operators developed little tricks to save time such as key word capabilities. When a key word such as 'TIC' appeared, an audible alarm sounded. The position of the TIC popped up on the force marshaller's screen and Morris would tell him to send a specific aircraft to that position. Once the aircraft was closing on the position the pilot would switch to the joint terminal air controller (JTAC) on the ground, who guided him onto the target.

With radar coverage of more than 75 per cent of the country and up to five radios on the go at any one time, the CRC had near total battle awareness.

'There were blind spots so we'd still have to rely on assets that were overhead, or tankers, to get comms down into those areas,' Morris says.

With more than 40 nationalities on the radio they sometimes had to ask for a repeat transmission.

'We may have had to ask someone what they wanted again once or twice, but I liken it to speaking to children — you can understand your own children but you can't understand anyone else's. So the more you listen to it the better you get,' Morris says.

The main adjustment was during the first two to three weeks when the operators had to adapt to camp life, different procedures, lower quality radios and lots of them.

'Just listening to all that information, taking it all in and trying to get it to the right people that need to know is quite challenging,' Morris says. 'I found it quite daunting and I thought, "Wow, this is a pretty big feat we are doing here and I hope I'm up to the task."'

For the commander of 41 Wing, Group Captain Daryl Hunter, the deployment of the mobile CRC and radar to Afghanistan was a major task.

The 42-year-old is in command of the RAAF's air battle management and air surveillance roles. That means he runs all the air surveillance of Australia and its near region and the mobile control and reporting function.

He says the intensity of the work in Kandahar, where the operators monitored two separate chat systems on multiple windows simultaneously, was incredible. There was no visual picture of the army on the ground, just a series of chat rooms providing details in text form. The RAAF mission commander and force marshaller would then have to interpret the chat and create the scenario on screen.

'If you were not on top of it, then the first breakdown was not getting the information [that was] needed before they could talk to the aircraft that were positioned and ready and waiting [and] before you could get them to move,' Hunter says.

In the cabin next door, the air surveillance operators kept tabs on the huge number of aircraft movements using a large spreadsheet to monitor all the aircraft call signs.

'The force marshaller would update the spreadsheet every time an aircraft checked in with the levels it was operating in, the airspace and any other pertinent remarks,' Hunter says. 'Not only were they talking to them, they were typing in the role and details so they maintained that record any time there was a call. That way they could go back and look … and the tanker plan was done the same way.'

If an aircraft was scheduled to refuel but was called off to support troops on the ground, it would not make the refuelling schedule. So another aircraft might have to replace it, otherwise it would run out of fuel.

'The busier it got on the ground, the more changes it forced back into the plan so the busier it got all around,' Hunter says.

Operators would be dragged out after three hours in the cabin and swear blind that they had only been in there for a few minutes. Yet everybody who worked at the CRC recalls their time there with great enthusiasm and fondness. Their call sign became well known among aircrews from all the nations and soldiers on the ground.

Chapter 24

AIR TRAFFIC CONTROLLERS

The war in Afghanistan is unique in many ways, but when it comes to controlling aircraft movement the rulebook has been rewritten. Afghanistan mixes military and civilian air traffic with barely a rudimentary air traffic control (ATC) system of its own.

Since the 2001 US-led intervention, the coalition has run the airspace using a network of military radars installed up and down the country and controlled from air bases at Kabul, Bagram and Kandahar. Like the Control and Reporting Centre (CRC) at Kandahar airfield they come under the overall control of the Combined Air Operations Centre (CAOC) outside Afghanistan, but unlike the CRC they do not control aircraft in the battlespace. Their job is to manage civilian aircraft transiting Afghan airspace and all aircraft — civil and military — that arrive and depart from airfields in Aghanistan. Hundreds of military aircraft movements a day have to be coordinated with dozens of civilian flights in and out of the country, as well as international flights transiting one of the busiest chunks of airspace on earth.

It has the potential to produce the 'perfect storm' of conflicting aircraft and in the high-stress world of air traffic controllers this is about as challenging as it gets.

The Afghan airspace threw up daily challenges for Squadron Leader Ruth Elsley well beyond anything she had experienced in her 15 years as a RAAF air traffic control officer.

Originally from Whyalla in South Australia, she was working as an airspace management adviser at the CAOC during 2009, alongside a British Royal Air Force air traffic expert. Their job was to ensure the safety of civil aircraft over Afghanistan while allowing the coalition air commander to achieve his military goals.

Another vital task was liaising with Afghanistan's civil air traffic organisation to help develop a national airspace model and establish a civil aviation authority responsible for all pillars of airspace regulation, from technical and airworthiness regulation to navigation aids and air traffic control.

'Afghanistan is a unique situation. Normally when you run a war you don't have civil aircraft running at the same time,' she says. 'Afghanistan is on the direct route between Asia, Australia and Europe so we need to be able to transit civil aircraft while still running an airspace war. It is very complicated because Afghanistan is such a poor country. It doesn't have the facilities,' she says.

More than 400,000 civilian aircraft transit Afghanistan's airspace each year and each one contributes $400 to the national coffers. That $160 million makes air movements one of the biggest contributors to the nation's struggling economy.

'It is incredibly important to have those airways available,' Elsley says.

During her four-month posting she had to try to progress the Afghan air traffic management system within the limits of a poor country, where air traffic controllers are paid just $50 a month.

'There is no incentive to be an air traffic controller. Their incentive to be an air traffic controller is to learn English so they can become a translator and earn oodles more money,' she says.

Despite the obstacles Elsley believes the Afghans are motivated to get their house in order. 'I met with Mr Romani this week. He's a deputy minister for civil aviation,' she says. 'He was educated in America and is a smart man, but he needs the resources to do it, and he's very keen to develop with the coalition a way forward for Afghanistan.'

The job was a dream posting for Elsley but it was not her first demanding overseas posting. In 2005 she spent seven months as contingent commander and aviation safety officer with the Australian detachment in the Sudan.

After losing her husband to cancer during her first posting at Nowra in New South Wales, she worked in a variety of jobs that culminated in the Sudan posting. She was the first Australian on the ground in Khartoum following the UN Resolution.

'They hadn't been able to get anyone in to do a scoping mission for us so I was basically put on a plane and told, "When you get there look for someone in a blue hat",' Elsley recalls. 'Fortunately, it wasn't that bad and we were met at the airport, but even the very first introduction to Sudan had its own challenges.

'Sudanese customs officers didn't want to give me my weapons, didn't want to release my weapons and medical kits to me. I stood my ground and told them I wasn't leaving the airport until they gave them to me, so phone calls went all the way up through government that night. Eventually government came down and said, "Just give them to her" so they did.'

While Sudan has a more developed aviation system than Afghanistan it was still very much a Third World situation.

'I couldn't take Australian procedures and safety levels and apply them to Sudan because it just wouldn't work,' she says. 'I was walking on airfields where you picked up part of the runway and underneath was just dirt. I was walking on airfields where you couldn't go off the sealed surface because the whole rest of the airfield was mined. There were contractors from a dozen different nations with different standards for their aircraft. On the third day I had to go out to the airfield and check because someone had messed with one of the safety pins on one aircraft, which happened to be two bottle caps stuck on with Blutac.

'I thought, "How am I supposed to do aviation safety here?" In the end you just run with it, but it was incredibly challenging.'

Elsley was also establishing the 15-strong Australian contingent, with her people spread right across the country. 'We had virtually no comms and very little medical or force protection support and I had to keep track of that.'

She was the only Australian in Khartoum, so was also the postal officer, administration officer, intelligence officer, welfare officer and even the chaplain.

The job opened up the world of multi-national operations to Elsley and the Middle East posting brought her to a whole new level of coalition war fighting operations.

Back at RAAF Base Williamtown, sorting out the complexities of air traffic movement and coordination is second nature to the commanding officer of 44 Wing, Group Captain Foster 'Fozz' Breckenridge.

Raised on a cattle farm in central Queensland and the youngest of four boys, both his parents had been in the air force during World War II and from a young age Fozz was determined to fly. Unfortunately he was not suited to RAAF pilot training, so after initial employment as a RAAF technician he became an air traffic controller in 1988. His first posting was to Darwin, followed by overseas jobs in Singapore and Butterworth, Malaysia, and postings to control towers around Australia.

These days, Breckenridge manages all of the RAAF's 250 air traffic controllers and the extensive air traffic control system. The Wing employs a total of about 500 people. In 2009 he was closely engaged with the government's plan to coordinate and harmonise civil and military air traffic management in Australia, culminating in a new aviation White Paper.

RAAF air traffic controllers are highly skilled and uniquely trained in both military and civil airspace management. They manage civil air movements in places such Darwin, Townsville and Williamtown and so they are prime targets for poaching by civil aviation organisations globally, which offer high salaries.

This means the RAAF is constantly fighting to retain enough experienced controllers to operate their 11 main military control towers around the nation. Overseas deployments stretch resources even further.

At the heart of the RAAF's air traffic control organisation is the School of Air Traffic Control at East Sale, which has carried the load for military air traffic control training in Australia since it started in 1947.

The 36 students each year are trained in three courses with 12 in each. The school's commanding officer, Wing Commander Andrew Gilbert, says the key issue is graduating the right number for the 11 control towers around the nation, because there are restrictions on the number of trainees who can work in a tower.

Gilbert, a 25-year RAAF veteran from Adelaide, says most people who train as air traffic controllers have a fundamental interest in aviation but are generally not suited to flying. 'The other issue is that generally at the end of the shift you take your headset off and you go home, whereas as a pilot you are stuck out at wherever you have landed your aircraft.'

Most students enter the 36-week initial course with little or no knowledge of aviation. They learn the basics of aviation theory, meteorology, theory of flight, rules of the air and air traffic control subjects. Before they graduate to the tower simulators they spend time in a computer lab that simulates all aspects of flight and learn how to control aircraft and operate speed control vectors.

The RAAF latest state-of-the-art tower simulators at East Sale include six 180-degree, one 252-degree and two 360-degree simulators. Instructors can dial in any airport and the graphics are so good that the students see exactly what they would see at, say, Darwin or Townsville. They can put any aircraft type into the circuit and simulate any situation.

'We can simulate fog, rain, snow, kangaroos that can hop around on the airfield, we've got fire vehicles for emergencies, we can put up different airfields,' Gilbert says. 'There is a radar screen, there is a meteorology screen for weather conditions and the console is very similar to what they experience out in the field.'

At the flick of a switch a Cessna in the circuit can be replaced by a C-17 transport jet and the scenarios and problems are limited only by the imagination of the instructors and programmers. With instructors who have served in Sudan, Aceh, Somalia, Solomon Islands, East Timor, Iraq and Afghanistan the scenarios that can be cooked up are limitless.

Flight Lieutenant Scott Mully is an experienced air traffic controller who deployed to East Timor in 2006 and he says a 360-degree simulator would have been invaluable to him, if it had been available back then.

'I was on the second Herc that landed, so we got off the Herc, ran across the airfield, up into the tower and we started to control helicopters and do all this other stuff, when there were no local controllers to give us any sort of information. We were just shooting from the hip,' he recalls.

Being able to simulate environments such as Komoro airport in Dili or Baghdad International Airport also allows instructors to identify problems and rectify them through further training.

'There were two or three controllers deployed to Baghdad who couldn't cut the mustard,' Gilbert says. 'They were sent home, so then you had to send someone else over. It's a bit embarrassing being deployed overseas and then not being able to cope with the traffic patterns, density, airfield configuration, weather conditions, whereas we can actually simulate all that here.'

Testing students and refreshing professionals can mean the difference between life and death and the RAAF's new suite of simulators means that 60 students a year can be trained if required.

While simulation and radar control is the high end of the business, air force controllers must be able to operate with just the basics.

'Controlling with a radar isn't that difficult once you get the hang of it,' Gilbert says. 'When you turn up [somewhere and] there is no radar [or] even a control tower, you are sitting in the back of a jeep controlling the aircraft. So you've got to learn without radar before you train with radar. In the 1950s they used to pay radar controllers more because they were using high-tech equipment but the reality is, controlling with radars is actually easier than controlling without.'

The RAAF's deployable air traffickers have to be ready to move at very short notice. During the 1999 East Timor operation they took over management of Dili's Komoro International Airport early on so that multiple aircraft from several countries could safely negotiate the small, cramped airfield.

In 2009, Group Captain Al Holtfreter was the RAAF's Director of Airspace Management. Originally a bank clerk from Norville, a small town in rural Western Australia, he joined as an air traffic controller and has been in that world for his entire 28-year career.

'I've flirted with leaving the air force and going out and doing [civilian] air traffic control, but really I've never been overly committed to do that either,' he says. 'I've applied for a job once or twice in my career and indeed got them, only to say, "No, I don't really want to leave this, I'm enjoying it too much." So I've been pretty happy. The air force has been very good to me.'

Looking back, he says, 'When I joined the air force [in 1981] I don't think there was a wing commander air traffic controller. Squadron leader was as far as you could get and you had to be in it for 30 years to get that high. That's changed over time as air traffic has morphed into something quite different ... over the time I've been in it. And that is really a consequence of the sort of ramping up of operations that started to occur in the 90s,' he says.

'Deployability' became the catchword as the air force developed a sophisticated capability that could be accessed by all three services in a joint operation. It required a much broader level of capability, developing controllers who could carry their skills onto the battlefield with the army or into the amphibious environment with the navy.

'We started to develop different ways of insertion,' he says. 'We have guys training with the paras in the army, so we can insert air traffic controllers very early on.'

This means being able to go into landing zones being secured by the army to provide elementary air traffic control.

'We then started to modularise the type of controller we developed, so it would be a couple of guys on the ground with a radio who had parachuted in, coordinating aircraft arrivals and departures,' Holtfreter says. 'Then we could bring in more equipment to build up mobile towers and we'd have a mobile air operations team getting in. They would pretty much do airfield control and management of immediate airspace throughout the airfield.'

The gradual build-up would continue until radars were brought in and there was a fully functioning air traffic management system available in even the most remote and hostile environment.

'The initial task that we had on the ground at Timor in 1999 was surface movement control — apron control — because the aprons at Komoro were particularly small,' Holtfreter recalls. 'With the amount of traffic that was coming in, management of the aprons, taxiways and runway was quite critical.'

The Indonesian civilian controllers had left by the time the RAAF team arrived so they had to rebuild the system from scratch. With just six or seven people the task was very demanding, especially once they took control of all air traffic movements into and out of Dili. Without radar, they relied on radios they had carried in, so could only offer a procedural service out to about 50 kilometres based on radio calls.

Holtfreter says there was a great deal of evaluation of training systems and methods following the East Timor deployment.

'We started to get a much larger group of controllers that were basically ready for deployment and we've sustained that kind of thinking ever since that time,' he says. 'We have a number of controllers now sitting on notices to move for any type of contingency. We rotate between controllers so that we don't have the same people continually at high readiness.'

If East Timor was challenging for Number 44 Wing, Baghdad in 2003 proved to be a whole new ball game for the Australian contingent of air traffic controllers.

The Iraq mission offered them a unique opportunity to apply their skills in a real war as they integrated civil aircraft movements into the battle space environment.

Baghdad International Airport was so huge, with so many players already in place, that just fitting in was a task in itself, according to Holtfreter. The airfield was managed jointly by the US air force (which ran the tower and fixed-wing aircraft operations) and the US army (which coordinated the vast number of helicopter movements and base security). The Australians had to liaise with the US army about everything happening on the ground and the US air force for anything in the air.

'We found ourselves as much in a liaison role as anything else,' Holtfreter says. 'The tower is the centre of the airfield. Everything happening around it — from the artillery that is being used on the airfield for air base protection and the coordination of that artillery; helicopter movements; civilian terminal movements; plus everything happening on the ground as far as vehicles and access and people crossing runways was concerned — was coordinated in the tower, which was us.'

One of the most difficult incidents occurred on 22 November 2003 when a DHL Airbus A300 cargo plane was hit by a surface-to-air missile soon after take-off. In a remarkable piece of flying the crew landed the plane successfully with only engine thrust available to control speed and direction.

The Baghdad tower was under Australian control at the time. Two RAAF controllers were running the tower and Holtfreter was also present when the jet was hit. Once the crew had regained control they very quickly got the Airbus lined up for a landing with a large chunk of its port (left) wing missing.

'There is not a lot you can do as an air traffic controller apart from your job, really, and stay calm,' he says. 'You make sure all the ground support is there when the aircraft gets on the ground, basically keep everybody else out of his way and try to keep him [the pilot] calm. That was the most difficult thing.

'He knew that he had a seriously damaged aeroplane that was not responding well ... so he had to make a decision about what he was going to do and he had to make that decision early. There was some discussion about trying to change where he was landing but he wasn't having a bar of that. He had picked a runway and he was coming to it and he wasn't about to change his mind.'

The controller needs to get all the information from the pilot and disseminate that to everybody on the ground who needs to know.

'But it is a really difficult thing in that stressful environment to know when you should be talking to the pilot and when you should be shutting up and letting him get on with business,' Holtfreter says. 'That creates a level of tension in controllers which is quite significant. They are aware that they need to get information out and they are also aware that the pilot is working hard, so they don't want to distract him.'

All other traffic in the Baghdad area was aware of the gravity of the situation so the two quite junior RAAF controllers were able to focus on helping the DHL crew survive. Fortunately the plane veered off the main runway and onto the dirt apron after it landed so the ensuing dust cloud extinguished a fire that might have destroyed the aircraft. Once it had stopped, the emergency chute deployed and the crew slid down straight into a mass of razor wire that had been snared as the plane left the runway. Luckily they sustained only minor injuries.

The pilots visited the control tower to thank the Australians personally for helping to save their lives.

'He [the captain] shook a lot of hands, spoke to the controllers who were involved, they spoke to him and were a little in awe of his flying skills to get that thing on the ground,' Holtfreter says. 'It was a remarkable feat. You could hear that from the aviators that were airborne at the time. They said it was the best landing they had ever seen. They had seen the damage to the wing.'

Another dramatic incident in Baghdad involved a British Tornado fighter jet with a massive fuel leak that landed without power. It was virtually 'towed' to the airfield by a tanker and then had to glide in for a landing. The pilot mistook a large taxiway for a runway and landed there. Because of the poor visibility due to dust and distance from the runway, the controller could not tell that the aircraft was on the taxiway until after it had landed. In addition to poor visibility, the Tornado crossed the fence at 70 knots (120 kilometres per hour) faster than normal on his glide approach.

Wing Commander Pat Cooper, who worked in the CAOC during 2003 but visited Baghdad International Airport, says it was lucky no aircraft were at that end of the taxiway at the time.

'In those conditions it can be very difficult to determine whether they are landing on the runway or not,' he says. 'You see them lined up they look like they are about right until they are almost ready to touchdown and then you get the perspective and you think, "He's not landing on the runway!"'

Cooper did not see the incident himself but he later met the Tornado pilots who had flown the aircraft and they were very appreciative of the priority and service they had received from the Australians in Baghdad Tower.

Holtfreter says the Australian controllers performed brilliantly in Baghdad and quickly won respect. 'We are such a small player with a specific capability and we have to win everybody's respect.'

It was tough in the early days as they pushed to have procedures introduced to cover things such as ground traffic movements and artillery fire control.

'When we got there the airfield was just a nightmare. There were people driving everywhere, people would enter the runway without clearances, they wouldn't talk to the tower,' he recalls.

There were also several artillery batteries inside the perimeter that just fired at will. 'Of course, they are firing from the airfield, so it is crossing the flight paths of aircraft. Once they pull the trigger it is too late, but it is stuff you can coordinate and it requires some really quick skills.'

The pressure can be enormous when artillery batteries want to return fire, special forces choppers want to leave the ground and large transport planes want to land all at the same time.

'It is that integration piece that is so important to what they [ATC] do,' Holtfreter says.

The Australians were often trying to control what was going on without knowing what was going on, because of the extremely tight American security.

'They set up these links where they discuss what is coming up and if you are not in the net, it is very hard to anticipate,' Holtfreter says.

That frequently meant little or no warning about special cargoes,

VIP visitors or other high-security operations. 'Lots of things happened that were quite remarkable and you'll never see again. For example, they changed the currency in Iraq not long after we arrived, so they are flying in money by the planeload! Billions of dollars of new Iraqi money being unloaded on the tarmac, with trucks literally driving out the gate with bags of money on them.'

The Australian controllers in Baghdad knew something big was happening one day when some burly African Americans with wires fitted to their ears and who talked to their wrists arrived and cleared the tower of all but vital personnel.

'We had a feeling it was someone fairly important because the security level had gone up a notch, both on the ground and in the air,' Holtfreter recalls.

No one had been told that US President George W. Bush would be visiting Baghdad. The regular US air force transport jet didn't morph into Air Force One until it crossed the airport fence.

PEOPLE

Chapter 25

VERY IMPORTANT PASSENGERS

There is no such thing as a typical week in the life of the RAAF's Number 34 VIP Squadron. One day they might fly the prime minister or governor-general into a busy capital city airport and the next be off to an isolated outback airfield or remote Pacific island.

Variety is central to the operational procedures of the pilots and crew attendants who rotate through the Canberra-based squadron. An ability to respond quickly and efficiently and deal with a multitude of demands and personalities are vital traits for the 30 or so pilots and 30 crew attendants. A thick skin and a flexible personality are also mandatory for dealing with busy national leaders, military chiefs or visiting heads of state. Discretion is also paramount.

The public image of the RAAF's VIP operation is of luxury jets fitted with gold taps and wine cellars bulging with Grange Hermitage. The reality is a leased fleet of two Boeing 737 Business Jets (BBJs) and three small Bombardier Challenger 604 jets. These are hardworking aircraft. While far removed from an economy cabin on a commercial airliner, luxury appointments are few and far between.

The nine-seat Challenger is a very fast jet with a functional but comfortable cabin. It has large timber tables stowed inside a wide, timber-lined compartment along the side. The tables pop up between six grey leather business-class swivel seats. There is also a three-person bench and a well-appointed toilet/bathroom at the rear.

The larger BBJ can carry 30 passengers but is not large enough to accommodate travelling media on international trips. In the past they travelled with the prime minister in a RAAF Boeing 707 but the Howard government decided to bump the journalists, who now travel on commercial flights.

That decision rebounded badly in 2007 when five Australians, including journalist Morgan Mellish and government officials Elizabeth O'Neill, Mark Scott, Brice Steele and Alison Sudrajat died when a Garuda Indonesia Boeing 737-400 crashed at Yogyakarta airport. They were travelling to an official meeting involving then foreign minister Alexander Downer, who had flown separately on a nine-seater Challenger. Another journalist, Cynthia Banham, was critically injured. That tragedy, which prompted severe criticism of the government, will no doubt influence the selection of the next fleet of VIP aircraft.

The BBJ offers more comfort than the Challenger. It has a VIP suite with a bedroom and bathroom forward of a separate working cabin fitted with first-class seating and a large conference table. There are also satellite communications.

The main cabin, where everyone else sits, is behind the VIP suite. It includes a first class section where senior staff or ministers sit in luxury reclining leather seats and a business class section to the rear for staff, officials, engineers or guests, such as the occasional journalist or photographer. In the old days, the prime minister always went down the back to brief the expectant media pack but these days rare media opportunities are conducted in the flying 'office'. There are two large, well-stocked bathrooms at the rear.

Alcohol is served on VIP flights but there is no Grange and even the famous Penfolds Bin 707 is a thing of the past. These days most people are too busy or tired to overindulge so drunkenness is rare. The flights are fully catered and on a long haul the passengers are fed a standard airline business-class menu on quality crockery with real cutlery.

Crew attendant team leader Warrant Officer Wendy McDonnell believes that identifying the correct balance of personality and willpower is crucial when selecting staff. She runs a section of 30 attendants and has a flight sergeant deputy and three sergeants to oversee the teams. She reports to the squadron commanding officer and has to ensure that there is enough staff for any task that is required.

Long-haul flights require several different crews and it can be quite difficult to find enough people. 'It's not nice to have to cancel somebody's leave [but] at the end of the day everybody loves the flying side of things so they are quite happy to change their plans and go on a task and take their leave later on.'

McDonnell often sits on selection boards. 'We are not looking for a Qantas flight attendant — someone who gets on, does a flight and gets off at the other end. We're obviously looking for someone that has an appreciation and understanding of military life for starters, somebody who understands the difference between a civilian flight attendant and a crew attendant in the air force.'

About half the crew attendants come from elsewhere in the RAAF and the rest from outside. The best candidate shows the potential to be assertive, think clearly under pressure and in emergencies, has a bubbly personality and can interact with the passengers.

There are five male cabin attendants but only two female pilots. Male interest in the job of cabin attendant has grown dramatically in recent years and at the last recruiting board McDonnell sat on, the genders of applicants were evenly divided. She foresees a time when men will outnumber women as cabin attendants.

'Most of the people who leave don't do so because they don't like the job any more,' she says. 'People are in my situation. They reach a stage in their life where they want to start a family and that's the reason why at the moment we have a few more senior males. They've hung around for a few extra years and the females ... have left to have families.'

She and her husband, also in the RAAF, had just enjoyed an 18-month co-posting to Canberra but that was soon to end.

'The ADF does try to co-locate couples, but sometimes that is just not feasible,' she says. 'My husband is posted to Melbourne in January at which time I will hopefully be on maternity leave, otherwise I'll take leave without pay to accompany him. I've absolutely loved my flying career and my 20 years in the air force and I don't really want to give it up, but my husband and hopefully my new family will take priority.'

As with the rest of the air force, attrition rates among crew attendants have been a concern over the years as the commercial airlines poached the RAAF's well-trained staff. However, in the past six or seven years the RAAF has improved conditions and pay and that has coincided with erosion of employment conditions in commercial airlines.

On gender, the commanding officer of 34 Squadron, Wing Commander Warren Crouch, says, 'I could have a squadron of 30 female pilots and 30 male crew attendants and it wouldn't make any difference to me. They are equally capable at the job; it's not an issue at all.'

Crouch is responsible for the operations and his job is to have the squadron's five VIP jets and crew ready to fly when the call comes from his colleague, Wing Commander Darren Goldie, who is the staff officer VIP Operations.

Goldie liaises between the 'clients' — Government House, the Australian Government and military chiefs — and 34 Squadron.

'They have a direct line across and when they say, "We'd like to do this," I turn that into air force language and hand it off to the squadron,' he says.

Goldie and his staff are co-located with the squadron headquarters at RAAF Fairbairn on the eastern side of the Canberra airport, so that the operation, from request to take-off, can be as seamless as possible. Efficient use of scarce resources is the key focus. The demands of VIP 'clients' are important but compromises have to be made. For example, if five separate parties want to fly from Canberra to Sydney on the same evening, the larger BBJ would be better than several shuttles with the smaller Challenger.

'We will allocate an aircraft based on what would be common sense to us, and then sometimes the squadron will ask to vary it,' Goldie explains. 'We might have a whole week of Challenger tasking when no one is travelling with more than five people, but the squadron might say, "For pilot training reasons we can either go out and fly an empty BBJ for training or we could take the PM to Sydney this afternoon," so you take the PM to Sydney [in the BBJ].'

The government is charged an hourly rate that is identical for the two types of aircraft even though the per-hour running costs and the cost of the leases are very different. The system is designed to avoid controversy.

The VIP aircraft are maintained by Qantas Defence Systems and both the RAAF and a private contractor undertake the catering. That system hit the headlines during 2009 when the then Prime Minister Kevin Rudd was forced to apologise for losing his cool with a crew attendant on a RAAF VIP international flight over catering difficulties.

Attendants are qualified to fly on both aircraft types but pilots are allocated to one or the other. They generally come from all parts of the air force, including pilot training school, but not fighter pilots. Junior flyers normally spend their first tour in the co-pilot's seat because of the lack of opportunities for training in this very busy operational squadron.

'Right at the end of that tour we try to give them very limited captaincy on the aeroplane,' Warren Crouch says. 'We then place a lot of restrictions on that captaincy and they typically won't fly a VIP passenger around. It will be training only or in support of other squadron movements, positioning the aeroplane, things like that.'

Most VIP aircraft captains are very experienced senior C-130, C-17 or AP-3C pilots. Fighter 'jocks' tend to stay away from the comparatively staid world, but Crouch, himself a former C-17 captain, Macchi jet trainer and Caribou pilot, says he would be more than happy to cramp their style and teach them how to fly a comfortable jet.

Like most pilots, he is yet to find an aircraft he doesn't enjoy flying. He flies the Challenger, 'a bit of a rocket ship'.

He is really impressed by the quality of the young people working as crew attendants. Some are younger than his own two daughters and he has been amazed at the qualities they bring to what can be a very demanding job.

'To watch them deal with the representational issues that go along with serving the most senior people in the country and the confidence [and enthusiasm] with which they do that is really quite impressive,' he says. 'That may involve being very direct with the PM or the GG or the CDF: "Sir or Ma'am, I need you to do this and I need you to do it now." First and foremost their role is one of safety on the aeroplane. The service they provide is very important but it is secondary to safety. These are a really impressive group of young people.'

Wendy McDonnell says VIP passengers abide by the rules most of the time and in nine out of 10 cases they respond without question.

'We have all done responsible service of alcohol training so we are able to identify if somebody has reached their limit,' she says. 'We usually don't get to that point because our passengers are quite busy people so they work a lot on the aircraft. They are not on there to have a party for 10 hours getting from A to B. They do a full day's work between A and B.

'People say to me, "With your experience, why don't you go to the airlines?" But I am quite happy in my job. I don't have to look after people's babies, we are not mobile crèches and our passengers have a high profile and they don't push the limits like a football team would.'

Regardless of the VIP's personality, the flight crew's job is to provide assurance that the entourage is in very capable and confident hands.

'It is important to us that we deliver them to whatever they need to do, or return them as well rested and well prepared as possible,' Crouch says. 'We certainly don't underestimate the importance of the work that is being done on behalf of the Australian people and our role in supporting that. Comfortable and discreet service is all part of that.'

Like her boss, Sergeant Kara Hoskin comes from a small South Australian town. Baraka has just 100 residents and a pub, so young Kara moved to Adelaide to finish her secondary studies before starting work in a travel agency. Six years later she applied to join the military police but during the interview someone mentioned a new program for directly recruited crew attendants. She joined one of the first intakes in 2002.

Her biggest early challenge was the compulsory combat survival training course at RAAF Townsville.

'That's where you do a lot of hill runs, escape and evasion training, get dropped off in helicopters, dropped into the ocean in a life raft — it was pretty tough,' she says. 'Because I had worked for six years before I joined the defence force, being treated like a child was very hard for me at first, but you just play the game. Once we'd finished our training and came down here [Canberra], everyone treated you like an equal.'

Hoskin joined the Challenger fleet for her first 18 months, flying around Australia and overseas, including nine trips to Jakarta. Because the Challenger can fly to obscure airports the catering can be tricky. At major airports they simply plug into the airline resupply system but in the outback or remote Pacific islands the options are few.

'We deal directly with the hotel, take our equipment with us to the hotel and sit down and talk through [with] the kitchen staff and the chefs about how we'd like our catering and they cook it for us,' she says. 'Quite often we'll eat at the hotel restaurant so you get a bit of an idea of what you should order and what you maybe shouldn't order. When we order from restaurants we'll receive their menu beforehand so that it is easier for them to cook the meals we require straight off their menu.'

Catering can be challenging, especially if there is a language barrier and, for example, 'stuffed chicken wings' arrive as whole chickens, but Hoskin says that when it all comes together and everyone is happily fed it is very rewarding.

There are often times when the local hotel simply can't do the job so the attendants shop at a local supermarket or deli and improvise the menu.

Busy periods such as during election campaigns can test the system to its limits. Tasks come up at very short notice with no time for the catering company to do its thing, so it is off to the squadron freezer and its supply of frozen meals or 'frozos'. One of the worst things that can happen is to be empty handed with a plane full of hungry passengers.

'Offering a passenger a shortbread biscuit for breakfast isn't ideal, but there would never be a situation where there would be absolutely nothing to offer them,' McDonnell says.

Most passengers are understanding about the pressures on the crew and treat them with respect and good humour.

★ ★ ★

Flying the racy Challenger 604 VIP jet made a welcome change for former Sydney boy, Flight Lieutenant Aaron Barker, who had spent the previous nine and a half years flying Hercules C-130 transport planes. After tours to the Middle East in 2005 and 2006 he moved to 34 Squadron for a change of scenery and a new challenge.

'I wanted to do some jet time and also the type of job here I think is interesting and exciting in a totally different way [from] Hercs,' he says.

During his C-130 days he flew the first Herc into Bali after the 2002 bombings and was shocked by the extent of the human devastation.

'It was quite confronting to see the state of some of the people. It was amazing that some of them were still alive so we just all pitched in and did what we could to get going and get them back home,' he recalls. 'I am not good with that sort of stuff but you just have to put your feelings behind you at the time and get on with the job.'

After the Herc, flying the Challenger is a little like going from driving a V8 Ute to a Porsche 911. It is faster than the BBJ and more automated than a Herc, so the flying is less hands-on and more systems management and button pushing.

'Flying the Challenger is a little bit more simple. You know, it is really just flying the aircraft from A to B, but I think it's also a fairly dynamic environment in terms of what we get asked to do,' Barker says. 'It can be a little bit trying and disruptive to your life, but I quite enjoy it.'

That 'dynamic environment' often means having to search for data on obscure airfields in out-of-the-way places.

'We do tend to get around to some fairly remote locations and you know it's a fairly autonomous operation and there is very little support in some of those places,' he says. 'You have to be well prepared and then sometimes, when things change, think on your feet as well. Sometimes we get asked to go into some places regionally that you might not visit on a holiday or with an airline, so there is a lot of preparation involved [and] digging for the information so you are as prepared as you can [be].'

That includes data on the airfield such as length, surface condition, taxiways, terminal, communications and the surrounding airspace. These can be hazardous, even though the dangers do not compare with flying a C-130 in the Middle East where the threat might take the form of a bullet or rocket-propelled grenade (RPG).

'Some airfields present their own threats in the form of high terrain, high elevation and limited procedures and facilities,' says Barker.

The pilots at 34 Squadron must prepare a plan to fly safely in and out of a remote location. Planning is crucial for flying thousands of kilometres from home base with no ground support and VIP passengers who can't afford to be stranded. Sometimes breakdowns occur and there is no choice but to wait for help to arrive.

'Some things are just out of your hands, and whilst it might make people unhappy or disrupt their schedule, all you can do is your best and maybe think of some options when you discuss the problem with the squadron,' Barker says.

Warren Crouch appreciates the variety that comes with the job.

'One day you can be flying from Canberra into Sydney in peak hour and then back to Canberra,' he says. 'There are a whole heap of issues attached to operating in such a busy air traffic environment, and particularly if you are a VIP-status aeroplane. You may be given some priority ahead of other aircraft, and along with that goes the obligation not to mess around ... The next day can be a trip out to a remote location where there is no traffic at all and very limited ground support available to us, so the variety can be extreme.'

A long-haul international mission on a BBJ presents a mammoth planning and logistical challenge. It is not simply a matter of loading up the jet and placing a couple of spare pilots down the back. RAAF crews have to be pre-positioned, diplomatic clearances obtained, security put in place and logistics support organised.

Squadron Leader Chris Martin is a BBJ crew commander whose job is to ensure the task is conducted safely and efficiently. A former Canadian air force AP-3C Orion pilot and 28-year flying veteran, he says the first major decision with an around-the-world VIP mission is where to pre-position the two or three additional crews to take over operating the BBJ. Unlike larger airliners there is no crew rest area on the BBJ, so duty hours have to be carefully juggled.

Most long-haul BBJ tasks require three crews, pre-positioned at refuelling points so they can get on board, do their checks and be airborne again within 90 minutes. This is known as 'crew slipping'.

'A lot also depends on the time the "customer" wants to spend in a location, because we have rules involving minimum crew hours or changes in time zone that require us to pre-position crews ahead of time,' Martin says.

Another complicating factor is that the twin-engine BBJ cannot transit airspace that a commercial jet with four engines can. A commercial airliner travelling from Sydney to London will commonly transit airspace over Afghanistan and Iraq because the four-engine aircraft can divert around danger zones in the event of mechanical trouble. Darren Goldie, Warren Crouch and their teams have to plan a more zigzag route.

Not all challenges are security-related. For example, when Governor-General Quentin Bryce wanted to fly to Poland at short notice in 2010 to attend the funeral of Polish President Lech Kaczynski, who ironically had been killed in a VIP plane crash, the request generated significant planning issues. As it turned out, she went to Poland via the Middle East, but the mission was disrupted when the Icelandic volcano erupted, throwing global aviation into turmoil.

Another factor is where to make refuelling stops. Flying a VIP home from London means the logical fuel stop is in a 'box' (of airspace) that includes Pakistan, India and the Maldives, south of India. Troops travelling between Australia and the Middle East have become familiar with a refuelling stop at Male airport in the Maldives, where they spend a couple of hours in its sparse international passenger terminal watching cartoons on flat screen TVs or dozing in plastic seats.

'But if the [VIP] jet breaks down it is less than ideal to have the GG sitting in the Maldives for several days,' Goldie says.

The juggling act is destined to continue with VIP operations, and as the lease runs out on the current fleet in 2014 public debate will rage anew. For 34 Squadron it will be a matter of providing advice up the command chain and waiting for the politicians, and ultimately the prime minister, to decide.

Crouch says, 'We will be asked our view in the context of a whole heap of other considerations, but the bottom line will always be what will work best, most safely and efficiently to allow us to deliver the services required of us.'

Chapter 26

SAVING LIVES

Group Captain Michael Paterson began training as a nurse with a handful of other blokes in 1979. It was an uncommon career choice for a young man in central Queensland where only 5 to 10 per cent of nursing students were male.

'Back in those days it was an unusual choice and I often tell the story when dealing with discrimination issues today that on my graduation certificate it says "she",' says the officer who commands the RAAF's Health Services Wing.

From assisting a woman in obstructed labour in an Iroquois helicopter in Bougainville to saving a soldier's life in Iraq, Paterson's 26-year career in the RAAF has taken him around the globe.

For a boy from a large Catholic family in Rockhampton it has been quite a journey from the local base hospital. Paterson's grandmother was a nurse and he had always been interested in first aid. He became a St John's Ambulance cadet at school and his family strongly supported his career choice. After completing postgraduate training at Rockhampton Base Hospital, the then 23-year-old was still living at home when a conversation with a colleague on night duty changed his life.

'Her boyfriend was a techo in the air force and she said there were nurses in the air force. So that sounded reasonably interesting to me,' he says.

Paterson had never seriously considered a military career and the only area that interested him was aeromedical evacuation (AME). Medical skills have always been sought after in the Australian Defence Force and for a trained nurse the path was never going to be very difficult. When the time came to make the move he knocked on the door of the air force recruiting office.

After completing officer training school in 1984 he was posted to the medical flight at RAAF Darwin, a busy place with 75 Squadron flying Mirages from there. It was also a busy time for Paterson, who undertook his basic AME course and operational health support course as well as going on numerous exercises.

He was often attached as a medic to the Airfield Defence Guards (ADG) and participated in many exercises with the ADG before being posted to 4 RAAF Hospital in Butterworth, Malaysia. The Butterworth deployment was downsizing with the removal of 79 Squadron back to Australia so eventually the hospital was disbanded and Paterson returned to home turf. In 1988 he was back at Amberley tending to the medical needs of about 3500 people working at the facility. During this period two profound events changed the direction of his career.

The first was the seventy-fifth anniversary of the Gallipoli landings in 1990. He was chosen as one of four AME support staff to accompany the last 60 or so surviving World War I veterans who were fit enough to travel on a pilgrimage to Turkey to commemorate the event that shaped the nation. Their job was to get the aged gentlemen to Gallipoli and back on multiple Qantas flights between Sydney, Singapore and Turkey and to provide emergency care and aeromedical support to an Iroquois helicopter stationed on the peninsula for the ceremony.

'Standing on the Gallipoli peninsula literally holding hands with a Gallipoli veteran, you can't have a moment like that and not think, "My God, Mike Paterson from Rocky, [you're] standing here with these men,"' he says. 'We became immersed with the DVA [Department of Veterans Affairs] team, so we helped the veterans before they went in our various [home] states and when we came home we stayed in contact with them. In fact I stayed in contact with the guys that I got close to, virtually until they died, over quite a few years, so for me, in a personal sense, that was just a gift that I didn't fully understand at the time. I have subsequently come to understand just what that gift was, and it is still very emotional for me.'

He was also selected to accompany four old diggers to the Western Front to receive France's highest award, the Legion of Honour. 'I was standing right beside the first veteran to receive his medal and that was just amazing.'

By this stage it was apparent that Paterson's file had been marked for bigger and better things. He became only the second RAAF Nursing Officer to be posted to the US flight nursing course, so that he could return to the operational health support and training flight at Richmond to teach AME skills to Australian Defence Force students.

'That's when I started to [develop] from being one of the many, many line flight lieutenants to having a bit of career direction,' he says. 'I didn't recognise it at the time apart from the fact I thought it was very good luck and I was happy to have the adventure of doing some flight nurse training and then coming back into an instructional role.'

One morning he was walking down a corridor at the base when he noticed a young nurse, Flying Officer Merilyn (Mel) White.

'Over time it dawned on me that I had found my wife in Mel and we had a very happy courtship in and around our various busy RAAF activities,' he says. 'Towards the end of our time in Richmond I asked her to marry me, so we headed down that direction.'

Unfortunately, the air force had other ideas and as the wedding plans gathered momentum, she was asked to deploy to Rwanda with an Australian team joining a United Nations mission.

'We were always going to be married, so it seemed to us the Rwanda trip was something she should do and I was very happy to support her going off and doing that,' Paterson says. His reward was a posting to RAAF Base Wagga as the officer in charge of the health flight for 12 months.

By the time the posting cycle had spun around and she had returned from an arduous deployment in the hell that was Rwanda, they were married and managed to snare a co-located deployment to RAAF Edinburgh in South Australia for four years of wedded bliss punctuated by the usual round of exercises.

Towards the end of their time in Adelaide, the Bougainville mission,

Operation Bel Isi, came up. It would be Paterson's first exposure to an army-led mission and some initial education was required on both sides. Once things settled down it became one of the most clinically challenging jobs of his career. He was working with his favourite AME platform, the UH-1 Iroquois (Huey) helicopter.

'Flying around in an orange Iroquois in amongst the spectacular scenery of Bougainville was a pretty nice way to spend some time,' Paterson says.

In addition to the health care challenges of the war between the Bougainville Revolutionary Army (BRA) and the Papua New Guinea (PNG) Government, the Australian medical detachment also played a political role in bridging the two sides.

'One of the privileges of health, because of what we do, is that we can migrate across those barriers with a lot more ease than other professions,' he says.

Once they had gained the trust of the locals, whose only previous experience with Hueys had been PNG military gunships, they operated in both camps, bringing vital health care to the long-suffering, poverty-stricken people of the island. He found himself treating everything from tropical diseases to gunshot and machete wounds and even obstetric emergencies in the Huey and back at the health facility at Loloho.

That unpredictable aspect of the work is one of the great attractions for military health professionals. Paterson has often gone to work in the morning and been in a different country that night, frantically trying to save lives and making tough decisions about people's immediate futures, based usually on quite limited resources.

'You have to accept there are going to be things that, professionally, you are extremely uncomfortable with, but that's the work that we do and you'd never survive it if you didn't understand that,' he says. 'It's quite different within Australia where we have enormous resources, but we have to understand that at times we are going to be in situations where we are just overwhelmed.'

That means making tough, split-second decisions and assessments.

The RAAF health wing is very well served by its active and specialist reserves, a large pool of medical specialists who sacrifice weeks and months away from their civilian practices to support the military and humanitarian work of the Australian Defence Force. They range from top specialists to critical care nurses, covering all medical disciplines from neurosurgery to ophthalmology.

One of Paterson's most important jobs is ensuring that the specialist medical reserve is preserved and renewed so that there is a strong pool of professionals ready to drop their lucrative practices at a moment's notice, don camouflage uniforms and sit in the back of a Herc for many hours to treat goodness-knows-what tragic cases when they hit the ground. There are even some specialist medical reserve officers who have done 10 operational deployments with the ADF.

'I have had the great privilege of working with them, particularly in places like Balad in Iraq where they really worked very hard and I got to appreciate exactly what was involved,' he says. 'They are not in it for the money or the medals; there is a spirit of service. Many of them have got very senior leadership roles in their respective health arenas and sometimes they might appear inflexible. So some parts of the organisation might say, "No, they can just wait to get on the Herc and if we can't bring them back for a week or two, well, that doesn't matter". But it actually does matter. We have got to respect these people who are really doing the very best they can … out of a strong sense of service.'

The pay-off for many is simply the type of trauma that they are called upon to treat — injuries that few surgeons in a civilian hospital would ever get to see let alone repair. In recent years, they have gone far beyond humanitarian missions in poor tropical countries, conducting mass amputations on gangrenous limbs in the frontline war zones in the Middle East.

Paterson led the Australian team into Balad, a massive US base of about 25,000 people about 80 kilometres north of Baghdad, with one of the busiest Role Three (specialist trauma care) field hospitals in the world at the time. His team was there for about six months and in that time the facility dealt with more than 5000 admissions. That is more than 30 a day, every day, building to 50 a day during operations such as the push by the US Marines into the insurgent hotbed of Fallujah.

As the commanding officer Paterson had to integrate his 25 people with the US air force team running the hospital and ensure that all possible force protection measures were put in place.

'I had a bunch of very precious people that I needed to do my very best to help survive and bring home. That sounds a bit melodramatic, but that's honestly how I saw it,' he says.

That job was not easy when the team was working in tents and much of the threat was in the form of rockets that rained down on the massive facility, but his attitude is pragmatic.

'When your number is up, your number is up,' he says.

The main challenge was remaining calm and he regards that as the most important part of his job.

'People were very focused. I just had to keep them going and look after them and give them support,' he says. 'I didn't have to do much, I just needed to be there and be calm.'

That is not easy when medical staff are dealing with badly injured children who might be about the same age as their own, or removing a dying soldier's helmet and finding a photo of a smiling woman and a couple of kids taped inside. 'Or you go to cannulate them and there is a wedding ring. While you do the job, you are very focused, but maybe later, when you've got a bit of time to think about it, you realise exactly what that means to a family.'

As his wife served in Rwanda, and many who went on that mission suffered serious post-traumatic stress, Paterson is a realist.

'I could never send anyone off to a deployment with the firm expectation that they would find it a professionally rewarding experience,' he says. 'I hope they do, and in most cases they do, but I am a realist and I understand people who will walk back in and say, "I'm never going to do that again."'

★ ★ ★

Two women who have lined up again and again to serve are Squadron Leader Nadia Wilson and Corporal Ayse Anderson. Over a cup of tea and Tim Tams in November 2009 at the expeditionary health facility at Al Minhad air base, the women appear totally relaxed about their jobs. There is something of the medical missionary in dedicated people such as these two, who approach their task with enthusiasm.

Wilson began her nursing career in her home state of Tasmania and after graduating and specialising in surgical nursing at Royal Hobart hospital she followed the sun north to Queensland and a job in private cosmetic medicine. After a while she realised that nips and tucks were not for her so she marched into the defence recruiting centre and joined the RAAF.

'I spoke to all three services — army, navy and air force,' Wilson says. 'Navy in particular for nursing officers is more admin orientated, they don't do a lot of clinical work and army was too structured. I was always keen on aviation and in nursing you get trained to be an aviation nurse, to do aeromedical evacuation retrieval and that seemed to be where I wanted to go.'

Ayse Anderson was born into an air force family in Ankara in Turkey. She migrated to Australia with her parents in 1989 and settled in Melbourne with virtually no English and with four years of nursing training that was not recognised in her new country.

Undeterred, she studied English and did volunteer work in a nursing home before she was able to enrol in a nursing course at Frankston TAFE. After completing the course she began working at a geriatric hospital while enrolling at university.

'It was very difficult to continue due to the commitment of work as well as home,' she admits. 'My parents were working two different shifts — Dad worked night shift at a plastics factory and Mum a day shift at a lingerie plant — just to start building our house and building our life in Australia. I started doing uni, then in 1998 I joined the air force.'

She had long thought about following her dad (who had been an F-16 radar technician in Turkey before emigrating) into the air force but had never imagined it would be in Australia. Like most migrant families life was tough for her parents Yucel and Sevinc and her little sister Ayla, who completed university and is now a marketing manager. Her father understood and was comfortable with her decision to join the RAAF, but her more traditional mother took a little more convincing that losing her elder daughter, before she was married, was a good idea.

After completing an advanced medics course at RAAF Base Williams, in Laverton, Victoria, Anderson was posted to Amberley to work in 1 Expeditionary Health Squadron. The attraction for her was the challenge of military medicine, which she says provides much more responsibility and autonomy than civilian nursing, and the opportunity to look after patients onboard big aircraft.

By far the most rewarding aspect of the job for both Wilson and Anderson is delivering wounded soldiers back home to their families. In September 2008 they both had to scramble with just six hours' notice for the first ever long-haul AME task in the new C-17 Globemaster aircraft. The job was to pick up five wounded SAS soldiers in Kuwait.

'It was a very long day. We had to drop people off at different parts of Australia and just having the family there who all just clapped ... I get emotional even now,' says Wilson, as tears well up in her eyes.

The C-17 represented a quantum leap in capability for aeromedical evacuations. Not only can it carry many more patients much further and faster than a C-130, it has piped oxygen and wired-in power sources so the medics don't have to lug heavy equipment such as oxygen cylinders on board.

Wilson says the need for a bigger and better AME capability was identified during the Bali bombing evacuations when the medics really struggled to do the job.

'From that it was realised that we needed some sort of mass casualty air medical response so when they purchased the C-17 they got the medical gear fitted as well,' she says. 'It is an amazing capability and we love it.'

The leap in capability was on display during an emergency in April 2009 when a C-17 evacuated six asylum seekers — four of them intubated to help them breathe — who were badly burnt after their sabotaged boat was engulfed in flames at Ashmore Reef. One of the challenges for RAAF medical staff on stand-by duty is juggling family life and both women are fortunate to have understanding husbands.

Anderson is married to a Gulf War veteran, Grant, and they have a six-year-old son, Aydin. The air force is a family affair for the Wilsons and Nadia's husband, Greg, is a former full-time and now reservist RAAF doctor, so their daughters Hope and Chase are well versed in the demands of military life and lengthy absences. Squadron Leader Greg Wilson was one of the first RAAF doctors into Bali after the 1998 bombing and was awarded the Conspicuous Service Cross for his work there.

'I was six months pregnant at the time,' says Nadia Wilson. 'They actually asked me to go and I said, "I'm sorry, I'm pregnant." So I worked for three days straight in the base command post organising the reception back home in Darwin, the ambulances, how many we needed and which hospitals they were going to.'

Both women are amazed at what they have achieved in their air force careers. Wilson has found an inner assertiveness that she could never have imagined.

'Sometimes it can be a male-dominated environment, especially at my level,' she says. 'I've just been promoted to squadron leader so I'm on a steep learning curve and [having] to be more assertive, not to be afraid to stand up for what I believe in. That has certainly come out of me on this deployment, that's for sure.'

Learning English was tough enough for Anderson but learning military-speak in the RAAF was even harder.

'There were so many words I didn't know and I thought, "Oh my God, what am I doing here?" But slowly you learn; you just adapt to it and build your career,' she says.

Her relatives back in Turkey are very proud of her. 'They are very excited that I am achieving these things. I'm Turkish and the second thing is, for a Muslim person, for a female, to achieve this is just incredible. That's why I think my dad is just so proud of the whole thing.'

Her younger female relatives back in Turkey see her as a role model as well, as they try and break the traditions of women marrying and staying at home to manage the family.

'Usually the women stay home and look after children and I'm doing the odd thing, the opposite for them completely,' she says. 'The ones that are growing up at the moment, they want to break that too and see how they can become an individual and achieve the best in their life. I do find I'm stronger, mentally and physically, than what I would have been outside or if I were back in Turkey, so I think I've challenged my life big time.'

Her Muslim faith has never been an issue for her and she has simply adapted to her circumstances. For example, she did not participate in Ramadan during her deployment because it would have affected her work.

'All the Muslims over here, host-nation personnel, they get up in the middle of the night, they eat something and have the day to recover from it because they sleep,' she says. 'My main job here is to be part of this team and continue what I'm here for, to do what I am here for. I can continue with my religion when I can do it, so no one is affected and no one has raised any comments regarding my religion.'

She practises her religion in the privacy of her own room but she does not believe you need to practise religion 100 per cent at all times to be a true believer. 'The doctors and other medical staff have supported me big time being a Muslim here. I had a big chat to the chaplain and he took some knowledge and information to make sure that other people understood how we operate and how Muslims are thinking.'

Having a Muslim woman on the base has been helpful as well in terms of understanding what various local customs and outfits mean.

'I understand the culture really well. There have been so many cases now with people asking about the women dressing up and men dressing up, or, "What is the man singing?"' Anderson says.

One of the most difficult aspects of a four-month deployment is the lack of contact with family. It can be an acute problem for medical staff who might find themselves back in Australia only briefly, escorting a patient home.

Wilson made the tough decision not to see her children during her 48-hour stopover, although she did spend a day with her husband, Greg.

'I was a bit concerned that people would think, "Oh, she's going back home for two days, well, why didn't she see her family — that is really strange", but I couldn't because it would have really upset them and me,' she says. 'I probably would have come back not as focused, so that was my decision and our other medic had to do the same thing. He was of the same opinion that he would not see his children because it would disrupt them, but he did see his wife.'

Managing the emotions of children over the phone from the other side of the world can also be tough. Anderson has found that chatting with her son can be something of a lottery.

'Some days they want to talk to us, some days they don't and they don't want to know you. They are angry and upset with you because you left them behind,' she says. 'So going home for a day is an opportunity to see each other, but they wouldn't understand at all. My husband was the same. He said, "If you do ever come here, please don't." I can understand where he is coming from.'

Family stresses take their toll and after 13 years in the RAAF, Wilson decided to take a break following her Middle East deployment.

'I do love the job but my family is taking more of a priority now. So when I get home I'm taking some long service leave to determine what I want to do in the future,' she says. 'This deployment has definitely been a highlight and it has really opened my eyes, in particular to what the army do, as well. Sometimes you just get single-service focus and you know what you are doing, but some of the members we've had to look after here are amazing people. What they've had to do over there [in Afghanistan], it's just mind blowing.'

Chapter 27

IN THE FACE OF TRAUMA

The tears well up in Flight Lieutenant Leigh Stalling's eyes as she recalls the night when nine wounded Australian SAS soldiers were brought into the field hospital at Tarin Kowt in Afghanistan.

The intensive care nursing specialist had seen plenty of trauma during her deployment to the Dutch-run Role 2 hospital at Camp Russell, but she was always agitated when she knew that badly wounded diggers were on their way in.

'I found it very emotional, especially when it is your own troops. It's quite strange,' she says. 'You treat everyone the same, but I would get exceptionally nervous, almost to the point where I'd want to cry, when I knew there were Aussies coming in. I know that is stupid but just the pressure you felt — these are our boys. I get emotional about it now,' she says as she dabs away the tears.

It is February 2010 at the Health Operational Conversion Unit at RAAF Base Amberley and Stalling is recalling her four-month tour to Tarin Kowt.

The SAS ambush in September 2008, for which Trooper Mark Donaldson was awarded the Victoria Cross, was the biggest mass casualty incident involving Australian troops since the Vietnam War.

As soon as the first gurney burst through the door of the intensive care unit carrying a gravely wounded digger suffering from serious gunshot wounds, Stalling's nerves vanished and it was down to business to save the most seriously hurt and deal with nine men who had been wounded during the fierce battle.

'I was on night duty that night. I was pulled out of bed to come in, so I was already a bit fatigued,' she recalls. 'But once you know our boys are coming then your adrenaline is through the roof.'

Fortunately the outcome was a positive one and the medical teams managed to save all the soldiers and see the most seriously hurt safely on their way to Kandahar and beyond for more specialised treatment. The family of the soldier suffering the worst wounds wrote an email to the trauma team at Tarin Kowt, thanking them for saving his life.

'It was nice follow-up and we usually wouldn't get that,' Stalling says.

They also treated the wounded handler of Sarbi, the 'wonder dog'. The handler was hit during the firefight and was suffering the added distress of having lost his faithful explosive ordnance detection dog. Sarbi fled during the battle after his master was wounded and turned up 14 months later after being found by an American soldier.

'When the news release came out about Sarbi we were all so happy. That was the end of something that happened over there,' Stalling says. She even joined the 'We love Sarbi' Facebook campaign.

Sarbi returned to Australia in December 2010 and in April 2011 was awarded the Royal Society for the Prevention of Cruelty to Animals (RSPCA) Purple Cross for exceptional bravery.

No amount of training can fully prepare a medical person for their first experience of the trauma of war or, in the case of Afghanistan, for the cultural void that makes people refuse treatment because amputation is against their religion, or because women cannot be allowed to make decisions or, in some cases, even be permitted to receive treatment at all. In many instances Australian medical staff in Afghanistan had to simply 'unplug' very ill patients and watch them walk out the door with their families, knowing that their mangled, festering limbs would soon kill them because that was seen as better than living with a part of their body missing. For people trained to do everything they could to save lives this was a traumatic experience.

'You know he will die but treatment has been withdrawn so you pull out the lines because he is going home and that is really quite confronting,' Stalling says.

There were very satisfying exceptions, such as the Afghan policeman who was admitted to the Role 2 field hospital at Tarin Kowt (TK) with three gunshot wounds that had perforated many vital organs and left his insides mangled. He was given only a 20 per cent chance of survival but after 22 days of around-the-clock treatment by the two Australian intensive care nurses working 12-hour shifts, he survived and recovered.

'The three gunshots had penetrated just about everything and it was really messy,' Stalling says. 'No one expected him to live, so we did really well to keep him alive.'

After the team had returned to Australia the policeman came back to the hospital and she saw photos of him. He was unrecognisable from the near corpse she had spent countless hours nursing. Fortunately for the policeman, there were no major casualty incidents involving the diggers during those 22 days so he could occupy an ICU bed throughout his treatment.

'Thank God we never got to the situation where we had to make a decision, but it was a scary thing to think about when you are holding onto somebody for that long,' she says.

Stalling grew up on the Central Coast of New South Wales and joined the army cadets when she was 13 years old. She had always planned to join the army. After completing Army Reserve training she went to university to study nursing and then undertook postgraduate studies in intensive care nursing. She applied for the army and the RAAF and was accepted into both, so she visited an army and an air force base before making her final decision.

'I just saw how happy the RAAF was and that it was doing more of the operational things I was interested in, and just the places they were going and what they could offer me. So I made the decision to join the air force,' she says.

That was in 2005 and the ensuing years have been busy and rewarding for her. 'They have really taken my skills and utilised them. They've sent me overseas to do a few courses and I have been very blessed with my deployments. I hadn't even seen a gunshot wound before I arrived at TK and suddenly that was my bread and butter.'

She lost 7 kilograms during her time in Afghanistan but says she put it all back on in the first week she was back at home.

Before she arrived at TK, a controversy had erupted about the timing of the coalition aeromedical evacuation (AME) flights delivering troops from the battlefield back to the hospital. There had been some delays outside the 'golden hour' after which time the chances of survival diminish rapidly, but by the time she arrived the system was working well. She was also amazed by the quality of the first aid applied to badly wounded soldiers by their mates in the field.

In one case, a Dutch soldier came into the hospital after an improvised explosive device (IED) had exploded right under his vehicle and blasted a massive hole in his perineum.

'The sergeant in the field actually put his fist into this guy's perineum and held it there and that was the only thing that got him alive back to where we were,' she recalls. 'We worked on him for 11 hours, gave him litres and litres of blood but still couldn't stop the bleeding. He eventually got to Kandahar; we ended up using QuikClot [a modern clotting agent], which has to be removed surgically, in order to stem the bleeding. He was very lucky to survive.'

The surgical team drafted a letter to the Dutch forces after this case and told them that without the first aid given on the ground the soldier would have died of shock before he reached the hospital.

Sergeant Robyn Baxter's deployment to Kandahar as the medic for the RAAF Control and Reporting Centre (CRC) was the culmination of years of training.

This was not so much because of what she had to do for her fellow Aussies as the sole medic at the facility but the incredible variety of work she undertook when she helped out at the trauma department at the Role 3 coalition field hospital on the other side of the vast airfield.

One of the busiest specialist trauma facilities in the world at the time, the Role 3 was where most critically injured coalition soldiers in the southern Afghanistan area of operations and badly injured locals from miles around were taken for intensive treatment. It was common for the hospital to deal with 20 or more seriously injured blast victims at once and it offered services from brain surgery to plastic surgery and everything in between.

During a mass casualty incident the medics, nurses, surgeons and other specialists operate like a well-oiled machine. The trauma bays function at maximum speed as patients are assessed and moved on to the specialist areas or operating theatres whose staff attempt to save their lives or stabilise and prepare them for the long AME flight to the huge US military hospital at Landstuhl in Germany for specialist treatment.

After leaving school in her hometown of Newcastle in New South Wales, Baxter completed an enrolled nursing certificate and began work in the cardiac unit at John Hunter Hospital, where she met a number of military reserve medical staff. They would show powerpoint presentations of their overseas deployments and that sparked her interest in aviation medicine.

'I very much like the emergency side of medicine where you don't know what is going to come through that door,' she says. 'You've got your mind racing and everything pumping to try and save someone's life.'

The overworked staff at the Role 3 would often call medics working around the base looking for volunteers to help with a mass casualty incident.

'Basically, any medical person available would be asked in, so I'd just drive around the airfield and go over and assist them with any traumas coming in,' Baxter says.

Trauma care was not on her list of daily duties at the CRC where her sick parades would deal with everything from coughs and colds to minor injuries and emotional support, but never massive gunshot or explosive trauma. Several insurgent rockets came over the fence at Kandahar but none landed inside the compound. Generally that meant she was free to go to the field hospital whenever they called, provided she was not away conducting a medical evacuation.

'The Role 3 was a very busy hospital so from time to time they would call up seeking assistance,' she says.

Her stay in Kandahar was seldom boring — indeed quite the opposite — as she had no idea what would come her way from one day to the next.

'The trauma we saw was incredible and way beyond anything that you would ever see in a hospital back at home,' she says. 'Working on those patients also helped me learn a lot more about myself and what I am capable of doing as a medic.'

Being part of a resuscitation team at the Role 3 facility was certainly beyond anything she had experienced before.

'You are given your position in the "resus" team and you just get in and do your job and it's not until afterwards that you think, "Wow, that was impressive." Seeing everyone do their bit and the outcome at the end, and some of them were pretty amazing, you think, "How on earth did we achieve that?"'

The teams usually found out what was coming through the doors when nine-line summaries of the patient's condition were radioed ahead from the inbound helicopters or ambulances. The waiting time between when the alert was sounded for incoming wounded and the arrival of the choppers was spent planning the treatment and going over in her mind exactly what she would need to do.

'When it does rock in the door you either think, "Okay, we've got this handled" or "Whoa, I was not expecting that,"' says Baxter. 'It is either worse than I thought or something more or less.'

From the resuscitation bays the patients were taken either directly to surgery, X-ray or the CT scanner. Some of the cases simply astounded her. 'Seeing what the specialists do to fix people up after they sustain serious gunshot or shrapnel wounds is simply amazing.'

The one aspect of the job that constantly astonished her was the random nature of casualties. Vehicles carrying four passengers would be hit with a roadside bomb and one soldier would not have a scratch on him, but the person sitting right next to him would be gravely wounded.

'It was amazing to see what these vehicles and what these IEDs were capable of,' she says. 'To find that one person would get no scratch on them and the other person would be badly hurt, you feel that person is so lucky and all they want to do is call home and say "I'm okay."'

Being so close to Kandahar city, a hotbed of insurgent activity, meant that the Role 3 was constantly dealing with local people caught up in the bloody and indiscriminate insurgency. On occasion the facility dealt with hundreds of casualties and was placed on standby for a fuel tanker explosion in Kandahar city, but mostly it was ones and twos with gunshot and blast wounds. Many of the victims were children caught in the crossfire or blown up playing with unexploded munitions.

'I have an 11-year-old daughter myself and I would imagine what it would be like if it was her,' Baxter says.

Both Stalling and Baxter were amazed at how tough and stoic the Afghan children were and how those with very serious injuries would lie quietly while the doctors and nurses got to work on them. Unfortunately, their families were not always so keen on the idea of their youngsters being treated by the Westerners, but the children themselves were always pleased to be in the hospital.

'The kids were always very happy, very positive, considering what was happening around them,' says Baxter. 'Even those kids with limbs blown off or serious gunshot wounds … were just happy to be alive.'

Like all the medical staff who dealt with the Afghanis there was a broad cultural gulf to overcome. It manifested itself in many ways, including the refusal of local men to deal with females, but the most difficult one for the Australian medics to get to grips with was the issue of amputation.

'Many of them would be unconscious when they got their limbs removed to save their lives, but when they woke up and realised they were no longer whole, they would ask to take the amputated limb with them so they could keep it and be buried whole when the time came,' Baxter says.

Another difficult aspect was the number of return cases who had been harmed by their own people because they had been treated by the foreign military. Even children who had lost both parents could only be kept at the hospital until they were stable and then they were released back into the community.

'It didn't matter what country you were from, just the fact that you were military meant that you were dirty,' she says. 'The patients would go back out and because they had let the military treat them they would be harmed again or have dirt put in their wounds so they would suffer serious infections.'

Cultural differences were often quite confronting for both Stalling and Baxter. The lack of respect for women was one thing but the cruelty was another altogether.

'We had a group of little girls, school girls, who were on their way to school in their school uniforms when a vehicle drove past and someone threw acid over them,' says Baxter. 'The interpreter told us it was to disfigure them so they could never get a husband as punishment for daring to go to school. That meant they were basically going to be slaves for the rest of their lives. As they were leaving they were so grateful and so positive and determined not to let it bring them down. They would still go to school because they wanted to be teachers.'

The one thing that really got under Stalling's skin was the cruelty to little children.

'We had a few kids come in who had quite significant burns on their feet requiring skin grafts,' she says. 'In that environment you expect that to be some kind of IED injury, but these were kids, not even two years old, who had misbehaved and then been held over the fire at home until the bottoms of their feet were burnt as a disciplinary thing. That really aggravated me and with all this senseless stuff going on, these are injuries that didn't need to happen. That was really hard to take. They were such cute kids.'

Inevitably another family member would bring the little ones to the hospital because they knew that such cruelty was unacceptable to Westerners. The Australian female medical staff were often spat on or abused by local men for daring to touch them or in some cases even just talk to them.

'We had to have security guards with us sometimes just so we could treat a male patient,' Baxter says. 'That was for our own protection and that of the patients because we didn't want them to injure themselves any more than the state they were in. Some of them did have very strong beliefs about females, especially the doctors because in their opinion a doctor should be a male and the male should be dominant, not a female.'

At least at Kandahar there were a lot of male staff who could swing into action to short-circuit the cultural malaise. At Tarin Kowt most of the medical staff were female including the nurses, the head surgeon and the hospital chief.

Stalling says a lot of time was spent explaining that everyone was a woman: 'Unless you want to speak to the wardsman here, you are going to have to deal with us.'

The gender divide was so great that during her four months at Tarin Kowt, Stalling saw just two female patients and both were at death's door.

'The ones that came had been cared for by their families but they were very sick by the time they got to us,' she says. 'They would have been dead within days.'

One of the most satisfying jobs for Baxter was the aeromedical evacuation of seriously hurt diggers from Tarin Kowt back to Kandahar and then on to Kuwait and home to Australia. She still keeps in contact with one of the soldiers whose lower leg was shattered by an IED blast.

'He was standing up in the gun position in one of the vehicles and an IED went up straight under him and basically shattered his leg from the knee down and he had to come back home for major surgery,' she says. 'It was quite emotional because before, they'd said goodbye to one of their soldiers who had been killed.'

The dead digger was in a second aircraft on the airstrip so it was an emotional but rewarding time for Baxter and her very grateful patient.

Despite the confronting nature of the work and the cultural challenges, both Stalling and Baxter say they would return to Afghanistan in a heartbeat.

THE FUTURE

Chapter 28

LIGHTNING STRIKES

Even the world's most advanced aerospace industry has found the task of building a brand new 'fifth-generation' stealth fighter aircraft, the Joint Strike Fighter, a daunting challenge.

On top of that, inviting eight other countries, including Australia, the United Kingdom and Canada, to join the project and participate in its development and construction has been an undertaking so complex that it makes NASA's moon landing look almost like a joy flight.

The Howard government decided very early that US defence giant Lockheed Martin's F-35 Joint Strike Fighter (JSF), designated 'Lightning II', was the right aircraft to carry Australia's air defences well into the 21st century.

With an estimated price tag of $12 billion to $16 billion, the JSF would be Australia's biggest single military purchase. It would attract vocal criticism, microscopic analysis and the government and Defence would be held to account if it were late, if costs blew out or the aircraft failed to meet the performance specifications guaranteed by Lockheed Martin's marketing department.

As the long-range F-111 was due for retirement and most of the RAAF's F/A-18 A/B Hornets were nearing the end of their lives, it was imperative to find a single aircraft type that could conduct the multiple roles required of an expeditionary air force protecting a huge island continent.

Lockheed Martin dominates the stealth jet market and builds two of the three full-stealth aircraft currently flying, the F-22 Raptor and the

F-35 JSF. The Raptor would have been a strong contender, but it was virtually unobtainable under US foreign military sales laws and the Australian Government probably couldn't afford it anyway. With the choices limited, the JSF partnership deal offered by far the greatest industrial opportunity and a quantum leap in technology and capability for Australia.

Some opponents had argued strongly that the life of the F-111 should be extended because it was still a competitive option in the Asia–Pacific air power mix. However, further extending the life of a half-century-old airframe would have been massively expensive and risky.

A longer life had already been granted to the RAAF's fleet of 75 or so classic F/A-18 A/B Hornets through various upgrades, so the then Minister for Defence, Senator Robert Hill, accepted the pro-JSF arguments from Defence and convinced the then Prime Minister John Howard and his cabinet that the new and still experimental American stealth fighter was the way to go.

Air Vice-Marshal John Harvey was the RAAF's 'Mr F-35' between 2002 and 2010, when he left the New Air Combat Capability project office to become Defence's head of capability development. Harvey watched the JSF from its conception as a paper plane to the early test flights in 2010 and he is certain it is right for Australia.

He says the biggest challenge for any project manger is to maintain perspective, to balance, on a daily basis, the swings between optimism and pessimism as the inevitable project issues arise, and to manage negative media by reporting the facts in an honest and balanced manner.

Most negative responses were coming from the F-111 and F-22 lobby. Defence has always been careful not to be too critical of them and former Chief of the Defence Force (CDF), Angus Houston, and others have publicly acknowledged the Raptor as the world's foremost fighter aircraft.

'However, it is basically specialised, it is very expensive and for us, we do think JSF will do the overall job in the best and the most cost-effective way,' Harvey says.

He and the RAAF always had an ace up their sleeves — the positive approach of the partner nations. Defence and the government wanted Australia to get into the fifth-generation jet fighter business and having another eight countries, including its closest allies, the US and UK, and other key partners such as Canada and the Netherlands as well as Denmark, Italy, Norway and Turkey all committed made the decision much easier.

'Instantly, you've got nine countries with the same aircraft making interoperability a lot easier,' he says.

Another key bargaining chip was the global supply chain model that Lockheed was establishing. By mid-2010 about 28 Australian firms had already been contracted for $220-million worth of JSF work and some estimates put the potential value of work for Australia at well over $2 billion. Unlike previous deals where, say, 100 Hornet fighters would be assembled in Australia, under the JSF arrangement local companies would plug into a global supply chain for more than 3000 aircraft.

The global financial crisis upped the competition, but Harvey says, 'We are still working to get some billions of dollars of work on the JSF. There are no guarantees but we are hopeful.'

He is less hopeful that Australia might house a regional support base for future JSF operators in the Asia–Pacific. Early discussions included the possibility but by mid-2010 the gloss was wearing off the idea. He believes other countries, like Australia, will strive for self-reliance when it comes to looking after such a critical asset.

Australia was the last partner to sign up in late 2002 and in 2006 the Howard government finally announced it would place all the RAAF's eggs in the JSF basket. Harvey likens the JSF's capability compared with other available fighters to the scene in the Indiana Jones movie where a ninja displays all his moves to Harrison Ford and then pulls out a knife before the hero nonchalantly takes out his gun and shoots him. The streetfighter's bible says never take a knife to a gunfight.

'Being a stealth aircraft, the things you'd do with the aircraft [JSF] you wouldn't think of doing with current generation aircraft,' he says. 'Attacking rather than running away from SAM [surface-to-air missile] systems, going to attack SAM systems with enemy air out there against you. The JSF can do all that without having to get other aircraft to help. The big thing is, pilots recognise they are stealthy. Just because you can see someone else doesn't mean they can see you. So if there is a threat out there, you point your nose at him rather than turning away.'

The first thing that strikes the novice pilot about the JSF simulator is how incredibly uncluttered it is. It is dominated by a single large screen, no dials, remarkably few switches, a joystick on the right and thrust lever on the left. The screen and helmet-mounted display provide data about everything from bomb and missile loads to maps, targeting information and the 'big picture' battle space.

Lockheed Martin's director of F-35 business development, Stephen O'Bryan, poses a fundamental question: 'Why did we build the F-35? Why not continue to build more fourth-generation aircraft?' The answer is that they did try.

'We did look at fourth-generation assets — F-16s, for instance. We added significant things to it, we continued to upgrade the capability over time, but we reached a point where the asset really couldn't do much more.'

The former US navy pilot spent 20 years flying F/A-18s, including eight years as a reservist. He accumulated 3000 hours including 700 carrier landings, or 'arrestments' that, as he puts it, 'didn't cause any damage to myself or the aircraft'.

In 1999 he joined the Lockheed Martin JSF program but in 2003 he was 'activated' again by the US navy for Operation Iraqi Freedom, flying off the USS *Roosevelt* aircraft carrier. He led a number of strikes, including the first US navy air strike out of the Mediterranean. If there is one thing O'Bryan understands firsthand, it is the importance of stealth.

'I can tell you from my experience, whenever I drop bombs on anybody, they tend to get angry at you,' he says. 'So when you drop them and they explode, you still have to leave the fight. You need to have a stealth signature [of] 360 degrees. One thing we learnt in Desert Storm, Bosnia and Iraqi Freedom is [that] all threats are mobile now, because fixed threats die the first day.

'Put yourself in the adversary's shoes: "I don't know where they are, I know there is stealth out there, I know it's an incredible capability. Do I continue droning ahead or just continue blissfully ignorant or not so blissfully ignorant? Or is it maybe time to go home and call it a day?" Either way, you've accomplished your mission.'

The F-35 also brings a new level of interoperability, something he knows from personal experience is badly needed.

'All the data links are going to be common. Imagine looking at the same picture that the UK coalition partner, the Norwegian coalition partner [is looking at], everybody is exchanging information. We don't have that today and this will provide that much better than any other program.'

The then Labor opposition was initially only lukewarm towards the JSF as a sole capability option and its defence spokesman, Joel Fitzgibbon, strongly favoured the F-22 Raptor. Its tune changed very quickly after it won government in November 2007 when the political difficulties with the US Congress and the massive cost of the F-22 were thrown into stark relief.

Soon after taking office as the Minister for Defence, Fitzgibbon spoke to US Defense Secretary Robert Gates and his American counterpart undertook to lobby the Congress to have the foreign sales ban overturned for Australia. The reality was that Fitzgibbon already knew the JSF was the only option. He says he was always interested in the F-22 Raptor but in the end he was just playing a game to try and improve Australia's bargaining position.

'As it was, we were just a country with no negotiating strength at all,' says Fitzgibbon. 'It was just, "Here is the aircraft, like it or lump it." At that point the JSF was only an experimental aircraft and we had no real idea about price or delivery schedule.'

Despite sitting on opposite sides of the political fence, Fitzgibbon and his coalition government predecessor, Brendan Nelson — who both received all the classified Defence briefings — agree that the JSF is the right capability for Australia.

In marketing terms the decision by Lockheed Martin and the US Department of Defense to open up the JSF project to eight partner countries was a stroke of genius. It was risky, but if they could pull it off they would have a ready-made market and an almost irresistible sales pitch for at least nine other interested nations, including Israel, South Korea, Japan and Singapore.

How best to purchase it and provide best value for money to Australian taxpayers has been a major part of Steve Gumley's job since he became head of the Australian Government's Defence Materiel Organisation (DMO) in 2004. Gumley has been a key player in the global JSF partnership and regards the purchasing model as the catalyst for a huge change in the international defence market.

He says the six-monthly project CEO conferences have allowed the key players to get together to monitor progress and thrash out strategies.

After long involvement with the project as head of the Defence purchasing agency, Gumley says those CEO conferences have been pivotal. 'It's turned into quite a fascinating example of international collaboration … I think the JSF, 20 years from now, will be seen as the project that really caused much greater integration of the global defence market, especially amongst the western democracies.'

All the key players — the JSF Joint Program Office, government representatives from all the partner countries, Lockheed Martin, BAE Systems, Northrop Grumman and the two engine makers — came together at those conferences to report progress. 'So from the point of view of project management, it was a wonderful way of getting everybody to start committing their data on time.'

To data junkies such as Gumley who, due to his engineering background, regards facts as the elixir of life, the conferences were manna from heaven. 'We could … go away with up-to-date information, no more than a week or two old. Looking back on it, [it was] pretty full and frank disclosure.'

It wasn't all about the data. Each country had bilateral discussions with the Americans and less formal and unique networking opportunities, including 'side-bar conversations' over meals, with key people in the program.

'You'd read people's body language when they were talking about problems with the project. You'd know if it was a minor thing or serious thing just by the way they treated it,' Gumley says. 'I know when I got back I had discussions with people back here. I was a strong supporter of the JSF — I still am — but I could see risks developing in the program.'

The unique JSF global partnership model would test the resolve of some of Lockheed Martin's most diplomatic and capable executives and one of the most respected is former US navy Top Gun pilot Tom Burbage.

In 2009 Burbage was the head of the JSF program for Lockheed Martin and the international face of the project, spending much of his time in commercial airliners criss-crossing the globe as he reassured nervous partners that the project was meeting its performance targets and staying on time and on budget.

It is a difficult message to sell in a marketplace littered with the corpses of aerospace executives who have failed to meet their undertakings. After numerous contracting debacles in recent years, the Australians were not alone in taking the promises of American defence contractors with a very large pinch of salt.

It was never going to be easy for Tom Burbage, a personable bloke with a ready smile, to convince nine buyers that his company could pull off the biggest advance in fighter aircraft in decades and sell it at a much lower cost than anything else, with numerous technical and industrial partnerships and billions of dollars of contracts up for grabs.

Retiring with 25 years of US navy service, he worked on Lockheed Martin's F-22 and C-130 programs before moving to Fort Worth and the F-35 in 2000.

'At the very beginning it was all about "How do we staff up a big program, how do we bring on international partners, how do we find roles for the industry to play and how do we design this aeroplane and then how do we refine that design?"' he recalls. 'Then we sort of shifted to, "Okay, now we've designed it, how do we build it?"'

They introduced a whole new way of building the aircraft 'to the engineering' rather than 'to the tool'. 'If you build to the engineering then you have a repeatable process; you can move parts between aeroplanes. If you build to the tool, which we've always done in the past, tools change over time and airplanes become unique.'

In other words, the tolerances for the mostly composite-skinned JSF are so precise that every jet is (and will be) exactly the same as every other.

More than 14,000 people work at the plant and the massive JSF production line is one mile and 25 feet long. The extra 25 feet were paid for by the city of Fort Worth to make it the longest single production line in the US because everything is bigger in Texas.

The shell of the building dates from World War II when it was used to build fighters and bombers, including the AP-3C8 Lightning and Hudson bombers, but everything inside the huge and spotless factory is state of the art. In July 2009 the second JSF for the US navy was moving down the deceptively quiet production line and Lockheed Martin executive George Standridge was as proud as a new dad as he pointed to its folding wings.

'This is the factory of the future; it's a very, very different way of building airplanes ... If I'm going to deliver this asset then the way it comes together is important,' he says as a tour group of wide-eyed school children wanders past. 'Some of those kids will fly this airplane ... because you are talking about something that will be in production and service [for] 30-plus years.'

The JSF comes in three models: the conventional take-off and landing (CTOL) version for the air force, the short take-off and vertical landing (STOVL) aircraft for the marine corps and the aircraft carrier version for the navy. Only the CTOL version is in current Australian planning. For the JSF, production was switched from the traditional horizontal production line to a more vertical system and the company even enlisted the help of Cirque du Soleil to understand how best to operate in the vertical environment. As well as moving along the line, the aircraft move up and down vertically between workstations.

This is a fundamental shift in aircraft production techniques. It required a huge investment from the company to re-tool and reconfigure virtually its entire production line to cater for the minuscule tolerances involved with stealth technology and the huge volumes that would be built when JSF production reached its peak after 2015. Much of the technology is leading edge and developed in the company's own laboratories. This includes robotic finishing, precision fabrication technologies and automated component movement matched to the moving production line.

The state-of-the-art technology is matched with the latest in radars and sensor technology from fellow American giant Northrop Grumman and electronic warfare, vertical landing, fuel system and crew escape technology from the British-based BAE Systems. It will be fitted with a single engine generating 40,000 pounds of thrust — the most powerful engine ever installed in a fighter jet.

According to Standridge, a former US navy pilot with 650 carrier landings under his belt, the main game changer with the JSF was not just the capability but also the economies of scale for smaller users such as Australia.

Standridge believes there are three key elements to the JSF program. First is the plane's true multi-role capability and stealth. Second are the strategic political and military relationships between partner countries. Third is the critical mass that a 3000-plus aircraft project brings to the table.

'That critical mass allows you to upgrade these airplanes throughout their lifetime,' he says.

One of the big challenges as large-scale production loomed and some countries began delaying their final orders was ensuring that the industrial infrastructure matched the volumes of aircraft to be built. By mid-2010 Australia had already signalled that it would delay its final order until further down the production schedule when experts such as Steve Gumley believed the aircraft would probably be cheaper and certainly more reliable. The decision by the Australian Government to buy Super Hornets as capability gap-fillers provided Gumley with an extra bargaining chip.

Whether or not that produces a significantly better deal for Australian taxpayers still remains to be seen, but it will affect the end result. Pricing has always been an extremely complex issue with expensive defence equipment purchased overseas. Exchange rates fluctuate, as does the price for aircraft along the acquisition chain. For example, the first 14 approved by the Rudd Government in early 2010 would be significantly more expensive than the final 14. In addition, there are several organisations calculating prices in different ways and an added complication is whether a contingency is factored in.

The costings are so confusing that Gumley is not surprised that even well-informed commentators have been arguing oranges and apples. Historically, defence projects are costed on the lowest price for political reasons.

Gumley believes the bottom line for 100 JSFs will be an average unit-recurring 'fly away' price of about AU$75 million (at an exchange rate of 0.92 in fiscal year 2008 dollars) per aircraft.

By mid-2010 the project cost was running, by his calculations, between 3 to 4 per cent above where it should have been. He says the big test for Lockheed Martin was whether they would set a fixed price for the jets Australia would buy. 'If they do that then you know the manufacturer now has confidence in the cost of his program. And once the manufacturer goes fixed price, you can actually start to get some confidence that the project is starting to get under control.'

He believed this would happen. He says Australia is only talking about buying 72 JSF aircraft under Phase 2 A/B of the New Air Combat Capability (NACC) project. 'Phase 2C, which hasn't even been considered by government yet, is the final 28 and that links back to how long our future government decides to keep the Super Hornets running.'

The biggest risk to pricing as of mid-2010 was the global financial crisis and its impact on partner countries.

'If the countries start deferring, prices will go up. So any country can cause damage to all its other partners by deferring. Someone has to pay those costs, so if you defer for reasons to save yourself a bit of money and go down the curve, all the people will pay more,' Gumley says. 'So they rush to the back of the queue, then the next person rushes to the back of the queue because his unit price is up. It's quite possible you end up where you started, two years late and everyone paying an extra $5 million for every aircraft just because of the behaviour of the partners.'

Lockheed Martin predicts it will build between 3000 and 4500 JSF aircraft at a maximum rate of about 240 a year during peak production. That is a massive step up from anything achieved outside wartime. The numbers are monumental when compared with the 20 F-22s coming off the Lockheed Martin production line in 2009 and the 42 F/A-18s that Boeing builds each year.

Gumley is confident that in capability the JSF will be a terrific addition for the RAAF but says, 'Just remember, the one limitation on JSF is it has less range than an F-15 or F-111, so that's why the tanker fleet is important to us. It's also why the Vigilare command and control system is important and why Wedgetail, as the eyes in the sky, is important. When you integrate the JSF [as the attack part] with those other air force systems, that's what really makes it a capability. So DMO is going to deliver everything the air force needs. We've got to deliver JSFs, tankers, Vigilare and Wedgetail.'

The JSF program is predicted to deliver 3173 aircraft to nine partner countries with a total budget of US$673 billion. Sustainment costs alone will be US$256 billion and the standard jet will cost US$10,300 an hour to operate.

The year 2009 was pivotal for the JSF because most of the test aircraft were completed and on the flight line. Meanwhile, 2010 and 2011 were to be heavy flight-testing years and Lockheed Martin had logged more than 1000 JSF test hours by the end of 2010.

In June 2009 Tom Burbage was confident enough to predict that the F-35 would quickly gain a reputation and become a modern-day classic.

Two profound and fundamental advances have been made for the pilot of the single-seat JSF aircraft. First, he (or she) will have the element of surprise. Stealth technology makes the jet hard to find and even if a ground controller picked it up visually, sensors looking straight at the aircraft would not see it. Pilots of existing stealth planes such as the Raptor say it is a weird feeling the first time they go up against conventional jets or ground radars and fly right past them undetected.

Second, the sensor systems are highly automated and integrated so the pilot operates inside a bubble of nearly total situational awareness, based around two screens that feature two large and four smaller displays accessible to the pilot in a heartbeat using voice commands.

In the early stages, Lockheed's flight physiologist was concerned that JSF pilots might lose their frame of reference within the actual airframe. Traditionally pilots have maintained a visual frame of reference using the structure of the aircraft. The JSF pilot will receive so much information from so many sources that he or she need never even glance outside the cockpit. Everything the pilot needs to know is displayed on one of two screens and on a helmet-mounted display (HMD) inside their helmet visor, so it remains in sight when the pilot's head is turned.

Another early fear was that JSF pilots might become disoriented when flying low and fast without an external visual reference, but Burbage says the opposite is the case.

'The guys love to fly with this system, low and fast, because you are seeing everything around you as you go,' he says. 'The level of detail these sensors can detect now is really incredible and we are flying them … so we have a level of maturity in our sensors and software that we've never had before.'

The JSF has also turned the relationship between ground- and flight-testing on its head. The company achieved a 'static stall test' on the aircraft in just 350 days compared with 1000 days for the F-22 and the F/A-18.

The static stall is the speed at which an aircraft's wings cease to have the forward momentum to maintain lift and they 'stall' or stop flying.

That means the JSF's flight envelope for stall (the safe limits of speed, altitude and acceleration) was fully opened before flight-testing even began. In the past that envelope was opened incrementally and test aircraft could only fly to a certain point before the next increment was opened.

Thanks to early investments in integrated lab facilities and a flying test-bed called a catbird (a heavily modified Boeing 737 that carries a complete JSF cockpit and all the systems), Lockheed is now achieving world-leading performance figures. For the first time, it can test all the JSF systems simultaneously. This will have a flow-on effect for customer nations who benefit from lower testing costs.

Maintenance is another area where the JSF tests traditional thinking. Traditionally, if an air force removes a part to get it repaired by a manufacturer, then it wants that same part back.

'That is not the way we are going to do this aeroplane,' Burbage says. 'This aeroplane will maintain a global parts pool and you shouldn't really care. If you are contracting with me to make sure eight of your 10 jets are ready to fly every morning and eight of the 10 jets are ready to fly every morning, you should be happy no matter what part is in it.'

JSF owners will have to dramatically alter their mindset about wanting to 'own' everything and think laterally when it comes to operating the Joint Strike Fighter. Burbage believes the JSF could trigger a revolution in how future coalition air operations are run. He says that if all contributing nations were JSF operators, there would be nothing to prevent them from deploying a 'coalition' squadron and rotating pilots from all the nations through that squadron, rather than every country taking their own aircraft to the fight.

'It certainly could be done and if I had 30 or 40 F-35s at some operating base I could just fund it with contributions from coalition partners, rotate pilots through but leave the same aeroplanes there,' he says. 'If the aeroplanes need to be changed up, change them up but change them as part of the operation, not as country "X" comes in and brings six aeroplanes.'

Whether nations such as Australia would allow their pilots to fly another country's aircraft under such an arrangement would be highly controversial but with up to 20 countries potentially flying the JSF, interoperability is destined be a strong feature of future coalition air operations around the globe.

Officer in command of the AP-3C Orion maritime patrol aircraft detachment in the Middle East in November 2009, Squadron Leader Roy Philpott with one of the RAAF's highly capable surveillance platforms at Al Minhad air base. *PHOTO IAN McPHEDRAN*

Commanding officer of the RAAF detachment to Joint Task Force 633 at Al Minhad air base near Dubai in November 2009, Group Captain Gary Martin, with a map showing the key air bases around the Middle East Area of Operations. *PHOTO IAN McPHEDRAN*

Then Chief of Air Force Air Marshal Mark Binskin (right) prepares for a familiarisation flight on board a US Air Force F-15 Eagle. *PHOTO ADF*

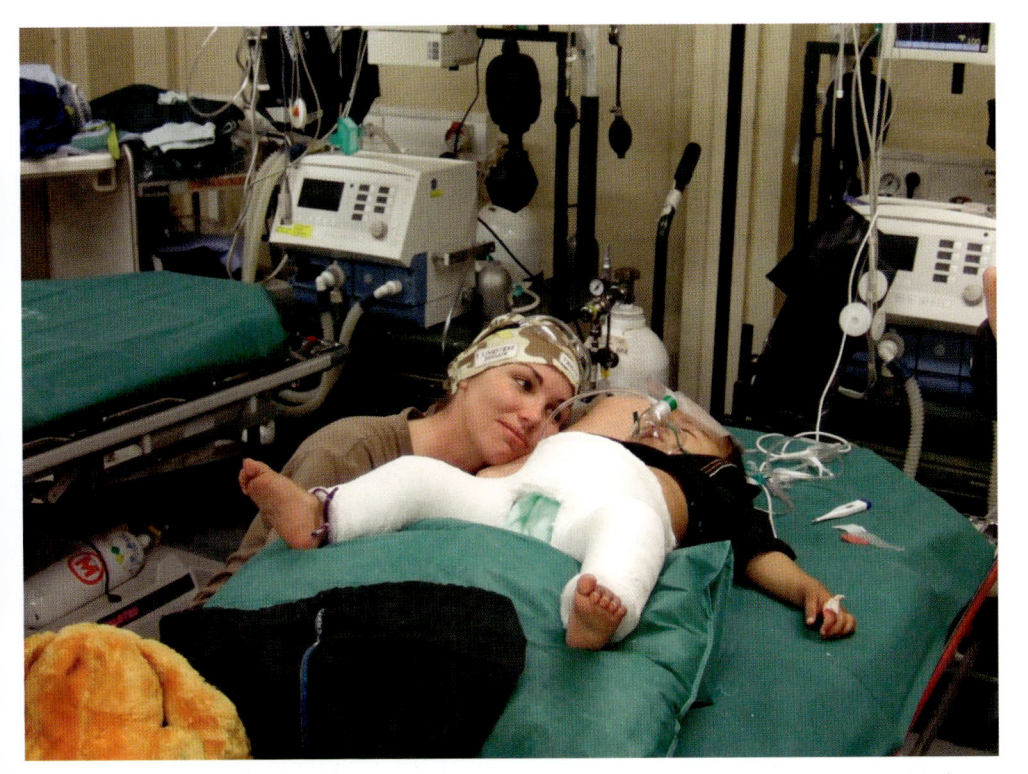

RAAF intensive care nurse, Flight Lieutenant Leigh Stalling, keeps a close eye on a seriously hurt Afghan youngster at the Dutch-run Role 2 field hospital at Camp Russell near Tarin Kowt. *PHOTO ADF*

Medical staff Corporal Ayse Anderson and Squadron Leader Nadia Wilson at the RAAF Expeditionary Health Facility at Al Minhad. *PHOTO IAN McPHEDRAN*

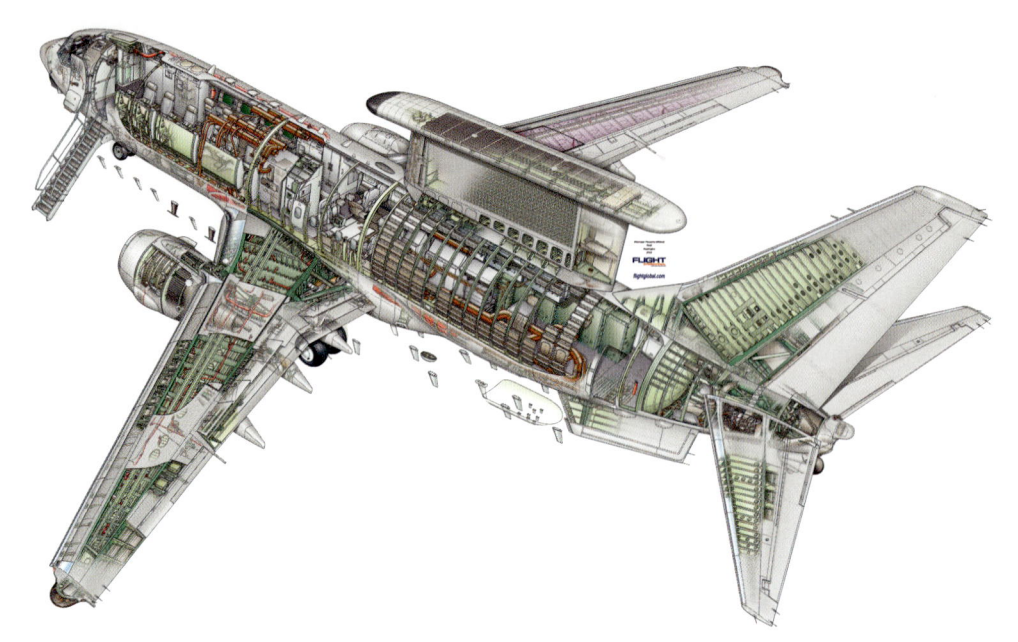

A cutaway drawing of a Wedgetail Airborne Early Warning and Control Aircraft showing its myriad of sensors and antennae that will make it the most effective airborne radar platform in the sky. *ARTWORK COURTESY FLIGHT INTERNATIONAL*

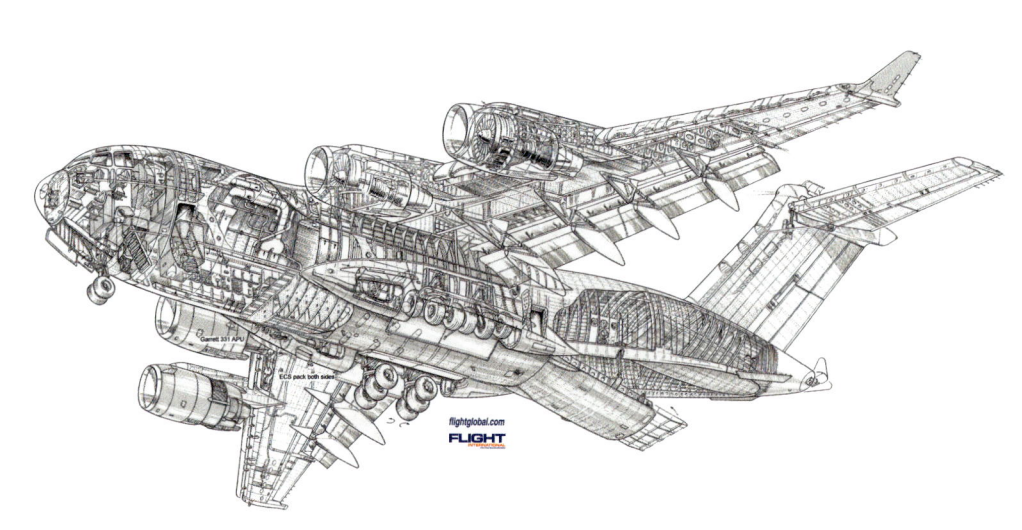

A true giant of the skies, the Boeing C-17 Globemaster jet transport aircraft. The cutaway drawing gives an insight into the complexity of a modern-day heavy airlifter. The RAAF purchased four of the C-17s under a seamless rapid acquisition deal. *ARTWORK COURTESY FLIGHT INTERNATIONAL*

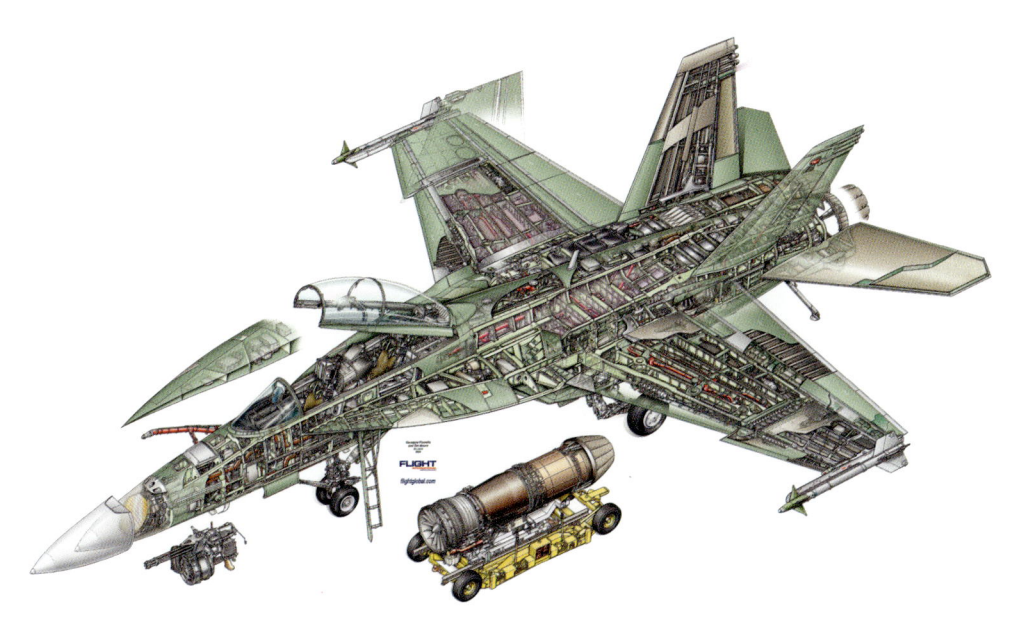

This cutaway of a Boeing F/A-18F Super Hornet provides a unique insight into the sheer power of the RAAF's latest multi-role fighter aircraft. *ARTWORK COURTESY FLIGHT INTERNATIONAL*

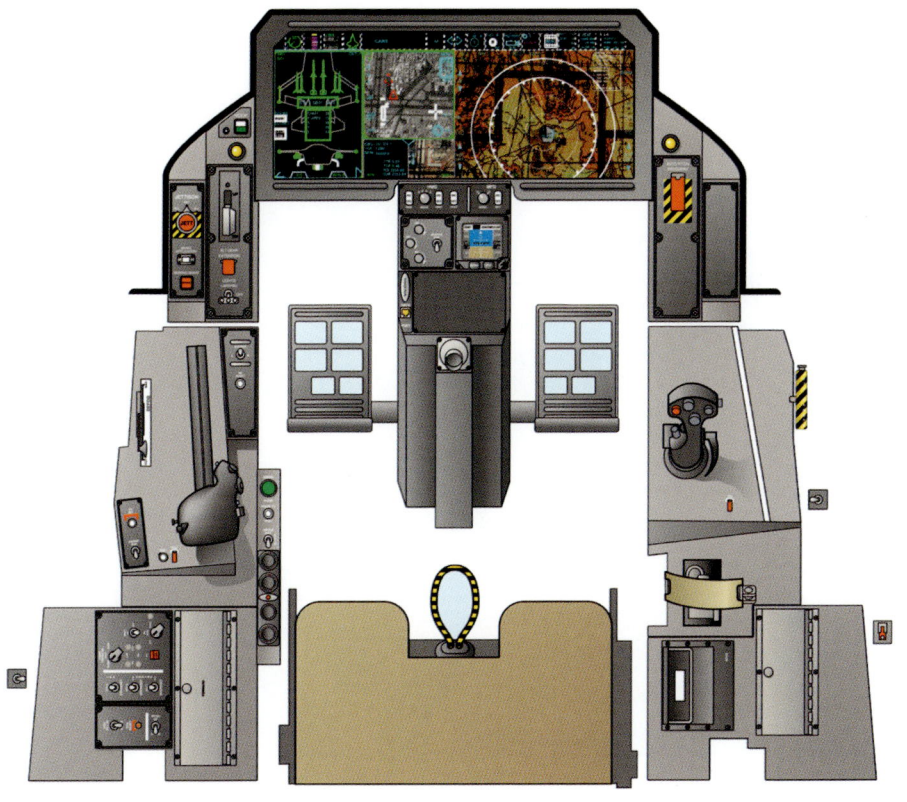

This drawing of the cockpit of a Joint Strike Fighter shows just how uncluttered the workspace for the next generation of RAAF fighter pilots will be. *ARTWORK COURTESY FLIGHT INTERNATIONAL*

Unmanned Aerial Vehicles (UAVs) are set to dominate the future air-battle space. One of the first long-range, high-altitude multi-role surveillance aircraft was Northrop Grumman's Global Hawk shown here at Edwards Air Force base in California. Ideally suited to Australian conditions, the Global Hawk is still under consideration for future service with the RAAF. *PHOTO IAN McPHEDRAN*

RAAF F/A-18F Super Hornet pilots Flight Lieutenant John Haly, Wing Commander Glen Braz and Commanding Officer of 82 Wing Group Captain Steve Roberton, with a US navy jet at the Lemoore Naval Air Station near Fresno in California. Australian pilots and maintainers conducted conversion training at the base. *PHOTO IAN McPHEDRAN*

A RAAF F/A-18 Hornet fighter leaving terra firma under full afterburner with both engines generating about 17,000 pounds of thrust. *PHOTO RAAF*

An F-35 Joint Strike Fighter aircraft on the production line at the state-of-the-art Lockheed Martin factory at Fort Worth, Texas. *PHOTO IAN McPHEDRAN*

A RAAF F/A-18F Super Hornet fighter jet creates its own vapour cloud as it executes a high 'G' banking turn during a low level training flight. *PHOTO ADF*

The author with an SR71 Blackbird at a museum near Eglin air force base in Florida. The Blackbird holds the record for the fastest speed by an air-breathing aircraft at 3500 km/hr. *PHOTO ANDREW McLAUGHLIN*

Chapter 29

TEST PILOTS

UFO spotters spend a lot of time in the Mojave desert north of Los Angeles hoping for 'sightings' of strange flying objects. The most productive time is after dark and they are more likely to hear rather than see unusual activity in the skies. But these are not visitors from another galaxy — rather, they are the latest military aircraft being flight-tested by US aerospace companies and the government.

Much of the trialling of new top-secret aviation technology is carried out at night, with lights blacked out, and the Palmdale facility and the Edwards Air Force Base further out in the desert in California have been crucial test locations since the 1950s.

Test pilots are a breed apart. Their input into any new aircraft project is crucial, but when that aircraft is set to alter fundamentally the way whole air forces do business, the test pilot's role takes on global significance.

Jon Beesley is one of the world's most experienced military test pilots. A former US air force fighter pilot, he is the chief test pilot with Lockheed Martin's Joint Strike Fighter project. In his long career he has logged more than 5500 flying hours on 50 different aircraft.

Growing up on a potato farm in south-eastern Idaho, he dreamed of flying. He had an uncle who had fought in World War II as a young fighter pilot and was killed in Italy in February 1945 after flying for just 18 months.

'I've always been close to airplanes. It's an interesting thing to have happen to you when you live in Idaho and you raise potatoes. But I always wanted to do that,' says Beesley, now an affable, down-to-earth father of six and grandfather of 14.

When it comes to stealth aircraft Beesley, who was also a US air force test pilot and operations officer on the top-secret F-117 Nighthawk stealth fighter project at Edwards Air Force Base, has probably flown more hours in so-called 'low observable' aircraft than any other pilot.

He spent two years testing the F-117 in what he calls the 'black hole' because of the secrecy.

'When someone asked me what I do, I would say "I fly aeroplanes" and then I would say, "What do you do?" Then I didn't have to talk again because they would normally start unloading about what they did,' Beesley says. 'It was hardest on the families because they didn't know. They knew we were doing things. I'd been here a couple of years when I called my wife and said, "Look on TV, that's what I was doing." That was after it was announced — and I'd been there two years before it was announced.'

To most outsiders the word 'excitement' probably sums up their view of the life of a test pilot. Hollywood movies such as *The Right Stuff* about test pilots involved in the early space program, including the legendary Chuck Yeager, have glamorised the job. The reality is very different for a test pilot strapped into an aircraft for its first test flight. They are very experienced pilots with thousands of hours of flying behind them, but it takes extra courage to test the envelope of a brand-new aeroplane that could literally fall out of the sky.

In 2000 Beesley was presented with the Chuck Yeager Award for his career achievements as a test pilot. He says his job is exciting all right, but those nervous first flights are the pinnacle of years of hard work.

On 15 December 2006 he became the first pilot ever to fly an F-35 Joint Strike Fighter (JSF).

'For four and a half years before we flew the flight we were very much involved in literally thousands and thousands of hours of simulations,' he says. 'There isn't really an opportunity in this business to go back and fix everything that you might not like. Therefore, you get engaged early so that it gets done right the first time, or as close as you possibly can. Fixing stuff is very expensive. And so the test pilots have been involved for five or six years in every aspect of the airplane making sure that things were the way they should be and the airplane flew the way it should.'

They trained with the team of control engineers and before flying the aircraft they went through a series of engine runs with the entire team involved.

'Then ultimately you go out to go for a flight in a single-seat airplane with 5000 of your best friends watching,' he says.

Before lifting the jet off terra firma Beesley had taxied it up to 120 knots (222 kilometres per hour) several times on the ground. He says his most important job during the first flight of a new jet is to pay 'real close attention'.

'As opposed to the people who were watching, I was pretty busy,' he says. 'When you get in these situations, you really have to grab hold of yourself and detach yourself because you can't lose focus. Probably the most interesting part is when the airplane comes off the ground. You really want to make sure it's not going to do the "funky chicken" about 10 feet into the air. Up till then it's very good theory, but nonetheless it's theory.'

During the first flight a caution message was received just before take-off. 'We had to figure that out — and that took an aeon, probably a tenth of a second to figure out — were we going to go flying?'

Beesley has never had to pull an ejection lever to explode out of a cockpit and for that he is very grateful. 'There's nothing sporty about them. They're pretty violent things.'

He says things would have to go very, very wrong before he would decide to eject. 'Ejection systems are interesting, in that you use them because if you don't, you're gonna die.'

Beesley's attraction to the job extends far beyond fascination with speed or danger. Like most people who have hazardous jobs he is much more interested in the detail — in his case, about why a particular aeroplane will be safe for him to fly — and in problem-solving.

'I keep learning. And that's the fun of it,' he says. 'It's really fascinating to work with really bright people because difficult problems are solved. Impossible things take a bit longer but the amazing thing is they are solved.'

Apart from the take-off the next most important thing about any flight is the landing. Nothing is left to chance during testing so all first flights are conducted with the landing gear deployed.

'The reason you don't raise the gear is because you've already got one problem [getting off the ground] so don't compound it and have another one,' Beesley says. 'The very first thing you do is you fly around with the gear down at different speeds and make sure the airplane's good to land. That's really what the focus of the first flight is.'

Each test flight expands the performance envelope in small increments, increasing airspeed and altitude until it is ready for a mid-air refuel and then it is a matter of ticking boxes until the entire flight envelope is certified safe to fly.

'All of these airplanes are innately unstable,' he explains. 'Left to their own devices they'll just pitch up and depart. There is no stable place for the airplane really, in many respects. We control them very tightly, so we have a very controllable, wonderfully flying airplane. But if you ever just turned off the flight control system it wouldn't just generally glide, it would pitch up or do something crazy. The thing you've got to watch very carefully is [that] the airplane feels very, very good, very, very good, very, very good and then it falls off the edge. And off the edge is where you run out of control.'

Beesley says one of the F-35's biggest advances was something they addressed early on. 'In the early days of the F-16 they referred to it as the electric chair … because it was the first airplane where the pilot grabbed on the stick and pulled and it wasn't actually hooked into any controls. He was hooked to a brain, an electric brain, and that told the controls what to do. Very different. Well, where we've gone is really another step and we now have not only an electric brain but [also] electric muscle. We have 270-volt power going out. So, as it turns out, fortuitously,

"Lightning" is a marvellous name for this aircraft. Because it really is an electric airplane.'

Beesley believes the RAAF pilots who are selected to fly the F-35 JSF will be in for a rare treat.

'I think they'll be very impressed with the performance and how easy it is to fly,' he says. 'They're going to find the cockpit a very friendly place. It will become easier for them and the reason for that is so they can think and make decisions.'

For US marine pilot Major Joseph 'OD' Bachmann, that decision-making time will be a luxury after years spent flying the Harrier jump jet, a notoriously difficult aircraft to pilot with the reputation of a 'widow maker'. The marines will be the first of the three US services to get the new stealth fighter.

Bachmann is the US government pilot for the F-35 Integrated Test Team and in his career he has accrued more than 2000 hours' flight time in more than 30 aircraft types. He flew two operational tours during the 2003 Iraq War.

Unlike the Harrier, the new jet is 'fly by wire' so there are no hydraulic or mechanical controls. The old system made the Harrier a brute to fly whereas the JSF requires a lot less energy from the pilot.

'That means more time spent actually executing the mission, which is killing the bad guy,' Bachmann says.

Beesley says the focus was on making flying the jet as natural as backing a car out of a garage. 'You don't give much thought to it. You pay attention, but the purpose of your trip is to drive the car some place and do something and come back,' he says.

Graham 'GT' Tomlinson is probably one of the most experienced vertical landing jet pilots on the planet. The former Royal Air Force Harrier pilot is chief test pilot with BAE Systems, a key partner in the JSF program, and has more time than any other pilot in the short take-off and vertical landing (STOVL) variant of the JSF, which Australia is not planning to buy. The easy-going Yorkshireman says the JSF is a much more complex aircraft than the Harrier, but much easier to fly and definitely safer.

'Whatever the [JSF] pilot tries to do he can't get into trouble. It is so close to being completely foolproof that a pilot is going to have to work exceptionally hard to kill himself.'

To Tomlinson, the ease of flight, situational awareness and stealth are the key attributes. 'You are aware of what is going on around you. The mission isn't just hugely more effective, it is [also] hugely easier. Stealth means you can throw things at the bad guy before he even knows you are there. Once the threat is eliminated then the need for stealth is eliminated.'

The stealth capability means that in any future conflict, instead of waiting for the air force to take out ground threats, the JSF could fly from aircraft carriers on day one, virtually invisible to enemy radars and so largely immune to missile threats. This is a major change to the power projection balance, providing a huge strategic advantage.

Former US air force fighter pilot David 'Doc' Nelson and ex-navy Top Gun Jeff 'Slim' Knowles both found testing the next generation of jet fighter a natural fit after lengthy and distinguished military careers.

Nelson has more than 4700 hours of flying time in 48 aircraft types and was the first operational test pilot for the F-22 Raptor and the third to fly an F-35 JSF. Knowles was Lockheed's chief test pilot on the F-117 Nighthawk program and is lead test pilot on the US navy's aircraft carrier version of the F-35 jet. Both men describe the JSF as a 'powerful and nimble' aircraft and extremely easy to fly.

'It likes to get up and go. It's a nice-handling airplane,' Knowles says. 'It's very nimble, kind of how you wanted your fighter aeroplane to handle, I guess. You know, [with] previous airplanes we didn't always have the luxury of electronic flight controls being able to modify the way the airplane handles, to make it meet your needs.'

Knowles says, 'Take a guy, a carrier pilot, and take him out to the simulator. After a couple of landings he'll be smiling, because it's going to be easy. Not too many other airplanes you can say that about, that it's easy to land on a ship. Now on a dark night it may not be so easy because nothing is, but … you're going to take some of the risk away from a young guy out there at night trying to find a ship and land on it, because we're making it easy to fly.'

Nelson says the most exciting thing about the JSF project is the fact that the US will be able to have an aircraft carrier full of stealth aeroplanes projecting power to wherever it needs to be projected.

That alone will change the face of modern warfare.

Nelson is a big fan of stealth. 'There are two people who really believe in stealth. One of them is the guy who flies the stealth airplane, and I can vouch for that. The other one is the guy who flies against it and tries to find it. Both of them get a sense that stealth really works. It's like boxing with a guy with a blindfold on.'

The former air force ace says the performance of the JSF is incredible. 'It has one engine and the engine makes about the same thrust as both F-15 engines made. You take off on [afterburner] and you fly them pretty much straight up, at least at a really steep angle,' he says. 'You carry the weapons internally, so whether it's got a full bomb load or it's empty, it will go right up against Mach 1 in pretty much a heartbeat. Other airplanes are fast and handle well if they are clean, but if you hang bombs, tanks or missiles on them, then that slows them down. So this internal bomb carriage is a significant big deal and that enables the stealth.'

Six core test pilots work on the JSF program and between them have experience on every allied jet fighter flown during the past 20 years. They are supplemented by overseas pilots such as Graham Tomlinson, but their diversity means that they can cater for the needs of all the pilots coming to the JSF from 'legacy' aircraft such as Harriers, F-16s and FA-18s.

'If their airplane did something, then our airplane has to do it too or else they're unhappy,' Nelson says.

The test pilots love to watch newcomers on the simulator flying missions they could never have dreamed of in their legacy planes, simply because they could not have flown safely into situations that the JSF can get into.

'We put them in the simulator for about three days of training and by the end of two weeks they've been successful at air-to-air and air-to-ground missions that their legacy airplane cannot do because it's just too easy to be attacked,' Nelson says. 'We can configure their radar cross-section in the simulator to be their legacy airplane and have them fly those same missions. I think that's when they are impressed. They can't do it [on their legacy aircraft].'

He says the big challenge for pilots stepping up from FA-18s or F-16s to the JSF is not in the actual flying of an aircraft with incredible thrust that handles like a sports car, but the amount of information. The JSF stick and throttle have exactly twice the number of switch positions as an F-16 and the pilot has 12 screens of information literally available at his or her command.

'To me the risk was, how are we going to fuse all these things to make it digestible to a simple-minded pilot's brain? And I think we've done it,' he says.

As for the job of test pilot, both men agree it is like living out a childhood dream.

'You know, I think that if all we did was come to work and fly it'd be hard to call it a job. It would be really embarrassing to get paid. But they let us have a few meetings to go to so that we'll have some self-esteem,' says Nelson with a laugh.

It has been an iterative process over the years with many meetings and working groups with operational pilots, nutting out problems and making compromises.

With well over 100 JSF flights between them, both Nelson and Knowles had developed a great fondness for a jet that they believe will be loved by its pilots and become one of history's great warplanes.

Knowles says, 'If it comes to fruition and we sell 3000 airplanes and populate however many air forces across the world, then it will go down as one of the big ones.'

Chapter 30

SUPER HORNET

If there is one aspect of the pre-flight briefing to which a nervous civilian pays very close attention before taking a ride in a jet fighter, it is the part about ejecting.

So when United States Navy Super Hornet pilot Lieutenant Christian 'Wink' Lockwood says, 'Now if we hit a bird and I am unconscious …' it is the cue to listen up and to learn about the yellow and red handle located between your legs.

'You need to remove this pin, turn this knob and pull this handle. Put your chin up and clench your elbows close to your body before you do it. You will go out first and I will follow 0.25 seconds later,' he says, with the confidence of a 29-year-old Top Gun pilot with 310 aircraft carrier landings and 1500 flying hours in an F/A-18F Super Hornet under his belt.

Confidence is seldom lacking in fighter pilots and you know Lockwood is on his game when he says there is no better feeling than taking off from a carrier in a Super Hornet on a dark and stormy night in the middle of the ocean, knowing that the only place on earth where you can land the $100 million machine is back on that small strip of bobbing steel.

'That is cool,' he says.

Lockwood was at the 2009 Australian International Airshow at Avalon near Geelong as part of Boeing's global roadshow to demonstrate the F/A-18F Super Hornet to existing and potential customers. A long list of RAAF pilots, from then Chief of Air Force, Air Marshal Mark Binskin, down and a small number of very lucky reporters, were slotted to take to the skies above western Victoria in one of two US navy demonstration Super Hornets.

The Howard government had signed up to buy 24 of the fighters in a $6 billion deal to fill any gaps between the retirement of the F-111 fleet and the arrival of the F-35 Joint Strike Fighter (JSF). The purchase was widely criticised at the time but with likely delays already appearing with JSF the Super Hornets, known as 'Rhinos', would ensure Australia's airpower needs were not compromised during the 2010–2015 period.

After squeezing a less-than-toned 52-year-old body into the largest flying suit as well as a G-suit, a G-tube and a portal harness, the next step is to be shoehorned into the rear seat of the two-seater jet. There are greetings from a line-up of high-fiving ground crew, some wearing a knowing grin, and then it is into a cockpit that is remarkably spacious and built for big folks. The harness includes ankle and thigh straps as well as a four-point lap-and-shoulder restraint.

After strapping in, it is time to find the one and only piece of equipment that might save two lives — the ejection handle. An excited passenger's sweaty hand tends never to wander far from it.

Outside, the smell of the jet exhaust fumes and deafening roar of the engines fuel the excitement of the crowds who line the runways. Inside, the air is pure and it is surprisingly quiet as we taxi out, thanks to the well-insulated headphones inside the flying helmet, where the noise is more of a background hum so that the voices on the radio come through loud and clear.

With the oxygen flowing and Lockwood's calm voice feeding gentle instructions through the intercom, the jet heads out to the active runway to begin the ride of a lifetime.

The issue of acceleration had been discussed during the pre-flight briefing but no words can adequately prepare you for the moment that the throttles are opened on the twin General Electric F414-GE-400 turbofans that can each produce 22,000 pounds of thrust with afterburner (where fuel is injected into the jet pipe 'after' the turbine to generate maximum thrust for supersonic flight, carrier take-offs or combat manoeuvres).

When the throttles are opened the noise through the headphones builds to a dull roar. This awesome amount of raw power launches two human beings and 14 tonnes of jet fighter off the deck with astonishing speed. Within seconds the jet has hit 162 knots (300 kilometres per hour) and is airborne, producing an interesting sensation of having your stomach wrapped around your spine.

The hour-long flight includes a comprehensive demonstration of the jet's capabilities including turns, loops and stalls up to 7.5 Gs, or seven-and-a-half-times the force of gravity.

At this point a novice passenger experiences eye flutter and can lose consciousness as the face is contorted and limbs feel as if they are glued to the seat. The G-suit inflates and deflates up and down the lower half of the body as the Gs kick in, to maintain blood flow and prevent unconsciousness.

Despite the knowing grins of the ground crew, the cockpit remains free of stomach contents on this flight.

Lockwood obtains an air traffic clearance for a run past Victoria's famed Twelve Apostles at 500 feet and about 324 knots (600 kilometres per hour). He had driven along the Great Ocean Road with his wife a few days earlier — a drive that takes about an hour — and was keen to see the famous rock formations from the air. Following a sinus-clogging descent from 15,000 to 500 feet in a matter of seconds, the rugged coastline and the apostles offer an incredible, if short-lived, sight through the bubble canopy of the speeding jet fighter.

As we zoom along the coastline, a sightseeing helicopter gets more than its passengers bargained for as it flies directly below the speeding jet. Then it's back up to 20,000 feet for the brief return flight, which takes just a few minutes.

Lockwood executes a silky-smooth landing and we taxi back to the Boeing facility where we are greeted by the expectant ground crew, who at least get the satisfaction of watching this passenger's legs buckle slightly at the bottom of the ladder.

The Boeing rep is also waiting there with a glossy photo of the grinning passenger taken pre-flight, rather like family snaps taken at a theme park, except that no thrill ride can measure up to an hour in the back seat of a Super Hornet.

The last Minister for Defence in the Howard government, Brendan Nelson, who himself had been for a joy flight in a Super Hornet in 2007, was almost single-handedly responsible for the acquisition of 24 of the jets for the RAAF.

Nelson, who served as the minister from 2006 to 2007, endured savage criticism for the decision, but with the F-111 fleet heading for retirement and blowouts looming in the cost and delivery schedule for the futuristic F-35 Joint Strike Fighter, he felt a deep responsibility to insure the nation against any gaps in its air defence.

Effective air power, particularly above the so-called 'sea-air gap' to the continent's north, is vital to Australia's national defence.

'I thought under no circumstances am I going to tolerate, or allow to be tolerated on my watch, the prospect that we carry a gap in air combat capability,' Nelson recalls. 'In terms of how you covered, how much you covered that gap, I looked at a number of things. I said, "Can you lease aircraft from somebody, can you borrow aircraft from another friendly country? What can we do?" There were very limited options, but the obvious one was Super Hornet.'

Nelson had been reassured on many occasions by senior air force officers that there would be no 'gap' and that the F-111s and classic F/A18 Hornets could carry the load well into 2013. However, with growing delays to vital pieces of the air defence puzzle, including Wedgetail Airborne Early Warning and Control (AEWAC) aircraft, Airbus A330 multi-role transport tankers, the troubled network-centric command and control system known as Project Vigilare and new missiles, the then minister felt compelled to act.

He recalls returning from the Northern Territory to Canberra on a Challenger VIP jet with the then Chief of the Defence Force, Air Chief Marshal Angus Houston, in April 2006. Nelson had already raised the possibility of a 'gap' with Houston and other top brass, but was not confident about their commitment to a Plan B.

'I said to him, "Look, I'm worried about this complex capability. I'm convinced the Joint Strike Fighter is the right aircraft for Australia ... but I'm very worried about all of this coming together on time,"' Nelson says. 'I [had] also come to appreciate [that] the biggest threat for the Joint Strike Fighter was not technology, nor the ability of Lockheed Martin to deliver — in fact, in many ways you could have more confidence in the Joint Strike Fighter coming in on time because many of those issues had been resolved with the F-22 Raptor — but my concern was that it had the potential to be held hostage in the US Congress and US political system in terms of financing for the program.'

Nelson felt strongly that Congress wanted to keep the production line at Lockheed open for the Raptor. If that happened, he believed it could come at the expense of the JSF and therefore Australia.

'While we are a very important ally to the US, in the end the US understandably is going to look after the US. So I had this conversation with Angus and I said, "I'm also very worried about Wedgetail." At that stage I wasn't really fully aware of just what the problems were that were emerging, but I was getting a feel for it. And at that stage I think Wedgetail was 24 months late, or 22 months late and Vigilare was also late, I think at that stage about two years, and Angus said to me, "Well look, we can keep the F-111s flying."

'Typical of military people — if there is a problem, well, "How can we deal with it?" So, you know, he was reassuring me we could tolerate a three-year delay with Wedgetail and Vigilare and that the F-111s could be kept flying beyond 2012.

'I said to Angus, "I am not going to go to Washington at the end of this year [2006] and sign the production sustainment follow-through and development [memorandum of understanding] on the Joint Strike Fighter until I am absolutely satisfied of two things. The first is that we've got a good industry participation program developed and signed off by the Americans for Australian industry and the second is I want to see the fully developed, fully costed contingent option if, for some reason, we face some sort of gap and we can cover it."

'Angus said to me, "Oh, Minister, don't worry, that's all done. We would go for Super Hornet." Obviously, I knew by that stage what the Super Hornet was, and I said "OK, well, I still want to see it. I want to see all the documentation and want to see it costed." And they gave me sufficient material to satisfy me and — this conversation I subsequently had with Geoff 'Shep' Shepherd who was Chief of Air Force — there was no doubt in the mind of our RAAF. If there was a problem, they would go to Super Hornet.'

In mid-2006, then Prime Minister John Howard was going to Washington and he requested detailed briefings from Nelson on key defence issues. The minister was shocked to find that the Defence briefs mentioned another six-month delay to the Boeing Wedgetail project, blowing it out to 28 months behind schedule. From there he dug more deeply to uncover the extent of the problem. During this time the F-111 fleet suffered two serious setbacks including an airborne fire emergency and alarm bells began to ring loudly in the minister's mind.

In July, Nelson met with Shepherd and asked him straight out, 'How long can we fly these F-111s?'

Nelson recalls Shepherd saying, 'No later than mid-2012.' The 2004 decision to withdraw the F-111s from service at the end of 2010 had already resulted in a wind-down of maintenance spares and the like.

'I'm thinking, well, with Vigilare [and] Wedgetail, issues were also emerging with [F/A-18] centre barrels … and I was starting to get nervous about the delays that were emerging. At the same time you've got the political machinations in the US Congress and the US Senate,' Nelson says.

His next stop was Washington for meetings with then US Defense Secretary Donald Rumsfeld and other key players including the head of Boeing Defense, Jim Albaugh.

During an at times robust exchange, an angry Nelson, fed up with Boeing's excuses, said to Albaugh, 'What do you want me to say to the Australian public, [to] Australian taxpayers?'

Albaugh admitted to Nelson that Boeing had let Australia down. The company had informed the markets just that morning that it was taking a $400 million write-down on Wedgetail.

'I said to Jim, "Look, my first priority is to get capability, it is not about liquidated damages, it is not about anything like that. My first priority is to get the capability. You've got to get the right people working on this project, you've got to put significant resources into it because it is a reputational issue for you, let alone the issues we have as a customer",' Nelson says.

The last question at the joint press conference with Rumsfeld at the Pentagon later that day was about Wedgetail and Nelson did not spare the giant American company.

'We are very disappointed with Boeing's performance on this project,' he said. 'I think Boeing has let the Australian government down, and I think they've let themselves down.'

In the aftermath of this unprecedented public attack, Boeing undertook to throw the required resources at the Wedgetail project and when, a year later, the newly elected Rudd government immediately named the company as number one on its defence industry shame file, the project received even more focus and was eventually delivered in 2010.

Back in Canberra, Nelson met again with Shepherd who, he says, told him the F-111s could now be flown for an extra year if necessary to mid-2013. This was just six weeks after he had said that 2012 was the absolute deadline.

Says Nelson, 'I thought to myself, "Hang on, there is a conspiracy of optimism at play here!" I said to him, "Six weeks ago you said we couldn't fly them any later than mid-2012. Now you are saying 2013." He said, "No, no minister, we can do that."'

'It's part of the character of Defence [to say] "We can do it." And I thought, "Right, these guys are desperate to make absolutely sure, that no one, no outsider, particularly no minister is going to fiddle, start playing with all the tapestry of the new air combat capability!"'

By now Nelson's interest in the Super Hornet had become very strong as he saw the probability of an air combat capability gap emerging before his eyes and on his watch. He told the then chairman of Boeing Australia, former Liberal leader Andrew Peacock, to start 'sharpening your pencils' on Super Hornet.

Nelson is adamant that up to that point no one from Boeing had even raised the possibility of Australia buying the US navy aircraft. He then raised his concerns with then Prime Minister John Howard and presented a detailed 'layman's' analysis of Australia's likely air combat outcomes between 2006 and 2020. Howard was concerned and bluntly asked Nelson what he wanted to do about it.

'I said, "I think we are going to have to buy a squadron of Super Hornets. And he said "Okay, get it ready and bring it to cabinet."'

By early December 2006 Nelson had in-principle support to buy 24 of the fighters for a through-life cost in excess of $6 billion. He again went to Washington to sign the JSF agreement and to tell Lockheed Martin's senior JSF executive, Tom Burbage, of the government's intention to have a serious look at purchasing the Boeing fighters. His plan was to buy the Super Hornets, sell them back to the US navy in 2020 and go to the fourth squadron of Joint Strike Fighters, provided everything else went to plan.

Nelson knew the news would leak quickly so he called the *Australian Financial Review* from Washington to announce his plan. By March 2007 he had the deal fully costed and was convinced that the risk of a 'gap' was too high a gamble.

'Having had the full classified briefing of the Super Hornet, this was no "dog of an aircraft", as its critics were describing it. It's obviously got active electronically scanned radar — it is a serious, serious aircraft.'

Nelson was disappointed that some senior people in the air force did not go out and sell the plan to buy 24 Super Hornets as robustly as he would have liked.

He gained a better understanding during a dinner in Melbourne in

March 2007 when he asked Geoff Shepherd whether he was happy with the government's decision. He recalls Shepherd saying that he was over the moon. The military had not believed Nelson could win extra resources to cover the $6.6 billion project cost. They were worried the money would be diverted from other air force budgets.

Shepherd left the Defence minister in no doubt that the RAAF feared a possible 50/50 split between Super Hornets and Joint Strike Fighters and that it might lose the fourth squadron of JSFs.

Nelson says, 'No one ever said it to me, but I think they were a bit miffed that I'd interfered with everything ... but when I got down to the pilot level I didn't strike any of them. There were some who were naturally sad about the retirement of F-111 but I didn't strike any of the pilots, our pilots flying now, who were anything other than enthusiastic about it.

'Steve Gumley said to me after we lost the election and I was cleaning out my desk, "Brendan, of all the decisions you have made, the one that will prove to be the most important for this country will be the Super Hornet decision."'

The idea of a gap-filler had begun to play on Gumley's mind when the JSF's weight problems started to surface late in 2004. The head of the Defence Materiel Organisation (DMO) knew that removing that weight from the fighter would inevitably prolong the production schedule. The F-111 retirement issue was bubbling along as well. 'And so it became clear, by about early 2006, that we couldn't leave Australia with an air capability gap.'

Nelson immediately seemed to spot the issue.

'I remember us going over to brief him and explaining to him about the weight, about the schedule, about the gap,' Gumley says. 'Right through this period it wasn't the JSF cost that was driving decisions, it was all schedules.'

That brought them to consider the choices. Gumley says DMO was not involved with the actual decision to go with the Super Hornet.

'The decision of the capability came out of Defence. DMO costed at an approximate level, not an exact level, a couple of things. We were

343

certainly not the decision-maker. We were the recommender,' he says. 'In fact, if we look at where Super Hornet has gone, Australia has got financially a very good deal. We got excellent FMS [Foreign Military Sales] pricing because we are buying off an established production line. The project has come in below budget and right on time, [in fact] a month or two ahead of time. We've got all the capability that we were promised and so for an air project … it has been quite different from the norm'.

Once the decision was made the project came under Gumley's wing. Under the American FMS terms, DMO would buy the jets from the US navy's production slots at the Boeing factory in St Louis and not directly from Boeing.

Historically, projects conducted under FMS rules have suffered cost blow-outs because the initial price had been underestimated. But Gumley was confident that Super Hornet would come in within the budget because of the extensive data analysis his team had done.

Like the earlier rapid acquisition of the C-17 transport jets, the Super Hornet was indeed right on time and budget, a vastly different outcome from other Boeing projects such as Wedgetail and the Vigilare command and control system, that both ran four years behind schedule. The project came in about $300 million below the forecast amount. There is still room for a blow-out of sorts because the price only included 10 years of sustainment costs but the plan is to sell the aircraft with 'very low kilometres on the clock' in 2020, thus avoiding additional costs. That, however, will depend on the delivery schedule for the JSF. It would be a brave person who predicted the RAAF would have 24 nearly new Super Hornets to sell by 2020.

Gumley says a future government might decide to postpone buying the final squadron of JSFs and extend the Super Hornets. 'If they do there will be another funding request to sustain them beyond the 10 years.'

He regards Nelson's decision to buy the Super Hornets as 'inspired'. The early indications about JSF schedule delays turned out to be accurate.

'He looked at the probabilities, there were a number of deep discussions about it, and he went with his instinct and his instinct proved entirely correct. It was an inspired decision, in some ways a courageous decision because it went against some of the contemporary wisdom.'

Despite some claims that the Super Hornet buy would directly affect JSF pricing, Gumley believes the two are not linked at all. 'The biggest impact on the price of the JSF was actually the JSF schedule delay.'

Despite public statements to the contrary, Shepherd admits the RAAF was concerned about the possibility of an air combat capability gap of up to five years.

'There were a number of options. The most expensive was clearly a new bridging fighter, the Super Hornet. The other option was "Can we extend F-111, can we stretch out our own (classic) Hornets?"'

Importantly, he says, the RAAF needed to retire the F-111 at a time of its choosing and not in the wake of a tragedy or because of further cost blow-outs.

Although a bridging fleet of Super Hornets was just one of the options that went to the Australian Government, the RAAF had been flying Hornets for 20 years and understood the US navy and how it ran Hornets.

'[The Super Hornet] is actually the best fourth-generation fighter out there, I believe that absolutely. It's got the best radar, best software and I've flown the Su-30 [the Russian-built Sukhoi Su-30], I've flown the Eurofighter Typhoon,' Shepherd says. 'It was a touch-and-go decision at the time [with] a lot of controversy. I think Nelson pushed it through and made the right decision. My only fear is that we keep it in too long. It clearly should be a bridging fighter. I don't want to sit here in 2025 and say we are going to keep the Super Hornet forever. I was also adamant that we get the two-seat F/A-18F, not the single-seat F/A-18E. The Super Hornet buy has to replace, and be seen to replace, the F-111 strike capability, and not be confused with the eventual JSF purchase.'

Even with the JSF schedule sliding, Shepherd believes a mixed Super Hornet/JSF fleet post 2020 would be wrong for the RAAF. He supported the Rudd government's decision to sign up for just 14 JSFs in the first instance, but strongly opposes using the Super Hornet as an excuse not to buy a fourth JSF squadron.

Shepherd was also perplexed by the decision to wire the second 12 Super Hornets in such a way that they could be upgraded to 'G' or 'Growler' models to provide electronic warfare (EW) support.

'You don't need electronic support aircraft with JSF. It does all that, so we don't need a squadron of Growler aeroplanes in 2025 to stay in service until whenever to support JSF on strike missions,' he says.

Steve Gumley disagrees. In his view there are certain missions the Growler could do well before the JSF comes on line. Much of the information about electronic warfare (EW) capability is classified but Gumley says having the jet fitted 'for, not with' the Growler wiring meant that the EW 'black boxes' and external pods could be fitted with a minimum of cost above the EW equipment itself.

'It would be impossibly expensive to reopen an entire Super Hornet and rewire it if you wanted to come back and fix the boxes later,' he says.

The next Minister for Defence, Joel Fitzgibbon, who had lambasted Brendan Nelson over the decision, came to praise it. Fitzgibbon remains convinced that the purchase was rushed after the decision was made to retire the F-111s. He argues that it left Australia vulnerable to Boeing's pricing structure and was the sort of bad planning that had left taxpayers vulnerable in other big-ticket Defence acquisitions such as the navy's Sea Sprite helicopters. Despite Gumley's assurances on price, many critics regarded the $6.6 billion price tag for 24 jets as excessive.

However, once elected to office the Rudd government accepted that the bridging capability was vital to national security and besides, walking away from the contract with Boeing would have been far too costly for long-suffering taxpayers to bear.

Nelson is convinced that his decision bought Australia an extra five years in the transition phase between F-111 and F/A-18 and the F-35 JSF. Given that by mid-2010 the JSF delivery date was slipping out towards 2018 it was just as well. 'For each year you delay the Joint Strike Fighter, in 2007 dollars you save half a billion, so we bought time [and] leverage in terms of our bargaining,' says Nelson.

As part of his induction into his new job as Australia's representative to NATO after leaving parliament, Nelson visited Lockheed Martin's Fort Worth plant again in early 2010 and met some senior US navy people who told him they were looking closely at what Australia was doing.

'I would not be surprised if the US navy bought more Super Hornets,' he says.

By the time his tenure as minister was over, Nelson was not only convinced his decision had been vindicated, but had also become a huge fan of the 'rapid acquisition' concept for buying defence equipment. He had witnessed the success of the Abrams tank purchase and the very smooth acquisition of four massive Boeing C-17 transport jets and had overseen the on-time and on-budget buy of 24 jet fighters.

Looking back, Shepherd says, 'Each minister has peccadilloes and each chief has peccadilloes and faults and all the rest of it — they are only human — [but] I think Nelson was brave in getting that decision through. History, I believe, would have proved the house of cards wouldn't have stayed balanced.'

On 29 April 2011 six of Australia's F/A-18F Super Hornets touched down at the Royal Malaysian Air Force Base in Butterworth. The 'Rhinos' were there to participate in their first overseas deployment — the five-nation Exercise Bersama Shield 2011, on the Malaysian peninsula and South China Sea.

It was a proud day for the RAAF.

Chapter 31

THE FLYERS

Group Captain Steve 'Zed' Roberton did not follow a typical path into the Royal Australian Air Force.

As a kid he didn't build model airplanes and his eyes didn't rush skywards whenever a plane flew overhead as he carried his surfboard along the beach at Bribie Island in Queensland. He didn't yearn to get into a cockpit either, and on the rare occasions when he did fly he was prone to air sickness.

His only family link with the military was his paternal grandfather who flew 67 combat missions in B-25 bombers during World War II and was shot down over Belgium. He never flew again after the war until 1990 when he jetted to Perth to see his grandson graduate as a jet fighter pilot. Upon landing back in Brisbane under broken clouds he declared that it was a 'good day for bombing'.

It was a leggy blonde and an aircraft without an engine that sparked Zed Roberton's interest in aviation. He was in the second year of a science degree at the University of Queensland and thinking about a career in medicine when he wandered into the university's great court during orientation week.

There he noticed a very attractive young woman standing next to a glider from the university's gliding club. 'She was a terrific girl. I dated her for a while and started flying and just loved it. I seemed to have a bit of a knack for it and that was it. I thought, "I'll have a crack at that."'

After overcoming his initial fears, he found he enjoyed flying a glider. 'I was really scared to death. I was a little prone to air sickness and

[in] gliding there is a lot of turning in the thermals but I found that when I was actually flying I wasn't getting sick,' he recalls. 'It was just so free. I guess gliding is the purest form of flying.'

He compares it to the difference between sailing and driving motorboats. 'If I couldn't fly fighters the only thing I'd want to fly is gliders.'

For all pilots the first solo flight is an experience that is never forgotten: the moment when they look across — or behind, in the case of a tandem glider — and realise there is nobody else there. Roberton's first solo took place at the Kingaroy gliding club on the Darling Downs, west of Brisbane.

'We had a wonderful instructor there, Don Scott, who had seen a lot of guys off to air force at different stages. He was a great instructor and he sent me off [solo] after about 7 hours or so. That seemed to be a couple of hours shorter than normal, and about 10 hours shorter than when I thought I was ready,' he says. 'He launched me off and it was quite exhilarating getting the thing back on the ground and realising I'd survived. I seem to remember the first landing wasn't all that pretty.'

The young student and part-time surfer and bakery assistant began to contemplate an air force career.

After completing his science degree, young Roberton borrowed a suit from his dad Peter and presented himself at the recruiting office in Edward Street, Brisbane.

'I remember being quite intimidated talking to the other candidates because they all seemed to know a lot more about flying and the air force and fighters and all sorts of things than I did,' he says. 'The interviewees would be sharing stories when they came out about what questions they got asked. Having sat on several of these boards now myself, one of the things we like to do is ask candidates something they don't know the answer to, to see whether or not they have the confidence to say, "I don't know," but then have a guess. These guys were getting asked questions like, "Why does the F/A-18 have tails that are canted outwards?" and things like this. I've got nearly 2500 hours on F/A-18s and I've only just figured that out myself.'

As a laid-back free spirit from the Sunshine Coast, Roberton also found military life slightly intimidating. He had what he thought was a short haircut for his final interview and another trim a week later before he walked in the door of the Number 1 Flying Training School (1FTS) at Point Cook, where he was told to have another haircut straight away.

'I remember the warrant officer disciplinary shouting at me for marching like I was carrying a surfboard. It was really quite foreign. It was also freezing cold at Point Cook … but [it was] a terrific bunch of people,' he says. 'I was on course with a really good group [including] Linda Corbould, who has gone on to basically be one of Australia's best air transport pilots and certainly our most accomplished female aviator. She and Mel Kilpatrick were the third and fourth female RAAF pilots to graduate.'

His early days at the 1FTS were quite intimidating for another reason as well. He and one other student were the only two who had never done any powered flying. Everyone else had either a commercial or private pilot licence and were therefore much more confident with radio calls and procedures. Nevertheless, things clicked into place and by the time he reached the Macchi jet trainers at 2FTS at Pearce, he had caught up to his peers. In fact, he had surpassed them and was pronounced dux of his fast jet training course, thus almost guaranteed to be posted to fighters. He was keen to go to F-111s after seeing the sleek swing-wing jets buzzing around his home skies.

The RAAF had different ideas. Roberton's aptitude was for single-seat fighters where dogfighting against enemy aircraft was still a key aspect of the operational profile. After several instruction flights in the tandem training aircraft, he clearly remembers his first solo flight in an F/A-18 Hornet fighter on a sunny afternoon in February 1993. That was also the year he married his childhood sweetheart, Libby Stokes. The couple now have three children, Isabella, 10, Corey, eight, and Benjamin, six.

'In a single-seater you look around behind you, there is no other seat, no one hiding back there … It's a little bit different in a two-seater because you've got this great lump of metal in front of you, but you sit in a [single-seater] fighter and you feel like you are strapped on the front of a bullet,' he says. 'You look back and the wings are way, way back behind you, you've got the leading edge extension just down the sides but your visibility is very good, down to about 45 degrees, all the way around.'

He remembers taxiing out at Williamtown. It was a beautiful afternoon as he pulled up into the holding point to do his pre take-off vital actions and to run through things. He had to take a few breaths and calm himself down. 'I remember thinking what a monumental folly it was that the government was paying me to take a $40 million jet flying when I didn't seem to have much of a clue about it. It was just brilliant, just fantastic.'

The next step was learning how to prosecute and prevail in a dogfight against other fighters.

'That was just a really big life-changing moment. It was so much fun, actually not just doing something that was scripted, you know, like aerobatic flying,' he says. 'I did the F/A-18 aerobatic flying for a couple of years and aerobatic flying, to a degree, is a little bit like instrument flying. It's not easy, it's very hard to do well, but it is all pre-planned — it's numbers, numbers, numbers. With aerobatic flying in the F/A-18 you need to have 210 knots [389 kilometres per hour] and it's a 4-G, 11-alpha pull to do the loop. You know your heights and your speeds and you just have to allow for winds and conditions to make it look good and smooth, but it's all pre-planned.

'When you do dogfighting, every fight is different and it changes every three seconds and that challenge of not reacting to somebody but making them react to you and just driving them down and then when they are ready, just killing it … I love that, it's just really dynamic.'

Unlike many RAAF pilots, Roberton has been fortunate to stay with F/A-18s and remain in operational squadrons for most of his career. That means he has never had to fly in the back seat of a two-seater while some 'bog rat' trainee pilot flew circuits.

In 2006 he was appointed staff officer to then Chief of Air Force, Air Marshal Geoff Shepherd, but just as he was on leave helping Libby unpack boxes back at their house in Canberra, he was asked to stand up the Air Combat Transition Office. It was about the best possible desk job for a fighter pilot who freely admits that he needed a break from the physical rigours of flying fighter jets.

'My body was hurting, my brain was hurting and [it was] a whole new challenge,' he says.

He was promoted to group captain later that month and in March 2007 the Howard government announced that it would buy 24 F/A-18F Super Hornet fighters as a 'bridging' capability.

It is a long way and half a lifetime from the University of Queensland Gliding Club to the US navy's Lemoore Naval Air Station near the town of Hanford in California's food bowl, the San Joaquin Valley.

In July 2009 Roberton — at age 41 one of the air force's youngest group captains — was in the US to undertake conversion training on to the F/A-18F Super Hornet and to attend the unveiling of the RAAF's very first fighter aircraft as it rolled off the Boeing production line in St Louis, with then Chief of Air Force (CAF), Air Marshal Mark Binskin.

'My main role has been the coordination and leadership for CAF of all the resources for air force for air combat transition planning, part of which, of course, was leading the Super Hornet conversion team, but more broadly bringing together all the resources and all the stove-pipe projects associated with air combat transitions planning for the RAAF,' Roberton explains.

In January 2009, the Amberley-based Number 1 Squadron — the operational squadron — ceased flying F-111s and began the move to Super Hornets. Zed Roberton became the officer in command of the Super Hornets.

Overseeing the introduction of a new aircraft type and then getting to fly and possibly command the wing would be a rare privilege in today's air force and the easygoing and likeable Roberton did not take it for granted.

'I'm incredibly privileged and I'm loving it, still absolutely loving it,' he says. 'Here we are in Lemoore in California and I'm about to start my conversion and go back and see 1 Squadron have its first jet roll off the line next week, which is really satisfying.'

With all the political shenanigans now a distant memory he believes the decision to buy the jet will be seen as enlightened and better than anyone in the RAAF would have anticipated.

He says the team has been able to shape roles and missions, as well as the workforce required to operate the advanced data links and sensor suites, such as the state-of the-art AESA (active electronically scanned array) radar. AESA is a major advance in radar technology and allows the aircraft to broadcast across a range of frequencies so it can 'paint' a much greater number of potential targets while being very difficult to detect over background noise. Data links will allow the jet to operate with classic Hornets, Wedgetail AEWACs and airborne fuel tankers, and alongside US aircraft in coalition operations.

'We get all that seven years earlier and we have now managed to stand up an entire wing, balanced around a high-security environment we always were going to face with the JSF. Now we get to do that, we learn all the lessons, we work closely with JSF teams so they understand what we've learnt as we go through it,' he says. 'It will be hard to ever put a figure on how much it saved us or how great a decision it's going to have been, but clearly a lot of the criticism has died off. The new government came in and fairly quickly fully ratified the decision as they've been exposed to what we are doing with it and it's bought us a lot of flexibility we wouldn't otherwise have had as we go through the big transition to JSF.'

As expected, Roberton took command of Number 82 Wing, which includes all the Super Hornets, in March 2010. By that time a dozen of the jets had arrived at Amberley with all 24 due to be in place by the end of 2011.

Air power comes in many forms and has numerous applications. The modern fighter pilot or air combat officer, who occupies the back seat of a tandem aircraft, are as much sensor operators and communicators as warriors. The data links between troops on the ground and aircraft are becoming so sophisticated that a soldier can use his laptop to view real-time images being recorded and transmitted down to him by a fighter jet or manned or unmanned spy plane circling above the battlefield.

This not only lengthens the so-called 'kill chain' by allowing troops to call in more accurate air strikes, but it also helps to prevent collateral damage. With conflict becoming increasingly political and every civilian death generating hostile headlines, this aspect of air power is extremely important in the 21st-century battle space.

Like his boss Roberton, Squadron Leader John Haly is from Brisbane and studied science before becoming a fighter pilot. Unlike Roberton, the Wynnum Manly boy joined ADFA direct from school to do his degree, with a particular emphasis on astro-physics.

He had done some private flying while still at school and had been already bitten by the aviation bug before he finished high school. A good mate who was keen to join the RAAF encouraged Haly to follow suit. Unfortunately his mate didn't make it but Haly has gone on to become one of the leading fighter pilots in the RAAF.

After graduation and flying training Haly was posted to Number 34 (VIP) Squadron at Fairbairn in Canberra flying Falcon 900 VIP jets for very important passengers, from the monarch, Queen Elizabeth II, down to generals, ministers and opposition MPs.

'The lifestyle was interesting for a young single guy, you know, cruising around the world and all that sort of stuff, but the flying was not in the least bit stimulating. It cured me of any desire to be an airline pilot,' he says.

After 18 months of piloting the VIP 'flying buses' he was back on fast jets and was one of the first students to fly the new British-built Hawk lead-in fighter trainer. After qualifying on the Hornet, Haly joined 75 Squadron at RAAF Base Tindal just in time for the 2003 Gulf War deployment to the Middle East.

Then it was down to Canberra as aide-de-camp to then Chief of Air Force Air Marshal Angus Houston before being posted to Number 3

Hornet Squadron at Williamtown. Next, he was selected for the US navy exchange program at Lemoore Naval Air Station where he became qualified to fly off US aircraft carriers by day and by night, and was so good at it that he became an instructor to teach US navy pilots and 'wissos'.

According to the commanding officer of VFA-122 (V denotes aviator squadron and FA stands for fighter attack), the Super Hornet squadron at Lemoore, US navy Captain Greg 'Hifi' Harris, Haly is an outstanding pilot.

'I think Squadron Leader Haly is one of the best we've seen, which was a little unnerving for some of our guys, but the capability is certainly there,' Harris says. He believes that the level of cooperation between the US navy's carrier-based Super Hornet operations and the RAAF Super Hornet community is now so entrenched and intimate that it should be expanded to the point where RAAF pilots are able to operate from US navy flat tops.

'My mindset has been the Australians are coming through as if they are going to operate on a US aircraft carrier tomorrow,' he says. 'I am treating them and training them just as if I was treating and training one of my brand-new aviators.'

There is virtually nothing that is off limits to the Australian crews as they pass through the vast training establishment in the middle of one of America's most fertile valleys on the edge of the Sierra Nevada mountains.

'I think the intriguing piece of that, as we move forward, [is] there is a timeframe when Australia might look to operate jointly with the US off an aircraft carrier, providing support via their own air force but operating off a US carrier,' Harris says. 'That is certainly a capability that could exist in the future, we've had Australian air force pilots earn their navy gold wings by qualifying day and night on the aircraft carrier.'

He says it is a matter for the political side of the house to decide how much integration there will be before militaries get together and decide where our best cooperation strategies lie and how to best utilise the capability.

'I think we are crazy sometimes ... if we think we are going to do anything alone. Having our allies there again, as I mentioned before, I think adds that measured response, that alternate experience and different viewpoint on how to look at things,' he says. 'There still are differences in the way we view certain things and the approach we might take, and that ... adds something unique to the mix and I think that common thread we have with Great Britain, Canada, Australia, that's a good balanced group of people to deal with.'

Harris believes the Super Hornet purchase has cemented an already close relationship between the RAAF and the US navy and will open the way for even closer cooperation when the JSF comes into service across three US services (air force, marines and navy).

Harris regards the RAAF as a kind of halfway house between the US navy and the US air force. 'I think somewhere in the middle is where we need to be operating and in my experience so far in dealing with the Royal Australian Air Force, it seems to be where they operate — strict adherence to rules but that openness to "Okay, how can we make an adjustment for this case?"'

John Haly is a big fan of the two-seat Super Hornet and the multiplier effect it offers the RAAF. He says the Block 2 machines (the second model of the jet) being purchased by Australia offer true 'multi-role' capability because they can conduct numerous tasks at once. The AESA radar in particular allows the crew to multi-task in a way that was not possible in earlier fighters.

'It's now near simultaneous multi-roles so the jet can be doing everything at exactly the same time across all the spectrums of its roles and capabilities,' he says. 'Now the biggest limitation is the man in the seat and if you just have one person there you are not able to do multiple things at once, like you can when there are two people working on potentially two totally different roles using the same sensors.'

The RAAF pilots who used to fly the F/A-18 A Classic Hornet find the conversion to Super Hornet much more straightforward than the F-111 crews. The Hornet pilots tend to feel comfortable with the larger

Super Hornet almost immediately because it looks and handles like a Classic Hornet. Conversion time in the US navy is just five hours and RAAF pilots are well and truly competent within that timeframe.

The conversion is harder for F-111 crews who are used to operating side-by-side in a much older airframe with completely different performance characteristics.

Learning how to fight using the Super Hornet's advanced sensors presents the biggest challenge to the Australian pilots.

'The high speed of the sensors and the capability of the radar are the biggest difference and becoming proficient at that takes much longer than learning how to fly,' Haly says.

Motivation is not generally a problem for young fighter pilots who are paid handsomely to fly jet aircraft around the sky at 540 knots (1000 kilometres per hour) and faster.

He says, 'It's an immensely rewarding job and on top of that we have a very self-critical and very introspective viewpoint of our performance and I think everyone's harshest critic is themselves. We are very open and honest in briefing and de-briefing. It is just the fighter-pilot culture that has evolved in air forces everywhere. Perfection is impossible to achieve. It is just perpetual motivation out there.'

Chapter 32

NEXT GENERATION

Air Marshal Mark Binskin says he has no need to gaze into a crystal ball to see the future of the Royal Australian Air Force.

In 2009 a staggering 87 per cent of the air force fleet was in the final 10 years of its life. By early 2011, the oldest plane at RAAF Base Amberley was a three-year-old C-17 Globemaster heavy lift jet while, nearby, the Super Hornet fighter had replaced the venerable F-111.

'You don't have to look too far into the future to realise it's already here. We've got Wedgetail coming into service at Williamtown; the classic Hornets, although they are 25 years old, have all new systems on board, all the latest weapons, so the future is already hitting there as well,' Binskin says.

The motorcycle-riding Vice Chief of the Defence Force joined the Royal Australian Navy as a trainee fighter pilot in 1978. Obsessed with aircraft as a youngster, he made countless model airplanes, joined the air force cadets as a teenager and after he left school his parents paid for him to undertake his restricted level pilot's licence in a Cessna 150 while he waited to hear whether he had been accepted into the air force or the navy. He had applied for both but the 'senior service' signed him up.

The navy's fleet air arm ceased fixed-wing aviation in June 1983 and pilots such as Binskin had two choices: move to helicopters or transfer to the RAAF. He chose the latter and the rest is history.

Looking to the next few years, Binskin says the Joint Strike Fighter (JSF) will come on line later this decade along with the new Boeing P-8 Maritime Patrol aircraft and a new battlefield air lifter (subject to government approval) as well as the other high-tech projects such as the Vigilare command and control system and new air traffic control and battle space management technologies.

'We talk a lot about how the future is going to be the next 10 to 12 years, but then in a lot of cases the future is already hitting us and everyone is starting to adapt to it to get the most out of our new systems. It's a great, great time to be in the air force,' he says.

A good example of world-first futuristic capability is the Wedgetail Airborne Early Warning and Control aircraft (AEWAC) that was years in the planning pipeline and substantially delayed before arriving at Number 2 Squadron at Williamtown in 2010. Although there were some high-end technical glitches to be ironed out with the complex radar system, the operators were already seasoned before the first jet landed.

'We have got a Wedgetail pilot with 1000 hours on the aircraft, yet we only accepted it in early 2010,' Binskin says.

With the government setting stringent benchmarks for new military projects and taxpayers increasingly well informed about delays and cost overruns, introducing high-tech projects such as Wedgetail is fraught with risk.

'Someone asked me, "When will we get the full technical maturity out of Wedgetail?" I answered "never" because it will just continue to grow and the capability will be far greater in 30 years than what it is now.'

The Super Hornet is another example of this highly planned approach. By the time the first jet arrived at Amberley in 2010, RAAF pilots and maintainers had been working at Lemoore US Naval Air Station in California for more than a year. Some pilots, such as John Haly, even became Super Hornet instructors with the US navy and were deployed on aircraft carriers. From that core group the new squadrons were born.

It is not all a bed of roses. On the people front, the recent period of high operational tempo has exacted quite a price, according to RAAF historian Chris Clark. While family disruption is part and parcel of military life, he suggests the period since the 1999 East Timor intervention has placed enormous strains on the air force and its people.

'I think people going back on repeated rotations within a short period of time, that's where you see Australians really coming out. They are working for long periods in theatre with very little relief [and] very little rest time. [If] people don't get to sleep, they make mistakes,' he says. 'The thing you observe most frequently in the air force now is that in those … areas of air force where we have commitments overseas, you find people are on their third or fourth deployment to the Middle East Area of Operations (MEAO). Translate that back to what that means in their domestic circumstances, you find an awful lot of marriage breakdowns. That's the sort of personal cost you talk about. People really are expected to display extraordinary devotion to their career over personal circumstances.'

Clark says the situation is unlikely to change given the constraints of a force that by early 2011 employed about 14,500 personnel, 3500 reservists and 900 civilian public servants. He believes that the biggest risk after more than a decade of high tempo operations is burnout.

The RAAF had 13,500 people when it went into East Timor in 1999.

'That same [core] group of people has been conducting and supporting operations across the globe constantly since 1999,' Clark says. 'Air force has gone through the process of working out, "Well, we'll do a reshape and rebalance, we'll work out where our numbers are [and] where we might have a surplus and see if we can redirect them to areas that are really under pressure."'

The then Chief of the Defence Force, Air Chief Marshal Angus Houston, was acutely aware that by 2010 elements of the air force, such as the AP-3C Orion and C-130 Hercules fleets, had been constantly on operations since 1999.

Houston, a decorated air force helicopter pilot, joined the RAAF when Australia was at war in Vietnam and retired in mid-2011 when the nation was at war again in Afghanistan. A tough leader with a warm public persona and quiet manner, he regards the RAAF as the equal of any air force, 'pound for pound'.

Apart from the technological advances, Houston says the biggest changes he has witnessed during his long career have been in safety and values. He says the safety culture combined with better equipment means far fewer losses and the focus on values means the RAAF has the highest number of women in its ranks of all three services.

'We have a values-based air force. That means behaviour has to be consistent with those values and the air force has made a lot of traction in that area,' Houston says. 'People are treated well, they are valued and the leadership culture is one that basically empowers people and encourages the people at the lower level to go and do the work themselves. That is a big difference now compared to when I started. I don't ever remember anybody saying anything values-based. Now we have a culture [and leadership] which has a very high priority on air-force values ... I think it works wonderfully well.'

Although the air force has become a much more female-friendly workplace, one of Houston's biggest disappointments was it still had no female fighter pilots. There are women flying C-130s, C-17s, AP-3C Orions and flying as air combat officers in F-111s and Super Hornets but no fighter jet pilots.

'We had our French friends come over to an exercise, Pitch Black, I think around 2004 and they came with a bunch of fighter pilots and had four Mirages and there was one woman air combat pilot,' Houston says. 'I'd love to see that in the Royal Australian Air Force. There have been a couple of women who started the training but haven't completed it.'

Traditions in the air force are more mutable than in army and navy. Legendary airplanes liked the C-130, Caribou or F-111 allowed the RAAF to develop traditions around the airframes themselves, but Clark says it is rare for the air force to hold on to aircraft for so long.

'These platforms are increasingly costly to replace but when you think of Mirages or Sabres, they had 10 to 15 years and out they go, so you don't have a lot of time to build up traditions around your squadrons because you are re-equipping with another, different type of aircraft,' he says.

Generations of current Australian aircrew were inspired as children by the F-111's spectacular and noisy 'dump and burn' routine at air shows and public gatherings around the nation. The next generation will not see the 'pig' in action any more, but they will still be awestruck by the skilful aerobatics of the Roulettes and the astonishing sight of newer fighter jets shooting skywards.

As the RAAF reached its ninetieth anniversary in 2011, former and current serving air men and women renewed their traditions with a range of ceremonies to mark the occasion. Even as the popular flypasts helped to inspire a new generation of interest in military aviation, many children who dream of breaking the bonds of gravity were already comfortable with advanced technology. Glued to home computer games, the pilots of tomorrow were conducting stealth 'missions' over enemy territory using a joystick remarkably similar to the real thing in the new-generation Joint Strike Fighter.

Index

A

'Aardvark' *see* F-111 strike bomber
acceleration 336–337
accidents *see also* crashes
    F-111s 91–92
    human error 213
    survival training 115
    VIP operations 287
acclimatisation training 111
active electronically scanned array (AESA) radar 353
ADG *see* Airfield Defence Guard
Advanced Medium-Range Air-to-Air Missiles (AMRAAMs) 129
aerial resupply 252–253
Aermacchi MB-326 jet trainer 31
aerobatics
    compared to dogfights 351
    manoeuvres 79
    Roulettes 77–81
    safety and risks 80
    training 80
aeromedical evacuations (AMEs)
    Bali 42, 44, 45, 47, 48–49, 50–51
    C-17s 297–298
    C-130 13
    Cairns 52
    Sinai desert 30
    Tarin Kowt 304
Afghanistan
    aircraft vulnerability 60
    C-17 235–237
    C-130 10
    CAOC 242, 256
    children 307, 308
    civilian aircraft 264, 265
    climate variations 57
    convoy overwatch 185–193
    CRC *see* Control and Reporting Centre
    cultural issues 302, 307–309
    Orions 180
    trauma care 300–309
    UAVs 198–199, 200–202
air battle management
    CRC 259, 262–263
    JTACs 255–257
    training 83
air campaign planning training 82

air combat officers (ACOs)
    responsibilities 105
    training 82
    UAVs and 203
Air Combat Transition Office 352
air dropping 233
Air Lift Group 32–35
Air Mobility mission 35
air racing 169–170
air strikes *see* bombs and bombing
air support
    close 252–253
    offensive 165–167
air traffic control (ATC) 264–275 *see also* joint terminal air controllers
    Baghdad 264–265, 271–275
    'deployability' 270
    East Timor 269–271
    radar 269
    Sudan 266–267
    training 267–269
airborne electronic analysts (AEAs) 180–181
Airbus A300 272–273, 338
aircraft carriers 333, 355
aircraft defence *see* Airfield Defence Guard (ADG)
aircraft maintenance *see* maintenance
aircraft production techniques 320
aircraft technicians 210
Airfield Defence Guard (ADG) 221–227
    as bodyguards 226
    East Timor 18, 224
    Iraq 226
    medical staff 291
    Middle East 225
    role 221, 222
    tactics 223
    training 222
    weaponry 223
    women in 226
airfields
    air traffic control *see* air traffic control
    defence *see* Airfield Defence Guard
    establishment 28
    management 249–250
    scheduling aircraft *see* air battle management
    threats 286–287
airsickness 68–69
Al Asad Air Base (Iraq) 124, 125

Al Minhad Air Base (UAE)
    ADG 225
    aircraft maintenance 209, 215
    catering 218
    Orions 185–186
Albaugh, Jim 340–341
Alcantara, Flight Sergeant Frank 48–52
aliens, Australian service personnel as 138–139
altitude issues 65
Amberley Base 92
ambushes, Taliban 189
AME *see* aeromedical evacuations (AMEs)
Anderson, Corporal Ayse 296–299
Anderson, Grant 298
animal traps 117
anti-aircraft artillery 145
anti-submarine warfare 182–184
ANZAC Day fly past 100
AP–3C *see* Orion AP–3C patrol aircraft
army
    Afghanistan 194, 198
    assumes control of helicopters 31
    infantry skills training for RAAF 117–120
    joint operations 127–128
    JTACs 254
    relations with ADG 224, 226
    rivalry with RAAF 117, 216
    Solomon Islands intervention 2003 71
    UAVs 202
arrival patterns 58
Ashford, Bruce 36–43
Ashford, Deanne 37, 39
Ashmore Reef disaster (2009) 180
Australian Defence Force joint operational model 127–128
Australian Light Armoured Vehicles (ASLAV) 185
Australian War Memorial 22
Autissier, Isabelle 33
avionics technicians 210

B

Bachmann, Major Joseph 'OD' 331
Baghdad
    ADG 226
    air traffic control 264–265, 271–275
    bombing 1–3, 141, 142–146
    US President's visit 275
Baghdad International Airport 11
Bagram (Afghanistan) 198
Balad (Iraq) 294–295
Bali bombing (2002) 36–52
    aeromedical evacuation 42, 44, 45, 47, 48–49, 50–51
    deaths 41
    demands on air crew 47
    Denpasar airport 38, 39, 44
    Hercules 286
    medical treatment at Denpasar 40–43
    psychological damage 47
    RAAF arrives 39, 44
    RAAF mobilised 37–38
    synchronising RAAF efforts 46
    victims treated at Darwin 43
Bali bombing (2005) 48–49
Banham, Cynthia 280
Barker, Flight Lieutenant Aaron 286
Basedow, Flight Lieutenant Matt 185, 187, 191, 194–195, 196
Basic Flying Training School 93
battle director, CAOC 245–246
battle management *see* air battle management
'battle worthiness' policy 33–34
battlefield air lifter 358
Baucau (East Timor) 17–20, 21
Baxter, Sergeant Robin 304–309
BBJs 279–280, 287–288
Beazley, Kim 24
Beesley, Jon 327–332
Bell, Corporal Geoffrey 223–224, 226–227
Bellenger, Wing Commander Sean 81
Benson, Squadron Leader Ross 22, 63, 65–68
bin Laden, Osama 135
Binskin, Air Marshal Mark VCDF
    appointed Chief of Air Force 94–95
    appointed Vice Chief of the Defence Force 28
    CAOC 242–243, 246
    future of the RAAF 358–359
    Super Hornet 335, 352
    view of East Timor campaign 28
Black Hawk helicopters 54
body armour 55
bodyguards 226
Boeing 707 crash (1991) 34
Boeing 737 Business Jets 279–280, 287–288
Boeing 737–400 crash (2007) 280
Boeing Australia 342
Boeing C–17 Globemaster *see* C–17 Globemaster
Boeing Corporation 197, 341
Boeing Scan Eagle 186, 200
Bolton, Flight Lieutenant Dean 45–46, 233
Bombardier Challenger 604 jets 279, 285, 286
bombs and bombing *see also* Bali bombing
    ACO's role 105
    Baghdad 1–3, 141, 142–146
    CAOC 243, 247
    coordinating 253
    dumb bombs 145
    East Timor 24
    F–111 107
    Iraq 129, 154–156, 165–166
    JSF 333
    laser-guided 129, 145
    Taliban 189
border protection 175–184
Border Protection Command 182
Bougainville 291–292
Breckenridge, Group Captain Foster 'Fozz' 267

364

Bridge, Warrant Officer Gary 215
Brown, Flight Lieutenant Brian 175, 182–183
Brown, Air Marshal Geoff CAF 126–129, 171–172
Brown, Air Commodore Jim 247–248
'brown outs' 118
Bryce, Governor-General Quentin 288
Burbage, Tom 319–320, 324–326
Burgess-Orton, Michael 68–71
Burr, Grant 170–171
Bush, President George W. 128–129, 275
bush survival course 110–113, 116–117
Butterworth, Malaysia 291

C

C–17 Globemaster 228–238
   acquisition 228–229, 233
   aeromedical evacuations 297–298
   Afghanistan 235–237
   air dropping 233
   Bali bombings 51
   capabilities 230–231, 235
   cargo 236–237
   Christchurch earthquake 237
   compared to Hercules 229–230
   Japanese earthquake and tsunami 237–238
   simulator 231–232
   training 231–232, 233
C–130 *see* Hercules C–130
cabin attendants
   applicants 281
   catering 285
   combat survival training 284–285
   gender balance 281–282
   qualifications 283
   quality of 283–284
   role 284
   selection 280
Cairns, Warrant Officer Rod 73–74
Cairns, aeromedical evacuation 52
Cambodia 32
cameras 187, 191
camp construction training 117
Campbell, Wing Commander Jake 82, 83, 202–203
Canadians 218
Canfield, Squadron Leader Glen 79–81
CAOC *see* Combined Air Operations Centre
capture 156–157
cargo *see also* loadmasters
   C–17 236–237
   Hercules C–130 8–9
Caribou DHC–4 62–74
   altitude issues 65
   cool to fly 64, 65–67, 74
   crashes 70
   East Timor 14, 21–23, 70
   flight control system 72
   fuel supply 73
   landing 66, 69, 70
   loadmasters 74
   navigation 64, 68
   oil leaks 72
   performance 23, 63, 64
   PNG 64–65, 69, 73
   repair and maintenance 63, 67, 71–73
   retired 62, 74
   safety 64, 65
   Solomon Islands 71
   versatility 67
Carmody, Shane 25
Castle Hill (Townsville) 110
casualties
   care *see* trauma care
   children 307, 308
   civilian 254–255, 307–309
   fatalities 103, 228, 280
catbird 325
catering for VIP operations 280, 285
Caterpillar Club 97–98
Central Flying School (CFS) 77
Challenger 604 jets 279, 285, 286
Chappell, Steve 158
'Chemical Ali' 129
Chief of Air Force
   ADG protection 226
   Binskin appointed 358
   Brown appointed 127
   CAOC director 242
   East Timor 28, 81
   Shepherd appointed 94–95
   Super Hornet and 335, 340, 352
children 307, 308
Chinook heavy-lift helicopters 31
Christchurch earthquake (2011) 237
Chuck Yeager Award 328
civilian aircraft 8, 264, 265
civilian casualties 254–255, 307–309
CIVPOL 14
Clark, Chris 28, 359–360
Clarke, Flying Officer Justin 175
climate, effect on safety 57
close air support 252–253
coastal survival training 117
cockpit, F–111 100–101
code word training 115
combat recovery training 118
combat survival training 109–120
   acclimatisation 111
   aircraft failure 115
   bush survival course 110–113, 116–117
   cabin attendants 284–285
   crashes 112–113
   evasion and rescue 114
   fire lighting 112
   food and water 111, 112
   importance 113–114
   infantry skills 117–120
   interrogation and torture resistance 115
   jungle survival 113

kits 116–117
navigation 112
physical fitness 115
priorities 119
snow survival 116
solo exercises 113, 119
stresses 111, 120
urban environment 114
women in 120
Combat Survival Training School (CSTS) 109–110, 116–117, 118
Combined Air Operations Centre (CAOC) 241–250
    air battle management 255–257
    airport management 249–250
    assets 245
    battle director 245–246
    bombing operations 243, 247
    coordination with JTACs 256, 257
    daily air tasking order 132
    management 242, 244–245, 247–248
    OHS considerations 249
    operations centre 242
    regional commands 246
    relations with CRC 261
    role 245, 248
    troops in contact (TIC) operation 243–244, 245
commandos 252, 254
Commonwealth Heads of Government Meeting (CHOGM) 160
computers 230, 235
contractors 216, 217
Control and Reporting Centre (CRC, Afghanistan) 259–263
    attacks on 260
    radar 262
    redevelopment 259
    relations with CAOC 261
    trauma care 304–305
    'troops in contact' volume 262
    working conditions 261–262, 263
conversion training
    F–111 100–101
    Super Hornet 352, 357
convoy overwatch, Afghanistan 185–193
cook 217–219
Cook, Steve 50
Cooper, Wing Commander Pat 273–274
Corbould, Wing Commander Linda 228, 350
Cosgrove, Major-General Peter 14, 25–26, 132–133
counter-interrogation training 115, 156–157
Craigie, Corporal Rod 219–220
Crane, Vice-Admiral Russ 95
crashes
    Boeing 707 34, 280
    Caribou 64, 70
    Mirages 96–97
    rescue training 118

survival training 112–113, 115
crew attendants *see* cabin attendants
crew resource management 82–83
'crew slipping' 288
Crouch, Wing Commander Warren 282, 283, 284, 287, 289
Cseh, Squadron Leader Peter 'Choady' 19–20
cultural issues, Afghanistan 302, 307–309

D

Darwin Hospital 37, 42–43, 44
Dassault Mirages 95
Davis, Wing Commander Peter 215–217
decoration *see* medals
decoy flares 10
Deeth, Terry 92
Defence Materiel Organisation (DMO) 343
defence of airfields *see* Airfield Defence Guard (ADG)
defensive counter-air (DCA) missions 123
demonstration pilots 87–88
Denpasar airport after Bali bombing 38, 39, 44
Denpasar Hospital 40–42
departure patterns 58
DHC–4 *see* Caribou DHC–4
Diego Garcia air force base (US) 130
Dili 14–17, 21–22
dispersal move (aerobatics) 80
dogfights 351
domestic pilots' dispute 1989 8
Doolittle, General James 'Jimmy' 98
door illustration at Amberley 92
Downer, Alexander 280
drones *see* unmanned aerial vehicles
drug smugglers 182
Dubai *see* Al Minhad Air Base
dumb bombs 145
'dump and burn' routine 99, 107

E

East Sale Base 81–82
East Timor conflict (1999) 14–28
    ADG 224
    air traffic control 269–271
    Australian diplomacy 24–26
    Caribou 70
    evacuation 15–17
    F–111 107
    food drops 20–21
    Hercules 81
    Indonesia's intentions 24–25
    lasting effects on RAAF 27–28
    loadies 54–55
    militia rampages 14–15, 21, 23
    Operation Spitfire 15–17
    Operation Warden 17–20
    Roulettes 81
    transport of captives 22–23
Edwards, Group Captain Brian 84–85
Edwards Air Force Base (US) 327

Efogo airstrip (PNG) 73
Egypt 30–31
ejections
　Mirages 97
　Roulettes 77
　Super Hornet 335
　test pilots 329
　training 115
Elder, Major General Bob 242–244
election campaigns 285
electrical maintenance 219–220
electronic countermeasures (ECM) 56
electronic warfare (EW) capability 346
electro-optical sensors 185, 191
Elsley, Squadron Leader Ruth 264–267
engagement, rules of 140–141
engines, Hercules C-130 8–9
English, Flight Lieutenant Steve 77
environmental law 133–134
environmental training *see* combat survival training
equipment acquisition 228
evacuation, medical *see* aeromedical evacuations
evasion exercises 114
Evers, Squadron Leader Col 109–114
Ewart, Flight Lieutenant Jim 248–249
Exercise Bersama Shield 2011 347
Exercise Red Flag 101

F
F-15 Strike Eagle aircraft 135, 142–146
F-22 Raptor 313, 317
F-35 Joint Strike Fighter (JSF) *see* Joint Strike Fighter
F-111 strike bomber 99–108
　awaiting Super Hornets 338–339, 341
　cockpit 100–101
　conversion training 100–101
　East Timor 24, 107
　fatalities 103
　'G' model bought 103
　low-level speed 102
　maintenance 107, 108
　nickname 99
　performance 101, 107
　public popularity 107–108
　radar 94, 100, 107
　replacement 314–315
　retired 99, 108, 345
　safety 103
　size 100
　support costs 107
　'swing-wings' 107
　training 93, 101–102, 104–105
　women crew 104–106
F-117 flight testing 328
F/A-18 fighter *see* Hornet F/A-18 fighter
F/A-18F Super Hornet *see* Super Hornet fighter
family issues 34, 61, 299–300, 359–360

famine relief mission, Somalia 32
fatalities
　F-111s 103
　repatriations 228
　VIP flight at Yogyakarta 280
fighter pilots 348–357
　dogfights 351
　F-111 92–93
　flight testing *see* test pilots
　JSF 324, 334
　Macchi instructors 31
　no women 361
　role 354
　Super Hornet 350–351, 352–354, 355–357
　training 86–90, 164–165, 350–351
　UAVs and 202, 203–204
fire lighting training 112, 117
fishing, illegal 181–182
fishing kits 116
Fitzgibbon, Joel 10, 317, 346
flight attendants *see* cabin attendants
flight control system, Caribou 72
flight deck, C-130 10
flight engineers 181
flight feeding 218
flight testing
　F-117 328
　JSF 323–325, 328–329, 331–332
　landing 330
　pilots *see* test pilots
　procedure 330
　stealth aircraft 328
　take-off 329
'fly-by-wire' aircraft 235, 331
FMS (Foreign Military Sales) pricing 344
Foley, Wing Commander Jack 244–246, 247
food search training 112, 117
Fort Worth (US) 320
'four ship' missions 142
Franks, General Tommy 128–129
Freebairn, Flight Lieutenant Samantha 43–45, 228–231
French 361
fuel supply, Caribou 73
Fukushima nuclear power plant 238
future of the RAAF 358–362

G
G force 78
Gallipoli anniversary 291
Garuda Indonesia Boeing 737-400 crash 280
Gates, Robert 317
General Dynamics F-111 *see* F-111 strike bomber
Gilbert, Wing Commander Andrew 268, 269
Gillard government opens ADF to women 226
gliders 348–349
Global Hawk UAV 200
Globemaster C-17 *see* C-17 Globemaster
Goldie, Wing Commander Darren 282, 288

367

ground fire 59
Growler wiring 346
guards *see* Airfield Defence Guard (ADG)
Gumley, Steve 318, 322–323, 343, 346

H
Habibie, President BJ 25
Hagstrom, Flight Lieutenant Allan 153, 154
Hall, Flight Lieutenant Matt 1–3, 135–151, 163–170
Haly, Squadron Leader John 123–126, 354–357, 359
'hard flying' 101
Harland, Jeff 25
Harper, Warrant Officer First Class Wayne 118–120
Harrier jump jet 331
Harris, Captain Greg 'Hifi' 355
Harrison, Dave 33
Harvey, Air Vice-Marshal John 99–100, 314
Hazeldine, Squadron Leader Lochie 185, 190
health professionals *see* medical staff; trauma care
heat stress 57–58, 209–211, 212
heavy air lift and drops 233, 237
Hegarty, Matt 27
'heli' boxes 180
helicopters
    Chinook 31
    loadies 54
    rescue training 118
    UH-1 Iroquois 29–30
helmets 55
Henry, Squadron Leader Steve 249–250
Hercules C-130 7–13
    Afghanistan 2008 10
    Bali bombing 2002 286
    'battle worthiness' policy 33–34
    cargo 8–9
    compared to C-17 229–230
    design 12
    Dili evacuation 15–17
    East Timor 14, 20–21, 81
    effect of climate and temperature 57–58
    electronic countermeasures 56
    engines 8–9
    flexibility 12
    flight deck 10
    Iraq 125
    loadies 53–54, 58
    maintenance 209–210
    Model J 11–12, 55
    models 11
    Operation Bali Assist 42, 44, 46–48, 50–51
    Operation Warden 17–20
    passenger conditions 7–8
    pilots' affection for 12–13
    primary role 7
    risks 56–57
    safety record 55
    Somalia 9–10

Heron UAVs 198, 199, 201–202
High Range military training area 62
Hill, Senator Robert 314
Holt, Wing Commander Lyle 199, 201
Holtfreter, Group Captain Al 269–273, 274–275
Honiara 71
Horn of Africa 195–196
Hornet F/A-18 fighter
    demonstration pilots 87
    East Timor conflict 24
    Iraq 123, 124–125, 131, 133, 135, 152–153
    pilots 350–351
    replacement 314–315
    targeting pods 131
Hornet F/A-18F fighter *see* Super Hornet fighter
Hoskin, Sergeant Kara 284–285
hostages 115
Houston, Air Chief Marshal Angus 204, 314, 338–340, 360
Houston, Liz 158
Howard, John 11, 24, 340, 342
Howard government
    JSF 313, 314, 315
    planning for Iraq 126
    Super Hornet 336, 338–340
    VIP flight operation 279–280
Hueys *see* Iroquois UH-1 helicopter
Hughes, Peter 42
humanitarian flights 13
Hunter, Group Captain Daryl 262–263
Hupfeld, Air Commodore Mel 115, 152–155, 157, 167, 170
Hussein, Saddam 136

I
improvised explosive devices (IEDs) 186, 189, 306–307
Indonesian military 14–15, 21
infantry *see* army
infantry skills training 117–120
information exchange 167
information management training 84
infrared sensors 187–188
injuries *see* trauma care
intelligence, surveillance and reconnaissance (ISR) 82, 185–195
intensive care nursing *see* trauma care
International Assistance Force in East Timor (INTERFET) 14, 17
international cooperation
    aircraft carrier 356
    COAC *see* Combined Air Operations Centre
    JSF 315, 318, 319
International Security Assistance Force (ISAF) 201, 225
interrogation resistance training 115, 156–157
Introductory Fighter Course 93

Iraq
- ADG 226
- air traffic control 264–265, 271–275
- Al Asad air base captured 124
- Australian sovereign control 133–134
- bombing missions 1–3, 129, 141, 142–146, 154–156, 165–166
- CAOC 242
- combatants' misgivings 166, 168–169, 170–172
- daily air tasking order 132
- dangers 34
- extent of air power 123–124
- Hall's experience 135–151
- Hornets 123, 124–125, 131, 133, 152–153
- invasion 136–146, 154
- medical staff 294–295
- Operation Falconer 130–131
- Orions 180
- planning for 126–128
- SAMs 147–149
- SAS 124–125
- 'Shock and Awe' operation 139–140
- size and scale of operation 159
- targets 133–134
- US in 128, 130–131, 136–146, 155, 159, 167, 168, 294–295
- US President's visit 275
- war declared 130, 164

Iroquois UH–1 helicopter
- loadies 54
- medical staff 293
- Sinai Peninsula 29–30

Irvin-brand parachute 98
Israel–Egypt Peace Treaty 1979 30
Ivanovic, Sergeant Paula 232–234

J

Japanese earthquake and tsunami (2011) 237–238
Jemaah Islamiyah 36
jet fighter pilots *see* fighter pilots
jet fighters *see* F–111 strike bomber
joint operations 127–128
Joint Strike Fighter (JSF) F–35 313–326
- capabilities 315–317
- CEO conferences 318–319
- contracts 199, 315
- cost 313, 314, 322–323, 345
- delivery fears 339–340
- flight testing 323–325, 328–329, 331–332
- flying challenge 334
- future 358
- global partnership 315, 318, 319
- maintenance 325
- models 320
- opposition to 314, 317
- performance 332–333
- pilot problems 324
- production 320–321, 323
- project management 314
- purchase in doubt 344
- radar 321
- range 323
- sensor systems 321, 324
- simulation training 316, 333–334
- Super Hornet and 353
- technological advances 330

joint terminal air controllers (JTAC) 251–258
- air battle management 256
- Army and SAS 254
- avoiding civilian casualties 254–255
- convoy overwatch 191
- coordination with CAOC 256, 257
- role 251, 252–253
- skills required 253–254

JSF *see* Joint Strike Fighter (JSF) F–35
JTAC *see* joint terminal air controllers
jumbo jets 162–163, 279–280, 287–288
jungle training 113, 117

K

Kabul airport 60
Kandahar (Afghanistan)
- CRC *see* Control and Reporting Centre
- trauma care 304–309
- UAVs 198

Kelly, Mark 'Grace' 137–138, 141–142
Kelly, Corporal Mick 92
Kelly, Flying Officer Trish 176–177
Kilpatrick, Mel 350
Kindler, Air Commodore John 243
King Airs 104–105
Knowles, Jeff 'Slim' 332–334
Komoro International Airport (Dili) 14, 16, 18–19, 20
Kosovo 199
Kupang (West Timor) 81

L

land surveillance missions
- Afghanistan 185–195
- Iraq 180

landing
- Caribou 66, 69, 70
- flight testing 330

laser-guided bombs 129, 145
latrine construction training 112
leadership culture 361
legal action 107
Legion of Honour 291
Lemoore Naval Air Station (US) 352, 355, 359
LIFT Youth Development Incorporated 89
'Lightning II' stealth fighter *see* Joint Strike Fighter
Lindbergh, Charles 98
'liquid lock' 72
LITENING AT targeting pods 131
Lloyd, Group Captain Pete 106–107

loadmasters 53–61
  Bali bombings 47
  C–17 232
  Caribou 74
  East Timor conflict 54–55
  effect of climate and temperature 57–58
  ground fire checks 59
  helicopters 54
  Hercules 53–54, 58
  operational procedures 58–59
  relations between soldiers and aircrew 55–56
  safety responsibilities 53, 59–60
  training 58
Lockheed Martin
  C–130 Hercules 7
  JSF 313–315, 316, 317–318, 319, 322–323, 324–325
  Orions 179
  Super Hornet 347
Lockwood, Lieutenant Christian 'Wink' 335–338
lone survival exercises 113, 119
long-haul international missions 287–288
'low level' flying 101
lubricants 210
Luke, Corporal Ben 211

M
McCaldin, Flight Lieutenant Jasper 100–103
McCarthy, Jason 42
'Macchi' MB–326 jet trainer 31
McDonnell, Warrant Officer Wendy 280–282, 284
McGreevy, Flight Lieutenant Mick 185–186, 190–191
Mackinnon, Wing Commander Terry 175, 177–179
McKnight, Sergeant Garreth 211–212
McNamara, Air Marshal Neville 28
mail runs 70
maintenance
  Caribou 63, 67, 71–73
  electrical 219–220
  F–111 strike bomber 107, 108
  Hercules 209–211
  JSF 325
  Middle East 209–217
  Orion 214
  Super Hornet 108
  targeting pods 131
  VIP breakdown 287
Malaysia 291
maritime patrol 175–184
Maritime Patrol aircraft 358
marriage breakdown 360
Marshal Base (Afghanistan) 198
Martin, Squadron Leader Chris 287–288
Martin, Group Captain Gary 236
Martin, Warrant Officer Paul 209–211, 212–213

Martin Baker Club 97
Masden, Squadron Leader Steve 255–258
Meadows, Warrant Officer Al 91–92
medals
  Legion of Honour 291
  US Air Medal 135
  United States Legion of Merit 172
media 280
medical evacuation (medivac) flights *see* aeromedical evacuations
medical staff 290–300
  ADG 291
  Bali bombings 47, 51
  Bougainville 291–292
  difficulties faced by 295
  nursing officers 291–292, 296–300
  specialists 294, 306
  training 291
  trauma care *see* trauma care
  veterans at Gallipoli and France 291–292
  women 296–300
  work variety 293
Medina Republican Guard 135, 142
Mellish, Morgan 280
mental stresses 111, 116, 120, 359–360
mentoring 88, 90
Mentoring and Reconstruction Task Force 185
Merriman, Flying Officer Adele 104–106
mess 218
Middle East Area of Operations (MEAO) 11 *see also* Afghanistan; Iraq
  ADG 225
  aircraft maintenance 209–217, 219–220
  CAOC *see* Combined Air Operations Centre
  loadies 53, 54, 56–58, 60
Millar, Group Captain David 'Doc' 103
Mirages 95
missile attacks
  Baghdad 272–273
  CRC 260
  Iraq 2, 142, 147–149, 154, 156
mission command skills training 83
Mitchell, Squadron Leader Brett 82
Morris, Squadron Leader Clinton 261–262
mortality *see* fatalities
Moseley, General Michael 'Buzz' 126, 128, 132
'motion desensitise training course' 68–69
Mount Hotham 116
Mully, Flight Lieutenant Scott 268–269
'Multinational Force and Observers' (Sinai Peninsula mission) 30
Murdani, Benny 24
Muslim staff 298–299

N
nanotechnology 199–200
navigation
  Caribou 64, 68
  F–111s 103

370

flight training 82
  ground training 112
navigator/communicator (NAVCOM) 176–177, 181
Nelson, Brendan 317, 338–344, 346–347
Nelson, David 'Doc' 332–334
New Zealand earthquake (2011) 237
Nicholas, Group Captain Paul 12–13, 15, 17, 26
night vision goggles 101
Noble, Leading Aircraftswoman Kina 217–219
Northrop Grumman 200, 321
'notion of tactical principles' 34
Number 1 Flying Training School 349
Number 2 Flying Training School (Pearce) 31, 77, 93
Number 6 Squadron 92
Number 34 Squadron 24, 279, 287
Number 35 Squadron 64
Number 36 Squadron 15–17, 33
Number 37 Squadron 32, 61
Number 38 Squadron 21–24, 62, 64
Number 75 Squadron 87
Number 77 Squadron 87, 88
Number 79 Squadron 93
Number 82 Wing 353
Number 86 Wing 32
Number 92 Wing 181
nursing officers 291–292, 296–300 see also trauma care
nutrition training 111

O
O'Bryan, Stephen 316–317
occupational health and safety at CAOC 249
ocean patrol 175–184
Oddie, Air Commodore John 15–16, 20, 27, 29–35, 46
O'Donnell, Squadron Leader Peter 'Stan' 108
offensive air support (OAS) 165–167
Officer Training School 31
oil leaks 72
O'Neill, Elizabeth 280
Ononge airfield, PNG 70
'op stops' 19
Operation Bali Assist (2002) see Bali bombing
Operation Bel Isi (Bougainville) 293
Operation Christchurch Assist (2011) 237
Operation Falconer (Iraq 2003) 130–131
Operation Pacific Assist (Japan 2011) 237–238
Operation Padang Assist (Sumatra 2009) 232–233
Operation Resolute (2009) 175–184
Operation Shock and Awe (Iraq) 1
Operation Spitfire (Dili, 1999) 14–17
Operation Warden (East Timor, 1999) 17–20, 21, 70
Operational Conversion Unit (OCU) 162
operations support 26–27
Orion AP–3C patrol aircraft
  Afghanistan 185–192
  anti-submarine warfare 182–184
  combating piracy 195–196
  illegal activity surveillance 175–176, 179–182
  Iraq 180
  maintenance 214–215
  radar 183
overwatch see convoy overwatch

P
P–8 Maritime Patrol aircraft 358
Palmdale facility (US) 327
Papua New Guinea
  Bougainville conflict 293
  Caribou 62, 64–65, 67, 69–70, 73
  flood mission 67
  relief missions 64–65, 69–70
  tsunami 1998 13
parachutes 97–98
Parson, Squadron Leader Steve 182
Paterson, Group Captain Michael 290–295
PC–9 Pilatus training aircraft 77–79, 81
peace keeping mission in the Sinai Peninsula 30
Peacock, Andrew 342
Pead, Flight Sergeant Daryl 72–73
Pegg, Lachlan 226
people smugglers 175–177, 181–182
Philpott, Squadron Leader Roy 186, 192, 195–196
Phnom Penh 32
physical fitness 115, 119–120
physical stresses 111
Pilatus PC–9 training aircraft 77–79, 81
Pilot Selection Agency 93
pilots
  domestic pilot's dispute (1989) 8
  flight testing see test pilots
  Iraq 1–3
  jet fighter see fighter pilots
  VIP operations 283
piracy 195–196
Pitch Black exercise 361
Pizzuto, Wing Commander Richard 259–261
poaching 181–182
political science 27
post-traumatic stress 295
Powell, Flight Lieutenant William 251–255
prisoners of war 115, 156
Project Vigilare 338, 344, 359
psychological damage of Bali bombings 47
Puk Puk airstrip 63

Q
Qantas 162
Qantas Defence Systems 283

R
radar
  air traffic control 269
  AP–3C 183

CRC 262
  F–111 94, 100, 107
  JSF 321
  Super Hornet 353
  UAVs 200
Raptor F–22 313, 317
Read, David 37, 40
reconnaissance system 187–188
Red Bull air race 169–170
Reed, Air Vice-Marshal Alan 92
refuelling 288
'regime change' policy 136
relief mission, PNG 64–65, 67
religion 298–299, 302
remedial instruction 90
remotely piloted vehicles (RPVs) 198
repair and maintenance *see* maintenance
repatriations 228
rescue training 114, 118
reservists 39
resupply, aerial 252–253
Rhinos *see* Super Hornet fighter
Richmond 32
risks
  aerobatics 80
  management 34
  mitigation 212
Roberton, Group Captain Steve 'Zed' 106, 348–354
rocket attacks *see* missile attacks
Role 3 coalition field hospital (Kandahar) 304–307
rotary-wing UAVs 200
Roulettes 77–81
rover kits 125–126
Royal Darwin Hospital 37, 42–43, 44
RQ–7B Shadow UAVs 198
Rudd, Kevin 283
Rudd government
  delays UAV radar purchase 200
  JSF and Super Hornet 322, 346
  troop protection deal 198
rules of engagement 140–141
Rumsfeld, Donald 340
runways, short-field 63
Rwanda 291

S
Saddam Hussein 1, 132, 136, 141, 142
safety
  aerobatics 80
  Caribou 64
  culture 361
  effect of climate and temperature 57
  F–111 103
  loadies' responsibilities 59–60
  loadmasters' responsibilities 54
safety record
  C–130 55
  Caribou 65

SAMs (surface-to-air missiles) *see* missile attacks
San Eagle unmanned reconnaissance vehicles 198
Sarbi the wonder dog 302
SAS *see* Special Air Service
Scan Eagle UAV 186, 200
Schmitt, Squadron Leader Warren 21–22, 63–65, 70
School of Air Traffic Control (East Sale) 267–269
Scott, Don 349
Scott, Mark 280
Scud missile attack 142
search and rescue (SAR) missions 13, 33, 180
Seaton, Andy 103
secret code word 115
'seekers' (laser-guided bombs) 145
sensor employment manager (SEM) 181
sensors 187–188, 321, 324
September 11 2001 attack 136
747 jumbo jets 162–163
Seymour Johnson Air Base (US) 135
Shadow UAVs 198
Shaw Air Force Base (US) 126
shelter construction training 117
Shepherd, Air Marshal Geoff
  East Timor conflict 25–26
  F–111 91–98
  on information exchange 167
  Iraq 132–134
  Roberton appointed to staff 351
  Super Hornet acquisition 341, 343, 345–346
'Shock and Awe' operation 139–140
short take-off and vertical landing (STOVL) aircraft 331
short-field runways 63
signal fires 117
Silverman, Warrant Officer Wayne 54–58
Simmons, Squadron Leader Paul 'Simmo' 85–90
Simmons, Sandy 89
Simpson, Heidi 152, 157–158
Simpson, Flight Lieutenant Ray 'Homer' 152, 154–161, 162–163, 171
simulation training
  air traffic control 268–269
  C–17 231–232
  F–111 101–102
  JSF 316, 333–334
  test pilots 328–329, 333–334
Sinai Peninsula 30–31
'slewing' 188
snow survival course 116
Solomon Islands intervention (2003) 25, 71
Somalia 9–10, 32, 195–196
sonar 183
spare parts 211–212

Special Air Service (SAS)
   Caribous 66
   Iraq 124–125
   JTACs 254
sport 215
stall testing on JSF 324–325
Stalling, Flight Lieutenant Leigh 301–304, 307
Standridge, George 320–321
'static stall test' 324–325
stealth technology
   aircraft carriers 333
   capability 332
   F–25 fighter *see* Joint Strike Fighter
   flight testing 328
   function 324
Steele, Brice 280
Stevens, Di 41
stress
   effect on personnel and families 359–360
   heat 57–58, 209–211, 212
   post-traumatic 295
   training 111
strike coordination and reconnaissance (SCAR) 165
Strike Eagle aircraft 135, 142–146
submarines 182–184
Sudan 266–267
Sudrajat, Alison 280
Sumatra earthquake (2009) 232–233
Super Hornet fighter 335–347
   acceleration 336–337
   acquisition 338–345, 346–347
   capabilities 345, 353, 356–357
   conversion training 352, 357
   cost 343–344, 346
   delivery 344, 347
   introduction 352–353
   maintenance 108
   passenger's experience 336–338
   pilots 352–354, 355–357
   planning for 359
   radar 353
   senior officers' misgivings 342
   training 83
   upgradeable to Growler 346
Super Missile Exclusion Zone ('Super MEZ', Iraq) 1, 140–141, 144, 147, 153
supply drops, PNG 69–70
surface-to-air missiles *see* missile attacks
surgeons 294, 304
surveillance
   land *see* land surveillance missions
   maritime 275–284
   UAVs 198
survival kits 116–117
survival training *see* combat survival training
'suspected irregular entry vessels' (SIEVs) 176
'swing-wings' 107
synthetic aperture radar 200

T
'tac' flying 11
Tactical Coordinator (TACCO) 175, 181
take-off
   flight testing 329
   loadmasters' responsibilities 59
Taliban 186, 189
Tapini airfield, PNG 69–70
target directives in Iraq 133
targeting pod technology 131
Tarin Kowt ('TK', Afghanistan) 10, 57, 235, 301–304
technicians, aircraft 210
Telfer, Squadron Leader Phil 214–215
temperature, effect of 57–58
'terrain masking' 102
terrain-following radar 94, 100, 107
terrorism, Bali *see* Bali bombing
test flights *see* flight testing
test pilots 327–334 *see also* flight testing
   ejection 329
   JSF program 328–329, 333
   movies about 328
   simulation training 328–329, 333–334
   vertical landing jets 331–332
Thorpe, Wing Commander Tony 67, 74
Tindal Base 24
TNI (Indonesian military) 14–15
Tomlinson, Graham 'GT' 331, 333
torture resistance training 115, 156
tower simulators 268
tradition 361
training
   ACOs 81–85
   aerobatics 80
   AGD 222
   air traffic control 267–269
   airsickness 68–69
   altitude 65
   C–17 231–232, 233
   counter-interrogation 115, 156–157
   ejection 115
   F–111 93, 100–101, 104–105
   fighter pilots 86–90, 93, 164–165, 350–351
   instructors 87–90
   Iraq 131–132
   loadmasters 58
   navigation 82, 112
   nursing officers 291
   remedial instruction 90
   Super Hornet 83
   survival *see* combat survival training
   war simulation *see* simulation training
   youth 89
trapping skills 117
trauma care 301–309
   children 307, 308
   civilians 307–309
   cultural issues 302–303, 307–309
   IEDs 306–307

Kandahar 304–309
successes 303, 304
Tarin Kowt 301–304
trialling *see* flight testing
troops in contact (TIC) operation
  COAC 243–244, 245
  convoy overwatch 192
  CRC 262
Tropical Cyclone Yasi 52

U

UH–1 Iroquois *see* Iroquois UH–1 helicopter
UNAMET 14
United Arab Emirates Al Minhad Air Base *see* Al Minhad Air Base
United Kingdom
  CAOC 242–243
  in Iraq 126, 131
United States
  Australian F–22 purchase 317–318
  CAOC *see* Combined Air Operations Centre
  F–111 107
  in Iraq 123, 128–129, 130–131, 136–146, 155, 159, 167, 168, 294–295
  Joint Strike Fighter 339
  navy exchange program 355
  relations with RAAF 356
  September 11 2001 attack 136
  Super Hornets 344, 352–353
  test pilots 327–331, 332–334
  UAVs 197
US Air Medal 135
United States Legion of Merit (Degree of Legionnaire) 172
unmanned aerial systems (UASs) 198
unmanned aerial vehicles (UAVs) 197–205
  Afghanistan 186, 198–199, 200–202
  CAOC 242
  development 197–199
  miniaturisation 199–200
  operators 202, 203–205
  rotary-wing 200

V

values focus 361
Van Haren, Squadron Leader Terry 130–132, 203–204
variable geometry 107
Vern, Pilot Officer Daniel 177
vertical landing jets 331–332
veterans 291–292
Vice Chief of the Defence Force (VCDF), Binskin appointed as 28
Vigilare Project 338, 344, 359
VIP operations 279–289
  aircraft 279
  aircraft allocation 280, 282–283
  aircraft maintenance 283
  attendants *see* cabin attendants
  captains 283
  catering 280, 285
  charges for 283
  'crew slipping' 288
  during election campaigns 285
  passengers 284
  pilots 283, 354
  refuelling 288
  route planning 288
'vomitron' 68–69

W

war simulation *see* simulation training
water production, survival training 111
weapons systems operator, pilot as 93–94
Wedgetail Airborne Early Warning and Control (AEWAC) aircraft 338, 339, 340, 341, 344, 359
Westney, Sergeant Eddie 221, 223, 224–225
White, Flying Officer Merilyn (Mel) 291
Willacott, Alissa 60–61
Willacott, John 60
Willacott, Warrant Officer Scott 16, 18–19, 47–48, 58–61
Wilson, Squadron Leader Greg 40, 42, 298
Wilson, Squadron Leader Nadia 296–300
Winter, Sue 37, 40
Wiranto, General 25
women aircrew
  ADG 226
  C–17 228–231, 232–234
  F–111 104–106
  no fighter pilots 361
  Orions 176–177
  proportion of 361
  survival training 120
Wood, Bruce 'Poodle' 96
Woolshed airstrip 63
workers compensation claims 107
World Trade Centre attack (2001) 136
wounded personnel *see* medical staff; trauma care

Y

Yogyakarta airport crash (Indonesia, 2007) 280
youth work 89